THE PARANORMAL
— IS NORMAL!

Ashton Wylie
CHARITABLE TRUST

The Paranormal – Is Normal! won the Book Category of the 2016 Ashton Wylie Mind Body Spirit Literary Awards, described by judges' convenor Adonia Wylie, as an outstanding body of work from within the genre. The judging panel of AWCT trustee Adonia Wylie, author Keith Hill and journalist Mike Alexander were unanimous in their overall choice of the winning book.

A recently received review -

"Everyone should read this book."

"The book should be given widespread publicity so that it somehow gets through the fog of mainstream reporting. Modern science is held in such high esteem that a book providing solid science in support of non-physical reality can be an eye opener and a life changer for many. It is an eloquent and erudite bridge between science and spirituality, providing a common ground upon and through which a meaningful dialog can take place. Plus, the immense amount of findings presented in this book from standard scientific research, presents daunting challenges to even the most materialistic of hard-nosed skeptics".

Dr Dennis Grega, Psychologist researcher and joint CEO/Convenor of the AfterlifeData.com website and services – the world's largest "afterlife" website.

THE PARA**NORMAL** – IS **NORMAL!**

*The Science Validation to Reincarnation,
the Paranormal and your Immortality*

ALASTAIR BRUCE SCOTT-HILL

To purchase another copy of this book, visit **www.copypress.co.nz**

Published 2016
by Xcell Books

ISBN 978-0-473-35275-2

The moral rights of the author are asserted

© Copyright Alastair Bruce Scott-Hill, B.E.(Elect.) 2016
All rights reserved.

Except for the purposes of fair reviewing, no part of this publication may be copied, reproduced, or transmitted in any form, or by any means, including via technology either already in existence or developed subsequent to publication without the express permission of the author.

Printed by The Copy Press, Nelson, New Zealand. www.copypress.co.nz

Dedicated to the many researchers in this field who have unstintingly done all they could to seek and pass on truth and knowledge to others.

In addition, I would like to thank members of my family and friends for all their encouragement, but in particular to my lifelong friend Doug Burrus, a fellow professional engineer for both his kind offer and provision of very useful detailed suggestions for change.

A Few Reviews

"Because Science can't see, identify, or find God in a microscope or telescope, many people rationalize that there is nothing more, after this material life - that there is no such thing as a soul that survives death in a spiritual world. Alastair (Bruce) Scott-Hill was of that mind-set until he began exploring scientifically areas outside the boundaries of mainstream science, territory beyond discernment with any man-made instrument. His explorations took him over some very rough terrain and through murky waters, territory in which only the most resolute survive. The few who do survive usually struggle to explain their findings in language that most can comprehend. But Scott-Hill, with skills honed in a 35-year career as a professional communication engineer and information technology systems designer, is able to translate the seemingly complex, into a relatively simple system. He tells of finding an afterlife - the survival of consciousness after death - supported by quantum physics and with scientific evidence founded in reincarnation research, mediumship, out-of-body experiences, and other paranormal phenomena. Where science generally offers only despair, Scott-Hill offers hope that goes beyond the blind faith of orthodox religion and into providing true afterlife validation and belief for us all."

Michael Tymn, Editor, The Journal for Spiritual and Consciousness Studies

Mike Tymn, a 1958 graduate of the School of Journalism (B.A. Public Relations) at San Jose State University, is considered one of the world's foremost living experts on evidential afterlife studies. In particular in the provision of an unparalleled coverage of evidence concerning mediumship over a very large historical time period in his six published books to date. A number of these are bestsellers. He has contributed more than 1,600 articles to some 40 newspapers, magazines, journals, together with his six afterlife books over the past 60 years. He won the 1999 Robert H. Ashby Memorial Award given by The Academy of Religion and Psychical Research for his essay on "Dying, Death, and After Death.

"A clearly written, well researched and richly detailed meditation on the reasons, scientific and experiential, for a belief in the survival of death and reincarnation. Against those who hold that modern science has invalidated such ideas, Bruce

Scott-Hill is surely right to insist on the many ways in which they are in fact supported by post-classical physics. A stimulating read!"

> **Robert McLuhan**, Robert McLuhan gained a First in English Literature at Oxford University, then worked as a foreign correspondent for the Guardian in Spain and Portugal before becoming a freelance journalist. He has been a member of the Society for Psychical Research since 1993. McLuhan writes columns for a number of English newspapers and has authored three books to date including his latest, *Randi's Prize: What Sceptics Say About the Paranormal, Why They Are Wrong, and Why It Matters*. He is editor of "Paranormia", a website which deals with consciousness, spirituality, and psychic research.

"Alastair (Bruce) Scott-Hill, a Professional Engineer, [...] has had a number of major paranormal experiences, and with his strong interest in open-minded science he has spent the past sixteen years intensively studying what quantum physics and other disciplines might have to explain these experiences and the paranormal in general. An especial interest of his has been the question of reincarnation. Bruce set himself the task of producing a "beyond all reasonable doubt" understanding of the truth of the matter.

As might be expected of such a writer, his presentation is clear, logical and concise: and I found it convincing. I find it illuminating, fascinating, and expect to refer to it, again and again. I have studied the field in which Scott-Hill writes for many years, and am glad to say that where previously I felt confused, I am now less so.

In his first Chapter of his book [...] Scott-Hill explores the issue of creation by design or by chance in great detail, and exposes the absurdity of the notion of "chance". Design implies conscious mind, and the rest of the book explores this from many points of view. I outline his arguments a little more fully, because denying Darwinism sounds heretical. I am however convinced by his arguments.

The idea of a Creator or creative process is considered in relation to Beauty, then the Laws of Physics, and especially the "Big Bang", the fine-tuning of the universe, the ever increasing complexity.

He summarises with:

> "**Principle 1** - A non-physical timeless (but contingent) quantum-like realm beyond our current physical existence is possible, where things and events respond directly to consciousness/intention.
>
> **Principle 2** - The Universe overwhelmingly exhibits design, information, intelligence and mind. It is also biocentric, therefore providing

compelling evidence not only for a creator/God as the first cause, but with its purpose including the creation of all life."

Chapter 2 – Non-Physical Reality, Independence of the Mind from the Brain, Consciousness and Immortality. Here he explores the realm depicted by physicists, non-local causation, including quantum-entanglement, the EPR effect, and the holographic universe. All familiar ground for me. But I was struck by this quote: "One of the most shattering concepts which follows from acceptance of a holographic universe theory is that, at the quantum or non-physical level, information does not travel through time and space from one 'physical' location to another; instead, the subatomic particles themselves simply seem to exist in a dimension which renders time and space (i.e. distance), irrelevant." Surely here lies a key to understanding a great many paranormal phenomena, otherwise inexplicable. Scott-Hill explores this in fascinating detail in an Annex to Chapter 4 "Further considerations of Time and Space."

Bruce then explores whether mind resides in the brain. His answer of course, is No, and he explores this at length, but keeping the reader eager to read what next is to follow. He then remarks, "In short, consciousness creates reality!" "we continuously and unconsciously actually create our own separateness and reality based in time" "the universe is purely mental: .. mind is fundamental; matter merely an illusion - and that this is physics, not philosophy (or religion)." "We are immortal!"

This review will be too long if I attempt to discuss the whole book. But I will quote the other "Principles" by which he summarises his main points as he proceeds:

> "**Principle 3 - Mind is primary, as with consciousness. Consciousness creates reality. We are immortal.**
>
> **Principle 4 - The physics exists, such that on death, our consciousness, mind, memory (i.e. one's psyche and soul) plus senses could transfer and exist in a timeless realm.**
>
> **Principle 5 - Recent scientific advancements can now explain the paranormal, psychic ability and the ability to communicate with discarnates or other entities in other realities.**

Principle 6 - The science of time and space supports belief in reincarnation.

[...]

Do explore this book."

Rev. Michael D S Cocks, a former Anglican Vicar, Christchurch, New Zealand. He gained Honours in Theology at Oxford, and Honours degrees in Philosophy and Psychology in New Zealand, and read at St Catherine's, and also at Ripon Hall - a modern theological college. Michael has published two books, "the Afterlife Teaching from Stephen the Martyr" and "Into the Wider Dream: Synchronicity in the Witness Box." For this book Michael was awarded finalist status in the 2015 Ashton-Wylie Book Prize. He is currently editor of "The Ground of Faith" website.

Contents

A Few Reviews		vii
Contents		xi
About the Author		xv
Author's Introductory Note		xvii
Foreword		xix
Preamble		**xxiii**
0.1	Science	xxv
0.2	Inspiration	xxviii
0.3	Revelation	xxviii

Section 1   **1**

Chapter 1	**The Case for a Creator/God**	**3**
1.1	The Theory of Cause and Effect	3
1.2	The Theory of Design, Evolution	7
1.3	The Origin of Life	13
1.4	Logical Consistency and Unity both in Nature and the Universe	17
1.5	Beauty in Nature	19
1.6	The Laws of Physics (i.e. the Universe, or Nature)	20
1.7	"The Big Bang" and Fine Tuning of the Universe	21
1.8	Complexity/ Progression of Life	27
1.9	Closing Chapter Comment	30

Chapter 2	**Non-Physical Reality, Independence of the Mind from the Brain, Consciousness and Immortality**	**33**
2.1	Non-Physical Reality	35
2.2	Whether the Mind resides in the Brain	38
2.3	Consciousness	43
2.4	Closing Chapter Comments	51

Chapter 3		**The Quantum Communication System (PCAR) Linking All Life, and Quantum Fields**	**55**
	3.1	Quantum Fields	56
	3.2	The Zero Point Field	60
	3.3	The Brain as a Filter	63
	3.4	The Collective Subconscious, and Group Consciousness	64
	3.5	Group Consciousness - Experiments Aimed at Detecting PK Phenomena and Group Consciousness	69
	3.6	The Subconscious – the Path to Universal Knowledge, and Resonance	72
	3.7	Self Resonating Quantum Fields	74
	3.8	Schempp's PCAR Universal Bio - Quantum Holographic Brain Processing and Communication System	77
	3.9	Further Experimental Evidence for Mind to Mind Communication between Different Lifeforms	79
	3.10	Non - Physical Reality - Senses	81
	3.11	The Ability for the Senses to Survive Death	82
	3.12	Reincarnational Aspects	84
	3.13	Closing Chapter Comments	86
Chapter 4		**The Commonality of Science Amongst all Paranormal Phenomena. Plus Time and Space**	**89**
	4.1	Introduction	89
	4.2	The Commonality of Science Amongst all Paranormal Phenomena	90
	4.3	Time and Space	104
	4.4	Discovery and Relevance of the PCAR System	111
	4.5	Closing Chapter Comments	113
	Annex	Further considerations of Time and Space	115

Section 2			**125**
Chapter 5		**Reasons for Reincarnation**	**127**
	5.1	Possible Reasons for Re-incarnation	127
	5.2	Views of Mystics	130
	5.3	Religious Re-incarnational Views	138
	5.4	Difficulties in Belief of Reincarnation	140
	5.5	Reasons for a creator/God's Creation, Particularly Reincarnation	142
	5.6	Closing Chapter Comments	146
	Annex 1	"Seth's" Introduction to Jane Roberts	149
	Annex 2	A Selection of Seth Quotes	153

Section 3			157
Chapter 6	ESP, "Remote viewing" and Non Ordinary States of Consciousness		159
	6.1	Telepathy	159
	6.2	Clairvoyance	163
	6.3	OOB states (out-of-body or OBE, out-of–body experiences)	169
	6.4	NDE's (Near Death Experiences)	180
	6.5	Closing Chapter Comments	186
Chapter 7	Past Life Recall - Spontaneous and via Hypnosis		189
	7.1	Spontaneous Past Life Recall of Children	189
	7.2	Hypnosis and Past Life Regression	200
	7.3	Closing Chapter Comments	221
Chapter 8	Psychics and Mediums		225
	8.1	Psychics and Mediums	225
	8.2	Closing Chapter Comments	248
Chapter 9	Life-between-Lives and Concluding Book Comments		251
	9.1	Life-Between-Life	251
	9.2	Closing Chapter Comments	264
	Annex	Reincarnation/Recycling, Our True Reality, Ideas and thoughts. Information and knowledge	271

Appendices			293
Appendix 1	Darwinism and Atheism		295
	A1.1	Darwinism	295
	A1.2	Atheism	309
Appendix 2	A List of Some Constants Affecting Earth		315
Appendix 3	The Double Slit Experiment		317
	References		319
	Index		333

About the Author

Alastair (Bruce) Scott-Hill, a Professional Engineer (now retired), graduated as a BE (Elect), Cant. and spent his career in communication technology, particularly in telecommunications and information technology. The main portion of his career was with Telecom New Zealand spanning some 35 years designing national telephone exchanges, and telecommunication networks. He also designed the first Telecom online nationwide supply computer system. Subsequently he then took up a position with Standards New Zealand, where he was responsible for all New Zealand Standards in Telecommunications, Information Technology and Acoustics.

He has had a lifetime interest in science.

Author's Introductory Note

I have always considered "science" is the only acceptable measure which should be used to validate any theory **or belief**, and this is surely vindicated by its success throughout the ages for mankind to both understand our "world" and also to gain and benefit from new discoveries. With my love and faith in science, this is why many years ago I decided to use science to research for myself the validity of reincarnation and the paranormal.

Although this is a science book, I have resisted the temptation to include any mathematics (apart from a few probability statements). In addition, despite the science base, I have taken particular care to ensure that is written in such a way that it should be of interest and readable to anyone - even those who have had no formal education in science.

This book is the result of my researches and labors to find sufficient evidence to overcome all my earlier doubts in the areas covered by the title and subtitle. I have though had a great informative journey in writing the book and increased my knowledge immensely. What I have found and passed on to you is simply a result of following wherever the evidence has led. When I started on my journey many years ago I had no realization then that my researches would for myself prove so successful in changing my earlier belief system. I hope it succeeds for you as well as it has for me, as not only has it been a great journey for myself, but the results have vastly exceeded my expectations.

Foreword

"...most people forget (and avoid) whatever does not fit within consensus realities."

Ingo Swann

It will be noted that the book comprises three parts:

Section 1   The Science behind Reincarnation, the Paranormal and your Immortality

Section 2   Reasons for Reincarnation

Section 3   Detailed science based evidence (i.e. data and case studies) supporting Reincarnation

Section 1 - The Science behind Reincarnation etc., - covers science areas not well known, which have not been dealt with to my knowledge in any other books on reincarnation. However I felt that sensibly, it was important that one should at least cover the science behind reincarnation which must exist, to even allow re-incarnation. I discovered much of this science is a result of only fairly recent developments in physics and biology, and hope you find as I do that these strongly support belief in an afterlife. The scientific evidence for a God/creator is also included, as for my own personal belief in the possibility of reincarnation, I felt it only reasonable that such a case must first be made for a superior entity such as a creator/God to exist - in order to have conceived of, and implemented the re-incarnation process. Section 1 therefore provides an initial introductory Chapter covering the scientific based case for a creator/God. It is emphasized however that this is not a religious book, so that any arguments for a creator/God ignore any religious beliefs, and instead are science based.

Two Chapters of Section 1 importantly deal with the issue that if a soul is to survive death, how can the mind exist independently of the brain, with consciousness and memory intact?

Section 2 – Reasons for Reincarnation, - covers discussion on the issue that if re-incarnation occurs, there must be logical reasons for this.

Section 3 – Detailed science based evidence (i.e. data and case studies) supporting Reincarnation, - deals with subjects pertinent to reincarnation such as telepathy, remote viewing, hypnotic regression, psychics/mediums etc. with background and case histories which can be explained by theoretical science concepts and experiments covered in Section 1.

Many years ago when I first encountered anecdotal evidence for re-incarnation, I discounted the stories completely on two accounts. Firstly, since these related to other's experiences, rather than mine, there was always a possibility that they could be both false and attributable to wishful thinking. Secondly, as a professional engineer with naturally higher demands for logical arguments than most; I felt I at least needed to have some better arguments for the existence of a creator, and the physics of the reincarnation process.

However, in recent years, after reading more books and articles on re-incarnation I felt both the weight and quality of evidence – in some cases, was stronger than I had first realised. In just the last ten years, there has been astonishingly breakthroughs in micro biology, cosmology and quantum physics which suggest our reality may be more about mind than matter, and which lends considerable support to the concept of reincarnation. It then struck me that this in itself could be the answer to my wish for acceptable proof. After all, the need to find irrefutable scientific evidence is not necessary for belief of guilt when convicting criminals. Neither is such rigor necessary to believe in the existence of Spain, despite the fact I have never been there.

I therefore realised - *it is simply necessary to present a sufficiently compelling case in order to exclude reasonable doubt*.

I have also been misguided by my colleague scientists who (usually) demand rigid scientific proof for belief, entailing appropriate experimentation and repeatability of results to vindicate a hypothesis. When I looked more thoroughly at current scientific belief, to my amazement many well held theories such as "string theory" or even biological Darwinian 'evolution' theory, lack scientific proof – which suggests that scientists do not always practice what they preach.

Some years ago in my early marriage years in circa 1963, as with many others, I read a number of books written by an American journalist Jane Roberts, purportedly containing trance information from a multidimensional entity called "Seth". They seemed interesting at the time, but I rejected them as nonsense until I recently returned to complete my writing of this book. Many statements in the "Seth" books correlated amazingly with quantum physics properties discovered only recently, but which were unknown at the time of Jane Roberts writing. I have therefore included a number of extracts of "Seth" sayings at appropriate points for you in the text to make your own minds up concerning their validity. I no longer consider them nonsense.

Preamble

I feel I must emphasize that this is not a religious book but rather a science book, and where it deals with God, the intention is solely to provide scientific evidence for a creator/God rather than a viewpoint based on any religious belief.

My approach in this book has been to use **preferentially (solid science) independent replicated laboratory experiments**, for evidence concerning any subject matter. Where this is simply impossible, probability analysis is used. Some further evidential material has also been added though, highlighted by the use of supplementary Annexes to three of the mainstream Chapters, where some esoteric material and in some cases observational science has been provided to add further weight to some area of discussion.

With such a contentious subject as the presentation of a case for a Creator, and for other issues raised in this book, it is first desirable to expand on the point made in the Foreword where I said that I wished *to present a **sufficiently compelling case in order to exclude reasonable doubt.***

Overwhelming proof in a scientific sense is probably more rigorous than most would appreciate. A good understanding of the issues is of critical importance, since, because the criteria for scientific proof is so stringent; it tends to make scientists skeptical of other views in areas where they feel they have a stake. In other areas, such as requirements for conviction in courts, or for their own personal beliefs including religious conviction, I am sure, on the whole, that scientists as with all of us, are willing to accept a degree of proof which they consider sufficient to exclude 'reasonable doubt'. As Fred Hoyle (himself a scientist) has stated:

> "I have always thought it curious that, while most scientists claim to eschew religion, it actually dominates their thoughts more than it does the clergy" [1]

The problem is that the 'official', skeptical, sometimes biased and even atheistic viewpoint of a number of scientists is often quoted and accepted by the media as gospel and judgment on behalf of the rest of us. Since to an extent we all tend to be 'followers', (at least on matters on which we lack expertise), their 'rulings' hold sway.

Scientists though are also human and, whereas some never believe unless they have personally carried out experiments themselves, others rightly can be accused of arranging facts to fit their theory, not the theory to the facts.

At its most extreme, scientific belief is encapsulated by the comment of Sir Brian Pippard Physicist, Cambridge University when he said:

"The one and only certainty each of us has is the certainty of his or her own existence."[2]

Kitty Ferguson in her book *Fire in the Equations* puts it rather well:

"Science doesn't make any claim to have discovered the ultimate truth about anything. Scientists speak instead of discovering predictability - of seeking deeper understanding of nature. They also talk in terms of models and 'the standard model', which means the model that nearly all experts agree on at the present time. They speak of 'approximate theories', which means theories that work satisfactorily in a certain area but do not claim to be the whole truth as it might apply to all areas. They speak of 'effective theories', which means something we can work with for the present while knowing that it isn't absolutely and unequivocally correct.

It is generally agreed that in science nothing can ever be proved. The best anyone can say of a theory is that it has not been disproved. No matter how many times something is confirmed by testing, there is still an infinite number of times it may be tested in the future. That means the number of chances left for it to be disproved will always outnumber the number of times it has been tested and verified. Scientists are sceptical people when it comes to anything which claims to be ultimate, unassailable truth. It may be this scepticism that keeps some scientists away from a belief in God, not the notion that science disproves God. The idea of anyone actually finding ultimate, unassailable truth has in a sense become foreign to the minds of many scientists, and to some of the rest of us as well, even though we may believe such truth exists."[3]

To gain acceptance of a theory as 'a standard model', the 'scientific method' (drummed into most of us at school) must be employed. You will recall that this first entails an initial hypothesis, which then must be vindicated by experiment. Finally, the experimental results need further independent experiment to both confirm the initial experiment results and also to support the hypothesis. Favourable peer review is then usually necessary before the results of the experiment are accepted for publication in a respected scientific publication.

Unfortunately many beliefs (such as the existence of a creator) cannot be subjected to experimentation via the scientific method, and therefore will never meet the required standard for scientific acceptability to be included in the 'standard model' of the universe.

Knowledge and Standards of "Proof"/Evidence

Knowledge is gained from:

1. Science (includes experiment, observation and discoveries),
2. Inspiration, and
3. Revelation.

The focus in this book is on science, whereas inspiration and revelation are mentioned only where this provides support or correlation.

0.1   SCIENCE

As far as "science" is concerned, use of the scientific method involving experiments (as covered above) is of course always the preferred source - as even though outcomes are always provisional subject to further review on the basis of further experimentation or new data, it is nevertheless the most dependable of all the three possible sources of knowledge. In this respect there are many recent experiments (not particularly well known and which may be a surprise to many), which conform to the scientific method but assist both in the belief of a creator/God, and reincarnation, and these will be covered.

By science though, I **also** mean mankind's past and recent **observation** of phenomenon which have led to hypotheses which over time and with **repeated observations** alone have led to their reasonable acceptance as truths, e.g. a darkening sky plus wind is likely to be followed by rain or a storm.

My definition of science must also include **discoveries**. For example, the now amusing past belief that the world was flat and "supported by turtles all the way down", disappeared rapidly when ships exploring over any horizon found that they could return to their starting point. A good example of knowledge banishing ignorance.

Careful and repeated observation of phenomena in a scientifically based manner, has often led in the past to a breakthrough in understanding and belief, e.g. Newton's discovery of gravity simply by watching a falling apple. In this case a scientist though would no doubt claim experimentation a superior method, and that repeated observation may affect belief but not certainty. For example. they might say that if this was an observed behavior of an apple in Newton's day, how could he be certain the apple would not fall, or behave differently tomorrow or 1000 years from then etc. However, as stated in the 'Foreword', my aim for this book is not to try to achieve the impossibility of providing sufficient evidence to attain unassailable truths, but merely to provide a strong enough case to satisfy a jury.

Before leaving science and moving on to discuss the other two sources of knowledge listed above, there are many other yardsticks or tools in science worthy of mention which help scientists measure the validity of hypotheses' - particularly where experiments can be shown to be impracticable e.g. the behaviour of sub atomic particles inside a black hole.

0.1.1 Logical Consistency

The most popular of these yardsticks amongst scientists is logical consistency. As far as logical consistency is concerned, one looks for a logical theory which is consistent within the area covered (e.g. with gases, a theory of expansion with heat would expect uniformity for all gases without exception, and for all volumes of gas). For the universe, one would expect any laws to be inviolate and not change in an arbitrary fashion from place to place, from minute to minute, or even millennium to millennium.

0.1.2 Mathematics

Mathematics has a special place amongst scientists. As Kitty Ferguson says "Our faith in mathematics and logic leads us to believe that if a thing isn't mathematically and logically consistent it can't be true"[4].

The belief is so strong by scientists, that many use this yardstick as a first premise to test the validity of their theory.

Mathematics is really symbolic logic where meanings or significance represented by symbols, are attached to objects to signify meaning in a particularly clear and concise way. It therefore makes it desirable to develop equations and carry out calculations for possible laws, which can then be tested by observation and experiment.

Because of this, it holds a unique position as the language of science and provides a logical direct correlation with reality. In fact there are simply no science theories which would be accepted as the "standard model" unless they can be described mathematically. Gödel's "Incompleteness Theorem" does show that there is the theoretical possibility of truths beyond the ability of mathematics to prove. However as Barrow points out that "'it may be the case that physical reality, even if it is ultimately mathematical, does not make use of the whole of arithmetic and so could be complete". [5]

Currently "String theory" has been developed using mathematics without any experimental or other evidence, and this is also the case for theories covering what happened before the "The Big Bang". In the case of "String Theory", the problem is that mathematics in this instance has given a number of different solutions - as with theories concerned with existence before the "The Big Bang". However in other cases such as quantum **mechanics**, mathematical theory has been verified by measurement to an astonishing degree of accuracy.

Finally, a particular branch of mathematics - 'Probability theory', is particularly useful as **a test for validity of a theory** and for making predictions. For example, the likely effects of global warming over future years, is now usefully presented solely on a probability basis using extrapolation of past climate and solar data inputs manipulated by various computer models. Meta-analysis of data and probability mathematics has also been found useful in analysing data for studies ranging from determining the likely effectiveness of medicine, to the outcome of telepathy experiments on large populations of subjects (dealt with in Section 3 of this book).

In areas of science where difficulty arises due to a number of competing theories, probability theory is a particularly useful approach, often to ensure rationality is not a victim of improbable ideas dressed up as science. Probability theory is used extensively in this book.

0.1.3 'Beauty' in physics

Beauty in physics implies simplicity, elegance, mathematical consistency and creativity. As the result of experience, many scientists consider that beauty in equations is often the best guide to the validity of a promising approach to a new discovery. James Watson mentions how beauty guided his discovery of the DNA code. Werner Heisenberg on his pioneering of Quantum theory said: "It was immediately found convincing by virtue of its completeness and abstract beauty" and Edwin Schrödinger said "Einstein's marvellous theory of gravitation … could only be discovered by a genius with a strong feeling for the simplicity and beauty of ideas". In a conversation with Einstein, Heisenberg once said "I believe just like you, that the simplicity of natural laws has an objective character that is not just the result of thought economy. If nature leads us to mathematical forms of great simplicity and beauty: …..we cannot help thinking they are true, that they reveal a genuine feature of nature."[6]

0.1.4 Parsimony

A criterion much loved by scientists by which they test their theories, is how economical (the technical term is 'parsimonious') is a proposed theory in refining ideas to a simpler, more self-evident form. An important point is that this is not a criterion confined to science; it reflects a logical methodology and is often used as a practical test for the efficiency of design e.g. of a bridge or an engineering process. We should never seek out a complicated explanation when there is a simple, self-evident one available. With nature, experience has shown the simplest explanation almost invariably turns out to be the right one. (Occam's razor.)

0.2   INSPIRATION

Unknown to many, a considerable number of scientific breakthroughs have been discovered by inspiration leading to new knowledge. In some cases, as a result of dreams, in others sudden flashes of inspiration have been claimed while awake but in a somewhat unfocused state. The most famous case of all was the ancient Greek Archimedes who while running a bath, inspirationally realised that one could determine density by noting how much water was displaced. [7]

More recently, Otto Loewi discovered that nerve impulses were transmitted chemically, not electronically, all thanks to a dream. In 1920, Loewi dreamed of an experiment he could do that would prove once and for all how nerve impulses were transmitted. He woke up in the middle of the night, excited and happy, scribbled the experiment down and went back to sleep. When he woke up, he couldn't read his notes. Luckily, he had the same dream the next night. The experiment and his later work earned him the title, the "Father of Neuroscience."[8]

Francis Crick, the discoverer of DNA structure in 1953, while shifting around cardboard cut-outs of the supposed positions of molecules on his office table, in a stroke of inspiration realised that each pair of bases must be held together by hydrogen bonds.[9]

Similarly, the famous 'Periodic Table of Elements' was discovered by the Russian chemist Dimitri Mendeleev while lying in bed day dreaming. Similar situations apply in the case of Niels Bohr's planetary model of the atom and Heisenberg's formulation of the basic principles of quantum physics and many other scientists who were either day dreaming or awakened from a dream where they achieved a flash of inspiration.

In each of these cases it will be noted that major breakthroughs were achieved in a partially or fully unconscious state where conscious reasoning was absent. All scientists mentioned above, claimed mystification for their insight, and disowned credit for their discoveries.

0.3   REVELATION

By 'revelationary' knowledge, what is meant is: "information" claimed as valid and gained from mystics, mediums in trance states etc. As above though, some valid information has been obtained by scientists in trance states. Since this is a science book, it therefore is only generally used in this book in cases where it supports other experimental replicated laboratory experiments for a proposition or theory. (An exception is an Annex to the final Chapter where esoteric wisdom is used in conjunction with some observational science concepts by the author to explain the phenomena and likely source of revelationary information/knowledge itself).

Section One

CHAPTER ONE

The Case for a Creator/God

The most powerful evidence for a creator/God (but often overlooked), is surely first to consider that there really are only two alternatives, and that this leads to a 50% probability for either i.e.:

- There is either a creator/God,
- Or, the universe and all life has happened spontaneously by chance.

By further argument therefore, it would seem only reasonable that one would simply have to provide a probability figure of well over 50% to provide a sufficiently convincing case to support the probability for a creator/ God.

My aim in this, as with the case I present for reincarnation, is to achieve a belief of at least over 90%.

I will now consider first traditional "proofs" for a creator/God, and then more recent scientific evidence on various matters, which support such belief.

First the traditional proofs or arguments are:

1.1 THE THEORY OF CAUSE AND EFFECT

This theory argues that every effect has a preceding cause. Therefore if one cycles through past effects and their causes (e.g. ones parents, their parents etc. .... a first human cell..... a first cell of life etc.) inevitably one ends with an unknowable first cause - which not unreasonably is called the first creator, or God.

It is difficult to refute this argument, although some scientists have suggested causality is not evident in certain quantum states. This follows from the fact that whereas causality is undeniable in Newtonian physics, at the level of atomic particles (i.e. called "quantum" states), Newtonian physics does not apply and random behavior is the norm. As stated by Paul Davies in his book *The Matter Myth*:

"Events occur without well-defined causes. Matter and motion become fuzzy and indistinct. Particles do not follow well defined paths, and forces do not produce dependable actions"[10]

However, John L. Casti (professor at the Technical University of Vienna and at the Santa Fe Institute) in an Article in Scientific American points out:

"Completeness of nature implies that a physical state cannot arise for no reason whatsoever; in short, there is a cause for every effect. Some analysts might object that quantum theory contradicts the claim that nature is consistent and complete. Actually, the equation governing the wave function of a quantum phenomenon provides a causal explanation for every observation (completeness) and is well defined at each instant in time (consistency)."[11]

Heisenberg's Uncertainty Principle describes our inability to simultaneously predict the location and speed of subatomic particles (e.g. electrons). This is often falsely quoted as suggesting the inevitability of chance events occurring at the quantum level - inferring these are uncaused, and therefore the universe is uncaused. This is incorrect, as Heisenberg's Uncertainty Principle does not prove that the movement of electrons is uncaused; it only describes our inability to predict their location and speed at any time.

Radioactivity too exhibits randomness to the extent that it is impossible to predict when a subatomic particle will be emitted. But just because randomness occurs at a quantum level does not necessarily mean there is not a cause e.g. if randomness is required for some reason to control events, then computers or microprocessors can be programmed to create random triggers. It seems more likely that each and every quantum random event has a cause unknown to us yet with our current scientific knowledge. Randomness is just one of the multitude of characteristics observable with quantum physics for which we currently have no explanation.

Also, large numbers of atoms obey the laws of statistics, and as mass increases such that large numbers of subatomic particles become solid objects, their cumulative effect becomes completely predictable.

No scientist therefore has ever encountered a **physical** reality (i.e. non-quantum) event he can claim exhibits indeterminacy. Furthermore all science experiments (apart from those at a quantum level) and the scientific method hallowed by scientists, absolutely depend on the predictability and repeatability inherent in the principle of cause and effect.

Denial of a first cause would therefore be inconsistent with all our experience, logic and observed consistency in the universe.

Fairly though it should be mentioned that since the current "standard model" of the universe agreed by cosmologists and physicists does not accept a creator /God, they have worked very hard in recent years to **theorise** that our universe originated not from God, but completely by chance as a result of a massive quantum fluctuation creating something out of nothing. The science follows from observations of particles materialising anywhere in empty space around us and then vanishing (quantum zero point vacuum fluctuations). "*Given enough time the claim is that one would expect such a fluctuation to involve so many particles that an entire universe would appear*"! [12]

"*Given enough time*" is an invalid argument unfortunately used far too widely by a number of scientists. Although infinite time is valid as a **mathematical concept**, it is of course unacceptable scientifically to assert that infinite time is available (and as a cause for anything) in any real life situation. Moreover, the concept of a **massive** quantum fluctuation is also an assertion without any supporting evidence whatsoever, as all **observed** quantum fluctuations are tiny and virtual, disappearing in nano seconds as soon as they appear. It is also inconsistent and unscientific to claim that a universe could emerge "*given enough time*" from a such a pre -"Big Bang" state, when the "standard model" of the universe, agreed by scientists themselves, concludes that based on evidence given below, that before "The Big Bang", **time simply did not exist**.

Further, if prior to "The Big Bang", the existence of energy or matter for a massive quantum fluctuation were somehow possible, how did these arise? Critically the **laws of physics** (including quantum physics), to even permit a random quantum fluctuation would also have had to precede "The Big Bang". So how did such laws arise then (or even be present with us today) - if not via a creator/God.

Clearly the massive quantum fluctuation theory makes no sense. Instead, it is merely speculation masquerading as science.

In contrast to this theory, a more recent theory (again without evidence, but suggested by Dr Param Singh (a respected physicist at the Perimeter Institute in Canada), is for a big bounce to (occur rather than a "Big Bang") - as the universe shrinks almost to nothing after first expanding to a point where gravity defeats the momentum of expansion. The concept is for such big bounces to continue forever. This would violate the Second law of Thermodynamics which indicates that energy of such a process would soon be dissipated. In addition, recent observations have indicated that expansion of the universe is accelerating due to 'dark flow', so there is little chance of a bounce (i.e. there is more evidence for a stretch!).

The director of the Institute, Neil Turok has yet another idea where he vehemently denies the "The Big Bang" theory. Instead he claims that string theory suggests our reality involves seven more space dimensions than our accepted three dimensions of space (and one of time), and leads to the concept that current inflation of our universe was caused by two "branes" (two separate universes separated by an extra space dimension) momentarily colliding to provide the necessary energy for the current expansion of our universe. Notably he claims before this event, time existed and probably lasts forever. He omits to explain how the "branes" arose, nor how time could exist prior to the Big Bang.

Sensibly in view of all this confusion of unsubstantiated theories, we should surely return to basics. Christian Doppler an Austrian Professor of mathematics, physics and mechanics, in 1841, identified that the colours of stars could be used to determine their velocity. This led to one of the greatest discoveries in cosmology and a precursor to "The Big Bang Theory" by the American astronomer Edwin Russell Hubble, who played a crucial role by showing that the recessional velocity of a galaxy increases with its distance from the earth, implying the universe is expanding and that the more distant a galaxy, the greater its velocity from a central point. Using this data to draw a straight line through points on simple graph of the velocity of galaxies against time and extrapolating backwards, easily shows that when the velocity of expansion was zero, time was also zero.

As any physicist knows, where zeros are encountered in physics, one has encountered a singularity - a term that identifies the state encountered is such that mathematics breaks down, and that events prior to the singularity cannot be determined. They are therefore **simply unknown**. Rather than speculate on unprovable possibilities, two things with some degree of certainty at least can be said about conditions prior to "The Big Bang" - time as we know it could not have existed, and since something cannot be created from nothing, there must have been 'something' prior to "The Big Bang".

We could though ignore time for a moment (as if it were not real, or did not exist), and instead note that, in all our experience, we observe that everything around us and **all events** are always dependent on something else. That is, everything is contingent as a sort of holistic dependency which links everything in a deterministic way. Events occur in a particular sequence order where when one such event concludes, another starts e.g. sub-atomic particles form atoms, atoms lead to molecules, molecules create solid substances etc. Similarly with the cosmos, gases condense into stars, which create planets, stars and planets then form into galaxies etc. This is called "The Contingency Argument" - which is a subset of the "Theory of Cause and Effect". With everything contingent upon something else, as with the "Theory of Cause and Effect"; there must have been a first contingent cause.

With this argument then, perhaps there is a possibility for a nonphysical realm containing a creator/ God existing totally without time, but with causality wholly dependent on the contingency we currently experience amongst all things and events. A theoretical physicist, Dr Fay Dowker of the Imperial College, London; points out two fundamental attributes associated with all quantum events - the first is they exhibit granularity e.g. subatomic particles are released **impulsively** rather than exhibiting the **continuous** nature of space and time evident in the macro universe. Secondly, equations in quantum mechanics surprisingly **have no need whatsoever to include time.**

Evidence will be provided later to support the fact that, that **at the quantum level**, time is simply an illusion and instead contingent events constantly create the present and future from the past.

Also as covered later, it will also be seen that in quantum physics, there is strong evidence for a link between **consciousness and intention**. This is exhibited by both repeatable scientific experiments (covered in Chapter 3). In addition there are instances of many well authenticated and documented events which until recently could not be explained prior to recent scientific discoveries which will be outlined in this book. These are areas currently regarded as paranormal such as telepathy, remote viewing (clairvoyance), Near Death Experiences (NDE's) etc.

PRINCIPLE 1 - A non-physical timeless (but contingent) quantum-like realm beyond our current physical existence may be possible, where things and events respond directly to consciousness/intention.

It is intended to suggest this as a possible principle/theory throughout this book. It is well supported by empirical and observational evidence presented later in this Section and also in Section 3.

It needs to be appreciated that there are severe difficulties facing cosmologists today in deriving an agreed materialist theory which can completely explain "The Big Bang", as the energies involved obviously preclude traditional scientific testing of theories under laboratory conditions. This gives rise to the situation described above where at the Perimeter Institute, there are many competing theories - each it is said with a typical life expectancy of just a few weeks. These are then rejected following a peer review in favor of other more promising theories. Most are supported by mathematical theory which has in the past been found to be spectacularly successful in predicting the success of theories. The problem is that mathematics itself often provides multiple solutions and in this case there is inadequate physical data available currently to choose one which fits reality.

1.2   THE THEORY OF DESIGN, EVOLUTION

The concept here is that there are many examples of design in nature e.g. the human eye strongly suggests design - with various components, lens, iris, receptor cells etc., all created to marvelously achieve the desirable facility of sight. Clearly we did not create such designs, so the theory proposes a creator/designer.

This idea received widespread support up until the late 1800's, as the result of publication of a book by the eighteenth-century theologian William Paley. He pointed to his watch as a proof of the existence of God, arguing that even a savage would recognize that such a complicated instrument must have a maker, and that this applies even more to man.[13]

William Paley was in fact no light weight as he was also a mathematician and naturalist, and he regarded the laws of gravitation (without which he considered life could not exist), as another strong piece of evidence for a creator/God.[14]

1.2.1 Evolution

The "*Theory of Design*" has been a staple for belief in God for many years now, but received a serious challenge in 1859 when Charles Darwin's book *On the Origin of Species* was published. This caused an immediate uproar by most religions and rather joyous acceptance by atheists. This is because it challenged the creation concepts of all religions by suggesting that, not only had species originated by chance rather than by God, but man evolved from amoeba type unicellular creatures by random chance mutations.

The Darwinian belief was that man along with all other life forms developed from a simple life form and then evolved on a purely chance random basis to form the prodigious range of species evident today. This suggested that **life itself** must also have arisen on a random chance basis plus the whole cosmos. Since it had the aura of science and has subsequently been supported strongly by many scientists; the idea of a creator/ God for many, became a biblical fable of wishful thinking. As stated by molecular biologist Michael Denton in his book *Evolution: A Theory in Crisis*:

> "The twentieth century would have been incomprehensible without the Darwinian revolution. The social and political currents which have swept the world in the past eighty years would have been impossible without its intellectual sanction…."
>
> "The influence of evolutionary theory on fields far removed from biology is one of the most spectacular examples in history of how a highly speculative idea for which there is no really hard scientific evidence can come into fashion and effect the thinking of a whole society and dominate the outlook of an age. Today it is perhaps the Darwinian view of nature, more than any other that is responsible for the agnostic and skeptical outlook of the twentieth century….. A theory that literally changed the world."
>
> "The decline in religious belief can probably be attributed more to the propagation and advocacy by the intellectual and scientific community of the Darwinian version of evolution, than to any other single factor." [15]

Also Cornell University's William Provine, a prominent evolutionist and atheist, said,

"That if Darwinism is true, then there are five inescapable conclusions: there's no evidence for God; there's no life after death; there's no absolute foundation for right and wrong; there's no ultimate meaning for life; and people don't have free will." [16]

Unquestionably there is strong support today for "Darwin's Theory of Evolution". However, there are many distinguished scientists, who today consider the widely accepted Darwinian evolutionary mechanism of both random mutation and natural selection are simply not supported by the evidence. Recent experiments in environmental effects (epigenetics) have brilliantly vindicated Darwin's belief in adaption to one's environment to a limited extent (within the genetic diversity of the available genome). However the mechanism has nothing whatsoever to do with mutation and cannot explain the appearance of new species, or life itself (see below). In fact, all experimental attempts aimed at determining whether mutations can cause beneficial results or species changes have shown the opposite - namely that random mutations massively degrade, rather than enhance organisms. Based on these experiments, probability theory also shows that if a few chance beneficial mutations occur, they simply cannot contribute to evolutionary change Ref: Appendix 1.

Since chance mutation cannot provide a mechanism for change to another species, there remains only two mechanisms known to date which can theoretically provide a variation of life forms. They are also fully supported by both the observed data in the fossil record and also by verifiable, repeatable scientific experiments. One is a cellular mechanism discovered as recently as 2001, involving gateway proteins on cell membranes exquisitely sensitive to various environmental effects which then triggers genes to switch on or off (called "epigenics"). The other is the well-known variability caused by gene shuffling during sexual reproduction (i.e. mating). However, variation by either of these methods could not obviously produce a completely new species or life form, as they are inevitably limited to the genetic diversity contained within the particular genome of a given species.

Gene sequencing to identify species, and the mechanism of gene shuffling to provide variety following mating were obviously unknown to Darwin. The critical point not known to Darwin (genes and DNA were discovered well after his death), but obvious to us today due to developments in information theory, is that following mating, the gene pool available between any two members of the same species provides the sum total diversity of information available to create change in the progeny (This is the biological equivalent of computer information being limited by the information-in/information-out concept). Also on an information theory basis, mutations cannot add to information in the genome. They simply add errors and thus destroy information.

Darwin therefore was misled by mistaking **subspecies** variation for the creation of new species e.g. he observed minor changes in beaks, colour of plumage in birds etc. in different environments and wrongly assumed these could lead to macro changes applicable to a new species. He also admitted himself he had no satisfactory explanation for biology's "*Big Bang*" - the Cambrian explosion, when most species were formed almost overnight (i.e. within a few million years compared with the 4.5 **billion** age of the earth). This definitely did not conform to his theory of necessary gradual random mutation changes over eons. He also claimed that although the fossil evidence showed no transitional species, he was "*sure this happened in the wild*". Today there are still no transitional species evident in the fossil record to support 'evolution'. Instead, all fossils appear as fully developed life forms. Nor is there currently a scientific explanation for the appearance of new species.

There is also a profound lack of evidence for the human species 'evolution' since the species first appeared. This was illustrated in a recent (2013) Horizon television documentary, where Dr Alice Roberts a Physical Anthropologist of the University of Reading, spoke of her recent examination of the oldest - 33,000 years old - discovered human bones in the United Kingdom, and said: "*that the variation found fits within the modern range of variation, therefore, there is nothing to suggest we have changed in a millennia*". This was supported by Dr Pardis Sabeti, Assistant Professor of Harvard University, who similarly claimed that he found changes amongst other races were only small predictable variations attributable to diet, hair and sweat characteristics in Asians, and disease resistance characteristics. Professor Stephen Stearns, looking at fertility patterns in humans, found increases in weight, but thought that such changes were only cyclic.

The different versions of early man e.g. Neanderthal, etc., are now thought to be mostly subspecies varieties, as evidenced by recent brain size studies that show differing cranial shapes but virtually the same brain size volume as modern man.[17]

(Since soft tissue is normally unavailable in fossil bones, obviously DNA cannot **usually** be recovered to test for the genome to identify whether or not it is the same or a different species from modern man).

Since the Pleistocene era, no new species of man or arrival of other life forms have occurred in the millions of years. Just species extinctions. To date man is the last and most complex of all species.

Critically there is no evidence whatsoever in the fossil record for the concept of Darwinian type "biological evolution" resulting in species improvement to form new species. At the beginning of the Cambrian era there were just unicellular organisms and worms, then miraculously fully formed trilobites arrived, followed by fully formed versions of virtually every phyla that exists or has ever existed - including the 30 or so groups of them still around today. Nowhere are there any transitional species exhibiting small Darwinian type 'evolutionary' changes. Just an amazing range of new fully formed and novel species - with an incredible and varying degree of complexity, filling every environmental niche.[18]

Many species which have survived until today are very ancient and are unchanged since prehistoric times. These include all reptiles, turtles, lungfish, spiders, cockroaches, silverfish etc. and many recently discovered which were thought extinct e.g. the coelacanth fish. In addition, all species which have survived until today are found to be immutable in the sense that they cannot change their genome into that of any other species. This is surely unsurprising, since successful mating cannot occur between different species. The concept of fish 'evolving', moving onto land to create new mammal species, then later returning to the sea to create whales and porpoises etc. is therefore sadly just a children's fairy story unsupported by either facts or logic.

All one can observe in the fossil record is both subspecies variation within the genome, and the arrival over time of a plethora of new species without any apparent cause - at least - as is known by science today. (Perhaps Darwin should have listened to his enlightened paleontologist colleagues such as "Cuvier, Owen, Agassiz, Barrande, Falconer, E. Forbes etc. and all the greatest geologists Lyall, Murchison, Sedgewick etc. As he says about them all in his book *On the Origin of Species* – "*...they have unanimously, often vehemently, maintained the immutability of the species*". [19]

To write further at this stage on the wealth of scientific evidence which shows that Darwinism is simply wrong and therefore an invalid argument against a creator/God, would seriously lose impetus in this Chapter for continuation of my arguments in favor of a creator/God. Since the false view portrayed by Darwinism has wrongly and adversely effected the belief of so many people in a God/creator since his 1856 publication of *On the Origin of Species*, it is of such importance that it rightly deserves a more comprehensive rebuttal treatment. I have therefore included detailed evidence against Darwinism in Appendix 1 entitled, "Darwinism and Atheism", for those who wish to investigate this further.

The above brief look at Darwinism deals with a necessary preliminary discussion to observe whether this defeats the argument for "The Theory of Design". Fairly, it is seen that the "Theory of Design" still remains unshakable, as Darwinism simply cannot explain the remarkable creation of new species, nor the amazing transformation from essentially unicellular organisms at the beginning of the Cambrian to an incredible increase in complexity at its end - most of which arrived in a mere three million years. As mentioned earlier, this "Biological Big Bang" of the Cambrian era, does by its interventional nature and massive changes to life itself, provide similarity to the "Cosmological Big Bang". An increase in complexity from earlier simplicity, does not necessarily suggest evolution - as is often thought; but instead, could be easily be regarded as a design intention to populate the earth first with simple lifeforms which then can act as food for the more complex species arrival later.

In summary, both recent scientific experiments plus the observation of the fossil record over now some 150 years, shows in a timed sequence manner of increasing complexity, the appearance of fully formed species equipped with ingenious mechanisms suitable to cope with varying environments. This relatively astonishingly brief period of time of increasingly complex life forms again does not demonstrate 'evolution'. Instead it suggests intelligence and planning. Surely this demonstrates purpose and design indicative of a creator. Needless to say there is no scientific evidence whatsoever for Darwinian type biological evolution, or a chance mechanism to account for the arrival of new species. Darwinism and evolution is therefore a sad myth which has hoodwinked so many since publication of Darwin's book *On the Origin of Species*.

Noteworthy and unquestionably though, our two known mechanisms for subspecies variation i.e. mating and epigenics, exhibit a program process function - just as much as that in a man invented computer. In the case of mating, the provision of two sexual partners provides an arbitrary gene mixing software program to provide a variable adaptive response of progeny to the environment. The gene mixing also assists gene defect repair of each partner. It also considerably assists survival of the species. Similarly, epigenics provides a complex software biological computer program of environmental triggers. When this program is run, it changes gene expression in accordance with the specified cellular membrane data list of environmental triggers. Such programs signify intelligence! Certainly never a pure chance random cause beloved by atheists. The fact that we do observe in the fossil record a time based arrival of fully formed new species up until the Pleistocene era when man arrived, is currently an unsolved enigma.

The relatively recent discovery of epigenics does however give some hope that one day further research and experiments will provide a science based answer. There is though some evidence given in Chapter 9 which gives a possible solution to the arrival of new species.

Given that there is no evidence whatsoever for chance driven biological 'evolution' of mankind, it is interesting to note that in the case of a highly developed complex and sentient species such as ourselves, biological evolution would - if designed and maintained up until now by a creator/God - may well be unnecessary for our future. This is because we are now rapidly developing our own capability by genetic manipulation and other scientific medical developments. As a result, we may be close to being able to radically evolve ourselves to an enhanced species of almost our own choosing. It may well be that such freedom of choice was intended by a creator/God and has already occurred elsewhere in the universe.

Apart from the often quoted example above of the human eye to support the

'Theory of Design', there are countless examples of cases in nature of such ingenuity and suggestion of created purpose, that to suggest they have occurred randomly, by chance, and without a designer - defies all logic.

For example, do not feathers plus the cleverly light, hollow bones of birds denote purpose and incredible design? And how about Venus Fly Traps and Pitcher plants as an ingenious way in which they can capture food? Did you know that if nitrogenous crystal secretions on fish scales were arranged beyond their micron alignment, fish would lose their iridescence and ability to appear invisible to most predators? Where did the angler fish get its 'angle' i.e. the rod protuberance above its mouth with an organic "fishing" line and red wiggly bait? How did electric eels know how to become electric, develop powerful banks of batteries and understand the physics of the electrocution process? Or for that matter how did snakes have prior knowledge of the chemical process of poisoning to "evolve" in that direction and yet ensure an ability to be resistant to their own venom? Also, how do plants know about hybrid vigour, where the humble dandelion provides a form of parachute to transport its seeds far on the wind, the sycamore chooses propeller design; and fruit and berry trees use irresistible flavorful fruit to seduce birds, beast and man to cunningly do their work for them? Does this not reek of intelligence – somewhere?

Biological 'Evolution' has been shown to be a myth unsupported by evidence or science. Instead the arrival of fully formed species with increasing complexity in a time based manner is fully supported by the evidence and suggests mind, intelligence and purpose. Similarly, instinctive behavior with its inherent association with mind and similarity with software instructions but accessible via the subconscious brain, also has the hallmarks of intelligence.

We now need to consider the remaining biological issue - the question of the 'Origin of Life' itself.

1.3 THE ORIGIN OF LIFE

Most scientist today, even those who accept Darwinian biological 'evolution', do not consider life arose spontaneously by chance occurrence. The number in this category rapidly increased with Nobel Prize winner Francis Crick's discovery of the structure DNA in 1953 - as it then became apparent that due to the complexity, and coding structure of DNA, it was improbable that it could arise by some chance process of self organisation. As Francis Crick himself (a former atheist) said:

> "An honest man, armed with all the knowledge available to us now, could only state that in some sense, the origin of life appears to be a miracle, so many are the conditions which would have had to be satisfied to get it going." [20]

Bill Gates himself said:

> "DNA is like a software program, only much more complex than anything we have ever devised." [21]

and,

Owen Gingerich, Professor of Science at Harvard University agreed with a previous Royal Astronomer and the late Sir Fred Hoyle, when he suggested that the formation of DNA is so improbable as to require a super intelligence. [22]

The fact is that DNA is a code system of genetic bases which together form a massive "library" of software instructions needed by cells to assemble and build protein molecules. The coding system uses the well-known chemical "bases" (or nucleotides) called Adenine (A), Guanine(G), Cytosine (C), and Thymine (T) - as a 4-character digital code. The genetic meaning of each sequence depends upon the code and its position in the sequence on the DNA strand. A key aspect is that although the **structure** of DNA depends on chemical attraction bonds between hydrogen, sugar and the phosphate molecules that form the two twisting helical backbones of the DNA molecule, there are no chemical bonds gripping the information coding chemicals comprising the nucleotide bases. This means that the individual bases of the four character A, G, C, T software instruction code set for assembly of proteins, cannot interact with each other and are totally interchangeable. Therefore, since there is nothing that forces them into any particular sequence, the sequencing and coding *'recipes'* of DNA have independence from the rest of the cell. This coding and sequencing on each DNA strand therefore has to come from somewhere. The individual codes and sequencing is such a vast accurate knowledge based library of meaningful and accurate body building information. It provides entirely different DNA encyclopedias for each species, that simply could not occur spontaneously or 'evolve'. It would have to be programmed. Who and where therefore is the programmer?

As stated by Scientist Stephen C. Meyer, a graduate of Cambridge University and a former geophysicist and college professor, who now directs the Centre for Science and Culture at the Discovery Institute in Seattle:

> "Whenever you have a sequential arrangement that's complex and corresponds to an independent pattern or functional requirement, this kind of information is always the product of intelligence." [23]

Also by George Sim Johnson in an article in the Wall Street Journal – "Did Darwin Get It Right":

"Human DNA contains more organised information than the Encyclopedia Britannica. If the full text of the encyclopedia were to arrive in computer code from outer space, most people would regard this as proof of the existence of extraterrestrial intelligence. But when seen in nature it is explained as the workings of random forces." [24]

It is impossible for chance, or self-organising systems to have causal power to provide information. Only intelligence can provide such information. In fact, for a short simple functional protein molecule to occur by chance, has been calculated as a probability of 1 in 10^{125}. (Note: The French mathematician Emile Borei, summed up the laws of probability in his Single Law of Chance where he found that, when the odds are 10^{15} against, then the chance of a single event happening is negligible on the terrestrial scale. When the odds get beyond 10^{50}, there is virtually no chance of it happening even on the cosmic scale.[25])

The impossible odds above refer to just a **single** short functional protein molecule. A minimally complex cell requires information from its DNA strand to manufacture between 300 and 500 protein molecules!

This of course is no problem for just any one of your cells typically six feet! of coiled DNA. During every moment of your life, DNA has to cater for an incredibly engineered largely error free cell replication. It is also busy supplying the 'recipes' for the cell's engine room to manufacture up to 20,500 different required proteins, any one of which requires typically 1,200 to 2000 bases out of the 3 billion human genome codes to produce. In fact, as far as memory is concerned, the DNA of one cell, stores far more information in a smaller space than the most advanced supercomputer on the planet.

Our discussion so far largely deals with DNA, but apart from DNA, the cell itself is the most complex and amazing information processing system known to man. A single cell (of diameter typically one tenth of a millimeter in size), not only provides a computer processing system beyond anything on earth, but has associated with it, a complex factory to manufacture cell material necessary to carry out all bodily functions required by any part of a particular species i.e. whether organs, limbs, brain etc. It also throws in added functions such as error detection and correction for manufacture and assembly, and an essential self-replication growth capability to fulfil all desired shape characteristics anywhere in the body. It is surrounded by a cell membrane which monitors and wards off possible invasions (the immune system). It also permits special environmental detectors (special proteins) on the cell membrane, to trigger appropriately and vary manufacture in accordance with an included knowledged based data set. A cell's factory is subservient to the needs of the body, but (unlike any factory on earth), each cell acts independently as a combined distributed processor/factory unit.

And, according to Darwinists all this is supposed to have occurred by chance? As said by J.W.G Johnson in his book *The Crumbling Theory of Evolution*:

> "The living cell is the most complex structure that exists; and its every part depends somehow on its other parts. When it is realised that a cell could not evolve part by part, but must exist in total or not at all, then it becomes clear that the propaganda about spontaneous generation of first life is unscientific wishful thinking." [27]

Also when we extract any of the parts or pieces of a cell for example - DNA, a ribosome (the manufacturing unit), any protein, or the membrane etc., we find they are nothing more than an organic molecule - but a completely lifeless molecule! Whatever life is, life coheres to the organised cell, the complete cell.

Appropriately, a number of scientists have used one of the most powerful science based tools, namely probability mathematics (as covered earlier) to determine the odds against life occurring spontaneously by chance. Sir Fred Hoyle and Chandra Wickramasinghe, Professor of Applied Mathematics and Astronomy at University College, Cardiff both calculated this independently, and the result they agreed on was - odds against of $10^{10^{40,000}}$ (Note: It will be recalled from the above that French mathematician Emile Borei calculated that when the odds get beyond 10^{50}, there is virtually no chance of it happening even on the cosmic scale[28]).

Sir Fred Hoyle, on the basis of his probability calculations more pictorially stated, that on the issue of the probable chance creation of life, that:

> "This would equate to the chance of "a tornado sweeping through a junk yard assembling a Boeing 747" [29]

The mathematical findings above add immense scientific weight to any observational conclusion that the mind boggling complexity of a cell could simply not have originated by chance. For anyone studying the micro biology of cell complexity and functions, they must inevitably face up to the fact that each tiny cell exhibits the characteristics of order, design, engineering, foresight and purpose, all of which suggest mind, and intelligence - but beyond anything we have experienced.

Debate on a "Theory of Design" is by no means exhausted, as evidence of design in the universe itself needs to be debated, together with proven evidence for evolution of nearly all of the chemical elements, stars, planets and galaxies.

So far in our quest to find whether there is sufficient evidence to support the "Theory of Design" and therefore the case for creator/God, we have covered the origin of life itself. This was followed by the arrival of new species over time including ingenious adaption mechanisms for all forms of life to their environment. Nowhere is there evidence for any of these matters concerning life to have arisen by chance. In fact probability theory as shown above indicates that this is impossible.

Apart from life issues, we now need to revert back to the "Universe" (where we started after looking at the Law of Cause and Effect), and determine whether chance is possible, or whether (as in life issues), we see everywhere design, intelligence and mind.

Before we deal with the "big" issues of the universe, such as 'The Big Bang' and fine tuning aspects of the laws and constants of physics, there are number of other cosmological issues below worthy of consideration, but often overlooked.

1.4 LOGICAL CONSISTENCY AND UNITY BOTH IN NATURE AND THE UNIVERSE

With casinos, early detection of fraud is critical to ensure profit margins are maintained. The key criteria used is a test for logical consistency. In his book *How Blind the Watchmaker*, David Wilcox points out:

> "As every casino operator knows, the success rate of random searches (for fraud) is less a matter of possibilities than of probabilities... **A rigged game can be deduced because of its excessive string of low probability outcomes**." [30]

On this basis, the universe would definitely appear to be "rigged" as most would argue that the universe is rational, objective, has pattern, symmetry, and predictability to it. As above, effect follows cause in a dependable manner. *Unity* is also a feature of the universe in that, as stated by Kitty Ferguson in her book *The Fire in the Equations* there is:

> "One system of logic is fundamental to everything. The universe operates by underlying laws which do not change in an arbitrary fashion from place to place, from minute to minute, or even millennium to millennium. There are no loose ends, no real contradictions. At some deep level, everything fits."[31]

There is also the surprising consistency in just about everything. Taking the case of subatomic particles, why should they each be exactly the same and why are there not at least very subtle differences - as could be expected in a random chance based universe? As Professor Swinburne points out in his book *Is There a God*, each electron behaves like every other electron in repelling every other electron with the same electrical force. Oak trees behave like other oak trees, and tigers like other tigers.

"If all the coins found on an archaeological site have the same markings, or all the documents in a room are written with the same characteristic handwriting, we look for an explanation in terms of a common source. The apparently coincidental cries out for explanation" [32].

Nature's preferences for certain numbers and sequences seems inexplicable (and incredible). The so-called Golden Mean - roughly equal to 1.62, and supposedly giving the most aesthetically pleasing dimensions for rectangles, has been found lurking in all kinds of places, from seashells to knots. The Fibonacci sequencee. - 1, 1, 2, 3, 5, 8 and so on, every digit being the sum of its two predecessors, crops up everywhere in nature, from the arrangement of leaves on plants to the pattern on pineapple skins. Use of the Fibonacci sequence by members of a plant, leaf or shoot, ensures that the alignment of stem positions gives a minimum of overshadowing and a maximum of exposure to light and air.(How do the plants know?).[33]

Paley, famous for his example of a watch supporting the Theory of Design (see above) went on to argue that **the universe itself** resembles a watch in its organisation and complexity - though on a vastly greater scale. Surely he argued, there must be a cosmic designer who arranged the universe this way for a purpose. "The contrivances of nature surpasses the contrivances of art, in the complexity, subtlety and curiosity of the mechanism."

Paul Davies famous author on Cosmology and Professor of Physics at a number of Universities, provides perhaps a far better example than that of Paley's watch. He depicts a monkey tinkering on the piano and points out that we all would surely agree that - "*the chances of his playing a well-known tune rather than a chaotic sequence of notes is minute.*" Expressed mathematically, Davies points out that the probability of a random choice leading to an ordered state declines exponentially with the degree of order.

> "Translated into a cosmological context…if the universe is simply an accident, the odds against it containing any appreciable order are vanishingly small. In other words, if "The Big Bang" was a random event, the probability would be absolutely overwhelming that the emerging cosmic material would be at thermodynamic equilibrium and in a totally disordered state."

Davies has given a mathematical example of what one might think a fairly low probability state compared with that of the incredibly high ordered state of our universe occurring by chance by indicating that "*the relatively low probability (compared as for example with the creation of the universe) of the more simple case of the chance event of a litre of air rushing momentarily to one end of a box, an amazingly low probability of* - $10^{10^{(20)}}$ *to one* [34].

Unquestionably since the universe is in now in such a highly ordered state (e.g. such as a single living cell), occurrence by chance is impossible. The only explanation left therefore is that it happened as a result of the actions of a creator/God.

Atheistic scientists wedded to the origin of everything happening by chance, seem to have no ability to explain the amazing logical consistency around us. Nor can they explain the obvious expectation that occurs to all of us, namely that our most likely expectation is that without a creator/God, we should observe chaos everywhere (or nothing, as we would not exist) - rather than order. Order universally suggests mind.

1.5   BEAUTY IN NATURE

There is in fact no suitable mechanistic explanation for beauty - whether observed in nature's laws, life or mathematics. Unquestionably beauty must be an inherent property of laws governing the universe. Since there is no necessity in it, and it is evident everywhere, there is no explanation as to how this could possibly have originated from chance. As physicist Henry Margenau explains:

> "We do not believe that beauty is only in the eye of the beholder. There are objective features underlying at least some experiences of beauty, such as the frequency ratios of the notes of a major chord, symmetry of geometric forms, or the aesthetic appeal of juxtaposed complementary colours. None of these have survival value, but all are prevalent in nature in a measure hardly compatible with chance. We marvel at the song of the birds, the colour scheme of flowers (do insects have a sense of aesthetics?), of birds feathers, and at the incomparable beauty of a fallen maple leaf, its deep red colouring, its blue veins, and its golden edges. Are these qualities useful for survival when the leaf is about to decay? [35]
>
> We note also pattern, geometry and splendour in nature from the incredible intricacy of feathers, or a snowflake; to the riot of colour in the plumage of a Macau parrot. Not all nature exhibits perfection in form though, as we sometimes encounter a certain asymmetry e.g. natural crystals are not perfect geometric shapes or tree trunks perfectly shaped. It seems that irregularities provide a necessary diversification, tension and balance to all things - just as we would find in art, where perfection of form or performance would provide boring constancy."

Also as mentioned above, for scientists there is vast beauty in the preciseness and form of mathematics. There is logical consistency, also great simplicity, and even elegance. There is also a sense that mathematics must be a fundamental part and perhaps an inherent property of the universe – since it shares such a rapport with nature and has been a prime factor in scientific progress and discovery. Certainly the universe is marvellously amenable to rational inquiry by mathematics.[36]

Peter Plichta, who recently discovered the long sought mathematical formula for the derivation of prime numbers, has found sequences of prime numbers in nature e.g. there is the pattern: 1+19 amino acids and 1+19 pure isotopes. In addition he believes he has found some evidence in nature for the decimal system[37]. Can all this arise from blind chance?

Ever since the days of prehistoric man, we have always gained a sense of accomplishment and pride in adding beauty to things we make e.g. we innately decorate a vase or a knife handle etc. (A bower bird also adds items around its nest to add beauty). We also enjoy producing art itself and observing it, as well as other forms of self-expression such as music, ballet etc. (obviously also a female peacock is smitten with the magnificent splendour of a male peacocks tail). Not only is creation of beauty an activity completely devoid of necessity, but it is very much associated with the intellect, or mind.

Beauty in nature therefore strongly suggests the mind of a creator/God. It also seems that we share the same love of beauty and are provided with the ability to appreciate it.

1.6 THE LAWS OF PHYSICS (I.E. THE UNIVERSE, OR NATURE)

Dating back to Isaac Newton and his discovery of the law of gravitation, scientists have never stopped attempting to discover "Laws of the Universe" to describe patterns observed in nature. What seems inexplicable, is the fact that first these laws are capable of discovery by us, and secondly that they can be described in mathematics which we have created for ourselves. They are also universal (i.e. they apply unfailingly everywhere in the universe), they are absolute (i.e. they do not depend on anything else), and they are eternal (i.e. as far as we know they never change even minutely over time). Rather than being merely useful for us, their reliability and predictive capability makes us certain that the laws depict real and fundamental truths about the cosmos.

As Paul Davies claims:

"If they are considered to have such status, then the laws are said to be transcendent, because they transcend the actual physical world itself." [38]

Interestingly Paul Davies therefore likens the Laws of the Universe to software and physical states to hardware i.e. all physical states are bound by the laws (i.e. the software 'programs' of the universe).

This surely suggests design, and a creator/ God of the 'program' of laws.

(I well remember watching a Television programme on April 9th 2012 featuring a discussion between Cardinal Pell of Sydney and the high priest of atheism and Darwinism, Richard Dawkins. Dawkins finally had to admit that the one area that made him doubt his atheistic viewpoint were "the Laws of the Universe", as he could not see how they could have occurred by chance.)

Complexity in nature seems to be very finely balanced, so that even very small changes in the form of the laws would apparently prevent this complexity from arising (as will be seen below in item 1.7 below dealing with "the Big Bang" and fine tuning of the universe). As Paul Davies observes:

> "A careful study suggests that the laws of the universe are remarkably felicitous for the emergence of richness and variety. In the case of living organisms, their existence seems to depend on a number of fortuitous coincidences that some scientists and philosophers have hailed as nothing short of astonishing" [39]

1.7 "THE BIG BANG" AND FINE TUNING OF THE UNIVERSE

1.7.1 "The Big Bang"

"The Big Bang" was mentioned at the beginning of this Chapter when dealing with the "Law of Cause and Effect". The issue then was that logically there had to be a first cause for the Universe, since one cannot create something out of nothing, prior to "The Big Bang". We now need to examine the "Big Bang" in more detail. Hopefully you will find as I do, that the detail below concerning "The Big Bang" and "Fine Tuning of the Universe" will reveal for you the most amazing and inescapable indication of design and intelligence in the whole area of Cosmology. And perhaps for you also, overwhelming belief based on the science, for a creator/God.

Background radiation revealed as static on radios and television plus the small temperature of some 2.73 degrees above absolute zero, has long been regarded as evidence of the remnant energy left over from "The Big Bang", and signalling that incredible moment about 13.7 billion years ago when "The Big Bang" occurred. Physicists believe a micro second after, all that we see around us now, some 100 billion stars and 100 billion galaxies, was squashed into the size of a mere grape.

Scientists had the opportunity to see for themselves how "The Big Bang" occurred by studying background radiation left over from "The Big Bang" using a Differential Microwave Radiometer. This took 360 degree pictures of the entire sky from a NASA's COBE (Cosmic Background Explorer) satellite launched in 1969 and specially built for the purpose. The CMB (Cosmic Microwave Background) is the oldest light we can see and amazingly depicts the remanent pattern of "The Big Bang". The CMB is affected by "The Big Bang" expansion, stretched out into the microwave part of the electromagnetic spectrum, and cooled to its present-day temperature. This residual radiation is critical to the study of cosmology because it bears on it the fossil imprint of those particles, a pattern of miniscule intensity variations from which we can decipher the vital statistics of the universe.

The results verified some predictions and beliefs from earlier studies, but nevertheless shocked the scientific world. Contrary to popular belief, instead of "The Big Bang" being a big bang, it was **not an explosion**. Explosions cause material to be ejected in a completely random manner and in a totally unpredictable way. What was pictorially obvious, was "The Big Bang" turned out to be a "Big Stretch". "The Big Bang" actually created everything that is: space, time, matter and energy blossoming forth at the speed of light. Physicists and cosmologists are amazed that such a violent event as "The Big Bang", could have been so balanced. This "big stretch" expansion, which is still going on around and beyond us today, was found to be **incredibly smooth and seemingly controlled**; quite the opposite of an explosion. Throughout the whole CMB map of the heavens, the most striking observation was an overall **evenness** of distribution of radiation, but with occasional blotchiness i.e. fluctuations.

As Paul Davies has pointed out:

"The level of fluctuations is critical. If variations were a bit bigger it would have caused black holes. Smaller fluctuations would mean less gravity, so that matter would never have clumped together. Therefore we have a "Goldilocks" situation where things are just right. If this were not the case, galaxies could not have formed." [40]

He also pointed out:

"That had the explosion differed in strength at the outset by one part in 10^{60} then, the universe as we perceive it could not exist. [41]

(Note: You may recall, from the above, that French mathematician Emile Borei calculated that when the odds get beyond 10^{50}, there it could not happen by chance even on the cosmic scale.)

Laura Danly an American astronomer and academic at the Griffith Observatory in Los Angeles asks us to imagine that this figure equates to the number of grains of sand on earth, and asks how many grains of sand we must throw away to wreck the Universe. The answer she gives is, you guessed it .... just one grain of sand! [42]

The initial conditions necessary before "The Big Bang" surely suggests design beyond comprehension. This, then followed by a "Big Stretch" to actualise the Universe itself we see all around us, surely seems to rule out any explanation that this was a chance event.

1.7.2   The Fine Tuning of the Universe

Although (as covered earlier in the Chapter), recent discoveries suggest that biological Darwinian type 'Evolution' - does not exist. On the other hand, evolution of matter by organising itself into more complex forms is undisputed. Due to gravitational attraction gas clouds form stars, which then form planets in a similar way. Stars unite into galaxies etc. All due to the known laws of physics.

A form of evolution is also exhibited with atoms, starting from the simplest, the hydrogen atom, which provides the energy to ignite a sun by fusing with helium. The sun, the factory of matter conversion, then fuses helium into carbon and so on, until heavier and heavier elements such as lead and uranium are finally produced. In this way the simplest atom is converted into the more complex atoms necessary for life itself. When the larger stars dissipate the majority of their energy, they often explode violently in a nova (or supernova) and the large range of elements produced over the life of the star are dissipated to coalesce again with other intergalactic gases to form new stars (suns) and possibly planets. In this way, finally over many millions of years, all the known stable elements are eventually produced. This process is often regarded as the evolution of chemical elements. Important very heavy elements to man are manganese and iron [43] and it is a sobering thought to realise that most of the atoms in your body have arisen from stellar explosions millions of years ago.

Perhaps the most remarkable method by which an element is produced in a sun's factory are the specific fusions forming carbon and oxygen. The process that creates carbon by fusion is complex and improbable, and yet carbon is one of the most abundant elements. All life of course depends on carbon and hydrocarbons. Two helium nuclei come together in stars to form the unstable beryllium nucleus isotope. Specific resonances within these helium and beryllium atomic nuclei enable parts to stick together rather than fly apart. This resonance 'glue' in the case of carbon just happens to match the combined energy of the beryllium atom and a colliding helium nucleus. Without it, there would be relatively few carbon atoms. Similarly, the internal details of the oxygen nucleus play a critical role. As related by Owen Gingerich, Professor of Science, Harvard University:

> "Had the resonance level in the carbon atom been 4 percent lower, there would be essentially no carbon. Had that level in the oxygen been only half a

percent higher, virtually all of the carbon would have been converted to oxygen. Without that carbon abundance, neither you nor I would be here now. I am told that Fred Hoyle, who together with Willy Fowler found this remarkable nuclear arrangement, said that nothing has shook his atheism as much as this discovery. Occasionally Fred Hoyle and I have sat down to discuss one or another astronomical or historical point, but I never had enough nerve to ask him if his atheism had really been shaken by finding the nuclear resonance structure of carbon and oxygen. However, the answer came rather clearly in the November 1981 issue of the Cal Tech alumni magazine, where he wrote:"

"Would you not say to yourself "Some super calculating intellect must have designed the properties of the carbon atom, otherwise the chance of my finding such an atom through the blind forces of nature would be utterly minuscule." Of course you would …….. A common sense interpretation of the facts suggests that a super intellect has monkeyed with physics, as well as with chemistry and biology, and that there are no blind forces worth speaking about in nature. The numbers one calculates from the facts, seem to me so overwhelming as to put this conclusion almost beyond question." [44]

None of the above would occur if it were not for the forces of nature i.e. the laws of physics. Associated with each though, is the concept accepted by many physicists of a sort of mathematical cosmic code. This is because the strength of these forces can be characterised in each case by numbers (i.e. codes) called fundamental constants.

There are many examples where the strength of a force of nature determined by its "code" i.e. the "constant", can have massive effects. As pointed out by physicist Freeman Dyson that:

"If the nuclear force were slightly stronger, hydrogen would be a rare element and stars would not exist. If substantially weaker, then hydrogen would not burn and there would be no heavy elements or life."

Surveying this broad pattern, he concludes that it argues purpose, not coincidence.

"The more I examine the universe and study the details of its architecture, the more evidence I find that the universe in some sense must have known we were coming".[45]

If gravity were only slightly less powerful, stars and galaxies could not have formed. Similarly if gravity were not the weakest of the four forces, neither would we have galaxies or planets. If the electric charge on an electron were only fractionally different, stars would not explode as supernovas and produce the evolution of chemical elements essential to all life. Apart from these examples involving constants embodied in formulae, there are other examples of unassociated 'constants' i.e. the speed of light in a vacuum and the mass and ratios of elementary particle masses whose value is critical to sustain the universe and life.

Surprisingly none of these 'constants' have dependencies on any known natural laws and therefore could take any arbitrary values.

Ervin Laszlo, Founder and Director of the General Evolution Research Group, founder and President of the Club of Budapest, Past President of the International Society for System Sciences, and advisor to the Director – General of Unesco, in his excellent book, *The Whispering Pond*, has no doubts that the fine tuning of the universe to the parameters of life is no accident. He points out that although matter forms a thin precipitate in space, it is of just the right density to permit life. If it were slightly greater than it is, interstellar encounters would knock life-carrying planets out of safe orbits and this would either freeze or vaporise all forms of life. If the nucleus binding force were merely a fraction *weaker* than it is, deuteron could not exist and stars such as the Sun could not shine. And if that force were slightly *stronger* than it is, the Sun and other active stars would inflate and perhaps explode. Also:

> "If the neutron did not outweigh the proton in the nucleus of atoms, the active lifetime of the Sun and other stars would be reduced to a few hundred years; if the electric charge of electrons and protons did not balance precisely, all configurations of matter would be unstable and the universe would consist of nothing more than radiation and a relatively uniform mixture of gases. And, if in the inflation that followed "The Big Bang" had not been precise small-scale departures from large-scale regularities, there would not be galaxies and stars today - and hence no planets".

Because of this he states:

> "The expansion rate of the universe and the values of the universal forces must have been determined already when this universe came into being. They could hardly have been adjusted to the process they initiated purely by chance[46]."

And for support he quotes Roger Penrose's calculations, where assuming our universe occurred by pure chance, $(10^{10})^{23}$ alternative universes would be required before finding a similar universe. Also Paul Davies calculations which show that the time required to achieve the level of order we now meet in the universe purely by random processes is of the order of at least $(10^{10})^{80}$ years! [47]

Of course this is an unbelievably vast time - but clearly therefore indicates the impossibility of such a chance event. In any case time is not thought to exist before "The Big Bang".

Penrose has worked out the probability of all these constants and the Big Bang occurring by chance as $(10^{10})^{23}$ - a figure well beyond the number of all subatomic particles in the universe, and beyond comprehension.

The number of fundamental constants, any one of which would have either made the universe impossible to exist or life itself as we know it, exceeds at least 150 - many of which are included in Yale educated Astrophysicist George Greenstein's book *The Symbiotic Universe*. The main ones **on which life depends** are included below, with a further 9 Included as Appendix 2.

1. Oxygen level: On earth, oxygen comprises 21 percent of the atmosphere. That precise figure is a constant that makes life on earth possible. If oxygen were 25 percent fires would erupt spontaneously; if it were 15 percent, human beings would suffocate.

2. Atmospheric Transparency: If the atmosphere were less transparent, not enough solar radiation would reach the earth's surface. If it were more transparent, we would be bombarded with too much solar radiation to survive.

3. Moon-Earth Gravitational Interaction: If the interaction were greater than it is, tidal effects on the oceans, atmosphere, and rotational period would be too severe, if it were less, orbital changes would cause climate instabilities. In either event life could not exist. If there was no moon, ocean tides would not exist, and without movement oceans would become toxic. Sulphurous and methane clouds resulting from hydrogen sulphide emanating from stasis and rotting of vegetation and fish in oceans would most likely wipe out all life.[48]

There are similar well known facets of nature on which life depends, e.g. the carbon cycle. Less well known is our dependence on lightning, as without the millions of lightning discharges each day there would be no life on this planet. Plants require fertilization with nitrates (much of which is synthesized by lightning) if they are to produce their 20 amino acids[49].

In biology there are many other key dependencies for life, such as photosynthesis in plants. There are also patterns – some overtly suggestive of purposeful intelligent design, such as the "rule of population biology" that dictates that males and females tend to be born in equal numbers[30]. Also apparently purposeful patterns of behaviour – who told the spider how to construct its web and why?

The universe clearly appears uniquely suited to life, which also seems very much to be its centre of purpose. Natural laws e.g. the inverse square law of gravity etc. and the constants mentioned above are very suggestive of 'software' crucial to make the universe (the computer) tick. With this analogy, 'mathematics' would play the role of the computer language necessary to write the programs.

Who then is the programmer?

You will recall earlier in this Chapter we learned Casino operators identify how a rigged game can be identified because of a string of low probability outcomes. Do we detect therefore that the universe and life itself is rigged?

It is difficult to avoid the conclusion that a rational universe aimed at fostering life implies mind and therefore a creator/God, who must have also written the computer language and programs.

(It is interesting to note that Stephen Hawking referred to the laws of nature as 'the mind of God'[50]).

1.8   COMPLEXITY/ PROGRESSION OF LIFE

Although there are a number of setbacks to our development and progression on earth, such as natural catastrophes; the overall trend for life can be observed as that of increased complexity. The fossil record shows life on earth initially arose as unicellular organisms. Since then more complex life forms have arisen with increased intelligence/ knowledge, as exemplified in man. It seems likely that this progression will continue, as physicist Professor Paul Davies has imagined:

> "One can envisage, for example, intelligent life, or even machine intelligence gradually becoming more advanced and spreading throughout the cosmos, gaining control over larger and larger portions until its manipulation of matter and energy is so refined that this intelligence would be indistinguishable from nature itself." [51]

To a microbe we are unquestionably a super intelligence. Therefore, as a species, are we so conceited that we cannot conceive of the very high probability of species with greater intelligence than ourselves and also a super intelligent/creator?

To use the old cliché – 'we only know what we know', so we could also be limited by our habituation with a physical environment and not appreciate that all possible life forms including **non-physical life forms** may exist and were actuated by nature's 'program'. It may be that a non-physical life form could have evolved far more rapidly without the restrictions of physical form - as with a creator/God.

This concept has a lot of impressive supporters including the astronomer Sir Fred

Hoyle, the physicist Frank Tipler and the writer Isaac Asimov. Professor Paul Davies has also raised the possibility of backward causation, whereby the super intelligence at the end of the universe acts backward in time to create the universe, as part of a self-consistent causal loop. Much and all as this appears fanciful, it is completely consistent with quantum mechanics. Ideas like this are similar to those espoused by both Sir Fred Hoyle and the physicist John Wheeler, possibly due to their awareness that time is an irrelevant factor in quantum theory which pervades all subatomic particle physics - as has been verified repeatedly by experiment.[52]

As mentioned earlier, since the formation of all the essential chemical elements for life requires some stars to first reach the supernovae stage, life anywhere in the universe can only arise after millions of years. Expansion of the universe over these millions of years has meant that distances between neighbouring stars are now so immense they have to be measured in light years. Our universe is rapidly expanding and current indications are that it will continue to expand at least in the indefinite future based on mass and dark matter calculations. Due to the inevitability of such vast distances occurring between stars and galaxies before life can flourish, John Barrow makes an interesting point in his book *Between Inner and Outer Space*, that "Should civilizations evolve in different parts of the universe, then, such civilizations would be forced to reach an appropriate degree of technology and social responsibility before they could communicate with other civilizations and exchange knowledge." He also suggests that vast distances would mitigate against wars and cultural imperialism by technologically superior civilizations. If this were not the case he suggests that knowledge of superior life forms, apart from the threat of wars could result in:

> "All motivation for human progress might be removed. Fundamental discoveries would be forever out of reach. A decadent, impoverished humanity might result[53]."

One could equally make a point about mankind's capability to travel throughout our own planet and more particularly development of technology over the years to aid weapon development. Surprisingly knowledge for improved technology seems always limited to the extent that it seems matched by a corresponding increase in our social responsibility, plus sufficient maturity for us to not quite destroy ourselves – yet! Rather than this being purely coincidence, one wonders whether this exhibits evidence of purpose and higher intelligence(s).

Speculation aside, unquestionably there is a remarkable apparent self-regulation of our planet earth's biosphere over many epochs, which is strongly suggestive of purposeful action aimed at continually maintaining an environment suitable for life. (This concept was first noted by James Lovelock who called it the "Gaia Hypothesis").

With the initial development of plant life and photosynthesis, earth's primeval atmosphere largely consisted of carbon dioxide and a very small component of oxygen. This was an unparalleled era of vegetation growth and forests flourished with this high carbon dioxide content which suited their respiration. Then as oxygen breathing animal life evolved and increased, correspondingly the atmospheric oxygen increased to 21% and amazingly has been maintained at that level ever since. If it dropped to below fifteen percent, *nothing* would burn. More importantly organisms could not breathe and would asphyxiate. If the oxygen in the air rose to above twenty-five percent, *everything* would burn. Combustion would occur spontaneously and fires would rage around the planet. In addition, a layer of ozone has gradually built up at the top of the atmosphere and from then on protected life on Earth from the Sun's dangerous ultra-violet rays. Life which was previously restricted to the oceans, was then able to flourish in the exposed conditions on land and this then set the stage for the arrival of animals including mankind[54].

Also as pointed out by Professor Paul Davies in his book *The Cosmic Blueprint*, despite the sun's luminosity increasing by about 30 per cent over earth's history, somehow the surface temperature also seems to have been self-regulated to remain remarkably constant over this time. The mechanism for this is related to the level of carbon dioxide in the atmosphere, as in primeval times, the large carbon dioxide content of the atmosphere acted as a blanket (i.e. the 'Greenhouse Effect') and kept the Earth warm in spite of the relatively weak sunlight of that era. Later when life formed and plants used carbon dioxide for their respiration and to form carbohydrates for growth, the level of carbon dioxide in the atmosphere declined. As Paul Davies explains:

> "This transformation in the chemical make-up of the Earth's atmosphere was most felicitous because it matched rather precisely the increasing output of heat from the Sun. As the Sun grew hotter, so the carbon dioxide blanket was gradually eaten away by life."

As James Lovelock put it:

> "So closely coupled is the evolution of living organisms with the evolution of their environment that together they constitute a single evolutionary process".

These concepts have led to a wide acceptance of the need to regard our planet as a holistic self-regulating system in which the activities of the biosphere cannot be untangled from the complex processes of geology, climatology and atmospheric physics.

PRINCIPLE 2 - **The Universe overwhelmingly exhibits design, information, intelligence and mind. It is also biocentric, therefore providing compelling evidence not only for a creator/God as the first cause, but with its purpose including the creation of all life.**

1.9 CLOSING CHAPTER COMMENT

When the evidence continually favours an intelligent and purposeful universe rather than a mechanistic/chaotic universe governed by chance, the argument for design, mind and a super intelligence surely seems overwhelming.

Not only is there simply no evidence for the counterview that chance produced "The Big Bang" - a universe replete with the laws of physics, and the associated fundamental constants finely tuned for life itself; but for 'chance' as the creator, we would have to accept the following:

- Nothing produces everything
- Non-life produces life
- Randomness produces fine tuning
- Chaos produces information
- Unconsciousness produces consciousness
- Non - reason produces reason [55]

In contrast:
As Kitty Ferguson has said in her best seller *The Fire in the Equations*:

"The arguments from design and rationality are still valid today. For whatever reason, valid or not, we still find inescapable the impression of a Mind behind the laws of this universe or inherent in them. Nowhere have we discovered mindlessness, not even in the unpredictable systems studied by chaos scientists, where there is mysterious, beautiful, pattern and structure."[56]

We have therefore two choices for you to make. You will recall I indicated at the beginning of this chapter that in looking at evidence for a creator/God there were really only two alternatives, and this led to a 50% probability for either:

- There is either a creator/God or,
- The universe and all life has happened spontaneously by chance.

I then set myself the task of providing a sufficiently compelling case to achieve a belief in favor of a creator/God of at least over 90%.

I hope I have succeeded.

CHAPTER 1 PRINCIPLES

PRINCIPLE 1 - **A non-physical timeless (but contingent) quantum-like realm beyond our current physical existence is possible, where things and events respond directly to consciousness/intention.**

PRINCIPLE 2 - **The Universe overwhelmingly exhibits design, information, intelligence and mind. It is also biocentric, therefore providing compelling evidence not only for a creator/God as the first cause, but with its purpose including the creation of all life.**

CHAPTER TWO

Non-Physical Reality, Independence of the Mind from the Brain, Consciousness and Immortality

Upsetting to many physicists, is that much and all that tremendous strides have been made in the last few 20 years trying to find the secrets of the universe, frustration mounts as the years tick by and little progress seems to have been made. This applies particularly to the elusive physics, the "Theory of Everything" (TOE), which is intended to meld all physics theories together (i.e. particularly Einstein's General theory of relativity, and Quantum Theory). Also the multitude of atomic particles discovered seems absurd and begs for simplification in line with beauty and parsimony (Occam's razor).

One of the most respected scientists in the world is Dr Robert Lanza from the different field of biology. He is described by a *"US News and World Report"* cover story as a genius, a renegade thinker and likened to Einstein, is not surprised at the lack of current advancement in physics. He has attacked the physicist's enclave of rigid materialism with the concept that they have ignored areas such as **life and consciousness** - which he regards as **primary**, and the keys to understanding the true nature of the universe. As he says in his introduction to his recent book *Biocentrism*:

> "Our understanding of the fundamentals of the universe is actually retreating before our eyes. The more data we gather, the more we've had to jiggle our theories or ignore findings that make no sense." [1]

One surely cannot help but agree with Lanza from the evidence in the last Chapter that life itself is the key and dominant factor in the development of the universe. All the fundamental constants of the universe, even "The Big Bang" itself inexplicably appears to have been controlled purposefully and tailor made to suit the emergence of life. Not only the universe, but even our own earth itself via the Gaia Hypothesis – the theory by eminent biologist, James Lovelock, asserting from observational evidence, that the earth itself has some form of consciousness and adapts and has changed over time in a cooperative and symbiotic way to produce a suitable environment for all of earth's species.

In a sense therefore we have found a major disconnect in science between belief systems of scientists **generally** and what readily available scientific evidence actually tells us.

In the area of "evolution", there is abundant evidence for subspecies adaption to one's environment. However no evidence whatsoever for neo - Darwinian chance based evolution of small adaptive changes leading to the observed arrival over time of earth's millions of new species. Examination of the evidence in Chapter 1 reveals there is not even a science based plausible explanation, instead most scientists and most of the world's population's erroneously believe it all happened by mutations - even though this is shown scientifically to be impossible!

In the area of cosmology, as indicated above, the universe itself arrived with "The Big Bang" in an incredibly controlled manner with just the right graininess to support condensation of matter into galaxies. Atomic particles interacted to form molecules in a myriad of ways to build rocks, humans etc. - all interacting with forces whose fundamental constants again were miraculously arranged to allow for life to appear. "*All this*", the majority of scientists say "*originated by chance*" - even when probability theory, as shown in each case in the last Chapter (so beloved by scientists and mathematicians), overwhelmingly indicates that this is impossible!

One aspect of the problem is pointed out by astrophysicist Bernard Haisch in his excellent book *The God Theory*:

> "Fundamental scientism, which has squelched a large portion of the scientific imagination, has many far reaching implications. Adherence to the creed fosters a conviction that the only possible reality is that explored or conjured up by physics and limited to matter and energy. It inculcates a belief (presented as fact), that science has proven God and immaterial intelligences to be merely left over antiquated myths".[2]

Not for a moment though do I consider this issue to be a malicious plot by mainstream materialist scientists to deny us all belief in the supernatural i.e. a creator/God - as many go to church regularly and no doubt some hold very strong religious beliefs (others though are vehemently atheists). Unfortunately it seems that the scientific culture that has followed Darwinism, is very much biased towards atheism. However this at least has ensured not unreasonably, that a scientist should always look for a scientific explanation first, rather than a supernatural one. Scientists who profess a possible supernatural explanation are also likely to be scorned by their colleagues.

Therefore even though they may find in some cases there is no alternative other than a supernatural explanation, it seems many will prefer to be illogical and stick to the old faithful nonsense explanation "*it all happened by chance*". Only if you are a scientist of the reputation of physicist Paul Davies, and Wheeler and many others, will you find scientists prepared to write books which hint at a supernatural explanation in some rare instances. It is also true almost without exception, that there has never been found likely material gain in researching non-physical areas such as the paranormal etc. - as all the most momentous discoveries in science to date, unquestionably have been on the basis of research into areas associated with the material nature of reality. The heart of the matter therefore is the issue of funding, where very little research in today's materialistic world is able to capture funding to explore fundamental research such as non-material aspects of reality. These include consciousness, memory, or investigations into the enigma of life itself i.e. **how does a cell exhibit life when its component parts are lifeless**?

I began this Chapter dealing with the physics TOE - the desired aim by physicists to link all known laws in physics with a single, coherent theory which can explain the material universe. If you are like me, this is simply not good enough. Instead I want a **Grand** Theory of Everything (GTE) not to just cover the physics of the material universe, but both the material and non-material universe combined - including life itself, consciousness and all paranormal phenomena. I believe there is sufficient scientific evidence now to support such a theory.

In the remainder of the Chapter we will cover in particular some aspects of quantum physics, which promises much hope for further research. It gives astonishing but not well known evidence to support the belief that mind and conscious are both primary, and responsible for the creation of all material things. Also that all paranormal phenomena are real, and can have science based explanations. Other relevant facets of science such as the discovery that the universe is holographic and field theories will also be covered together with neuroscience and consciousness research.

2.1   NON-PHYSICAL REALITY

Lewis Carroll – *Through the Looking Glass*

> "I can't believe that," said Alice
> "Can't you," the Queen said in a pitying tone. "Try again, draw a long breath and shut your eyes."

We need to see if physics theory and research can support continuance of our existence in non-physical form, following death, for a reincarnational existence. The issue of whether telepathy is valid also becomes crucial, as without physical form, clearly this would appear the only possible method in an afterlife (i.e. life-between-lives) by which communication could occur between ourselves.

Folklore throughout perhaps all countries embodies the concept of two forms of reality - a physical and non-physical reality. By definition, non-physical reality would have to be pretty insubstantial. Traditionally folklore also embellishes a non-physical or spiritual realm as having magical properties quite unlike those we are used to in our normal physical reality.

As scientists, if we were looking to find properties like these and unlike those normally encountered, our attention could not help being drawn to the physics of different states of matter and non-matter, where surprisingly completely different properties are often observed. Two examples are plasmas and super liquids.

Ironically the best bet for the strangest of all physical states is all around us and very familiar. Apart from having very strange properties, it is very insubstantial stuff. Who would have guessed - it happens to be subatomic particles, the basic building blocks of all matter, plus fields surrounding objects (including ourselves), which some scientists now believe are involved in the creation of matter.[3]

In contrast to the day to day reality we all observe, covered by Newton's laws of physics and Einstein's relativity theory; the behavior of subatomic particles (quanta) and their surrounding fields is so strange that the physicist Dirac in 1928 had to develop a completely new theory to explain it - he called it "Quantum Theory". Interesting therefore, (but perhaps coincidently), there is a happy degree of correlation between folklore and a modern scientist's concept of non-physical reality.

A 'field' aspect of non-physical reality has an important bearing on our understanding of telepathy and other paranormal phenomena, as we will see later. However there are other key and unusual aspects of non-physical reality - among them is that it seems that 'time' is not necessary, and forms no part of quantum theory or equations.

In 1935, Albert Einstein, Boris Podolsky and Nathan Rosen theorized a holistic effect of all non-physical reality - namely that subatomic level 'events', which appear to us as separate, are actually **connected** in some unknown way. They predicted that whatever happened to one sub-atomic particle would be reflected in its twin, even if billions of miles apart - a property of quantum physics called "entanglement" (i.e. the two particles are said to be entangled). Also that when any action (e.g. spin) is applied to one particle, it is mirrored instantly to the other regardless of distance. This independence of distance is (as we will find later) is of considerable importance and applies even if the distance involved is **on the other side of the universe!** Experimental confirmation of this theory first took place in 1972 when Stuart Freeman and John Clauser at Berkeley showed quanta of light are correlated instantly and independent of distance. It has been verified repeatedly since.[4]

Note: the word 'correlate' has a specific and important meaning in physics, it means:

Having a constant phase relationship, (Oxford Dictionary) i.e. when two waves synchronistically merge so that they are both in phase.

The property of subatomic particles where location ceases to be relevant (termed "non-locality") is also a characteristic of holograph images. Most people have had experience of holographic three dimensional images, but do not realise that if a small portion of the original image is removed, the removed portion retains every detail of the whole image, just as before - albeit at a reduced energy intensity. In scientific terms, every fractional part of a holographic image has the necessary information to replicate the whole. It can therefore be seen that the distance between any two objects in the holographic image is meaningless, as it depends on an arbitrary holographic image size, portions of which could occur anywhere and in any case be vanishingly small!

Following the Stuart Freeman and John Clauser's experimental confirmation of non-locality (mentioned above) involving the **instant** communication between subatomic particles over immense physical distances, physicists worldwide became perplexed as they knew that according to Einstein's theory of relativity, nothing could travel faster than light and "instant" clearly meant this had to be faster than light. It took the genius of David Bohm, Albert Einstein's brightest and ablest prodigy (formerly of Princeton University, and Emeritus Professor of Physics at Birkbeck College at the University of London), to finally see the relationship between the non-locality of quanta and holograms. He proposed that the cause was due to a newly perceived holographic property of quanta. He wrote extensively on this and even produced a definitive textbook entitled *Quantum Theory*. He is credited as the founder of the holographic universe theory, and had wide acceptance amongst physicists for this theory.

His theory was confirmed in 1982 when a research team led by physicist Alan Aspect, at the Institute of Theoretical and Applied Optics, in Paris, demonstrated that subatomic particles exhibit a holographic property.[5]

One of the most shattering concepts which follows from acceptance of a holographic universe theory is that, at the quantum or non-physical level, **information** does not travel through time and space from one 'physical' location to another; instead, the subatomic particles themselves simply seem to exist in a dimension which renders time and space (i.e. distance) irrelevant.

Unfortunately this is not widely known. As Joe Lewels writes in his book the *God Hypothesis*, following publication of Bohm's text book nearly half a century ago:

"......scientific and educational institutions have continued, for the most part, as if quantum physics did not even exist. In fact, rather than accept the implications of subatomic laws and incorporate them into their own fields, **most scientists** continue to simply ignore these findings, preferring to believe that quantum reality applies only to electrons, photons, neutrons and the myriad of other subatomic particles so far discovered, rather than to human reality. This belief, an effort to cling to the existing paradigm at all costs, conveniently ignores the fact that subatomic particles, the smallest elements known to science, are the basic building blocks of all matter and permeate the entire universe".[6]

The above discussed holographic and non-locality properties of quantum physics provides the science; which as we will learn shortly, can fully explain telepathy. This is because entanglement plus holography **allows for information to be transferred at the quantum level instantly and regardless of distance.** This becomes particularly evident in this and later Chapters, where it will be seen that experimentally, telepathy has not only been found to be **scientifically** valid, but replicable, instant and completely independent of distance. Additionally, in Chapter 3, quantum brain processing is covered (which has only recently been identified) together with identification of the likely specific quantum communication system responsible for enabling instantaneous transfer of information mind to mind between all life.

2.2 WHETHER THE MIND RESIDES IN THE BRAIN

The normally accepted scientific mainstream viewpoint is that consciousness and the mind, are synonymous and simply a **product** of physiological processes taking place inside the brain. Not widely known, however, is the fact that this is completely at odds with recent research, and even with investigations carried out as long ago as the 1930's by a former Canadian neurosurgeon Wilder Penfield.

Accidentally, in 1933, Penfield found while electrically stimulating directly certain areas of the brain of a conscious patient with an electrode, that flashbacks of memory occurred. One astonishing result was that stimulation of certain areas enabled the patient **to relate incredible detail of past events long since forgotten**. More astonishing was that when stimulation of other areas caused involuntary movements, the patient advised or indicated his complete mind independence to what was occurring in his brain - e.g. in some cases when the electrode caused the right hand to move, the patient reached over with his left hand to oppose the action.[7] **Mind therefore was in control, not the brain.**

He also observed with other patients that when they described past events, they were **even** able to relate what was in their **mind thoughts** at the time![8] Penfield also found that, although later he had mapped all areas of the brain responsible for speech, movement and all the internal and external senses; **neither the mind nor the will could be located in any part of the brain.**[9]

In other words Penfield found (contrary to erroneous belief even today), that rather than mind being a subset of the brain; his experimental evidence has conclusively shown that mind is not only separate from the brain, but strangely it does not even appear that it resides in the body.

He stated:

"None of the actions that we attribute to the mind has been initiated by electrode stimulation. There is no place in the cerebral cortex where electrical stimulation will cause a patient to believe or decide".

The electrode could trigger physical actions and provide access to stored memory, but not even the simplest elements of reasoning.

However with regard to memory, Penfield concluded from his research that simply everything we have ever experienced is recorded in our memory, from "*every stranger's face we have glanced at in a crowd to every spider web we gazed at as a child*". He reasoned that this was why memories of so many insignificant events kept cropping up in his sampling.[10]

In many ways therefore the functions of the brain and mind in controlling our body, can be likened to the bridge of a ship where the captain's **mind/consciousness plus memory** can either operate levers or a computer keyboard to control via the ships computer (the brain) which accesses and controls the rudder and engines (the body). As we age, deterioration of the brain can be likened to the computer access keyboard becoming worn, perhaps losing a few keys and interfering with access to memory.

The issue is - where exactly is the part which identifies the uniqueness of a person - namely the mind i.e. the portion where consciousness, intent and reasoning takes place together with memory storage.

If not in the brain or body, there is obviously a strong suggestion that it must reside elsewhere. From what we have learned already from holographic quantum effects, then consciousness/memory could therefore easily be located anywhere in space, yet interact instantly with the brain. It seems reasonable (and evidence is provided later), to suggest that perhaps consciousness and memory reside **relatively close in a quantum field adjacent to each particular object and lifeform.**

If this is the case, then death of the physical body should leave the mind/ consciousness intact.

In Chapter 3 we will also surprisingly find scientific support for our **senses** to also exist following death, and continue unaffected externally in an afterlife non-physical environment.

Neuroscientist Sir John Eccles also had this view when he stated "*Mind and will are arguably not subject in death to the disintegration that affects......both the body and the brain*"[11].

However, sensibly, we should look for further experimental evidence than that of just Penfield.

Another neurosurgeon Dr Pilbram of Stanford University, together with the great neuropsychologist Karl Lashey at the Yerkes Laboratory of Primate Biology, then in Orange Park, Florida, in 1946 carried out research on memory on rats. After training rats to perform a variety of tasks he surgically removed various portions of the rat's brains and re-tested them. Despite removing massive portions of their brains, which often impaired their motor skills, he found he could not eradicate their memories. At Yale University he reflected on the fact that likewise, individuals who had received head injuries in car crashes and other accidents suffered no long term memory gaps. A chance reading of a Scientific American magazine in the mid 1980's describing the first construction of a hologram, led him to conclude that stored brain memories were holographic with the usual characteristic of non-locality and that any portion of the holograph contains all the information of the whole.[12] He later theorized, "that the brain responds to vibrations both from the world of stimuli through senses **as well as from the world of ideas that exists in another dimension**".[13]

Surprisingly his work on memories was soon to be verified by an avowed skeptic - Indiana Universities' biologist Paul Pietch - who chose salamanders for brain research; as his earlier experiments had found that rather than die, they would remain in a stupor if their brain were removed. He reasoned if memories were holographic (which he didn't believe), then a behavior such as feeding, which was dependent on memory, should be unaffected if the salamander's brain was replaced in just a different orientation. After transposing the left and right hemispheres and allowing the salamander to recover, to his dismay it reverted to normal feeding. In desperation in over 700 operations he sliced, flipped, shuffled and finally minced the entire brains of his victims, with the same result - after restoring the brain in position and allowing the salamander to recover, the feeding habit was always seen to be totally unaffected. To his chagrin, he had experimentally proved memories were holographic.[14]

Pilbram's discovery of the holographic nature of the mind/consciousness was first published in an article in 1966. Since then many researchers have also pointed out there are many long standing puzzles associated with memories which can readily be explained by holograms. For example the speed of memory recall is normally instantaneous, which suggests non-locality and could be analogous to shining a laser beam of light on a piece of holographic film. When we are unable to recall something, this may be equivalent to failing to find the right angle of light shining on the piece of film, necessary to gain a response. Also brain researchers have struggled continuously to come up with a mechanism for storing the some 2.8×10^{20} bits of information that the brilliant mathematician John Von Neumann conservatively calculated would be typically stored by the mind over the course of a lifetime. There seems a direct and unique correlation with holographic properties, as the information storage capabilities of holograms are known to be potentially almost limitless e.g. a micron thick 2.5 cm square holographic film can store the information content of at least 50 Bibles! [15]

It has also been suggested (by prominent scientists, among them physicist David Bohm, physiologist Karl Pribram, Cambridge University Nobel laureate Brian Josephson, Oxford University mathematician Sir Roger Penrose, and neuroscientist Benjamin Libet), that the mind may exhibit quantum process behavior which could be responsible for some further puzzling aspects of consciousness such as the unitary sense of self, the sense of free will and non-algorithmic "intuitive" insights.[16]

(Note – importantly the deterministic nature of physical reality disappears with the random nature characteristic of quantum physics. This uncertainty and random behavior of quantum physics can also be seen to allow a **free will** capability in our otherwise fully deterministic universe.)

Most scientists, presumably unaware of this research, obdurately believe that memory, although holographic, will eventually be found by later research to be still located in the brain. Interestingly this is just supposition, and there is no evidence for it. The opposing school (termed panpsychism[17]) feels that mind, memory and consciousness reside in every facet of nature - and at cellular and subatomic level amongst not only humans but all life and material forms. This has been espoused by Tailhard de Chardin, and more recently by the physicist Freeman Dyson, who writes:

> "I think our consciousness is not just a passive epiphenomenon carried along by the chemical events in our brains, but is an active agent forcing the molecular complexes to make choices between one quantum state and another. In other words, mind is already inherent in every electron…"[18]

There is incontrovertible evidence to support the concept that consciousness exists at electron level, as very early in Bohm's career, in 1943, he observed at the Lawrence Berkeley Radiation Laboratory, lifelike virus type behavior of electrons forming a plasma, where it surrounded all impurities with a sheath so as to isolate them. In 1947, Bohm while at Princeton University as an Assistant Professor, extended his research to the study of electrons in metals. He soon found that the seemingly haphazard movements of individual electrons managed to produce highly organised overall effects in a similar fashion to the plasmas that he had studied at Berkeley. Entire oceans of particles were involved, incredibly each behaving as if it knew what untold trillions of others were doing. Bohm called such collective movements of electrons plasmons, and their discovery established his reputation as a physicist. [19]

Bohm's experimental evidence of the conscious behavior of electrons is given further support by experiments by Gary Steinman and Marian Cole at the Pennsylvania University, where evidence was found that molecules significant for life were made preferentially.[20]

Even such lowly and tiny life forms such as bacteria exhibit consciousness in that they perceive certain characteristics within their environment. They sense chemical differences in their surroundings and, accordingly, swim towards sugar and away from acid; they sense and avoid heat, move away from light or towards it, and some bacteria can even detect magnetic fields. [21]

Similar behaviour is also well known in plants. Despite the fact that no nervous system as such has ever been detected in plants, a Russian, A. Merkulov of the State University in Alma Ata claims he has confirmed the long-held view that plants have short term memories by using galvanometer polygraph tests. These indicated that plants repeated the frequency of flashes from a xenon-hydrogen lamp after a pause as long as eighteen hours.[22]

Mud wasps learn to recognise and memorise the location of their nests, otherwise they would be unable to find their way back when they returned from fetching mud or hunting caterpillars.[23]

Animals unquestionably exhibit purposeful behaviour and have memories (the memory of elephants is legendary). It would seem inconsistent, presumptuous and arrogant therefore to suggest that purposive behaviour of all life is not indicative of intelligence/mind; and instead argue that mankind only has mind, consciousness and memory, with all other life relying purely on instinctive behaviour.

If mind/conscious is not in the brain, then where is it? Medieval man considered all passions and intent (i.e. mind stuff) as residing in the heart. Strangely we feel we have made considerable progress by ridiculing this and with some degree of certainty (yet no evidence) instead postulate that the mind is in the brain. Recent scientific views however take a holistic view and regard any organism as a society of molecules which somehow co-operate and integrate their individual behaviour into a coherent order. Each constituent part of the hierarchy - molecule, cell nucleus etc., organ - could be regarded a separate entity (with perhaps the possibility of each having a separate mind/consciousness), as well as being a member of a larger whole - a person, or plant etc. With such an arrangement it seems reasonable to suppose, that there is also a hierarchy of consciousness dependent upon function i.e. **a cellular consciousness at one level and an overarching consciousness with responsibility for the complete entity**. This then can explain cases where not all organisms exhibit independent behaviour and instead tend to act as a group. Those in this category such as termites, ants, wasps and bees, not only behave as if they have a group mind, but experiments have shown that killing the queen destroys all current purposeful action throughout members of the colony regardless of distance from the queen[24]. This leads to astonishing but somewhat inevitable conclusion that these organisms have a form of group or collective mind, with the queen as the focus, yet individual bee's minds as well.

Before leaving "mind stuff", there is further supportive evidence to consider regarding what links our minds/consciousness with information fields - which certainly has little to do with the physical body. Additionally, to give further perspective to re-incarnation, it is desirable to outline how pervasive, yet largely unknown, is the effect of non-physical reality on our daily lives - particularly the concept of access to universal knowledge. For this we need to look more closely at consciousness, also the "unconscious" and consider recent discoveries concerning possible new non-physical fields.

2.3 CONSCIOUSNESS

Before we get too far into consciousness, although we have mentioned it previously in passing, to ensure it is clear what we mean, it deserves a definition. Perhaps the simplest definition is that a *conscious state is an inner qualitative subjective state of awareness or sentience.* Self-consciousness (or self-awareness) is a very special form of consciousness, which may be peculiar to humans and the higher animals.[25]

Other important attributes are also associated with consciousness, such as a sense of individuality or selfhood and the ability to reason, have feelings (including moods, emotions and sensations), and also a sense of intent (or will). Clearly this is all 'mind stuff' and the attributes, together with memory, that we associate with the mind.

i.e. mind = consciousness + memory

Most of the time we are involved in unconscious thought where we operate intuitively, making judgments and arriving at conclusions without knowing why. With conscious thought, it also seems that attention and degrees of attention cause a corresponding greater or lesser degree of waking consciousness - and our focus to be fixed on physical reality. While day dreaming or sleeping, however, there is a definite sense that our consciousness is placed elsewhere. (Later, the argument will be made for the 'unconscious mind' - to be very much focused in non-physical reality, **and therefore subject to quantum properties**). However, our sense of self also seems intact whether involved in conscious or unconscious thought.

By defining consciousness, and outlining its attributes and focus we have gained some understanding of its character. However none of this tells us exactly what consciousness is. Yet this is of considerable importance as it is doubtless the key criteria of what gives us our individuality as a person or entity (i.e. psyche or soul).

To answer this question, we need to refer to the views of Dr. David J. Chalmers - considered as perhaps the world's authority on the subject. (Dr. Chalmers studied mathematics at Adelaide University was a Rhodes Scholar at the University of Oxford and is currently Professor of Philosophy and Director of the Centre for Consciousness at the Australian National University. He is also Professor of Philosophy at New York University. He had a fascination with consciousness which led him into philosophy and cognitive science.) As with physicist Steven Weinberg, he considers that consciousness does not seem to be derivable from physical laws. He therefore **considers it to be a fundamental property of the universe** similar to space-time, mass and charge, etc., all of which cannot be reduced to anything more basic. He points out that - since in the 19th Century, electromagnetic phenomena could likewise not be explained in terms of previously known principles, but is now accepted as a fundamental entity - the same approach should be used for consciousness.[26]

As stated by physicist Fred Alan Woolf:

"In a universe, the places where (quantum) waves coincide, events occur. Something physical appears. And with the appearance of a physical object, a subatomic particle, an atom, a molecule, a group of molecules, a structural arrangement of molecules, a cell, a group of cells, and practically everything else in what we call the universe, there is also something else. That something else is intelligence, order, and consciousness."[27]

There is therefore the concept that matter cannot exist without an association of mind/consciousness. As Nobel laureate Erwin Schrödinger described it:

"Consciousness is that by which this world first becomes manifest, by which indeed, we can quite calmly say, it first becomes present; that the world *consists* of the elements of consciousness."[28]

Edwin Schrödinger would have every reason to come to such a conclusion, as it was he who achieved a breakthrough in discovering the mathematical formula which describes quantum probability waves - the Schrödinger probability function. Before we can examine further a relationship between consciousness and the critical importance of this probability function, we need to go back to basics and study in more detail the incredible weirdness of the base units of quantum theory. In fact we need to consider the base units of physical reality i.e. subatomic particles themselves.

Contrary to most people's understanding of a mere fundamental particle such as an electron, we don't really have much of an idea of what they are.

A classic experiment called "the double - slit" experiment. This was first carried out by Thomas Young as long ago as 1903, in order to examine whether sub atomic particles are waves or particles - as there were suspicions they could behave as either. The experiment comprised beaming sub-atomic particles, typically electrons (as in a TV set) at a barrier – a base-board containing two narrow parallel slits, and observing the result on a target screen beyond the barrier.

The outcome of the experiment provided a shocking result, since confirmed by other experiments. It was not the fact that the experiment quickly successfully revealed that all sub atomic particles can exhibit **either** a wave or a particle nature, but the fact that the experiment showed that until such time as the experimenter observed the outcome on the target screen, the electrons merely existed as probabilities. Verification of the probabilistic nature of subatomic particles was confirmed later by the discovery of quantum **mathematics** (called quantum **mechanics**), where all such probable paths can be predicted to an astonishing degree of accuracy. The only way the behavior of electrons in the double slit experiment could therefore be explained was to accept the amazing fact that interaction and conscious observation by the experimenter was itself solely responsible for changing the probabilistic nature of any given electron's path into an actuality. Or in more scientific terminology - observation by a living being i.e. conscious attention, collapsed the Schrödinger probability function to create physical reality. As pointed out by Amit Goswami, in his recent book, *Physics of the Soul*:

> "Quantum objects exist as a superposition of possibilities until our observation brings about actuality from potentiality, **one actual, localised event** from the many potential events. If the event has a great probability to actualise, upon observation, there the possibility wave is strong; where the wave is weak, the probability is small for its corresponding possibility to actualise."[29]

(For those interested, more detail on the double-slit experiment is given in Appendix 3)

In short, consciousness creates reality!

It must be emphasised again that up until the moment of observation/measurement, certain properties of quantum phenomena, such as location, momentum, and spin etc. simply exist as nothing other than a collection of probabilities, known as the wave function. Therefore prior to observation by a conscious observer there is simply **no physicality such as mass,** and therefore **no electron as we know it.** When interaction by a conscious observer takes place, the wave function collapses and the electron is actualised into reality. It is also important to realise that at the moment of choice, it is thought that unconsciously we make an instant choice between probabilities to determine our probable future as an **automatic unconscious action** - just as we make **unconscious** decisions on many other matters daily and instantly but without any conscious awareness.

Putting it another way to emphasise the point. We have no awareness whatsoever of the millions of incredible decisions our unconsciousness makes for us daily in operating our body, protecting us from harm by instinctive and automatic actions - none of which sneak through to our conscious mind. Likewise, our unconscious minds are thought to perform for us unwittingly as part of the same process, the task of unconsciously observing probable future outcomes continuously as they are presented to us, and selecting almost instantly those which are most likely to fulfil our desires in material reality. This action individually and collectively makes us creators (using free will) of our reality for ourselves within our universe system.

Robert Jahn, a highly respected researcher who founded the Princeton Engineering Anomalies Research Lab (PEAR) in 1979, relates this to a useful concept of consciousness, space and time. He considers that pure energy, as it exists at the quantum level does not have the separateness of space or time; but exists as a vast continuum of fluctuating charge. In contrast, our consciousness has the dual capability of exhibiting either a particle type nature with a definite position in space or time, or a quantum probability wave characteristic, independent of space or time. By the simple act of **conscious perception and choice**, we bring our conscious energy to create separate objects that exist in space and time. By this means therefore we continuously and unconsciously actually create our own separateness and reality based in time.[30] (The issue of space and time will be covered in more detail in Chapter 4 for both physical and non-physical reality).

While you are still reeling, 'wait there's more'. The experiment has been repeated thousands of times, even using particles as large as small molecules ("buckyballs"), and in every case the result is the same. Since molecules and all subatomic particles form all matter in the universe, including all life itself; **all** physical reality is created by consciousness. **Mind therefore is primary, and matter a creation of mind.**

Therefore we have our 3rd principle:

PRINCIPLE 3 - Mind is primary, as with consciousness. Consciousness creates reality.

"It is almost absurd prejudice to suppose that existence can only be physical. As a matter of fact, the only form of existence of which we have immediate knowledge is in the mind. We might as well say, on the contrary, that physical existence is a mere inference, since we know of matter only in so far as we perceive images mediated by the senses." - Carl Jung [31]

Other quantum experiments provide similar results. In 1977 George Sudershan and Baidyanath Misra of the University of Texas discovered that if one continually observes an unstable particle, **it will never decay**. The phenomenon is called "Zeno's Paradox in quantum theory". The concept is that conscious observation continuously without ceasing (i.e. sustained attention), maintains uncertainty in accordance with Heisenberg's Uncertainty Principle, so that a shift to a final state cannot occur. As soon as attention wavers, the wave function collapses and radioactive particles are emitted. As quantum physicist and neurologist William Bray says "*we paint the universe with our consciousness by observing, and then not observing*". (Verification of the effect is indisputable as this quantum property has to be taken into account in the current research, and design towards the current development of quantum computers.)

Moreover Von Neuman, the genius, mathematician, quantum physicist and brilliant logician, was the first to postulate **the primacy of consciousness** and stated that:

> "The entire physical world is quantum mechanical, so the process that collapses the wave functions cannot be a physical process; instead, the intervention of something outside of physics is required. Something non-physical….. i.e. consciousness."

As stated by Richard Conn Henry, Professor of Physics and Astronomy at the John Hopkins University:

> "It is not matter that creates an illusion of consciousness, but consciousness that creates an illusion of matter. That is correct physics: it is not controversial in the *slightest* degree that there is no reality; this has been demonstrated in both theory and experiment.
>
> And yet in how many physic classes today, are students made aware of this most fundamental discovery? In all my classes I assure you; but I am confident that this is not common. The illusion of matter which is to say the illusion of a really existing world is so strong, that I think most scientists are not able to overcome it. It took *me* decades to finally realise that this is not a joke, **and that the universe is purely mental: that mind is fundamental**; matter merely an illusion - and that this is physics, not philosophy (or religion)."[32]

As quantum theorist Henry Stapp remarked:

"in quantum theory, the purely physically described aspects for real events are no longer thought of as having the qualities assigned to rocks by classical physics; 'In quantum theory the purely physically described aspects are mere potentialities for real events to occur. A potentiality is more like an idea than a persisting material substance, and is treated in the theory '**as an idea that might happen**'".

This new conception of matter is what physicist James Jeans was referring to when he wrote " *the universe begins to look more like a great thought than like a machine*"

The concept that consciousness creates reality should not really be too much of a surprise to us, as daily in every activity we carry out, we are using our consciousness to make decisions for us instantly on how to **physically** manipulate matter in various ways (e.g. combing our hair, getting in a car). What therefore is new, is that experiments in quantum physics have overwhelmingly shown that likewise (**unconsciously**) all 'living things' consciousness, additionally also daily performs the function of instantly converting wavelike probabilistic subatomic particles into our desired actuality. All physical matter is therefore a mental construct. In other words, what we perceive now visually, is what we constructed mentally earlier. Further, no energy is thought necessary or involved in the process, as consciousness is involved in nothing other than making at a decision between available choices. Later (in the next Chapter, Chapter 3), we will cover the likely communication system involved in the process.

As a useful comparison, not generally realised, our visualisation that generally everything around us is solid, is but an illusion. Instead, our classical physical reality is really composed of nothing but energy fields of various kinds. This is why Richard Conn Henry, Professor of Physics and Astronomy at the John Hopkins University (above) stated our perception is flawed to the extent that "(our) *consciousness creates an illusion of matter*". Even the fundamental subatomic particles which form atoms, then molecules then all visible matter, are thought to be merely different forms of 'knots' in energy fields.[33] Subatomic particles such as electrons due to their behavior of circulating the nucleus of an atom in a probabilistic random way, must intrinsically appear visually as a cloud. As all matter comprises such atoms bonded into molecules, solidarity must be an illusion, as all matter must visually similarly appear as insubstantial clouds. The reason for the illusion is that our senses are cleverly and exquisitely designed to deliberately give a false perception of solidity which seems very much and sensibly designed to maximise our protection from danger - specifically to suit our particular species' attributes. For example as a predator, a perception of solidity - is largely suggested by a false visual indication of density plus largely grey or brown type colour ranges for most animals we encounter. Touch also encounters repulsive molecular force fields which again falsely suggests density and impenetrability - yet in anything "solid" we know from science there is mostly space, not substance. Our eyesight too, rather than providing vision which would provide a more truthful, realistic and an exact representation of the energy fields surrounding us, instead provides a distorted colour depiction. Design of certain specific frequency ranges seems deliberately biased in our vision receptors to particularly highlight the specific colours likely to suggest and warn us of a possible threat. The colours yellow and red seen in fires and the coloration of many snakes and poison substances, are obviously severe threats to our species and expected lifestyles. They are therefore given the greatest intensity bias of all colours. Similarly with sounds, contrary to our expectations, the answer to the famous conundrum – "If no one is present, does a falling tree make a noise"? The answer is emphatically no. The reality is far different. In fact, there **is no sound whatsoever from a falling tree**, instead just a soundless compression of air impinging upon our ear drums as a result of the movement of the displaced air from the tree "softly" "crashing" to the ground. We of course hear a frightening "bang" - helpfully amplified by our senses to warn of a possible threat or danger, as with similar sounds in this frequency range. These illusions are particularly well covered by the Einstein of biology Robert Lanza as referred to previously in his book (*Biocentrism*) where he has devoted to it, a whole Chapter.[34]

As above, we are deceived by our senses to even perceive everything around as substantial, but the underlying basic reality is that everything around us comprises merely energy fields and energy knots bound together by forces in different ways.

Paul Davies has explained that prior to observation, an electron in orbit around an atom cannot be considered to have a well-defined position in space at every moment. It should not be regarded as circling the atomic nucleus along a definite path, but instead as smeared out in an indeterminate cloud like manner around the nucleus. Although applicable for electrons orbiting atoms, this is not the case with macroscopic objects. Planets for example have a definite orbit around the sun. However, as with all macro objects they are still subject to quantum mechanics although to a lesser extent than subatomic particles. Obviously immediately following "The Big Bang", when the universe was very small, there was **nothing but subatomic particles** and matter had not yet condensed. Therefore at the point prior to macroscopic objects appearing to form galaxies, planets etc.; the whole universe must have been engulfed by quantum uncertainty.[35]

An issue often conveniently ignored by most physicists, is that a conscious mind at some point thereafter the Big Bang must have caused collapse of the whole universe wave function; to initiate the appearance of our classical world's non-quantum physicality and before life appeared in the universe. This suggests the active participation after "the Big Bang" by a super intelligence creator/God.

Matter, particularly subatomic particles, can be shown to be subject to a constant and unique vibratory jitter - exhibiting the wave characteristic of all matter, regardless of size and as described by the Schrödinger wave function. Just as we find major physical changes occur in many state transitions observed in physical systems, such as with falling temperatures the conversion of insubstantial steam to water then to the hard solid of ice; as subatomic particles form more massive material substances, the wave frequency of the resulting object decreases, resulting in reduced observable quantum effects. Also with solid objects and increased mass, our familiar classical physical universe is observed, but subject to Newton's and Einstein's physics. Here time and space matter, determinism prevails and velocity of everything is limited to the speed of light. This does not alter the concept of the primacy of mind, and the fact that consciousness creates reality, just that the quantum effects, though still present in all matter, reduces with larger mass presumably due to its increased wavelength.

The fact that the wavelengths increase with larger chunks of matter is just as well, as pointed out by Paul Davies - since with quantum tunneling, objects can only tunnel through a barrier comparable in thickness to their respective wavelengths. Therefore, if this were not the case, people would fall through the chairs they were sitting on.[36]

When first discovered, collapse of the wave function was thought to affect all matter not just subatomic objects. Recent experiments though, suggest that not only is there a reduced effect for macro objects as described above, but the collapse of the quantum wave forms caused by consciousness, only applies to those objects in **dynamic states** (i.e. in motion or change of position, momentum and direction of spin) and not those having definite and constant values for any observation.[37]

Further, William James (as long ago as 1911) pointed out that:

> "Our conscious perception either perceives nothing, or something there in a sensible amount, as is known in the laws of psychology as the laws of the 'threshold'. .... Your acquaintance with reality grows literally by buds or drops of perception."

Physicist Henry P Stapp considers that this form of 'discreteness' is also the signature of quantum phenomena. In the same way he points out that a similar parallel exists with psychological observations and quantum reality, in that the percepts that actually enter into a stream of consciousness, depend strongly on the **intention** of the probing mind i.e. there is either nothing (no intention), or something (intention). **A person then tends to experience what he or she is looking for**, but only if the potentiality for that experience is present. What is very different from physical reality built out of bits of matter, is that with quantum increments, they are built out of quanta information bits (qubits) - the conscious intention (i.e. thoughts) for certain discrete, **whole actual events** to occur. Chris Carter, author of the recent book *Science and* *the Near-Death Experience: How Consciousness Survives Death*, points out that recent experiments by Schmidt and others have also provided experimental evidence that the interaction of consciousness does not cause collapse of the wave function randomly as once thought. Instead, we all make actual **unconscious** choices between probable **alternative** outcomes prior to the wave function collapse as mentioned previously (these experiments by Herman Schmidt and others are covered in the next Chapter).[38]

Not only does conscious observation and a choice by a subject cause collapse of the probability wave function, but as Russian quantum physicist Michael B Mensky indicates, in his recent (2013) paper ("Logic of Quantum Mechanics and Consciousness"):

> "That if consciousness equals a separation of the alternatives from each other, then the absence of consciousness equals the absence of separation. Therefore, turning off consciousness (in sleeping, trance or meditation) opens access to all classical alternatives......Thus, when going over to the unconsciousness state, one obtains the information, or knowledge, which is in principle unavailable in the usual conscious state."[39]

(Note: Obviously semantics are very important here, as Mensky is unfortunately using the incorrect but usual convention of expression of suggesting that we lose consciousness during sleep etc. This is obviously incorrect as during sleeping, trance or meditation, we simply change the focus of our mental attention elsewhere other than our immediate environment. e.g. rather than being "unconscious", in contrast often in trance states, or in sleep, our mental activity is at a peak - as easily verified by electroencephalographs).

Another way of looking at Mensky's above proposition, and as suggested by others (e.g. Robert Jahn, and his colleagues at Princeton University), is Jahn's view mentioned above, that consciousness too, has complementary states where in ordinary states, the mind is more particle like and in quantum states, when the focus of intention is via the "unconscious mind", it exhibits the probabilistic wave nature.

Due to the **timeless character** of quantum reality, Mensky also claims that this would even allow access to information from any time moments in future and past - which must also include inspirational insights (including scientific insights).

2.4 CLOSING CHAPTER COMMENTS

We learned above that with conscious observation (particularly with intention), in a quantum superposition state (i.e. the non-physical state where we can select from **many** different probabilities), we choose our immediate future amongst probable available choices. In contrast, while meditating, sleeping etc. with consciousness turned off, we have access and links to all reality i.e. interconnectedness, a holistic character, and access to all information due to the holographic quality of ourselves and the universe. (It will be found later in the next Chapter and in Section 3 particularly, that these quantum principles and experiments are overwhelmingly supported by observation and experimental evidence.)

The ability for consciousness to collapse the wave function of all matter to create our reality - strongly for subatomic particles, but with a lesser effect for macroscopic objects, reveals the primacy of consciousness as the dominant factor for all life and everything that exists in the universe. When particles are small we observe solely quantum reality - with all the odd characteristics of quantum physics. In contrast, when particles are of macro size and held together by the usual classical physical forces, the quantum nature of reality still applies, but only to a **very** limited extent. The nature and properties of quantum physics suggest that matter while at the very small level of subatomic particle size, exists in a very different and timeless dimension from physical macroscopic matter - as is likely the case with consciousness, mind and memory. (Note: there is also the possibility that our mind/consciousness exists within one, or a number of different dimensions, as the most favored current version of 'string theory' postulates 11 dimensions, as opposed to the usual three spatial dimensions and the fourth dimension of time).

It is therefore not difficult to imagine that there may well be parallel realms within our universe very different from ours. In particular, a number of various realms where quantum reality is more dominant and where our consciousness can collapse the probability wave function of all probable matter around us to create our own universe collectively with others – **instantly, and in whatever manner we wish**.

It seems reasonable to suggest that our minds, consciousness, and memory (i.e. our souls) like other quantum entities (e.g. subatomic particles), are likely to be vanishingly small and of low mass (perhaps no mass at all - similar to photons). Also, like other quantum non-physical entities, they must unquestionably be holographic. This means that when we die, its holographic property would allow the uniqueness of ourselves, our character, consciousness and memory (even the memory of multiple lives) to be retained independent of memory size. Being non-physical, decay would be improbable; and instead, as covered further below and later in the book, the quantum characteristics in the particular case of mind/consciousness/memory can be shown to be most likely immortal.

At death, there would therefore be the very real possibility of our earth consciousness transferring to a more fully quantum dominant realm where we continue in our existence in a life-between-life manner. As will be shown in subsequent Chapters this is supported by all esoteric wisdom and also completely by observational experience in areas such as regressive hypnosis into past lives, NDE's (Near Death Experiences etc.).

2.4.1   **We are Immortal!**

If you are shocked by such an assertion, this follows very much from the above and the following are three arguments which support this:

1. Quantum physicist William Bray with impeccable logic, argues that since our universe is a physical construct of consciousness and had a beginning, it is finite i.e. it cannot be timeless. However, since the universe is a construct of consciousness, consciousness must have preceded it. Consciousness therefore, **including all forms of consciousness, including ourselves, must be timeless.**[40]

2. Tackling the issue yet in a different way - as we learned earlier, in quantum reality space and time are irrelevant. Therefore, since consciousness itself has been shown to be quantum, it must have a timeless nature!

3. Finally Paul Williams provides yet another argument for our immortality by brilliant reasoning in the form of a poem:

Here we are, set in the midst of an infinity of time
- the chances are infinitely against us that we
should be alive at any specific time. But here we are.

The only way we can get rid of an infinity of chances
which are against us, is to assume - that we too
are infinite.

J. Paul Williams

(As an aside, the above can be considered as observational science. Just because this is not experimental evidence, it should not be thought to detract from its validity. We have already described unarguably in this Chapter that in quantum states time does not exist. In addition, later the longevity of certain quantum particle states is explored which similarly indicates immortality.)

To our Principles 1 and 2 in Chapter 1, we are now ready to add Principle 3 - see below:

PRINCIPLE 1 - A non-physical timeless (but contingent) quantum-like realm beyond our current physical existence may be possible, where things and events respond directly to consciousness/intention.

PRINCIPLE 2 - The Universe overwhelmingly exhibits design, information, intelligence and mind. It is also bio-centric, therefore providing compelling evidence not only for a creator/God as the first cause, but with its purpose including the creation of all life.

PRINCIPLE 3 - Mind is primary, as with consciousness. Consciousness creates reality. We are immortal.

CHAPTER THREE

The Quantum Communication System (PCAR)* Linking All Life, and Quantum Fields

(also, the Subconscious, the Location for Memory, and Whether Senses Can Exist Outside the Body)

> "No - one understands quantum mechanics. It's effects are impossible, absolutely impossible to explain based on human experience" - *said Richard P. Feynman, Nobel laureate and inventor of quantum mechanics.*[1]

In the last Chapter we learned the astonishing fact that our consciousness creates our reality. One cannot of course help but ask how? For example in order to collapse probability waves in our immediate environment there would have to be an unconscious communication signaling system emanating from our mind/consciousness (probably controlled by our vision), to choose amongst all quantum probabilistic possible events. Additionally, subsequent return communication responses would be expected in order to verify that our choice had been actioned.

Our brain also thinks and needs to communicate directions down to cell level in some way. We may know too from our experience that telepathic communication is real, (it also can be detected readily scientifically, as discussed experimentally below); so there has to be some explanation as to how the brain can communicate and pass on information in a mind-to-mind manner amongst others. Additionally, we need to find the likely answer to the question - where does memory reside if it is not in the brain, and how is it accessed by the mind. All of this suggests that there would have to be a communication system pretty remarkable in the brain to achieve this. But also it would surely have to be a system so powerful and technically advanced that it could achieve functionality beyond anything we have ever encountered - as it would need to cater for not only telepathy, but all other paranormal activity. Obviously from what

---

*   phase-conjugate-adaptive-resonance system (pcar)

we have learned earlier, we would expect the answers to all this to lie in non-physical reality and involve quantum physics and fields.

Covered in this Chapter is the story of how we have now reached considerable understanding of the processes involved. It is an exciting science story involving many brilliant scientists (often working collectively), and only fairly recently has the most important link of been all has been discovered, a quantum bio-communication system (PCAR - phase-conjugate-adaptive-resonance system). Since the communication system is complex, there are a number of preliminary issues that need to be covered in some depth. First, we must look more closely at quantum fields.

3.1 QUANTUM FIELDS

Physical fields and quantum (non-physical) fields have very different properties.

On the one hand physical fields exhibit a definite location in space and time and predictable behavior. In contrast, as we found in Chapter 2, quantum fields are holographic and exhibit an indefinite locality in space and time.

These quantum fields are created by every object as a result of a characteristic vibration or jitter which emits non-local quanta energy containing information about the object as part of the field. Similarly all objects absorb surrounding quantum wave energy and information.

Quantum emissions and fields are also probabilistic (which surely seems somewhat indicative of an intended provision by a creator/God of a free will capability in an otherwise deterministic universe). They also do not actually exist physically in space-time like classical gravitational and electromagnetic fields and are therefore difficult to detect – particularly subtle matter fields. Additionally and importantly, the holographic non-locality character provides an instant **information** transfer capability regardless of distance, not present in normal classical physical electromagnetic fields.[2] This then is thought to allow conscious or subconscious intent by a living being in one place, to instantly influence another elsewhere irrespective of distance - as will be discussed below by experiments involving receipt of brain waves sent from one person to another i.e. telepathy.

Indicative of Rupert Sheldrake's morphogenetic field theory (which will be covered later in the Chapter), quantum fields contain **the template pattern or shape of any matter they surround**; and in the case of subatomic particles, similarly their probabilistic pattern and shape.

We have covered the fact that consciousness collapses the wave function of quantum waves externally beyond the brain to form matter. We therefore are now ready at last to look for possible evidence within the brain itself to see if there are scientific experiments and observations which can explain how this happens. For example, are there quantum consciousness waves emanating from the brain?

In the 1970's, microscopic-sized cylindrical structures termed "cytoskeletal microtubules" were unexpectedly discovered in brain neurons but their possible purpose remained illusory for many years. However in 1994, anaesthesiologist, Stuart Hameroff, from the University of Arizona, proposed that the microtubules could be a possible site for quantum effects in the brain. He considered they were about the right size to sustain quantum coherence (constant relative phase), and provide an interface with consciousness.

Since then, further investigations with colleagues Rich Watt, Steen Rasmussen, and others have provided support for Hameroff's original discovery. As Hameroff points out, he and his team found similar micro-tubular structures in tiny unicellular paramecium and despite the fact that unlike us, such tiny creatures (only some 10 microns long) do not have our complex brain at all, yet:

> "they could swim gracefully, avoid objects and predators. Learn and remember, find food and mates and have sex".

Together with other colleague scientists he found that for paramecium:

> "Sensory input and movement, cell division (mitosis), cell growth, synapse formation and all aspects of co-ordinated functions are accomplished by microtubules, cylindrical polymers of the protein tubulin arranged in hexagonal lattices comprising the cylinder wall". [3]

His team also found cooperative interactions amongst tubulin subunits suggestive of "cellular automata" computer simulations (i.e. computer programs with simple laws aimed at forming patterns mimicking cell growth).

Obviously therefore but previously unknown, the pairs of microtubules opposing each other across the synapse of each neuron in a human brain must carry out a similar quantum processing function to that of paramecium, as a supplement to the brain's well known chemical synaptic neuron processing. Calculations by Hameroff's team indicated that the cooperative interaction processing among tubulin subunits in microtubule pairs on each side of the synapse were capable of providing the same potential information processing in each neuron as *"the **entire brain** at the synaptic level"*.

Quantum particles/waves emanating or received at a neuron level via these microtubules in our brains, as with any quantum coupling, creates quantum entanglements, which could then be generated between the brain and its environment. These entanglements would have the effect of sharing quantum information with other areas of the brain, or transferring it to the immediate surroundings to form matter. In other words there is evidence in brain neurons for initiating and collapsing probability waves in the environment, plus the alternative option when required, to process data from physical origins in the body using the conventional chemical synapse system.

An experiment performed in 1994 by University of Mexico neurophysiologist Jacobo Grinberg-Zylberbaum and his collaborators directly showed conclusive evidence of the ability of correlated and entangled human mind directed quantum waves from one subject to be detected in the brain waves of another subject. In other words **this provided direct and repeatable scientific experimental evidence for telepathy.**

In the experiment two subjects were instructed to interrelate together i.e. chat for a period of twenty minutes in order to establish a degree of entanglement. While still communicating together for the duration of experiment by head phones, they then entered separate Faraday chambers (metallic chambers aimed at blocking all electromagnetic signals). One subject was then exposed to a series of light flashes. In about one in four cases the unstimulated brain of the other subject exhibited a transferred potential in their EEG reading attached to their scalp of comparable strength and phase (70% overlap) to the original subjects EEG response to the flashes. Control subjects not interrelated initially, never showed any ability to transfer an evoked EEG potential. (Experimenters used an average of about 100 flashes in order to eliminate "noise." It was thought that conscious **intentionality** (to behave as one) was a critical factor in the experiment to maintain correlation (i.e. entanglement)) [4]

Grinberg-Zylberbaum's experimental results and conclusions have since been replicated (for auditory stimuli) in London by neuropsychiatrist Peter Fenwick in 1999.

Although such experiments as this above are easily replicated, only rarely is the recipient consciously aware of telepathy. Conscious awareness seems reliant on the degree of intent by the sender together with the degree of emotional content.

Thus there is evidence that mental intention can affect others (when correlated as shown above) by the receipt of EEG wave forms. We ourselves probably have no idea to what extent our thoughts and that of others might affect our own body and others, nor do we know just how much other's thoughts affect us. We are well used to the fact that mind does influence our body to an extent e.g. if depressed we are more likely to catch colds etc. Also we are all well aware of the placebo effect of the ability of mind over matter. However these are minor influences of mind effecting matter. At the other extreme we have to accept that in some cultures a witch doctor need "only to point the bone" and the unlucky victim at the receiving end usually dies. Hypnotists too can (fortunately only temporarily) completely change our belief system and sense of reality by mere suggestion.

Interestingly, a breakthrough occurred in 1976 when Fritz-Albert Popp, a theoretical biophysicist at the University of Marburg, found that photons (i.e. quantum entities) and their wave nature, were responsible for signalling between different **cells** throughout the body. This provided the solution to one of the greatest mysteries of life, namely the way in which cells communicate with each other by forming quantum wave interference patterns. This is thought to be the likely way in which the brain consciousness (i.e. mind) also communicates throughout the body. These 'bio-photon emissions' were identified as the critical communication system whereby their wave characteristics were used to perform certain signalling control functions (dependent upon a particular range of frequencies) - including cell speciation, self-regulation and repair of all cell and body growth. This also included photon emissions from DNA - presumably to pass on genetic information and instructions to other cells throughout the body. Later experiments by Popp and his assistants on photon emissions with pairs of water fleas, fish and sunflowers; showed that wave interference was not only used to communicate **inside** the body, but **externally**, between living things. Popp considered such external communication could explain how schools of fish or flocks of birds achieve almost instantaneous coordination (characteristic of quantum non-locality). Other experiments also indicated such quantum fields could also be responsible for the homing ability in some animal pets (e.g. dogs and cats etc.) to enable them to find their owners when separated. Popp felt these quantum fields might even also explain homeopathy and acupuncture.[5]

Other scientists previously had detected field phenomena in living beings including Neuroanatomist Harold S Burr, from Yale University in the 1940's who found, measured and studied electric fields around salamanders. He also found the same salamander blueprint even existed surrounding salamander unfertilised eggs and found similar fields around all sorts of organisms ranging from salamanders and frogs, to **humans**.

Herbert Frohlich of the University of Liverpool, even found that once energy reaches a certain threshold, complete molecules (e.g. proteins) begin to vibrate in unison, until they reach a high level of quantum like coherence characteristic of holography and information transfer. Italian physicist Russian Renalto Nobili obtained experimental confirmation of this, namely that electromagnetic quantum waves emanating from brain cells if correlated sufficiently, have the capability of passing on information when interrelating with other waves. Even water in body cells, was found to exhibit waveforms with the same well known waveform patterns characteristic of brain EEG readings.[6]

Later we will find that these experiments vindicate a quantum physicist and mathematics professor Walter Schempp's work by verifying that the interchange of quantum interference wave patterns is the signalling method utilised by all life forms for transfer of information internally between cells (including brain cells) **and externally**. Two outstanding mysteries though still remain - while the close proximity of cells to each other in the body easily explains internal transfer of information via quantum effects, **how is the transfer of intention from the mind/brain connection achieved over distances externally**? Also, even though this (as with all quantum reality) is holographic and therefore non-local, so that quantum waves could travel instantly regardless of distance; where is memory stored? If external to the brain (as shown previously), is it stored in fields adjacent to our body?

For this we need to look at the biggest field of all.

3.2 THE ZERO POINT FIELD

Physicists for many years have been aware that even in a vacuum there is a ceaseless form of energy still present around us all, an ocean of subatomic virtual particles that represents the ground (i.e. zero energy) state of all matter. Sub atomic particles (mainly photons) appear in the field seemingly out of nowhere, combining, interacting and annihilating each other in an instant. The discovery of the field in 1926 and up until recently left scientists unmoved, as it was not regarded as of much interest and simply the base energy state of the universe at a temperature of absolute zero.

It is now regarded very differently due to research and investigations by Hal Putoff, a Laser physicist in the 1970's, and later by the astrophysicist Bernie Haisch in July 1992. Both are now endeavouring to tap into the prodigious energy provided by the field to meet future world energy needs. Haisch regards the field as the cause of inertia and recent research indicates it also seems likely that the zero point field can also participate in gravity (and therefore perhaps a science based capability which could possibly explain cases claiming levitation).

Hal Putoff in a paper presented to the publication *Physics Review* said:

> "The zero point field is a kind of self-generating ground state of the universe, which constantly refreshes itself and remains constant unless disturbed in some way. It also means that we and all the matter of the universe are literally connected to the furthest reaches of the cosmos through the zero point field waves of the grandest dimensions."

In her book on the subject, unsurprisingly called, *The Field*; well known science writer Lynne McTaggart, following discussion, with Hal Putoff says in her book:

"If all subatomic matter in the world is interacting constantly with this ambient ground-state energy field, the subatomic waves of 'The Field' are constantly imprinting a record of the shape of everything. As the harbinger and imprinter of all wavelengths and all frequencies, the Zero Point Field is a kind of shadow of the Universe for all time, a mirror image and record of all that ever was. In a sense the beginning and the end of everything in the universe."[7]

Haisch describes it as if, "the universe is floating on a sea of light". (Even though the field is radiating energy in the light spectrum, we don't see it as such, as it is outside our vision capability.) A key point concerning its properties is that since the field is comprised solely of subatomic particles, it is obviously the largest quantum field in the universe. Its quantum nature means not only does it have the capability to exchange information via correlated quantum waves interactions, but since it is holographic, it obviously has the incredible memory capability claimed by Lynne Mc Taggard above, of providing a "record of all that ever was".

We therefore have a likely storage library and source for the memory of all life forms, and a possible facility whereby memory could not only be stored during one's lifetime, but also during the lifetimes of reincarnation selves for at least the life of the universe.

Walter Schempp, a mathematics professor from the University of Siegan in Germany in 1992 provided an incredible breakthrough in quantum physics. Earlier he had developed a mathematical theory which he felt could explain how 3D images could be derived from radio waves (or any such electromagnetic waves). He considered that this theory could be the basis of how information processing in the brain/mind of any life form might work. Illustrating his theory by taking a particular case, but in a reverse scenario - his concept was that 3D visual images from the retina, passed via the optic nerve to the brain might be first be converted in the brain prior to subsequent processing into the entirely different medium of quantum waves. Similarly the nerve impulses arriving at the brain emanating from other senses such as hearing, smell and sound, would likewise be first converted by the brain into quantum waves before further processing. The converted quantum waves would then resonate and interact via entanglement instantly with other areas of the brain, and for memory access to and from the zero point field - and presumably for telepathy, externally to another brain of the same species.

Determined to test this theory in a practical situation, he successfully verified his mathematics and theory by working on and massively improving the design of functional Magnetic Resonance Imaging (fMRI) systems. Up until then, quantum entanglement had only been experimentally proved for subatomic particles, and then only at a specific range of **low** temperatures and pressure.[8]

His theory, mathematical analysis and work on Magnetic Resonance Imaging showed that quantum entanglement not only happened at a subatomic level, **but applies to all macro systems - including for humans, our complete body and brain.**

The "Quantum Hologram (QH)" was the name given to his discovery, namely that the event history of all macro scale matter is **continuously** emitted (broadcast) non-locally and is received by and interacts with other matter through a process of exchange of quantum information. The waves emitted by moving objects excite and modulate the zero point field, creating wavefronts which propagate in the field, meet, and interfere with others. The interference patterns that result, carry information at their nodes relating to the physical properties of the objects that created the waves. Because the zero point field is a seamless medium that extends throughout space, the information carried by the interference patterns produced, extends throughout all space as would be expected with normal spaceless characteristics of holography i.e. independence from distance.[9]

As stated by Lynne McTaggart in her book *The Field*:

"Walter Schempp's explosive discovery about quantum memory set off the most outrageous idea of all; short and long term memory doesn't reside in our brain at all. But instead is stored in the zero point field. ..... A number of scientists, including system theorist Ervin Laszlo, would go on to argue that the brain is simply the retrieval and read out mechanism of the ultimate storage medium - the zero point field."[10]

Neurosurgeon Dr Wilder Penfield (referred to earlier) was the first of these scientists to work out a theory of the brain (later vindicated by Walter Schempp's work and many other experiments), where he considered the prime processing function of the brain, is to act as a frequency analyser. Schempp's later work, followed by recent experiments carried out by many others, have shown that that all sensory information received by the brain is quickly converted by the brain from images, vibrations from eardrums etc. into what is now regarded as the universal language of the zero point field and therefore the universe - **namely quantum interference patterns**. Since these are quantum, **the interference patterns exhibit holography (and its inherent ability to contain vast quantities of information)**. Likewise their interactions can be transferred instantly to the zero point field, which would then be similarly instantly capable of being retrieved from anywhere in the universe. Therefore an imprint for each of us, all our actions, what we see, hear touch and smell, and even think, is no doubt constantly being passed onto to the zero point field enveloping us all, and the universe.

The zero point field is surely the internet of the universe for both mind and matter!

3.3   THE BRAIN AS A FILTER

Aldeous Huxley widely acknowledged as one of the pre-eminent intellectuals of his time. In his book, *The Doors of Perception* he described how his sense perception and his perception of existence itself shifted while using mescaline, a drug used for centuries by Indians of the Southwest and Mexico. As a meticulous observer and articulate reporter he claimed that while taking the drug he experienced "mind at large" - a concept that consciousness was literally unlimited, as if each individual were a manifestation of an infinite consciousness. This led him to a belief that our brains contain a filter whose function is to filter out everything other than immediate consensual reality. In his words:

> "To make biological survival possible, "Mind at Large" has to be funneled through the reducing valve of the brain and nervous system. What comes out is a measly trickle of the kind of consciousness which will help us to stay alive on the surface of this particular planet."[11]

There are many examples which supports the concept that our everyday brain consciousness is linked to, or a part of an infinite holographic interconnected consciousness, but filtered so that we are concentrated on our current reality and responsive to any dangers which might confront us.

You will recall, the experimental evidence of neurosurgeon Dr. Wilder Penfield in Chapter 2, where he encountered flashbacks of memory while electrically stimulating certain areas of the brain of a conscious patient, the patient had perfect recall of events that had happened on any day, to the point that the patient was even able to remember **what was in their mind at the time**. Clearly while such recall is impossible under normal conscious states, the brain does have the potential to access this information under certain circumstances.

Rather than a filter as such, the recent breakthrough by Walter Schempp above, on his theory of macro (particularly brain) quantum effects and "the Quantum Hologram(QH)", suggests that in a normal conscious state, the brain has access to only a limited range of frequencies to source information from the zero point field. But when asleep, in a semi-conscious state, or in emergencies; the brain's frequency range widens to allow access to a greater frequency range of information from the zero point field. Effectively therefore access to a variable range of frequencies forms a form of selective filter.

Such a situation occurs readily at least - namely "*a limited slice of the infinite sourced from the zero point field*" for some afflicted with autism known as "autistic savants" who perform amazing mental feats. Such a person is David Tammet, reported in the

British newspaper Guardian; who although cannot drive a car or even tell right from left, but can multiply any two three digit numbers while carrying on a conversation. He claims he sees the numbers as "shapes" that change and evolve into another "shape" that is the correct number. He can also recite the value of *pi* to 22,514 decimal places (which took five hours to recite). There are many other examples of the amazing feats of autistic savants.

There are other similar cases which are a variation of the above, namely that such mental feats have originated as the result of brain damage associated with injury to the head; but prior to the injury, the person's mental capabilities were normal. It therefore appears the "brain filter" was damaged to the point where knowledge normally not available to us was found to be accessible.

While a filter effect occurs with our minds while in a conscious state, it appears there are no such limitations in the unconscious state, as pointed out by the Russian quantum physicist Michael B Mensky, mentioned earlier. The obvious evidence of this is that this ability explains dreams; which can now be regarded as the exploration by our minds into other realms of reality - or to use the term Mensky prefers, where we explore "different 'classical' realities'". He also points out that a half conscious relaxed state, is more likely to be rewarded in gaining knowledge than fully asleep.

(Further examples of this are given below).

3.4 THE COLLECTIVE SUBCONSCIOUS, AND GROUP CONSCIOUSNESS

Most have heard of the concept of the "Collective Subconscious" which generally receives fairly wide support. The idea was first put forward by the famous psychiatrist Carl Jung. He believed the unconscious comprised an impersonal or collective unconscious, where the contents were considered as not personal but **collective**. In other words "not belonging to one individual alone but to a whole group of individuals and generally to a whole nation, or even to the whole of mankind" (also to other different species). He believed the contents of the collective subconscious were not acquired during an individual's lifetime but comprised innate forms, patterns and instincts appropriate to each species.

His views were based largely on his own experience with patients, together with study of Professor J.B. Rhine's telepathy experiments (covered in detail in Section 3, Chapter 6.) at Duke University in 1932. These made a deep impression on him as he believed they gave statistical, scientifically respectable, confirmation of the reality of both extrasensory perception (ESP) and psychokinesis (PK). He was particularly impressed that Rhine's experimental evidence showed ESP occurred regardless of distance and seemed independent of time.

He also came to the conclusion that although a child possesses no inborn ideas, it nevertheless at birth, has a highly developed mind which has access to the "deposit of the psychic functioning of the whole human race". He felt the instincts were preformed, together with primordial images which he thought had always been the basis of man's thinking and evident sometimes in dreams. For support of this he pointed out that mythological ideas were often seen in cases of mental derangement, especially in schizophrenia. Also that insane people frequently produce combinations of ideas and symbols that could never be accounted for by experiences in their individual lives, but only by a stored and common history of the human mind.

He considered that space and time "'did not exist in themselves but were only "postulated" by the conscious mind". Knowledge of events at a distance or in the future he reasoned was possible, as he believed that **within the unconscious psyche**, they all "co-exist timelessly and spacelessly". He also believed the subconscious mind had access to "absolute knowledge ... a knowledge not mediated by the sense organs".[12]

It will be evident that Jung's empirical evidence for both the existence and mental access to a store of "absolute" knowledge, aligns with both our Chapter 2 David Bohm's discovery of the holographic nature of the universe and recent discoveries that memory and all information and knowledge is contained within the universe holograph and internet - the zero point field (with the usual non-local quantum properties of independence from distance or time). Since Pribram also discovered that the brain is similarly holographic; it is not altogether surprising that Jung should separately find both sufficient evidence for, and also conclude that under certain circumstances the brain has access to all information /knowledge.

Although all who generally accept Jung's 'Collective Consciousness Theory', do not accept (or know of) all of his views as stated above; there are countless instances which provide striking supporting evidence for subconscious access to universal knowledge, some of which are as follows:

Instinct, and Instinctive behaviour: There are limitless instances of instinctive group behaviour, but most of us accept this without question and are usually oblivious to the fact that instinctive behaviour is always within a range which is unique and specific to each species. Also we have become so inured to it generally that rather than question why and how it occurs, we tend to blindly accept it as if its reality itself explains it - rather like a tautology. Some instincts are within our own human species experience, such as our automatic defensive reactions to danger i.e. increase in heart rate and release of adrenaline e.g. when encountering a snake (there is an almost universal reaction amongst all animals to a 'hiss' noise, suggestive of a snake).

Squirrels store nuts in advance of winter. Many bird species migrate at specific times of the year. Their close formation flying and ability (as with fish in shoals) to instantly change direction as a group, overwhelmingly suggests they are operating momentarily in a group consciousness coherent quantum state, linked via the subconscious.

Characteristically, it seems almost self-evident that during bird migrations and for situations concerning fish in shoals, that such a group action over long periods and with attendant boredom, favours slipping into a semi-conscious state. The ideal situation (as stated by Mensky in Chapter 2) where the subconscious dominates and where brains are likely to have a greater quantum coherence with the zero point field. (**Intention** of participants to engage in a group function is also seen as highly relevant - see the properties of Group Consciousness summarised below).

There also seems a parallel with ourselves where after learning actions such as driving a car and repeated many times, our subconscious invariably takes over such functions which then become automatic. If repeated by many of us and over many lifetimes by a large segment of our population, it seems that such a function gradually becomes associated with our species in a species specific collective memory within the zero point field. It perhaps could then become another of our instinctive species behaviours. Thus newcomers to driving a car in the future, will then innately find they have a high instinctive capability to drive a car with minimal instruction and with little concentration.

Interestingly, life forms other than humans; particularly insects, and bacteria etc. seem to spend a greater proportion of their lives exhibiting instinctive behaviour – which suggests they spend more of their time relying on their subconscious rather than using rational conscious thinking. Noteworthy also is that each of the various **types** of instinctive behaviour exhibited, almost invariably lie within an exclusive range, most of which are unique to each particular species, or phylum - confirming Jung's concept of 'collective' unconsciousness.

Inspiration: Most people can relate instances where, when struggling to solve a problem, they unexpectedly come up with an answer. Usually this occurs while the person is in a 'non-ordinary state of consciousness' such as day dreaming or dreaming, exhaustion etc. Examples are the case of Friedrich von Kekule, who had a sudden vision of the chemical formula for benzene while gazing into his fireplace coals - an insight that gave birth to modern organic chemistry. Similarly, the Russian chemist Dimitri Mendeleev envisioned his famous periodic table of elements while he was lying in bed exhausted after a long struggle to categorize these elements according to their atomic weight. Similar situations apply in the case of Niels Bohr's planetary model of the atom, Heisenberg's formulation of the basic principles of quantum physics, and the discovery of chemical transmission of neuronal impulses for which Otto Loewl received a Nobel Prize.

Mozart often claimed he found his symphonies in his head. William Blake said of his work '*Milton*': "I have written this poem from immediate dictation, twelve or sometimes twenty or thirty lines at a time, without premeditation, and even against my will." [13]

There are many others.

Savants and Inexplicable abilities: V.S. Ramachandran and Sandra Blakeslee, in their book, *Phantoms in the Brain* relate the case of Tom, a thirteen year old boy who was blind and incapable of tying his own shoelaces. Although he had never been instructed in music or educated in any way, he learned the piano by hearing others play. He absorbed arias and tunes from hearing them sung and could play any piece of music on the first try as well as the most accomplished performer. Amazingly he routinely performed three pieces of music at once by playing "Fishers Horn pipe" with one hand, "Yankee Doodle Dandy" with the other, and singing "Dixie".

Nadia despite an IQ measured between 60 and 70 was an artistic genius who produced sketches good enough to hang in the Madison Avenue Gallery.

Amongst the capabilities of other savants mentioned, was a boy who could tell the time of day to the exact second without referring to any time piece - even in his sleep, sometimes mumbling the exact time while dreaming. Another was able to estimate the exact width of an object from 20 feet away to an accuracy of one quarter of an inch.[14]

There are also many normal people who have the prodigious capability of carrying out unbelievable calculations in their head. Invariably when asked how they do this, they claim they have no idea and instead say the answer just popped into their heads!

Psychometry: Many so called sensitives or psychics claim they can pick up the thoughts and emotions associated with objects. Thus by holding a ring or any small personal belonging, they can give information about its owner or owners, and of the major incidents associated with them.

There are in fact indisputable cases where some such sensitives have been subjected to rigorous laboratory tests and proved to have these abilities, among them the famous Dutch psychic Gerald Croiset who often used his talents to help police solve crimes. In a series of experiments conducted in the 1960s, W. H. C. Tenhaeg, the director of the Parapsychological Institute of the State University of Utrecht, and Marius Valkhoff, dean of the faculty of arts at the University of Witwatersrand, Johannesburg, South Africa, found that Croiset, could psychometrize even the smallest fragment of bone and accurately describe its past.[15]

Clairvoyance: Norman Emerson, a professor of anthropology at the University of Toronto and founding vice president of the Canadian Archaeological Association, often used a truck driver named George McMullen to find and mark out archaeological sites, as he claimed he could tune into the past. Emerson relates an instance among many where McMullen located the site of an ancient Iroquois longhouse. Emerson was able to verify this by later uncovering the ancient structure exactly where McMullen said it would be.[16]

(Other cases of clairvoyance are dealt with in Chapter 4 and Section 3)

Divining: There are many instances where divining using rods or even a plumb bob are used to detect water, oil, or minerals. Abilities seem very variable. However the fact that diviners are employed by a number of oil companies with known successes, indicates some have undoubted talents. Others have been able to find water in areas where previously artesian water had never been found.

Twins: Apart from physical similarity, twins often are amazingly alike in many ways. There are many instances where twins separated at birth have exhibited a whole range of remarkable synchronicities. Examples are some twins who have been separated at birth and who have later met again where they have shown the same taste in clothes and food, and in some cases have even married people who have similar names and backgrounds.[17] Twins of course are unique in having a closely matched DNA sequence to each other, which suggests this is a major factor in explaining these synchronicities. Also, such synchronicities are further highlighted in cases where twins live in close proximity - which facilitates constant communication with each other. It seems in such cases it seems to result in their minds becoming quantum entangled (via zero point field linkage), leading to the frequently observed ability to be strongly telepathic and speak in unison as if they were sharing the same or a group mind.

Spontaneous Culture Links: Similar achievements seem to have been produced by entire cultures even though they were not in ordinary communication with each other, and may not even have known of each other's existence. Giant pyramids were built in ancient Egypt and in pre-Columbian America with remarkable agreement in design. Crafts, such as pottery-making, have taken much the same form in all cultures. Ignazio Masulli, a reputable historian at the University of Bologna found that there is no reasonable explanation for the striking recurrence of their basic design. Direct contact between these cultures is dismissed by archaeological research.[18]

The "Collective Unconscious", and "Group Consciousness" have many similarities such as that they both are states where the mind is clearly not focussed at all on physical reality, but instead is in a completely unfocussed relaxed state. Also, both types of consciousness demonstrate the entangled holistic character of quantum reality, rather the separateness associated with a normal conscious state. With the Collective

Unconsciousness, it seems that the mind must access a deeper level of the zero point field to gain information (including instinctive behaviour information patterns) not normally available in a conscious state. In the case of instinctive behaviour, the memory is species specific, whereas inspiration and savant type information seems general type information. (This savant type information perhaps with sufficient intention and persistence may possibly be available to us all. See below).

Access to Collective Unconsciousness information seems very suggestive of a species variable filter access to zero point field information (as mentioned above) of nested quantum waves, dependent as a group upon frequency range matching. In contrast, with Group Consciousness, minds are **linked** (e.g. twins) and entangled with the strength of the linkage (wave correlation) possibly dependent upon intention and attention. (Obviously such a mind linkage between twins is one of the many common verifications of the existence of telepathy).

Interestingly, some species minds seem almost permanently linked together e.g. termites, ants and most bees. Others occasionally exhibit Group Consciousness e.g. twins, birds in flocks, fish in shoals, locusts during plagues (in this case, experiments have shown that the release of the chemical "serotonin" acts as the trigger for group action when a threshold number gather together).

We will later find out that a light trance and training, seems to widen the frequency range of the "filter" to allow the subconscious to dominate, which then aids use of the PCAR communication system (mentioned earlier in the Chapter) to retrieve information normally not available. This applies particularly to the cases above usually associated with psychics, where psychometry, and clairvoyance, is involved, but also with divining ability and those of savants.

3.5   GROUP CONSCIOUSNESS - EXPERIMENTS AIMED AT DETECTING PK PHENOMENA AND GROUP CONSCIOUSNESS

Herman Schmidt, a professor of physics at the University of Cologne, is the world's leading exponent of modern PK research. (The meaning of PK or psychokinesis, is the influence of mind on matter).

In the early 1970's, he was impressed with J.B. Rhine's experiments on precognition and extrasensory perception at Duke University using card tests (covered extensively in Section 3). He believed he could contribute to Rhine's work by using a machine approach to see if he could detect the influence of consciousness on classical physical reality i.e. an experimental machine. The particular approach he chose was to design an experimental machine which could test whether participant's intention could influence random events at a quantum level.[19]

The experimental device he invented is called a random number generator (RNG), (subsequently called random event generators (REG's)). The concept he used was to engineer an electronic equivalent of a "flipping" a coin to provide a sequence of "heads" and "tails". A very high rate of "flips" (i.e. games) was provided in the design by employing a rapidly cycling clock to flip between two assigned imaginary "states", usually identified as the binary numbers "zero" or "one". A counter was included to count only instances where a "flip" actually matched the receipt of an emission of an electron from a radioactive isotope (strontium). In such cases it was arranged to record both the number of the event and the particular state (i.e. "zero" or "one") registered at the same time by the clock and display.

The point of using radioactive decay was simply to introduce randomness into the experiment, so that a participant could try to mentally influence by attention and intent, the REG to bias the result in favor of the experimenter's particular choice of state i.e. "zero" or "one". A graphical output provided by a computer was aimed at providing a display which could clearly show any deviations from randomness above a base line.

The outcomes of Schmidt's experiments and subsequently by all others using his REG machines (or variations) was a completely unqualified success. 832 PK studies alone investigated by Dean Radin and Roger Nelson at Princeton University were carried out by 68 different investigators between 1959 and 1987. Using meta-analysis on databases from the experiments, the investigation gave a resulting average hit rate of 51 percent, and odds against chance of beyond a trillion to one. (This replication rate was found statistically as good as exemplary experiments in psychology and physics.)

Interesting, meta-analysis by Princeton University on data available from experiments aimed at trying to mentally influence the results of throwing dice carried out over half a century previously, revealed similar results (51.2 percent hits), with an astonishing odds against chance of more than a billion to one. The manual nature of these experiments had let to the unfair criticism by sceptics of possible fraud. Therefore this led to these experiments being previously discounted.[20]

With now REG machines being readily available at a reasonable cost, hundreds of experiments are today being carried out continuously throughout the world. Portable versions have been created and they are often even used for demonstrations in lecture halls. These allow audience participation in the tests so they can see for themselves first hand and instantly, the positive results of their own mind/matter influence.

Soon after initial REG experiments, it was discovered that in the absence of participants, although graphical outputs generally depicted flat lining (the expected randomness in the absence of locally directed intention), minor fluctuations were detected. Amazingly these were soon found to correlate with all major world events of interest e.g. strong readings coincided with the twin towers terrorist attack of

9/11. The cause is now accepted as being due to the fact that the focus by millions of minds throughout the world on such an event causes a temporary slight drop in overall world quantum randomness as detected by any REG's anywhere, regardless of location.

REG experiments with participants showed significant and differing influencing capabilities amongst sexes. Larger effects were invariably obtained for more than one participant working together, and bonded couples such as partners or close members of the same family exhibited the best results (presumably due to greater entanglement correlation between them). Their results were four times that of individuals. Experiments also showed no discernable difference in experimental results even when participants were located thousands of miles away from the REG, or incredibly whether carried out many hours before or after the actual operation of the REG devices (illustrating time interdependence of quantum reality).

When running REG's in situations in the absence of any active participants, when results would normally be expected to be completely random; venues that were found to be particularly conducive to showing results above chance, included small intimate groups, group rituals, sacred sites, musical and theatrical performances, and other charismatic events. In contrast, data generated during most academic conferences, business meetings, or other mundane venues showed little deviation from chance.[21] The poor results associated with rather boring events, seems to highlight that attention and intention are likely to provide the best results.

Coverage in the literature of worldwide use of REG's is now well detailed, particularly in Dean Radin's book *The Conscious Universe*. In addition, Lynne McTaggart has written a whole book on it called *The Intention Experiment* and she has created a website of the same name where, if they wish, participants can also choose to join in ongoing intention experiments.[22]

Clearly Schmidt's experimental breakthrough absolutely verifies the ability for mind/consciousness to affect matter. In more detail though, it shows that consciousness plus our individual conscious intention exhibits the quantum property of non-locality by demonstrating that it repeatedly can cause effects beyond the body, instantaneously and regardless of distance (i.e. the quantum holograph (QH). It also demonstrates Group Consciousness, where multiple effects of many minds can effect reality (i.e. the REG experimental results).

Noteworthy also is the fact, that consciousness does not just effect matter in some minor, simple, or random way; but in an unknown manner, it always influences matter in accordance with the **intention** i.e. the specific mental will and direction of the experimenter.

The following is a useful summary (provided by Dr Dean Radin) of the properties of consciousness as determined by Schmidt and his other researchers:

1. it extends beyond the individual, and has quantum field-like properties, in that it effects the probabilities of events.

2. consciousness injects order into systems in proportion to the strength of the consciousness present.

3. the strength of consciousness in an individual fluctuates from moment to moment, and is regulated by focus of **attention**.

4. A group of individuals can be said to have group consciousness. Group consciousness strengthens when the group's attention is focused on a common object or event, and this creates coherence among the group. If the group's attention is scattered, then the group's mental coherence is also scattered. [23]

This can also help explain the group behavior of migratory birds and shoals of fish as mentioned previously. In both cases, not only are participants in a relaxed unfocussed and trance like state, but the mental intention to participate in a common behavior presumably creates coherence/entanglement and widens the frequency response of all together such that they share the same consciousness intention.

3.6   THE SUBCONSCIOUS – THE PATH TO UNIVERSAL KNOWLEDGE, AND RESONANCE

Since the facts fit the theory, the examples given above on inspiration, instinctive behavior, group conscious, savants, twins etc. provides compelling evidence for our acceptance that the subconscious mind has the ability to access universal knowledge sourced from the zero point field. However, it might reasonably be asked why we are not all walking encyclopedias? Also why don't we also share the abilities of autistic savants, be subject daily to wonderful inspiration and be blessed with the remarkable gifts of some of the people mentioned above?

Psychologist Robert M. Anderson, Jnr., of the Rensselaer Polytechnic Institute in Troy, New York, believes it is because we are only able to tap into information that is directly relevant to our own personal memories (i.e. events). Anderson calls this selective process "**personal resonance**" and likens it to the fact that a vibrating tuning fork will resonate with (or set up a vibration in) another tuning fork only if the second tuning fork possesses a similar structure, shape, and size which can create the same frequency signature:

"Due to personal resonance, relatively few of the almost infinite variety of 'images' in the holographic structure of the universe are available to an individual's personal consciousness," says Anderson. [24]

A tuning fork has a unique single frequency characteristic, as do all physical objects (as determined by the Schrödinger equation). All life forms similarly have unique but different frequencies (or perhaps group frequency patterns) including each and every one of us, so that all entities have their signature frequency identity. This is therefore a kind of address on the quantum internet highway in the zero point field - to source personal memory, or to interrelate with other entities directly via quantum fields.

The quantum holograph (QH) is similar, but entirely different from that created by a holograph formed by light interacting with electromagnetic fields; in that resonance in **classical physical** states merely allows maximum energy transfer. Rather than energy transfer, resonance associated with quantum holography is thought to involve coherent quantum wave interactions capable of not only exchanging information, but also consciousness type parameters such as **thought, emotion and intention**.

Our events and thoughts in the quantum non-physical world, are thought to be just as much "things", as are atoms in our world of classical physical reality.

In the case of twins, mentioned earlier, they each are so genetically alike that they seem to be linked (i.e. resonate) so that at a unconscious level they can share the same resonating set of frequencies and therefore gain access to each other's minds apparently at will. In this respect as noted above they often speak in unison and share the same opinions and thoughts, and behave generally as if they have the same group consciousness.

With other cases above, **such as inspiration, autistic savants, etc**. a similar process of linkage (i.e. resonance) at a subconscious level seems to occur, but on this occasion rather than linking with another mind (i.e. a twin), the subject appears to link with the collective wisdom of the universe contained within the zero point field in order to gain completely new knowledge. Linkage only seems to occur critically based on association with particular thoughts occurring in the mind of the subject at the time on any subject. In addition, information is usually only gained after persistent almost obsessive concentration on the subject.

It is important to note that this is **not personal "memory" type information** which relies on frequency matching of **personal** "events" in one's life or Sheldrakes's morphic fields which provide **personal** body template shapes rather than universe type collective information/knowledge itself. Access to this type of information is covered extensively in an Annex to the final Chapter of this book, Chapter 9.

The process again confirms the quantum holography of the brain, in a similar fashion where experimentally only a particular wavelength of light impinging on a commercially produced holograph will elicit a response. Inspiration would seem to occur in this fashion and as mentioned above, it seems invariably associated with day dreaming or dreaming. Likewise an autistic savant may exhibit a low IQ in a conscious state (exhibiting perhaps a damaged or unformed fully conscious brain), but be a real 'whiz' at a subconscious level and readily able to tap into memory, knowledge and untaught abilities such as playing the piano - a skill which relies very much upon concentration, intent, subconscious focus and accessing memory.

3.7　SELF RESONATING QUANTUM FIELDS

Before even Walter Schempp's mathematical and scientific breakthrough work on functional Magnetic Resonance Imaging (fMRI), systems biologist Rupert Sheldrake, had developed his own impressive theory of **information fields** and **self-resonance**. His theory is called morphic resonance, and provides the likely explanation as to how the structure and form (morphology) of all living organisms is attained by cells adhering to patterns provided by resonant and information fields to follow for growth and repair. In his model, developing organisms are shaped by fields which exist **within** and around them and these fields contain the intended species form and shape of the organism. He also suggested among these fields, that there are additional nested information/ memory fields which store **memories** of habits. Over time these habits strengthen with use and also importantly can influence following generations, perhaps to the point that if these habits become shared by others, they become instincts. (e.g. hunting strategies). The field's structure therefore would have a cumulative memory, based on what has happened to the species in the past. Sheldrake's concept of a morphic field therefore, also includes not only information fields of form, but also **behaviour**.

It will be noted that due to work carried out by Schempp and others, these fields are now accepted as quantum in nature; and to both reside, and exist as fields located within the zero point field.

As Sheldrake points out in his book, *The Rebirth of Nature*; according to his theory, it would be expected that when some members of a species acquire a new pattern of behaviour (e.g. learning a new trick), they would unconsciously create a new species behavioural information field. He believes that once the field was first established, it would facilitate others subsequently learning the behaviour. Also that the field would gain greater intensity (rather like increasing magnetism in a bar magnet), the more the trick was repeated. It would therefore follow that the more members of the species learn it, the stronger this effect is likely to be experience everywhere. Thus, for example, if laboratory rats learn a new trick in America, rats in laboratories elsewhere should show a tendency to learn it faster.

The following demonstrates that there is considerable evidence to support Sheldrake's theory:

In the early 1920s, people in Southampton, England, found that cardboard caps on the tops of their milk bottles were being torn off by birds (called "tits"), and the cream at the top of the milk was being drunk. Despite the fact the birds do not usually venture more than a few miles from their breeding grounds, the phenomenon soon started in other parts of the British Isles. On each occasion it seemed to have occurred independently. It soon spread throughout Britain. This cream-stealing habit spread to tits in Sweden, Denmark, and Holland. Milk deliveries ceased during the Second World War, and began again only in 1947-48. However, despite the fact that the pre-war tits would have all died out by 1947-48, nevertheless attacks on bottles rapidly recommenced in Britain in 1947. The habit soon re-established itself all over the Netherlands.

In another similar case, temple monks on the Japanese island Itsukushima, claimed they had observed a first instance of a particularly intelligent monkey learning to wash off any sand on oranges (provided by tourists) in the sea before eating. The habit soon spread seemingly by imitation to other monkeys on the island. The monks however were baffled to discover after some weeks that the habit had spread to all monkeys on the mainland, despite the complete physical isolation of the monkeys on the island.

Naturalist Eugene Marais found that termites could speedily repair damage to their mounds, rebuilding tunnels and arches, working from both sides of a breach, and meeting up perfectly in the middle - even though the individual insects are blind. He then experimented by breaking off a large part of the termite mound and dividing it vertically with a large steel plate. The termites soon repaired the breach and the two halves matched perfectly despite the fact the termites could not see and their mound was completely separated by the steel plate. He reached the ultimate conclusion that somewhere there exists a preconceived plan, (which we would now regard as a quantum field template located in the zero point field surrounding everything), which the termites merely execute. [25]

Cases cited by Rupert Sheldrake applicable to his concept of morphic fields and self-resonance include not only cases similar to those above, but cases involving information transfer of the **shape and growth** template/pattern unique to each organism i.e. bacteria, plants, birds, fish, and animals etc. including man, and also individual organs. The evidence for his theory is particularly strong, as up until now there has been no explanation as to how cell speciation occurs. Also cases such as how flatworms when cut in half, can regrow, or metamorphosis of a chrysalis into a butterfly occurs. These cases have previously defied rational explanation. His theory also applies to formation and growth of crystals where crystals of a new substance are typically initially found very difficult to form. Once initially successful and repeated however, crystallization then can occur instantly anywhere in the world (as has been often been experienced after first discovering a new chemical compound, followed by an initial lengthy and difficult process in creating crystals). He calls the process "morphic resonance" -"the influence of like upon like through space and time". He also notes the effect does not fall off with distance.

You will recall we have previously learned to identify this independence of distance (and instantaneous transfer of information), as "non-locality", characteristic of quantum fields and the quantum holograph (QH). Also, once a new information field is established as suggested by Sheldrake, it is easy to see that **only** other members of the same species would have exclusive access to information in the new field, due to their subconscious brain linking with the species exclusive new field frequency pattern via coherent interference quantum wave mingling and resonance.[26]

(Note: There are many familiar electromagnetic communication systems (e.g. frequency wave modulation/demodulation systems) based on classical physics, by which massive amounts of information is **transferred** routinely around our planet to give us television and other services. It is important to note though, that with quantum wave interference with other quantum waves, this quantum communication system itself extracts information for **direct** use by life-forms for cognitive processing. In contrast, in classical physical communication systems, information must first be input by an electronic man-made system into electromechanical waves, and then later extracted by demodulation equipment in a suitable form for television, computers etc.). Surely this suggests that via quantum waves, the universe is brilliantly designed for information processing and for communication between all life forms.)

Walter Schempp's theories, mathematics and work on functional Magnetic Resonance Imaging (fMRI) systems covered above is now thought - not only to have provided a complete explanation as to how Rupert Sheldrake's earlier ideas of morphic resonance fields work, but is the quantum field theory and system now regarded as that universally used by nature for all living beings for sense perception, brain processing information, and for communication with one's environment. This has also led to a growing certainty by many, that Schempp's original work and further contributions by other scientist (such as Pribram, Yasue, Hammeroff, Hagen, Marcer and Mitchell), now provides understanding of the physics - including a universal communication system which underlies all paranormal phenomena.

As stated by scientist Dr Edgar Mitchell:

"Intuition, telepathy, clairvoyance and many similar information phenomena seem easily explained by means of the non-local quantum hologram."

Unquestionably the non-local quantum hologram (QH) breakthrough discovered by Walter Schempp is the heart of the system. However the associated communication system (called the PCAR system - see below), which provides access to all the distributed non-local quantum holographs contained both within the brain and also the zero point field, are both perhaps equally important.

3.8 SCHEMPP'S PCAR UNIVERSAL BIO - QUANTUM HOLOGRAPHIC BRAIN PROCESSING AND COMMUNICATION SYSTEM

The quantum non-local communication system discovered by Schempp relies on transmission and receipt of information quantum waves of many different frequencies, with the information contained in both the amplitude and the phase relationships of the interference patterns. Following an emitted wave, a returned reference wave allows resonance and standing waves to occur which then enables cognitive decoding and processing of the information. As covered in the title to this Chapter the technical term for the system has the rather daunting name of a phase-conjugate-adaptive-resonance system (PCAR)).

The system also includes the concept of non-local storage of information in a quantum holograph (QH), with individual holographs associated with each and every macro object as part of the zero point field.[27]

There is evidence to suggest that all life forms, even plants, universally use this same quantum communication system. (Replicated experiments with plants, have indicated that effects depend on quantum correlation/entanglement, and occur independent of distance, as covered below).

Other interesting facets of the system are:

- The return signal loop resonating system is somewhat similar to the more simple non-quantum and **physical** sonar information retrieval system of bats, dolphins, whales who use sound to send out signals and receive reflections back to locate targets.

- It will be recalled that non-locality allows transmission of information **instantaneously and independent of distance**. Therefore, once the brain has processed information, conscious intention commands to limbs in the body, or even externally, obviously can occur at an astonishing speed. This therefore can easily at last explain the remarkable survival reaction and attack speeds of both insects and predators in either defence, or hunting modes. Rapid speech also exhibits the instantaneous access to memory contained within one's personal vocabulary store in the zero point field.

- An organism's personal quantum hologram (QH) can be regarded as its non-local information store in the zero point field that is created from all the quantum emissions of every atom, molecule and cell in the organism. Every physical experience, along with every subjective experience is believed to be stored in our own personal hologram and we are in constant resonance with it. Each of us has our own unique resonant frequencies contained within our unique quantum hologram which acts as a "fingerprint" to identify our non-local information store.

- The link between any object (including the case of humans and other living entities) and it's zero point field is so strong and ubiquitous in enveloping the object, that visual and other perceptions encountered in cases such as remote viewing/healing, or psychometry, is thought to occur by conscious interrelation with the particular object's (or entities') quantum hologram (QH) in the zero point field. Remote viewing therefore, as with other forms of clairvoyance is not thought to **normally*** occur by consciousness actually travelling to the distant location concerned. Instead it is thought one's consciousness accesses the target remotely via a form of visual perception with the zero point field (see below). Similarly psychometry where touch is involved (e.g. with a necklace belonging to the person), links directly with the object's and then the subject's identity in the zero point field. Linkage and resonance with the zero point field can also easily explain how a baby in the womb links with the mother's quantum hologram (QH) in the zero point field, to inherit her species specific instinctive behaviour, and also her learned behaviour ("Lamarckian" type) acquired from her mother's life experience.

    Clearly, at each level the organism is utilizing information (i.e. quantum fields containing patterns of energy and matter) obtained from its environment. This implies that there is a process (e.g. our mind/consciousness) that (unconsciously) uses and assigns meaning to this information. Note that "meaning" is also information, and regarded as a type of "thing" for processing in its context, for use by the organism.

- In early experiments studying the quantum non-locality nature of subatomic particles, it was found that retention of coherence/entanglement could only be preserved with particularly specific **low temperature and pressure constraints**. Surprisingly therefore, it was found that despite known quantum processing within microtubules in the brain and with the PCAR - communication system, that non-locality was found to be a normal and typical condition of the rather warm

---

* Note: in some cases e.g. "remote viewing" and perhaps where detailed and superior vision is required, there is strong evidence that consciousness itself can actually travel to a remote target to source data. This is covered in Chapter 6, Section 3.

and wet macro-sized brain. Later research suggested that in the brain there were networks of quanta where the particles had to be "woven" or "braided" in a way that is sufficiently robust to maintain coherence at body temperatures. Confirmation of quantum processing in the brain was later found to be re-affirmed and rather obvious, in that where particularly high ambient temperatures are experienced by the brain (i.e. hyperthermia), cognition cannot cope and is always adversely effected. This typically occurs in cases such as hot deserts where temperatures over 40 degrees are often experienced and results in even simple mental tasks becoming error ridden and frustratingly difficult.[28]

Unlike the body and brain, the evidence above constantly supports the concept that the mind (including memory) and consciousness are not fixed in physical reality. It is noteworthy that the zero point field, which likely stores both the memory of all life forms, and stores a record of all that has ever happened; consists of a cauldron of nothing other than sub atomic particles and fields. It is therefore obviously solely quantum in nature. Also, rather than simply a materialistic universe; the prominence, and our daily use of these resonating holographic quantum information fields, suggests a large proportion of our lives is already firmly and surprisingly based in non-physical reality, with our brains and consciousness very much involved in processing quantum interference patterns linked by resonance to the zero point field.

3.9 FURTHER EXPERIMENTAL EVIDENCE FOR MIND TO MIND COMMUNICATION BETWEEN DIFFERENT LIFEFORMS

The idea that **mind can affect the physical body** is becoming more acceptable to the public, but still receives little interest by mainstream science. Hypnotherapy, (essentially using mind to influence matter - our bodies), for years has been used successfully to treat psychosomatic illnesses, intractable cases of pain, also hypertension, warts, epilepsy, neurodermatitis, and many other physical conditions. Less well known is that with countless experiments, the placebo effect alone, has been shown to effect a cure rate of between 20-40%!

Also, all known studies of distant mental healing and prayer have shown positive results. For example, a study in 1988 on praying for coronary patients at San Francisco Hospital found compared with a control group, those prayed for were five times less likely to require antibiotics and three times less likely to develop pulmonary edema. None of the prayed-for group required endotracheal intubation and fewer patents in the prayed for group died.

In 1963, research consciousness pioneer Charles Tart, commenced many successful sender - receiver distant mind - mind controlled experiments involving skin conductance, blood volume, heart rate etc. All achieved significant results. His finger blood volume experiments were later independently verified by Erlendur Haralldsson of the University of Utrecht (and others), as occurring instantly, and in many cases over thousands of miles away. William Braud carried out similar experiments over seventeen years with results showing 57 % of experiments were independently significant, with odds better than twenty to one - where only five percent would be expected by chance.

Faraday type caging around the sender was often used in such experiments to verify that the mental interaction could not involve electro-magnetic waves. This, and fact that the intention effects occurred instantly and independent of distance, obviously indicates that the method of communication used is the PCAR quantum system. Despite the fact that in the majority of cases definite and positive effects were received and detected by measuring apparatus, in no cases though, was there any evidence that recipients were **consciously** aware of the events. This supports the case that for humans and in our material universe comprised largely of macro high mass objects, mind-mind contact and the **effect** of intention, normally is only slight and operates solely at a subconscious level - except, where presumably correlation/resonance is particularly strong. This would apply in crisis situations, or in cases of psychics - our mind "filter" seems to widen to allow mind-mind communication to break through into consciousness.[29]

This is in marked contrast with similar experiments carried out with plants, which demonstrate a sophistication to perceive and react to their environment far surpassing that of humans. The first experiments, were carried out as long ago as 1966 by Cleve Backster using a Polygraph (i.e. a lie detector) with the electrodes connected to his favorite house plant "*Dracaena massangeana*". He found consistent strong reactions whenever he made threats to harm the plant. Later, he found a strong reaction occurred even when the plant perceived any likely harm e.g. when a dog entered the room. He was also able to detect a response from the plant at the very instant when he decided to return home from a visit some 15 miles away. Others later were unable to replicate the experiments, unless they spent some time first in gaining rapport with the plants. We would now identify this as necessary to achieve a sufficient degree of correlation. Later experiments by Backster and other researchers showed that measurable communication, independent of distance and virtually instantaneously could occur between any life forms including bacteria. A typical example occurs between two eggs where when one shell was cracked, an immediate reaction was observed in another some distance away. Amazingly in none of these examples including plants, did any of the life forms have even a nervous system, let alone a brain. As is seen above, communication in all cases though still exhibits all the characteristics of the holographic, non-local PCAR communication system.[30]

3.10 NON - PHYSICAL REALITY - SENSES

With vision, for the brain to merely present to our consciousness, a two dimensional image as it appears on the retina, would be an inadequate and poor representation for us of physical reality. Instead, the incredible universal brain communication system mentioned above (PCAR), provides for us a full four dimensional (i.e. three space dimensions and one of time) simulated and virtual representation of a perceived object out in space and exactly in the same place as the actual object, so that the object and our perception of the object coincide. This is of course a critical survival criterion as it allows an organism to accurately see and locate objects (especially predators, and food) in three dimensional space.

When we first perceive something visually, the PCAR system processes the waveform of the image received on our retina, to send a quantum virtual mirror image wave back to the object to produce a resonant holograph type standing wave. This allows the brain to process the wave interference pattern information contained in the amplitude, frequencies and the phase relationships of the underlying interference patterns of the resonant standing wave, so as to completely represent and locate the object in three dimensional space.

The system not only applies to visual perception, but in a similar way, all other senses are processed in exactly the same way - just as vision is first converted into quantum holograph type visual images, sound is first converted into acoustic images, and touch into tactile images, and hearing into sonic images, etc.

For remote viewing (clairvoyance), the normal senses input waveform carrying location information (e.g. light waves received on the retina or sound waves etc.) necessary to allow the PCAR standing waves to form, obviously do not exist. Therefore, in its place, a **substitute** PCAR reference wave signal is required to locate the target in classical physical reality and establish resonance. Significantly the specific geographical coordinates of the target are now always provided to all remote viewing participants before attempting an experiment. This or any other means (e.g. a photograph of the target) seems to allow the mind to form the required reference wave necessary for the system to gain information from the target. (Detailed examples of remote viewing are covered in Section 3 of this book).

In the case of accessing one's own memory in the zero point field, for example when trying to remember a particular word; similarly, an "icon" i.e. a mental "cue", meaning a visual mind association of any kind - seems sufficient to allow the mind to focus on the word, and to establish the resonance condition required to decode the specific word's quantum hologram within the zero point field. In the case of psychics, they have often demonstrated the uncanny ability to locate the location of the body of a murder victim on a map, or lead police to the grave. In all cases though, it appears "icons or "cues" are first obtained by psychics often holding a photograph of the victim or an item belonging to them or by being given the name of the victim. Any of these "cues", therefore seems to similarly fulfil the PCAR requirements to establish the return reference wave necessary for resonance and information decoding.

3.11 THE ABILITY FOR THE SENSES TO SURVIVE DEATH

You will recall the neuropsychologist Karl Lashey who worked with Dr Pribram in the removal of portions of rat's brains in an unsuccessful attempt to locate memory.

He later carried out similar research on rats eyes to determine whether vision was holographic. He found that the visual centres of the brain were also surprisingly resistant to surgical excision, as even after removing as much as 90 percent of a rat's visual cortex (the part of the brain that receives and interprets what the eye sees), he found it could still perform tasks requiring complex visual skills. Similarly, research conducted by Pribram revealed that as much as 98 percent of a cats optic nerves can be severed without seriously impairing its ability to perform complex visual tasks. [31]

David Eisenberg, M.D., a clinical research fellow at the Harvard Medical School, published an account of two school-age Chinese sisters in Beijing who can "see" well enough by using merely the skin in their armpits to read notes and identify colours. [32]

In Italy the neurologist Cesare Lombroso studied a blind girl who could see with the tip of her nose, her arm, or the lobe of her left ear.[33]

In the 1960s the Soviet Academy of Science investigated a Russian peasant woman named Rosa Kuleshova, who could see photographs and read newspapers with the tips of her fingers, and pronounced her abilities genuine. Significantly, the Soviets ruled out the possibility that Kuleshova was simply detecting the varying amounts of stored heat different colours emanate, as she could read a black and white newspaper even when it was covered with a sheet of heated glass. [34]

The first example above, describing Karl Lashy's somewhat macabre ongoing penchant for exercising portions of brains (rats in this case), perhaps demonstrates that even with the visual cortex severely damaged, the PCAR system exhibits remarkable robustness to still provide the mind with some degree of vision. It suggests though, that the damage might only have affected the PCAR systems ability to identify the object's location absolutely exactly in space. The remaining other examples support this as well, as no **eyesight** at all is involved. However in all these remaining examples, it is noteworthy that either touch or a finger held close to a field near the object was involved. This therefore could operate as an icon or cue to allow the required PCAR reference return wave from the zero point field to be established and permit **some** degree of vision.

There are other examples of completely blind creatures such as fish in pools in underground caves, who have adapted to their constantly dark environment and do not have eyes. However they obviously have some vision necessary to cope in their environment, but clearly do not require the precise spatial vision provided by eyes. Similarly in the example above, where a steel plate is placed vertically through a termites nest, termites must still have some form of vision (most likely solely provided from the quantum wave templates contained within the zero point field), as they are still able to align passageways brilliantly through the nests on either side of the steel plate without the need for eyes.

In view of this, in an **afterlife** situation, it seems that as long as a quantum PCAR system were still available for information processing plus access to the zero point field; then the capability for vision would still be possible. Also, concerning the other senses, they all similarly operate using the same Schempp's PCAR system, which independently from Schempp's work, has been verified by a number of separate experiments by Pribram's on cats. He found that smell, touch and hearing also operate by the brain analysing holographic resonating frequencies.

Although in an afterlife, food would be unnecessary, a discarnate would still be able to detect different tastes and smells. Recent research by Dr Jennifer Brooks of the University of London, has shown that the earlier belief that discrimination for taste and smell operated purely on a chemical basis was found inadequate. Instead, quantum vibration of these bonds was found the key. This then vindicates that the quantum PCAR system[35] is the standard used for all lifeforms **sensory** communication (as well as for all other forms of communication i.e. vision, telepathy etc.).

As mentioned earlier, telepathy instead of speech would be necessary as a method of communication between non-physical entities. It has the advantages of instantaneous transmission, independence of distance and freedom from use of sense organs (it requires only mind-to-mind transmission). In fact it is so suited to communication between non-physical entities, **that its very existence must go some way towards indicating that it establishes itself a case for after death survival.**

The science for telepathy seems very much supported by the physics of quantum non-locality and the resonance concepts of Sheldrake. Mental visualisation (**attention**) of the recipient to identify their entities "object" resonant signature and conscious **intention** to communicate (as shown by so many of Dean Radin's experiments), are probably key elements in linking quantum wave non-local transmission of information telepathically between each other via the zero point field.

Telepathy is such a key function necessary for communication in an afterlife, that it deserves specific detailed consideration. Therefore experimental evidence and case studies necessary to verify the existence of telepathy beyond question, together with other PK functions and non-ordinary states of consciousness relevant to reincarnation are covered in Section 3.

3.12 REINCARNATIONAL ASPECTS

> "…….when we die, our life becomes a "perennial flower that returns to bloom in the multiverse"
>
> *- Professor Robert Lanza*

There are three key facets of quantum physics crucially relevant to an afterlife;-

- Small portions of holographs contain all the characteristics and information contained in the whole holograph.

- One's personal hologram containing our short and long term memory, is one field among many contained within the zero point field.

- Since mind/consciousness exhibits all timeless and spaceless attributes of quantum reality (e.g. non-local instantaneous action at a distance, holography (QH) etc.), **it most certainly is itself entirely quantum in nature**. Also, since in quantum states, space and scale become irrelevant, the specific size of our consciousness/mind would seem particularly capable of occupying **a very small space indeed** in our particular **physical** reality and most likely to be of subatomic size. (It will be recalled as described in Chapter 2, that Bohm found that even electrons in plasma exhibit a degree of consciousness by exhibiting purposeful behaviour).

This suggests that at death - if all that remains is only a tiny "consciousness/soul" portion - a remnant "knot" (but linked to our personal hologram field contained within the zero point field), then this would be all that would be necessary and sufficient for it to leave the body and return to a fully quantum life-between-life existence. In this way we all (including possibly all life-forms) could survive death and continue an **immortal** existence. Obviously, the consciousness/soul "knot" would need to contain an extremely capable brain type processing function. However this could be physically very small, as even a paramecium, with a total average length of 10 microns (about 100th of a millimetre), has a microtubular quantum processing and attendant PCAR communicating system.

As consciousness and mind is prime and creates physical reality, it must itself have preceded matter. This therefore shows our mind/consciousness **as one's soul** must therefore be capable of complete independence from physical reality. As mentioned earlier, it may even be likely that it is divorced entirely from physical reality and exists in one of our 11 universe dimensions mathematically predicted by scientists as part of "string theory". (As an aside, it is also of interest to note that esoteric literature regards a so called "mental" dimension and permanent "home" to the soul, named as the "5th Dimension".) Evidence is also provided in Section 3 to suggest that there is always a core of individual consciousness which remains in a non-physical life-between-life environment location - which can perhaps be regarded as the super-soul mentioned by Jane Robert's channeled entity "Seth" (see Chapter 5)).

Also, following our death (as supported scientifically above), an afterlife mind/consciousness (i.e. soul), could be expected to survive death with a full cognitive capability and instant access to memory in the zero point field. Additionally and critically though, the above indicates that we are all equipped with appropriate sensory systems to cater for both physical and non-physical realities, together with a communication system (the PCAR system) which is incredibly feature rich to cope with (presumably) every eventuality. Since consciousness has been shown in Chapter 2 to be quantum in nature, mind/consciousness and soul are timeless. **Physical death therefore is irrelevant, and as concluded previously in Chapter 2, we are all therefore immortal.**

Another key relevant reincarnational aspect of quantum physics, is that (as we saw earlier in Chapter 2), that as mass increases to form macro objects such as ourselves, quantum effects - so intense at the level of sub atomic particles - decreases with increasing mass. This has been very evident in practice, as we have seen that paranormal activity for us, being relatively massive and large, compared with subatomic particles; is somewhat feeble. This contrasts markedly with the strong paranormal activity in the case of ghosts or poltergeists reported in the literature over many years. We might therefore expect that in an afterlife scenario, then we would have a far greater individual and collective capability of telepathy, group consciousness etc., plus unlimited creativity and ability to create our own reality at will.

It is also possible in an afterlife situation that our current strong focus on conscious physical reality required to cope and alert us to with dangers, would no longer be relevant as a survival mechanism to protect us from harm. Therefore, our normal afterlife condition would not require the dominance of a brain type "filter" mentioned earlier. We could then without constraint be able to focus instantly on any chosen reality we please.

Considerable evidence to support the above will be presented in Section 3.

We can now establish our fourth Principal based on experimental evidence:

PRINCIPLE 4 - The physics exists, such that on death, our consciousness, mind, memory (i.e. one's psyche and soul) plus senses could transfer and exist in a timeless realm.

3.13   CLOSING CHAPTER COMMENTS

- Physics depicts a non-physical reality which is manifest at a subatomic level and exhibits the quantum properties of independence from both distance and time. Scientific experiments show that mind, consciousness and memory (which form the psyche/soul) share these properties and therefore must be independent from physical reality. The evidence therefore strongly supports that these, together with vision, and other senses can survive death.

- All our individual memories and information concerning growth patterns and habits etc. have been shown by experiment to be holographic, exhibit non-locality and are located within sub fields within the zero point field. They therefore are quantum, must reside in non-physical reality and in an afterlife situation would obviously remain accessible to us in spite of our death. The fact that growth patterns necessary as pre-cursors in the first place to create our physical form, resides in non-physical reality, demonstrates that our personal physical reality itself together with all physical reality can only be created and formed from non-physical reality. This inescapable logic, therefore also adds further proof to that shown by the double slit experiment - that mind/consciousness is prime and that **mind must create physical reality, not the other way around**.

- Breakthroughs in science over recent years, have provided both theoretical and experimental evidence which can explain most paranormal phenomena. Their experimentally observed independence from space and time, indicates that these must themselves be regarded as real, normal and scientifically explainable properties of **non-physical** reality. (This is covered in detail in the next Chapter).

Although some conclusions reached may be felt surprising and unfamiliar, one should reflect that the evidence is largely a result of laboratory experiments whose outcome has been verified by subsequent repetition. And where empirical evidence has been presented it is deliberately sourced from acknowledged world experts in their field.

In the next Chapter, having now looked at a number of scientific properties relevant to quantum physics i.e. the realm of non-physical reality, we now need to examine how these would seem to be able to explain the paranormal. Many reports of paranormal activity suggest phenomena such as ghosts, poltergeists etc. all of which align with reincarnational belief and suggest an afterlife, so we need to see if the science covered so far can provide believable explanations for this. We also need to look at whether science can support the activity of psychics and mediums who supposedly communicate with discarnates for validation of an afterlife for relatives. The next Chapter also looks at the vexatious issue of time, and how a timeless/spaceless afterlife environment has very recently received further strong scientific support.

To our earlier three Principles, we can now add Principle 4

PRINCIPLE 1 - A non-physical timeless (but contingent) quantum-like realm beyond our current physical existence, may be possible where things and events respond directly to consciousness/intention.

PRINCIPLE 2 - The Universe overwhelmingly exhibits design, information, intelligence and mind. It is also bio-centric, therefore providing compelling evidence not only for a creator/God as the first cause, but with its purpose including the creation of all life.

PRINCIPLE 3 - Mind is primary, as with consciousness. Consciousness creates reality. We are immortal.

PRINCIPLE 4 - The physics exists, such that on death, our consciousness, mind, memory (i.e. one's psyche and soul) *plus* senses could transfer and exist in a timeless realm.

CHAPTER FOUR

The Commonality of Science Amongst all Paranormal Phenomena. Plus Time and Space

"Assertions of impossibility are based on the metaphysical creeds of the scientists of the day"

C. J. Ducasse

4.1 INTRODUCTION

The first subject for this Chapter covers the observation of the **commonality of a science base** amongst what is termed - "paranormal" phenomena (the definition of the word paranormal, of course means "*beyond normal*" or "*not scientifically explainable*"). After reading this book, it is hoped that others (like myself) might then find this word "paranormal" no longer acceptable and instead unsuitable and contentious - as I now believe all phenomena currently called "paranormal" are scientifically explainable, understandable and common.

To be fair, while these phenomena may have been aptly considered "beyond normal" or "not scientifically explainable" some years ago, recent science developments now suggest that that this is no longer the case.

A few authors have suggested a link between paranormal phenomena and quantum physics. However, as far as I am aware, none to my knowledge have attempted (as in this book) to explain the underlying science relevant to the paranormal and reincarnation. I find this lack of attempting to find a correlation with available science surprising and disappointing, as I have simply followed the simple and ancient tradition of **observational science**, looking for repetitive occurrences observed by many and over long time periods, then attempting to find the underlying science.

Key specific **case studies** of paranormal activity relevant to reincarnation are covered in Section 3. I could deal with the science basis for these case studies on a repetitive and individual manner. However, due to the commonality of the science amongst them all; it seems more sensible to deal with their science base collectively, as has been done below. Also, as will be seen, this approach highlights their science commonality. Which in itself obviously assists in demonstrating its scientific validity.

The other main subject for this Chapter - is the big issue of time (and of space), which is one of the greatest enigmas in science. As far as re-incarnational belief is concerned, it is of critical importance. This is because repetitive reports of a timeless and spaceless environment in a life-between-lives environment together with the ability to **travel** freely in time - is reported in countless accounts and case studies of mystics, psychics and regressional hypnotherapists. This is covered in Chapter 5 and Section 3). If time does not exist in a life-between-life scenario, it is difficult to understand how motion could take place. Because of these apparent conundrums, they demand credible science based explanations. They therefore are worthy of discussion in this book.

4.2 THE COMMONALITY OF SCIENCE AMONGST ALL PARANORMAL PHENOMENA

The main commonalities which will be dealt with in separate sections below are:

4.2.1 The remarkable (and significant) alignment, between Paranormal and Quantum properties.

4.2.2 Unconscious non-verbal communication between all Lifeforms, and all realities, use the PCAR (Phase-Conjugate-Adaptive-Resonance) system.

4.2.3 Inspirational knowledge, and access to other realities for humans, is primarily obtained via Trance States.

(Note: Correlation with esoteric, reincarnational and in many cases religious beliefs, is covered in the next Chapter).

4.2.1 The remarkable (and significant) alignment of both the Paranormal and Quantum properties.

"To put it bluntly, science no longer contains absolute truths….the old distinction between the natural and the supernatural has become spurious"
Henry Margenenau, Professor Emeritus of Physics at Yale University.

As indicated in the previous Chapter, there are striking instances of similarity and examples where some unique property or attribute of quantum physics provides an explanation for the paranormal. An example is quantum non-locality - where distances become irrelevant. Although certainly not a factor in classical physics, this is both a striking characteristic of quantum physics, but also telepathy. This distance independence seems also characteristic of claimed abilities of some psychics. (This will be discussed in depth in the next Chapter.) There is also the question of time independence - where information can supposedly be gained by psychics concerning the future or past from those who have passed on. As mentioned in Chapter 3, often such information, has proved valid and instrumental in solving unsolvable murders. Likewise USA defense force personnel claimed to use remote-viewing paranormal properties to gain otherwise unattainable information by spying successfully on the Russians in World War II. Also "dowsing" - to find deposits of water, oil or minerals, has similarly been found to provide in many instances, valuable but previously unknown resource information to the benefit of many, especially petroleum and mineral companies. Noteworthy with all these examples is (as described early in Chapter 3), the fundamental and unique attribute of quantum fields and waves being able to directly gain information, but also the quantum non-local holographic characteristic of independence from distance.

Even when one takes into account the quantum nature of **consciousness;** surprisingly the mystical nature of most paranormal phenomenon seems to fade away completely, in favor of a likely science based explanation. For example, Schmidt's RNG replicable and independent experiments also clearly indicates the quantum characteristics, not only of the consciousness of participants to effect an outcome over the probabilistic uncertainty of the random generators (which are designed to produce quantum uncertainty), but also importantly, a collective outcome in favor of all of the participants specific joint personal intentions (whether consciously or unconsciously). Since this action occurs at, and irrespective of distance, this again exhibits the non-local characteristic of quantum physics.

This is also evident in quoted cases of the paranormal telekinesis ability to achieve mind-object influence i.e. moving a physical object by mind alone. This seems easily explainable as a quantum effect caused by the consciousness of some exceptional and gifted people (or even young children) focused to such an extent that they are able to collapse the probability event waveforms to create their own reality to their whim. Even to the extent of being able to levitate small objects (discussed further below).

Dr J.G. Taylor of Kings College, University of London carried out experiments on 50 persons (**mainly children**) and claimed experimental ability to succeed in mind-matter influence. He gained excellent results by achieving false readings on compasses, Geiger counters and measuring instruments. As he said in his book, *Superminds. A Scientist Looks at the Paranormal* (New York: Viking Press, 1975)[1].

From the 1960s to 1990 Russian Nina Kulagina demonstrated repeatedly and with impressive ability, the psychokinetic mind-matter ability to move objects using mind alone. She was tested and purportedly found to be genuine by many Russian and Western scientists. To eliminate any possibility of fraud, her demonstrations (films are available on "YouTube") often involved use of a large Plexiglass cube. Objects used inside included match boxes, Ping-Pong balls etc. or matches which were seen to move but also to dance from side to side in the container, and even levitate and to hover in the air. Physicist Dr V.F. Shvetz also reported her ability to make burn marks appear on paper. On occasions she was also able to transfer the outline of a picture she had seen, onto photo paper.[2]

Some children as well can exhibit truly exception abilities as psychics - particularly in cases of teenagers approaching puberty - where poltergeist activity occurs around them. In such cases evidence supports the belief that they act as the focus and energy source for **discarnates** who produce mind-matter effects far stronger than are possible by human psychics alone. This is of course, as would be expected with an anticipated stronger and practiced capability of discarnates to create a desired mind-matter outcome in a **fully** quantum life-between-life environment. It is noteworthy as well, that such teenagers identified as the source of poltergeist activity universally claim no knowledge whatsoever of the mayhem and the amazing levitation effects characteristic of poltergeist activity that is found to only occur in their presence.[3]

This is in complete contrast to the few successful but comparatively feeble cases quoted of human psychic's reported ability to levitate small objects, spoon bending, etc. In such cases there is simply no doubt that they are perpetrators of the phenomena, as they are in control, and can repeat demonstrations on command and under laboratory conditions. Characteristically also, only very small objects (e.g. a matchbox) are ever involved, and they invariably find the effort involved extremely tiring.[4]

Since poltergeist activity has been observed so often by scientifically qualified observers, it is overwhelmingly accepted as real. **It therefore provides itself strong evidence for a life-hereafter and re-incarnation**. As with discussion on mediums, it will be dealt with further in Section 3.

The teenage capability associated with poltergeist activity seems to disappear when they become adults.

There also seems a parallel, with those children (as covered later in Section 3) who are reported as remembering past lives, since this ability invariably also fades as they become older. In this case fading of such memories is generally considered to be due to cultural conditioning, as will be dealt with further below.

From all these examples, it can be seen that quantum physics provides a science based explanation behind probably all events classified as paranormal. In addition though, it also provides a degree of explanation for some other areas, not necessarily classified as paranormal, but nevertheless not fully understood e.g. hypnosis, dreams, memory (covered previously), precognition, intuition etc., as is covered below.

A final matter worthy of discussion is that most scientists (and people generally) have little interest in and are often dismissive of quantum physics. They consider that it's almost magical and weird behavior is simply restricted to the very small i.e. they believe that subatomic particles properties have no particular observable influence on classical physics or large scale macro objects such as ourselves. Obviously this is not the case, as is we learned in previous Chapters.

The fact though is that all matter is made up of such quantum entities as electrons, protons, neutrons etc., and these are all usually linked together in molecules which constitute everything we perceive. It is therefore not surprising that quantum reality effects all of us and our lives (as is particularly evident with the PCAR communication system covered in the last Chapter). Therefore it should not really be remarkable that this odd behavior of quantum particles should permeate large scale matter as the cause of what we perhaps wrongly describe as "paranormal" phenomena.

As indicated in the introduction to this Chapter, while to me the link of quantum properties with those of the paranormal is widespread and rather obvious, yet it is barely mentioned in the literature. To date sadly I have found just these few scientists have noted it in but a few publications Dr Charles Tart, Dr Dean Radin, Michael B Mensky, Dr Edgar Mitchell, Chris Carter and William Bray.[5]

One could go on exhaustively comparing quantum effects with paranormal activity, however most paranormal links with quantum reality have already been covered in previous Chapters. The point though surely has been made above, and in earlier Chapters, that cases of so called "paranormal activity", seem very explainable by quantum physics. For those interested in further reading, recommended are Dr Dean Radin's 2006 book entitled *Entangled Minds: Extrasensory Experiences in a Quantum Reality* which gives detailed experimental evidence support for ESP and suggests a mind relationship to quantum theory, also Charles T. Tart's new book, *The End of Materialism* which provides his own unequalled experimental evidence for the validity of the paranormal, and Michael Schmicker's book, *Best Evidence* which provides an excellent overview of scientific observational and experimental verification of the validity of paranormal phenomena.

4.2.2 Unconscious non-verbal Communication between all Lifeforms and all realities uses the PCAR system

"Many of the theories coming out of quantum theory are far weirder than psychic phenomena."

Marcha Fox "SF Author"

The only recently discovered PCAR communication system is complex in some respects, and simple in others, but unimaginably feature rich - with amazing capabilities so well suited to assist all life forms in many ways. In this respect Stuart Hameroff as mentioned in Chapter 3, found tubulins (which are thought to allow quantum processing) present in microscopically sized paramecium. So in a more rudimentary form but similar way, quantum processing is likely to be also present in less complex lifeforms even down to bacteria size - since even plasma (ionized air or gas) has been experimentally proven, as mentioned in Chapter 2, to demonstrate purposeful behavior and exhibit a degree of responsive to its environment.

As humans, we vastly exceed all other of earth's creatures in our **verbal/audible** ability to communicate. Others may have some verbal communication capability and perhaps most have none at all. We have become so dependent upon verbal communication, that most of us believe this is our sole method of communication with others and that our overall communication ability is superior to that of all other existing life-forms.

There is much evidence indicating that this is not the case, and that the non-local holography and resonance provided by the PCAR system is the communication/information system responsible for the occasional glimpses of superior communication and information processing capabilities demonstrated non-verbally by other animals. For example at Sheldrake's suggestion experiments have been successfully carried out to verify that dogs can detect the very moment that their owners decide to return home. We also learned in Chapter 3 that Cleve Backster found a similar ability with plants. Although this capability seems beyond that ever reported of humans, it is perhaps common to dogs, plants and many other life-forms. It therefore seems that our excellent ability and focus on verbal communication may well have left us at a disadvantage compared with many other life-forms.

With humans, telepathy is common and indisputable experimentally (as covered earlier) - at least as far as the ability to detect the arrival of a sender's signal by EEG detection (also by other physiological tests such as changes in blood pressure using a sphygmomanometer).[6] As mentioned previously though, normally the receiver is consciously completely unaware of the communication.

In crisis situations however, there are many striking cases cited in the literature where fully conscious telepathic **awareness and knowledge** by a human receiver has occurred. This often concerns a situation where an accident of some kind has occurred and a close relative (parent or child) obtains some instant spontaneous knowledge of the event. Typically it is found by the recipient, that the time of receipt of the information exactly matches the occurrence of the event. Where death has occurred, cases have even been reported of what is termed "crisis apparitions" i.e. a ghostly figure or appearance of the person concerned interacts or is seen by the recipient. In this case the ghost like appearance could easily be interpreted as both a deliberate mind construct by the recently deceased and use of the PCAR system for sensory functions and communication.

It therefore appears that in crisis situations, **intense** emotion is the trigger that allows telepathy to break though into our consciousness and on occasions even allows us to perceive "crisis apparitions" i.e. ghosts. Such often quoted instances are of particular significance to this book on reincarnation, as they demonstrate that we all do have a **full** telepathic capability for non-verbal communication in an afterlife. Moreover, since receipt of a message is received from a discarnate, it surely assists our belief that we too, just as the discarnate, can continue our current existence in a soul/consciousness form in a life hereafter.

The unceasing reports over the ages, across the whole world have been full of what seems for many in our civilized world, ridiculous tales of ghosts. Today, rather than sensibly being open minded, we seem to live in a world of presumption and instant rejection whenever reports are received of phenomena that appear fanciful. The certainty that reports are nonsense, is unscientifically assumed, without even analyzing the data to determine whether it is spurious or consistent. The once fertile area and acceptance by our ancestors of the importance of **observational** science is ignored and forgotten. Instead, anti-scientific skepticism and skeptics (including sadly most mainstream scientists) holds sway. This certainly seems to be the case - particularly with reports of ghosts, and the generally believed absurdity to any suggestion that ghosts might be real, have the ability to act like humans, and can even pass through walls.

Today unlike days of old where observers did not have the advantages of modern science, we often marvel while engrossed at a science fiction movie, watching a rotating simulated three-dimensional holograph image of a person. Since this is an example of holography, is generated by **photons** (i.e. quantum particles) and controlled by a computer (similar to a brain cognitive processing function), few may realize that it may differ little scientifically and technically from the image sent to a recipient in PCAR form as a ghostly image by a discarnate.

What follows then, in contrast to the above, is an example of the difference if one instead adopts an open-minded approach **based on science**:

We have established the premise that a life-between-lives scenario may be possible. We also have the proven scientific discovery covered earlier in this book, that we create unconsciously, continuously, and collectively our own reality. It then follows, that a human entity in a life-between-life existence who has recently died, has every possibility to be able to appear to loved ones. First, both communication and our senses cognition can scientifically be seen to be a function of the remarkable PCAR system. As for the frequently reported instances of ghosts being able to pass through unaffected by walls, this easily follows from quantum physics - as consciousness; with a probable almost massless quantum photon characteristic remaining after death (as covered in Chapter 3), can be likened to small masses such as subatomic particles. Obviously with a quantum nature, we would expect quantum behavior. Therefore their corresponding smaller wavelengths can easily fit between the spaces of larger masses (as pointed out by a reverse argument by cosmologist/physicist Paul Davies quoted in Chapter 2). This is the explanation for the frequently observed and well known tunneling property of quantum physics.

It will be recalled in Chapter 3 from the extensive experiments carried out by Schmidt and other researchers and summarized by Dean Radin on the properties of consciousness; that the strength of **attention** and **intention** are pivotal to improving the success with telepathy. Also to increasing the efficiency of clairvoyance and effecting change to one's reality. For example the use of prayer. This too is a use of the PCAR system. It therefore should follow, that if we change our focus of attention away from distractions, strive to increase our strength of intent, and do this regularly and consistently, we might be better able to mimic those animals around us who seem vastly more proficient than ourselves in their use of quantum PCAR non-verbal communication system.

Regardless (presumably) of any knowledge of experimentally derived consciousness properties, this approach is in fact that adopted and claimed my many psychics. It is covered in more detail in Section 3. In fact techniques such as this has given rise in some countries to training colleges and institutions (e.g. The Arthur Findlay College in England),[7] aimed at improving latent abilities of psychics. Some gifted individuals though do seem to naturally have strong psychic abilities at birth, or even as the results of accidents.

A number of psychics also exhibit an amazing range of so called paranormal capabilities, particularly those used by police forces through the world to assist in solving previously unsolvable murder cases. An example of one such psychic (typical of many), is an American psychic called Nancy Weber, who often stars on a long running American Television Show "Psychic Detectives". Since murder is involved and cases have been found previously unsolvable, information to solve all such cases and by all psychics carrying out this type of work, is (rather logically) universally sought by the psychics, psychically from the deceased person involved. It is of course immediately apparent if such messages supposedly occur and lead to successful solving of cases, then the psychic's efforts have not only aided the police and society, but are strongly evidential in establishing a case that an afterlife existence exists.

The reality is that there are many psychics who appear on this show, where time and again, supposed information they claim they receive in visions from the murder victim, has itself proved the key to solving the case and achieving justice. The program has now running for many years, and as with the psychics' ability, been found to be very successful. Such success over a long period without any suggestion of distortion, complicity or fraud by the producers or participants, obviously provides additional credibility to the case for an afterlife.

There is a similar television program which ran in New Zealand for a number of series in recent years called "Sensing Murder" where the producers ensured the psychics were totally controlled regarding the availability of information concerning the murder case, both before and during investigations. A selection of the most able psychics in New Zealand and Australia was made before each series (Deb Webber from Australia, Sue Nicholson from New Zealand, and Kelvin Cruickshank, also from New Zealand). Old murder cases were chosen to ensure it was unlikely they had any prior knowledge of each case. In addition, some of the two psychics for each case were chosen from Australia, met at a New Zealand airport in a city they had never visited before, given a map on arrival and asked to determine themselves from the map where the victim was murdered. After advising their driver of the location, the potential murder site chosen by the psychic was visited and if not also the place of burial, the same procedure then followed using the map etc. Finally the psychics were given photographs of the murder victim and asked for details of the murder and the name of the person murdered. At each location and test, they were kept apart and separately asked to describe what events occurred which led to the death and characteristics and personality of the victim - all while being recorded for television. No comment was made on their responses on all occasions - except affirmation if they were correct.

The psychics were amazingly correct on all occasions, with obviously one psychic being better than the other or providing more detail, but each adding correctly to the description of the victim. They were also able to agree on the manner in which the victim had met his fate. This agreement was reached even though they were separated completely, and were not permitted to ever meet during an investigation, or told anything about the case at all. On some occasions they even agreed on the **name** of the suspect/murderer.

Of particular interest in terms of correlations with quantum properties and the PCAR system, was the fact that in all such programmes, the psychic participants were able to successfully provide from claimed visions and intuition, valid information such as the site of the murder and the burial site (if different). Their descriptions of the death itself were credible and even aligned generally with the known murder weapon. Vision often was claimed to be as seen **as by the victim**, and their described personality agreed with what was stated by close relatives appearing on the programme. Noteworthy is the fact that the cases were old, yet the ability of psychics to obtain details years in the past was unaffected. Often a single photograph given of a victim was incredibly first left face down by the psychic, but only touched. By this approach using psychometry, considerable information concerning the case or the victim (e.g. their personality) was usually obtained and described by the psychic while recorded in real time on television. Then, after turning the photo over face up, additional information again from the scene of the murder was given by the psychic. Often information (subsequently verified) was received regarding what would happen in the future e.g. where the body would be found! Thus the quantum characteristic of time invariance was also exhibited, with information provided from both the past, and what turned out later to be the future.

The PCAR theory indicates that actual touch plus visual perception is a methodology that would assist in establishing both a necessary classical physical and also a quantum reference cue for PCAR processing. This then provides the necessary resonance to be established with a participant to allow an exchange of information, audibly, visually in four dimensions, in colour and in motion as an event history commencing and ending at any chosen point in time.[8] Significantly, this also aligned with the psychics' descriptions, as their visualisation's were always described as a movie as seen from the victim's perspective.

In summary, the ability of an exceptional psychic such as used in the cases above to successfully obtain valid **new knowledge and information** from discarnates long since dead, aligns with a large number of the total number of known properties of quantum physics i.e. the quantum non-local independence of distance and time, together with all the characteristics of the PCAR system. It also aligns perfectly with a large number of the described descriptions of paranormal phenomena, commonly labelled as telepathy, clairvoyance, psychometry, mediumship/channeling, and intuition.

Many exceptional psychics claim they had relatively strong capabilities at birth which developed further with practice over many years. The establishment of psychic training schools in some countries and their success, is testimony to the fact that their ability can demonstrably be strengthened by this method. This was evident particularly during World War II where normal servicemen were tested and trained both at Stanford University and on site, to become remote viewing adepts. These were used to spy on Russians during the cold war (covered in some depth in Section 3). There is strong evidence (in Section 3) to suggest that we all have an excellent psychic capabilities when born, but lose this as mentioned above due to cultural "conditioning". In many cases this cultural conditioning, causing loss of psychic abilities might result from active dissuasion and even ridicule by parents or peers, but also result presumably as their speech becomes their dominant form of communication. Some children today who show particular talent (called "indigo children") are voluntarily assisted, encouraged and trained by professional psychics (as shown on the USA television program "Psychic Children") to overcome these difficulties with considerable success.

Research into the PCAR effects and process, suggests that those who later re-learn their lost birth psychic capability to gain access to non-local information, do so by focusing their attention and quieting their left brain. This then allows the whole brain to achieve enhanced coherence and coordination between the hemispheres.[9]

This concept was taken up and discovered independently and brilliantly by a millionaire engineer researcher called Robert Monroe. He discovered a method of attaining readily a focused, yet OOB (Out Of Body) type of trance state to explore different realities by achieving hemisphere sound synchronization, using headphones and special apparatus. Many who were skeptics prior to using his equipment, (which includes other experimenters, and the public), later became enthusiastic believers and strong advocates; not just for the existence of other parallel realities to ours, but also for an afterlife. Additionally, as almost a side issue, his work experimentally and observationally over 40 years, vindicates repeatedly the alignment and importance of quantum physics ability to explain paranormal activity. (The results of experiments experiences are covered more adequately and in detail in Section 3, but it is intended to only deal with the PCAR system here).

In OOB trance states, participants in the experiments normally encountered entities from other realities. But also in some cases (and regularly), also entities in a life-between-life situation. All communication with entities in other realities from which they gained information - was found intelligent, interactive and credible.

In all cases communication was telepathic i.e. non-verbal, and knowledge and information gained via a communication system whose properties were identical to what we now identify as that of the PCAR system. Robert Monroe provides a somewhat detailed description of this system in his three books. The properties he describe align completely with the capability of most advanced psychics described above, where they too can instantly gain new information from claimed dead people which they then use to solve murder cases. In many cases he describes that on meeting an entity apart from conversing non-verbally, he was thrown a "rote" (the term he uses for what he colloquially calls a "ball" of information (just like a psychic touching or looking at a photograph of a murder victim, or seeking strongly to link with them).

The PCAR system development by Walter Schempp (in 1993) occurred subsequent to Monroe's investigations (commenced in 1958), so it is unfortunate that Monroe would have no idea of a quantum science based explanation for his experiences. Thousands of people, including professionals in many spheres and scientists (who performed many of the experimental work for Monroe) have related identical experiences during OOB states while using the special equipment at the "Monroe"

Institute in Virginia, USA[10]. This institute was founded by Monroe to continue experiments and allow others to attend courses there and share on the same experience of OOB travel. The institute is thriving and still operational today.

From the above it will be apparent that we are all equipped with the PCAR system at birth - **as with all life-forms**. Importantly, the evidence given above strongly indicates the system flourishes for consciousness/souls in a life-between-life environment. It therefore follows that the system must be prime for all life-forms in the sense that it is ubiquitous and must have preceded all classical physical reality. It is also supported by the fact that Hammeroff's microtubules appear as adaptions which may have had to be added to avoid decoherence of brain probabilistic processing at the normal environmental temperatures we encounter in classical physical reality. We would therefore expect it to perform better in a less mass, cooler temperature situation, fully quantum state. Most certainly in a life-between-life environment (as is supported above, but also by evidence provided in Section 3), and also perhaps in other probable non-physical realms.

There seems no end to applications of the PCAR system. This certainly seems to be the case, as at last it seems we have a scientific explanation for "epigenics", mentioned in Chapter 1. This was where subspecies variation rather than being attributable to mutations as asserted by Darwin is caused by a cognitive type process called epigenics involving DNA and cellular interactions. Physicist Peter Marcer, quantum physicist who currently holds a Research Fellowship in the Department of Physics at the University of Liverpool (and also, Chairman British Computer Society Cybernetic Machine specialist Group) considers the epigenics process is purely quantum, and yet another function of the PCAR system. He claims DNA base-pairing's main role is communication with the environment and fundamental to life on earth. It's non-local quantum holographic communication system is also used for DNA and cells to constantly link with their external environment to make suitable adaptive epigenic type evolutionary type changes which can be passed on to progeny.[11] Therefore instead of the impossibility of mutations leading to subspecies variation wrongly asserted by Darwin, the PCAR system now seems likely to be the true cause of all environmental adaptions for all lifeforms. Notably it logically appears to be a designed function inherent in the PCAR system, rather than the random nature based invalid idea of "mutations" as postulated by Darwin.

We can now establish our fifth Principal based on experimental evidence:

PRINCIPLE 5 – Correlations between quantum properties and the Paranormal provide strong evidence to support belief in an after-life, immortality and reincarnation.

4.2.3 Inspirational Knowledge, and access to other realities for humans, is primarily obtained in Trance States

It will be recalled in Chapter 2, that Russian quantum physicist Michael B. Mensky, succinctly stated:

"That if consciousness equals a separation of the alternatives from each other, then the absence of consciousness equals the absence of separation."

He then explained this by saying:

"Thus, when going over to the unconsciousness state, one obtains the information, or knowledge, which is in principle unavailable in the usual conscious state."

Based on discussion in subsequent chapters we can now expand on this more fully as follows:

When consciousness is focused on classical physical reality, there is normally no hint of holographic interconnectedness of all things or of non-locality. However, in contrast, when in a slight trance, our subconscious is to the fore and armed with quantum attributes. In this state we can easily focus our consciousness successfully on other realities and gain knowledge via the characteristics of the PCAR system.

This then can be seen as the key to all ancient esoteric information, where in a trance state or meditation, a participant is often advised by shamans etc. to focus attention for a prolonged period until they feel a merging of themselves and the object of attention.[12]

In today's world with our knowledge of quantum physics and the PCAR system, this of course is amazingly accurate advice. It shows how to best focus our consciousness in non-reality and invoke a non-local quantum consciousness state to access non-reality and source information via the PCAR system.

As mentioned above, a greater capacity to normally achieve a wider quantum-like "awake" consciousness is not uncommon amongst children but usually disappears later in life. Some remember previous lives and others often have "imaginary friends" as playmates (there is evidence to suggest that this could be a child psychic contact with a discarnate child as a companion).

Within humans themselves, surprisingly there are cultural differences which have an effect. In Western traditions, educational and rationality have ensured greater focus/utilization of the left brain attributes. Whereas in Eastern countries (e.g. Japan), there has been the more traditional emphasis on the intuitive and artistic right brain characteristic.

This variability is highlighted by those who are gifted as psychics from almost birth, as they seem even in normal **waking** consciousness states, to have a widened access to quantum non-physical reality. As indicated by Bob Monroe's experiments, those that naturally have or develop an ability to synchronise their left brain/right brain hemispheres, would be expected to perform better as psychics than the rest of us. Also, those that make a living from their gifts clearly spend many waking hours seeking information from discarnates – which suggests that since they claim their ability has increased over time, that practice leads to increased ability. Noteworthy, some psychics often claim (Deb Webber, Kelvin Cruickshank) that their proficiency as practicing mediums has increased even to the point where they are particularly bothered by people in life-between-life situations constantly clamoring for attention for them to contact loved ones. The validity of these claims seems supported by the fact that training at psychic colleges (as mentioned above) has been shown effective in increasing the ability of those with lesser psychic ability.

Robert Monroe's breakthrough successful research in mechanically enabling both hemispheres of the brain to become synchronized, even allows any normal humans with no particular psychic ability to temporarily match the talents of professional psychics. This can be to the point where they can achieve OOB capabilities and retrieve information from discarnates and entities in other realities.

In all the above cases, although we may realise that perception in our three dimensional world requires and utilizes the PCAR system, most of us normally do not bring non-local information to consciousness awareness when we are fully awake and conscious during the day operating in three dimensional reality.

In contrast though, in a slight trance as mentioned above, but in a **focused and attentive state**, things are very different. Then, we all can match the talents of shamans and psychics – at least in terms of retrieval of information using the PCAR communication system.

Inspiration is the most commonly claimed attribute for light trance states and (as mentioned previously in Chapter 3) even Nobel Prize winners have denied in some instances credit for their prize winning ideas. Usually a revelation is said to be achieved only after considerable effort, thought and striving to find an answer is involved. Then after relaxing somewhat, the answer comes. Scientifically it seems that the process probably occurs along these lines:

The intensity of thought focusses the query via the PCAR system in the needed frequency range of the zero point QH hologram and the sufficiently long duration of thought allows resonance to occur. Finally information is extracted from the coherent quantum waves by the brain's frequency analyser and interpreted by cognitive processing (the whole process taking place almost instantly - as is typical of non-local quantum physics).

As mentioned above, named information gaining attributes of psychics such as psychometry, clairvoyance, divining, mediumship/channeling, and many more can all be easily be claimed as scientifically explained by this system. Even some areas mentioned earlier such as spontaneous culture links, and savants - whose brains seem to have sacrificed cognitive capabilities in favour of an incredible ability to gain instantaneous facts (but rather undirected facts), on just about anything.

Even for example hypnosis, and precognition and perhaps other areas I haven't thought of, have easily derived scientific explanations based on properties of quantum physics. Hypnosis is deliberately aimed at achieving a trance state where the participant is invited to do the wishes of the hypnotist. In a sense, the subject voluntary (but only temporarily), gives up completely his conscious mind's control in favor of that of the hypnotist. Therefore in humorous stage presentations, the participant can if he wishes to allow his conscious perceptions to be readily changed and distorted by the hypnotist. Even to the extent that the hypnotized subject can even imagine or achieve some functions at odds with the subject's normal conscious belief system. For example, to accept that that an onion could taste like an orange, or to be able to become sufficiently rigid, that the hypnotized subject can be supported between two chairs by only the feet and head, and yet support a volunteer standing on their stomach without collapse.

In contrast though, **if hypnotic regression** by a **professional** hypnotist is involved to regress the subject to one's existing or past lives, **due to a deep trance state**, under the hypnotist's direction, it is therefore not surprising that the participant achieves a state of consciousness where access to non-physical reality is achieved. Unlike a stage hypnotist, a professionally trained hypnotherapist uses special techniques described later (in Section 3) to achieve a particularly deep trance and testable trance state which enables for most subjects access to non-reality states. In this condition the subject acts seemingly just as well as a legitimate psychic, and is able to recall his life in previous times unconsciously using the PCAR quantum system to retrieve his valid memories/information from the zero-point field. Due to quantum time independence, information gained from the past via the PCAR quantum system can normally readily be obtained. (Case studies on this are extensively covered in Section 3). Due to time independence, **future** information is also possible, however in this case though a future is always uncertain, subject to a possible change in one's future "event-line" choices (Further explanatory discussion on this is covered below, on "Time and Space" issues).

Finally considering our daily major trance state - "sleep". There is general belief that its purpose is to restore vitality with rest, but also perhaps for the psyche to sift and review the day's activity to allocate memory priorities, and to subconsciously plan for the future.

Nevertheless, there is also extremely strong evidence from OOB research and regressions that OOB states are common during many periods of deep every night amongst everyone, where interaction/experience and knowledge is gained in other realities.

4.3 TIME AND SPACE

(This discussion, is particularly helpful in establishing the science case for an afterlife and reincarnation. However it may prove a little difficult for some. It is stressed however that no mathematics is involved. It is suggested therefore if there is difficulty in understanding, skip this and continue to the next Chapter).

Most of us consider only the present is really "there", and the past and future unattainable and merely concepts. Physicists surprisingly have a very different view. Based on Einsteinian physics they consider time is so irrevocably linked to space, that just like distances (i.e. spaces) defining a map, time in the same way is space orientated and extends in either direction of space from any present moment. In one direction, is the past and in the other direction, the future. It is reasoned on this basis therefore, that the past and future must be accessible, and accessible from the present! [13]

4.3.1 Definition of "time"

Time can be defined in a number of ways - such "as *a measure of the interval between events, using units we have chosen for the purpose.*"

You will recall in Chapter 1 we introduced the concept that each of our realities could well be considered as comprising a series of contingent events. **We will find this "event" concept applicable to each of us and our lives and future particularly useful and important.** Also a key aspect of time, is that it inherently always involves the concept of "**motion**" e.g. such as the time to run a race, or how frequently our earth spins around its axis etc. In this respect it is notable that since time is always associated with motion, all aspects of time could instead be described equally well by equations for velocity and direction. (As will be seen later, this has some importance).

As noted above, Einstein's classical physics indicates that time extends in either direction from any present moment, as a time-line in space. In one direction along the time-line, we regard as the past and in the other direction, the future. This suggests that the past and future seem accessible from our present.

To date, attempts to find the secret of time travel have failed. It therefore seems out of the question as far as classical physics and our physical reality are concerned. In contrast, this is very much within the laws and observed behavior of quantum physics and mechanics. Here, the ability to travel in time (e.g. with subatomic particles) seems to be far more flexible and the norm and there seems nothing to impede the ability of all subatomic and quantum interactions to freely move between the past, present and future (see also below).[14]

In Chapter 1 we learned the expansion of the universe is still continuing, so that equally for all Galaxies and our own (which includes the earth), we are all travelling in space away from "The Big Bang" located at the center of the expansion. If we imagine we could look inward from our present position in space towards the initiation of the Big Bang, **we would be perceiving the past**. Similarly if we look in the opposite direction i.e. **the direction of expansion, we perceive the future**. This demonstrates rather well, the space dependency of time. It took amazingly the genius of Einstein to appreciate this, but once understood, it seems rather obvious. Given that it indicates that a time previously experienced has a certain locality in space, it also explains the belief that time travel is possible. It also shows the correct way of determining the direction of our personal time-line is to associate the past towards the center of "The Big Bang" "explosion" and the future away from it.

Regarding the space based nature of time (at least in our classical physical reality), in science, one looks for experimental validity of a hypothesis. This was achieved brilliantly with the launching of the first COBE (Cosmic Background Explorer satellite (see Chapter 1). This was used by NASA to measure the infrared cosmic background microwave radiation of the universe. The result was stunning photographs of the birth of our whole universe. These provided the immediate availability of vital information from the photographs showing how the early universe formed immediately following "The Big Bang" and up until now, by analysis of different frequencies of light. This confirmed the space relationship with time. Thus photons ("light" subatomic particles) in our past from "The Big Bang", travelled to a point in their future - our present. For these photons though, they travelled from **their** present to us - their future. The indeterminacy of the past or future - depending solely on one's personal position in the universe - suggests that they are invalid concepts, as we will explore further below.

Whenever one attempts to reflect on what time or space is, inevitably perhaps, if this is the first time and never considered in depth before, confusion reigns; as one would soon admit to being at a loss and have little understanding whatever, as to what each of them really are. Our main certainty surely is the reality of present time, even if we are unsure of the reality of past and future. The second, is a real sense of the flow of time. Perhaps another certainty might be that time cannot be illusory, as without time we would consider change impossible.

As will be seen later in this discussion of time and later in the book, it might be surprising to learn that all changes around us (including even changes in our own personal physical appearance over time) likely could be largely independent of time as we understand it and instead, dependent on our belief, consciousness and will.

In Newtonian Physics when the cosmos seemed relatively simple, space and time were thought of as completely separate. This all changed with Albert Einstein, perhaps our greatest scientist ever, with the publication of his "Theory of Relativity".

Ignoring momentarily the physics of the very small in our physical reality (i.e. at a quantum, subatomic level), today we know from Einstein's theory, that the Newtonian model is valid only for large mass objects where velocities are small compared to the speed of light. At higher velocities, thanks to Einstein and subsequent experimental observation/verification, we have now become aware that the earlier Newtonian view of space and time being separate, was inaccurate. This concept of separateness, although providing fairly accurate calculations at low velocities, is but an approximation. The Newtonian model is therefore incomplete.

Time therefore **in our physical reality** as covered above is inexorably linked to space, and is now therefore described by physicists as "space-time" - comprising the usual three dimensions of space, and one of time. For high velocities involving rapid changes of distance over time, it is therefore essential to take into account this space-time relationship in order to calculate the time to travel various distances across space. It is now realised that time is different for each observer when apart, or when either or both are in motion. So that, as often depicted in science fiction stories and television shows, a space traveler returning to earth some 10 years (in his time) after he left; if traveling far enough during that time, would find on return, all his friends and relatives he knew on earth had long since expired.[15]

This illustrates very clearly that there is no such thing as universal time. Also that our concept of time depends very much on a personal level as to our velocity and position in space (but also on mass/gravity, distance and direction) compared to elsewhere. It is therefore apparent as an inevitable and logical conclusion, that as an inherent part of Einsteinian physics; **there is no universal present, nor past or future**. In fact, despite our concept of the reality of our personal past, present and future; somewhere else in space, is the certainty that our personal past is yet another's future. Given this, it can be said that our concept of a universal past or future is also an invalid concept.

In defiance to this though, we see clocks all around us telling an impossibility and suggesting that there is a universal time at least for time zones when clearly this must be a nonsense, as even Greenwich time cannot be the same anywhere on Mars or elsewhere in the universe. Obviously Einstein must have come to the same conclusion, where as reported, he once rode to work daily in a tram to his position early in life as a patent office clerk. At the end of the tram terminus was a large clock. So that inescapably this was in his line of vision as the tram approached every day for some years. He must also have concluded as we would, that clock time is really but an accidental artifice, and no more than a convenient tool intended to provide a time framework for reference to be useful to us all.

This is why Einstein said "the distinction between past, present and future is only an illusion".

To be fair though, it agrees largely with what most of us rather feel, namely that the idea of a future or past is merely a concept. If we were not to use the concept of a past or future, we would instead on each occasion be burdened with having to say every-time we wish to talk about a direction on one's time-line to say "in the direction of "The Big Bang" or "away from it". Such is the usefulness of this artifice though, that the fact that there is really no future or past for each of us, just a time-line of continuous personal "nows"; is immaterial to most of us, except scientists. This similarly is the case with "clock-time".

In view of this, I will continue using the normal practice of using the terms future and past in reference to one or other directions of a time-line towards or away from "The Big Bang", but recognizing that there is no real future or past as commonly meant – **just these unbroken single time-lines for each of us of consecutive "nows"**.

We have shown above that time is relative (hence Einstein's Theories of Relativity). Therefore, we must carefully define any consideration with respect to the object concerned i.e. spaceship, person, cell or subatomic particle etc. We also note that not only is our concept of time relative, but particular values of time for objects in motion in space vary considerably dependent on their velocity (but also mass/gravity). This applies particularly at speeds approaching light speed. Compare this particularly with the relatively slow speed of our galaxy (together with **our individual bodies**), retreating into the void from "The Big Bang". In such cases our relatively low speed allows the Newton's equations to give good accuracy for calculating time durations travelled. We can therefore consider that, for earth itself, and for the bodies of all its residents; their realities could be visualised as each having similar but different time-lines of their contingent events mapped out in space in a direction away from the location center of "The Big Bang" while stationary on earth.

Einstein's equations only reveal dramatic changes to time becoming effective at speeds approaching the speed of light. Therefore if a **large mass** such as a space ship should accelerate close to the speed of light (we wish), it would appear slightly quantum-like by experiencing time slowing dramatically. But in contrast, for photons which have **zero mass**, time would disappear completely. Therefore for photons they cannot be described as having a timeline, but instead solely an event-line. This therefore exhibits the variability of time dependent on speed and the necessity when discussing time to carefully identify "**what is the object in question**".

This then leads us to the big discovery in this Chapter, namely that if we apply this concept to ourselves, then we must first identify the object in question. As far as we are concerned we have **both a body and a consciousness/soul, which we could identify as a science based duality.** If we consider the time-line of our consciousness, it is obviously quantum – as determined previously. Therefore our consciousness/soul, as with photons must be timeless and therefore immortal. Consciousness however - in terms of exhibiting purposeful behavior (as we saw in Chapter 2) is seen in cells, bacteria and even plasma - though obviously to a much lesser degree of perception or capability than ourselves. It therefore seems that whatever conscious perception exists in these and all such life-forms, it must be immersed in quantum reality and like ours subject to quantum laws. On the other hand all the larger masses of their bodies and ours must also obey the laws of physics and conform to Newtonian type laws of physics, or more accurately Einsteinian physics.

This dichotomy though strange, must therefore be correct. Summing up, each of our bodies (as for all life-forms) is subject to time, but not our consciousness's. Instantly we see that this fits well with our experience in that all physical bodies eventually decay and their vitality and consciousness seems to disappear at death. But hopefully from reading this book we now know that it does not really disappear at death, since the consciousness itself of all life-forms is retained forever in quantum reality.

Despite the contention that our **perceptions** as a consciousness/soul must exist in a timeless reality, nevertheless we do seem to feel an innate passage of time or flow of time. Due to mathematical symmetry considerations, scientists have long believed conceptionally there should be no preference to an "arrow of time" in any direction. But unsurprisingly only recently, they now consider there is, due to "The Big Bang". In particular by the fact that just before "The Big Bang" order was maximized, but later expansion then resulted in inevitable increasing disorder (i.e. entropy) of matter by its ongoing dispersion to the limits of our expanding universe. This has ensured the arrow of time therefore flows outward from the site of "The Big Bang", towards the future in the direction of expansion. Interestingly, this theory highlights the observation (via COBE research) of the reality of maximum order content at the beginning of the universe. This makes a mockery of any suggestion of a chance random quantum fluctuation as the cause of the universe - the belief much loved by atheists (see Chapter 1). Instead, maximum order at the commencement of the Big Bang aligns with what we would expect, namely the existence of an incredible arrangement and design of initial conditions absolutely necessary to create a universe, the laws of the universe and a suitable environment for life itself. Rather than a chance quantum event preceding the birth of our universe, instead maximum order logically suggests the Universe is attributable to the actions of a super intelligence and mind i.e. a creator/God.

With the arrow of time commencing at the **beginning** of the "The Big Bang"- as concluded earlier in Chapter 1 (by extrapolation of the velocity of the universe backwards in time), what we know as physical (or astronomical) time could not exist

before "The Big Bang". This suggests a non-physical timeless/spaceless reality prior to "The Big Bang" which would surely be an environment ideally appropriate for an **immortal** creator/God. (In any case the flash point temperature of "The Big Bang" would be so great that matter could only condense, cool and therefore exist only after a reasonable duration subsequent to "The Big Bang").

Eventually a physical universe must suffer a heat death, where nothing is likely to be left but random movement of subatomic particles i.e. a quantum state. Since such a state both precedes creation of our universe but also remains after its eventual heat death, this reinforces the fact that non-reality must be prime. It also fits and reinforces the concept that despite the future demise of the universe, all that is left, namely a quantum, non-physical timeless/spaceless environmental reality, would still remain as appropriate and suitable for an **eternal immortal** creator/God. This again supports the contention in Chapter 1 that the Law of Cause and Effect - dominant within our universe, justifiably can be regressed to a first creator/God cause for the creation of our universe. Metaphysically this can be postulated as the first cause, since (although we may never understand how), such a creator/God may have always existed.

Moving on to considerations of space.

Since time and space are irrevocably linked, it similarly follows from the above, that since time does not exist as we know it in quantum states, and space-time is linked, the same must apply to space in non-physical reality. We would therefore expect both a spaceless and timeless environment to be the case in a fully non-physical quantum "life-between-lives" reality - which is verified again and again by observations in past life regressions and in all types of OOB ("Out of Body") experiences as covered in Section 3.

(Note: quantum mechanics calculations involving interactions of subatomic particles, often show paths moving both forwards and backwards in time. As stated by *"The* Frijof Capra in his book *Tao of Physics*, "However when (resulting) space-time diagrams are taken as four-dimensional patterns without any definite direction of time attached to them, there is no 'before' and no 'after'...") i.e. they then depict an eternal now/spacious present.[16]

"Your real environment is innocent of space and time as you know them."
"In your real environment, you have no need for words, for communication is instantaneous. In your real environment you form the physical world that you know."
    Seth, the (supposed) multidimensional entity channeled by Jane Roberts. [17]

"Consciousness does not take up space."

Seth[18]

Interestingly, repetitively in OOB (out-of-body) experiences (discussed in Section 3) and also resulting constantly from regressional hypnosis (also detailed in Section 3), consciousness i.e. souls/non-physical life forms encountered in a life-between-life state, are universally described as appearing in various frequencies/colours of light i.e. photons.[19]

As we have learned before, photons have no mass and therefore travel at the fixed speed of light. The contention is that **photons, as with consciousness, last forever**. As vindication that, even near light speed, relatively low mass quantum subatomic particles exhibit amazingly long lives - the following details the predicted lives for protons and electrons:

> "The half-life of a proton is certainly no shorter than 10^{32} years which is more than a trillion times the age of the universe. The half-life of an electron is at least 3.2×10^{24} which is about 200 trillion times longer than the age of the universe."
>
> *Subatomic Particles, Nuclear Structure and Chemistry, Sandor Nagy*[20]

These of course are only estimated half-lives for protons and derived from the limited knowledge we have.

Therefore there is no reason to suggest that our mind, consciousness, and memory i.e. soul itself does not last forever in a timeless, spaceless reality.

Cosmologist/Physicist Paul Davies makes a useful addition to this discussion by saying that physicists could easily regard space-time as enfolded by, or embedded in four-dimensional space (three dimensions of space and one of time) - much as a two dimensional surface or sheet is embedded in three dimensional space. He goes on (surprisingly for a world renowned physicist/cosmologist) to say:

> "Might the soul inhabit a location in this higher dimensional space which is still (geometrically speaking) close to our physical space-time, but not actually in it? From this higher dimensional vantage point the soul could 'lock on' to the body of an individual in space-time without itself being part of space-time". [21]

Finishing this section with a few other relevant quotes:

> "With physical reality, death is inevitable whereas, in non-physical reality, all entities inherently are thought immortal."
>
> Far Journeys, *Robert Monroe*[22]

> "I simply believe that some part of the human Self or Soul is not subject to the laws of space and time"
>
> *Carl Gustav Jung*

As mentioned in the beginning of this discussion, this is but a necessary brief treatment on Time and Space.

However an Annex appended to this Chapter has been included for those who might be interested in a more expanded treatment. In particular, it covers a possible scientific explanation as to how changes (in particular, motion) can take place irrespective of time in a fully quantum life-between-life environment. Also, recent science developments give indications that quantum entanglement may well be responsible for our experience of time in our universe. In addition, that although time certainly exists in our classical physical reality, (shockingly) it cannot be a dimension, as once thought.

Ending our brief look at time and space, and summing up - it seems that for us and other life-forms, that reality must occur for each of us progressing via a personal consecutive series of unbroken contingent events - either made up of a series of **time-lines for physical existence, or event-lines - when in a quantum reality, life-between-lives existence.**

It can easily therefore be seen that at any point from a life-between-life event-line environment in this unbroken consecutive series of one's personal event-lines; one could return to earth and at birth continue the series as a time-line; until another death, and so on. In this way all, living entities would therefore be immortal.

This, then by itself, completely supports the concept of immortality via reincarnation.

This then leads to our **final** Principle for this book:

PRINCIPLE 6 - The science of time and space supports belief in reincarnation

Note: **"Change"** (covered in the Annex to this Chapter) in **motion, distance** etc., is mentioned above on a science basis to be likely independent of time - in either a physical or quantum reality. However as mentioned in previous Chapters, **physical** changes in our reality and future, can also occur on a personal basis (and even to our appearance), simply as a function of consciousness and its ability to collapse the probability wave-form to change **our personal reality** - simply by our individual conscious will and intent.

4.4 DISCOVERY AND RELEVANCE OF THE PCAR SYSTEM

Before leaving the PCAR system, it needs to be said that it is difficult to believe that Walter Schempp, who discovered the system, has not received the Nobel Prize. The validity of his discovery in my view, has no parallels in scientific adherence to the scientific method, or worth - in possibly future flow-on benefits, both to human welfare and for our understanding of the science base for our bio-centric universe.

1. *First he established his holographic theory based on observations at the time of an early development of MRI scanning machines.*

   At the time, no one understood why they worked. They were in black and white, gave fuzzy images and took typically some four hours of sitting still for an acceptable scan.

2. *He then successfully derived the necessary mathematics to support his theory.*

   This led him to such an understanding of how the raw and limited system worked, that he was determined to vindicate his theory and mathematics by modifying and improving the design. At 50 years of age, he then studied medicine, biology and radiology and finally qualified as a Doctor - as no facility would otherwise allow him to modify one of their incredibly expensive machines.

3. *As they say, the rest is history; he then proved his theory completely by modifying an MRI scanner up to today's standard.*

   These give a three dimensional colour image capability and with a scan rate of typically just a few minutes.

Of course two observations on the above must inevitably follow. The first, is that since his modifications vindicated his PCAR discovery, thousands of patients have already benefited medically from improvements to fMRI technology around the globe. Also clearly more will benefit exponentially in the future. The second observation is that the adherence of his discovery to the standard science model is so pristine, that whatever inevitable denial sceptics might make to the validity of this discovery, should, one hopes surely fall on deaf ears.

A fitting conclusion to this Chapter, is the following summary of my understanding of the relevance and attributes of the system.

4.4.1　Suggested List of the Relevance and Attributes of the PCAR System

- The system is used by our consciousness, unconsciously, to choose between probable events to create our reality; but it is also that used for the same purpose unconsciously by all other life-forms and in any reality.

- It is the prime non-verbal method by which all life in the Universe communicates with each and every other. This therefore is the non-verbal communication system used for us to communicate with all within our race, but also if desired with alien entities, and with discarnates in a life-between-life environment.

- It is the system used continuously by all life-forms to access all **knowledge**, including knowledge concerning all events in the past and future. This depends of course upon the expertise in the use of the system by the life-forms involved, e.g. those particularly skilled include, shamans, savants, psychics, prophets, etc. It follows that this is the mechanism that allows access to extract information continuously from the zero point field. This includes one's personal memory, instinctive memory particular to one's species and other information extracted after intense attention and intent i.e. inspirational information.

- It is similarly used by all life-forms to interrelate with the environment to provide the feedback to allow continuous epigenic **adaptive** DNA optimised changes appropriate to foster all life.

- The communication is non-verbal, it is instantaneous, it is independent of time or space and its strength depends on attention, and intent.

- The system allows the functioning of all perception (i.e. senses) for all life-forms developed in a physical environment. In a quantum reality, it retains the same function, but is not dependent on the existence of organs.

4.5 CLOSING CHAPTER COMMENTS

The next Section, Section 2 - "Reasons for Reincarnation", deserves a special Section with but a single Chapter, Chapter 5.

This is because it is desirable first to have reached this stage in understanding the science base for reincarnation, before looking at the reasonableness of some core beliefs in reincarnation and relevant documented support by some major mystics and the esoteric wisdom of the ages - which forms the majority content of Chapter 5.

Having then achieved much of the science base for reincarnation in Section 1 and by adding reasons for incarnation, esoteric wisdom and history of reincarnation in Section 2, Section 3 Chapters will then add further key Chapters expanding on issues already mentioned. These will include subjects such as children's Recall of Past lives (primarily children), OOB and Near Death Experiences, Hypnotism and regressive hypnotism information claimed to have been received from past lives. Additionally a more acceptable but outstanding possible cause for the enigmatic issue of how **new** species were likely created. This is in contrast to Darwin's discredited argument erroneously citing mutations.

To our earlier Principles we can now add the **final** two to this book, Principles 5 and 6

PRINCIPLE 1 - A non-physical timeless (but contingent) quantum-like realm beyond our current physical existence, may be possible, where things and events respond directly to consciousness/intention.

PRINCIPLE 2 - The Universe overwhelmingly exhibits design, information, intelligence and mind. It is also bio-centric, therefore providing compelling evidence not only for a creator/God as the first cause, but with its purpose including the creation of all life.

PRINCIPLE 3 - Mind is primary, as with consciousness. Consciousness creates reality. We are immortal.

PRINCIPLE 4 - The physics exists, such that on death, our consciousness, mind, memory (i.e. one's psyche and soul) plus senses could transfer and exist in a timeless realm.

PRINCIPLE 5 - Recent scientific advancements can now explain the paranormal, psychic ability and the ability to communicate with discarnates or other entities in other realities.

PRINCIPLE 6 - The science of time and space supports belief in reincarnation.

Chapter Four Annex

Further considerations of Time and Space

In summary, one of the apparent facets of all reality arising from the discussion above on time and space is that when motion gets really fast, time stands still. Inexplicably though, motion still occurs **without time as we perceive it**. Photons, our consciousness and other low mass subatomic particles can move around unencumbered without a concept of distance, but presumably still in space. We therefore need solutions to these conundrums. A possible explanation for motion regardless of time is given below.

Esoteric literature suggests that in a life-between-life fully quantum non-physical environment, that not only does time not exist, but nor does space exist as we know it. On this basis it is possible that space, just like material objects, is a mental construct of our consciousness; and being subject to free will, increases in any manner as desired to meet our collective or individual intent. In other words just as consciousness creates matter, consciousness also creates space.

Time if desired, could be equally flexible and be manipulated at will. The properties of consciousness are by no means understood, so it could itself not even take up any space (this is supported by esoteric literature). Any of these concepts would also be consistent with a belief that consciousness being independent of time (and space) can travel anywhere instantly including backwards and forward in time. It is also consistent with the concept that consciousness is prime. With matter and energy being subservient to consciousness, why not time and space?

Dealing with a possible answer as to how can change occur without time?

As mentioned early in this Chapter, time is always defined by motion. Perhaps our perception of velocity (i.e. motion) is also attributable to yet another misconception we have about time. This is due to concern expressed even by Isaac Newton in understanding that once force is applied to (say) an arrow; after the first instant, the arrow continues to fly without continuation of any force (termed "Zeno's Paradox"). Nor can a force be felt by one personally after the initial application (e.g. travelling in a lift). In recent years, in an attempt to explain the continuation of the arrow's flight, it has been explained as being due to "impetus". However it will be noted that this is just a word and fails to explain anything (i.e. it is a tautology).

Theoretical quantum physicist Shan Gao in his recent Kindle book *God Does Play Dice with the Universe*, has a novel explanation for Zeno's Paradox in that he believes that not only is the misconception criticism valid, but the error is due to regarding motion as continuous. Instead he believes that all motion is essentially discontinuous by being formed instead by almost instantaneous (characteristically) quantum jumps of random actual **events** (as is evident with the emission of photons from atoms). Motion therefore only appears continuous when observed over a larger finite period.

The following "Seth" quote supports this (most likely unknown to Shan Gao):

> "Only from unpredictability can any system emerge that can be predictable within itself. Only within complete freedom of motion, is any ordered motion truly possible." [2]
>
> Seth

Gao gives two examples to support his case. The first is the different diffraction pattern one encounters in the double-slit experiment when a single photon is fired through two slits and the second, the partial reflection of light - both of which he claims exhibit the randomness of motion.

This seems plausible when one considers this mirrors very well our new view of how material reality is formed - namely by consciousness of all life-forms collectively and unconsciously choosing between a superposition of available alternatives to collapse Schrödinger probability functions. As mentioned earlier, this only applies to dynamic states, which obviously very much means motion.

I recall that esoteric literature has mentioned previously the concept that the whole universe cycles i.e. blinks on and off between existence and non-existence at a very rapid constant rate.[3]

Therefore, our conscious choice of reality could unconsciously and automatically create events in an individual and discrete manner, just like the frames of a movie film passing through a projector produces the perception of continuous motion.

As reported by Professor Keith Mayes in his article "*What is Time?*"[4], experiments have already been initiated to study whether this behaviour is likely by investigating whether a universal time cycle between events can be detected. Unfortunately, as he explains, experimental investigations to date have not been successful, which could be due to a number of factors. However, according to quantum theory, the inherent uncertainty characteristic of quantum behaviour means that time cannot be measured to infinite accuracy, since it flows ' fuzzily' on the quantum scale. Therefore Mayes has said *"If it moves in discrete steps we have not yet reached a level small enough to observe it"*

Cycling of the universe in a metronomic manner by this theory is envisaged as providing an essential function by dividing events into discrete regular time intervals to allow such change to occur (by our unconscious will and intent) to form discontinuous motion. Discontinuous motion perceived over any relatively large comparatively finite interval, just as in a movie, would then have the customary appearance of being continuous. If correct, this would answer the imponderable issue highlighted above of how change can occur without time.

If valid, one important concept that may follow from the possibility of the whole universe blinking on and off at very high rate is that in the interval between cycles, this could allow for other realities to exist in our same space as ourselves - both of these ideas are contained in readily available esoteric literature. Again another "Seth" quote:

> "Time as you think of it does not exist ... an atom phases in and out, it fluctuates in a highly predictable pattern and rhythm. ... in those periods of non-physical projection, the off periods of fluctuation, the atoms appear in another reality"
>
> *Seth* [5]

Professional communication engineers such as myself would very much identify this as a well-practiced communication scientific approach called "time-division multiplex" (TDM) to increase capacity by enabling simultaneous use of the same frequency spectrum by time interval cycling of channels of information.

In terms of realities and our universe however, it would easily and conveniently allow a creator /God to use the same space for another universe or multiple universes and realities at once. Given its elegance and utility it is difficult to imagine that a creator/God who would wish to allow all probabilities to be actualised, would not have implemented this idea.

> "Between each ticking of the clock
> Long centuries pass
> In universes hidden from our own."
>
> *Jane Roberts, medium for "Seth"* [6]

Leaving this unaccustomed speculation in this book and to return to our usual validated science, to stretch one's credulity yet again, the brilliant cosmologist Paul Davies adds yet another conundrum in his book *God and the New Physics* by saying:

> "The quantum theory requires a sort of reversed time causality, inasmuch as an observation performed today can contribute to the construction of reality in the remote past. The point has been emphasized by the physicist John Wheeler:

The quantum principal shows that there is a sense in which what the observer will do in the future defines what happens in the past - even a past so remote that life then did not exist." [7]

(Wheeler by using the word "observer"- is expressing the effect of our consciousness in creating our collective reality - as is reflected in using the word "observer" as the key component cited as affecting change in the descriptions of the double-slit experiment).

While many may feel this unbelievable, it is completely supported by both quantum science and mathematical quantum mechanics, which as stated previously has been found to be an astonishingly accurate area of science. It might also be identified of course as area often speculated about in magazine articles - particularly the paradox, that if a time traveler travelled backwards in time and killed your grandfather, then it is presumed you might suddenly vanish. Regardless of the paradox however the science is impeccable.

A likely explanation simply follows from the concept - that we choose our own reality, with no buts! Therefore, by conscious attention, plus intent and belief, it must equally be possible to change our future and our past. Changing our past is most unlikely, although not impossible, as very few people would believe it possible and are therefore unlikely to try. We most certainly can change the future though, as we not only daydream about it continually but possibly dream as well about it, just about every day of our lives - even if we only dream mostly about the next day.

In essence therefore, a probable future may be chosen and wished for at all times in our event-line, subject of course to any changes of heart we might have in our choices for our future - until our future time-line becomes actualized as a present reality. This is vindicated by the ability of some psychics to make remarkable predictions about the future for their clients i.e. it explains precognition. It also explains how some psychics find unhappily that their predictions are completely wrong. (Again this concept is fully supported by esoteric wisdom.) [8]

Sadly we are still not finished with our conundrums of time and space.

If we examine our definition of time above, (repeated here) - **very, very carefully**:

Definition of "time".

Time can be defined in a number of ways - such "as *a measure of the interval between* **events**, *using units we have chosen for the purpose.*"

And put our thinking caps on, we might suddenly discover another thing about time that is shocking and embarrassing to say the least – namely that, as was covered in two *Physics Essays* in 2011 by Amrit Sorli, Davide Fiscaletti, and Dusan Klinar from the Scientific Research Centre Bistra in Ptuj, Slovenia, that:

> ***"time" has only a measurement function and therefore cannot be a dimension, in spite of the fact that it has been wrongly regarded in this light for eons.***

Therefore our viewpoint of our physical reality comprising three dimensions and one of time is fundamentally wrong. It now seems that we only have three dimensions of space, but for spacetime add a measurement function "time". As stated in the papers referred to it above, it was known to Einstein who reportedly made this comment:

> "Einstein said, '*Time has no independent existence apart from the order of events by which we measure it. Time is exactly (a measure) of the order of events: this is my conclusion.*"

The article goes on to say: *"The concept of time as a way to measure the duration of events is not only deeply intuitive, it also plays an important role in our mathematical descriptions of physical systems. For instance, we define an object's speed as its displacement per a given time. But some researchers theorize that this Newtonian idea of time as an absolute quantity that flows on its own, along with the idea that time is the fourth dimension of space-time, are incorrect. The authors propose to replace these concepts of time with a view that corresponds more accurately to the physical world: time as a measure of the numerical order of change.*

They begin by explaining how we usually assume that **time** *is an absolute physical quantity that plays the role of the independent variable (time, t, is often the x-axis on graphs that show the evolution of a physical system). But, as they note, we never really measure t. What we do measure is an object's frequency, speed, etc. In other words, what experimentally exists are the motion of an object and the tick of a clock, and we compare the object's motion to the tick of a clock to measure the object's frequency, speed, etc. By itself, t has only a mathematical value, and no primary physical existence.*

This view doesn't mean that time does not exist, but that time has more to do with space than with the idea of an absolute time. So while 4D space-time is usually considered to consist of three dimensions of space and one dimension of time, the researchers' view suggests that it's more correct to imagine space-time as four dimensions of space. In other words, as they say, the universe is "timeless". [9]

In summary: **"time" rightly must be regarded as being merely a measure of the numerical order of material change in our physical universe.**

It will be seen that even though our concept of "time" was incorrect previously, this in no way diminishes its importance in **physical reality**, but **only** as a useful measurement function it provides. This is because it is extremely useful to indicate when we travel throughout the universe between any two spacial points in space, against a handy comparative reference tick of a clock. Also as indicated above "The Big Bang" has given us a valid spacial direction for each of our event-lines. If we travel in any direction either towards or away from the source of the "Big Bang" we will most assuredly will travel either forwards or backwards on our event line, but not in "time" because there is no such thing – it is simply a measurement function, not a dimension. Therefore as we learned earlier, without "time" in the sense we currently understand it, there really is no such thing as a past or future just a series of "nows" in a spacious present.

Also it follows that (as indicated above) our ultimate reality outside the universe is timeless.

Theoretical quantum physicist Shan Gao's concept of a metronomic pulse of the universe (and our consciousness) is probably valid and responsible for our sense of the flow of time. Additionally, (and unfortunately) the entropic dissipation of energy and thus order since the Big Bang, leads inevitably to imperfect cellular repair with the indisputable effect of deterioration of all our bodies.

This concept interestingly has support from another recent science article which suggests that theory (by theoretical physicists Don Page and William Wootter in 1983) had shown that time is an emergent phenomenon that comes about because of the nature of entanglement. And it exists only for observers inside the universe. An observer outside would see a static, unchanging universe - as Wheeler-DeWitt equations would predict. Physicists Ekaterina Moreva at the Istituto Nazionale di Ricerca Metrologica (INRIM) in Turin, Italy, in 2013 successfully performed the first experimental test, vindicating Page and Wootters theory.[10]

In view of the above it certainly seems that we have got the whole idea of time completely wrong.

Taking the above further and summarising, we have now reached the position that "time" as we understand it is but a mathematical measure, with no other validity whatsoever. Our current belief of time is completely wrong, and should be discarded. As covered earlier, in this universe and in physical reality though, individually we all nevertheless experience a **sense** of time. It seems this is due to the rapid switching of the universe on and off at a rate currently unable to be detected which divides events and ensures events follow causes i.e. this creates and is possibly the cause of causality in our classical physical world. When our timelines are intersected by those of others, we obviously share the same sense of "time" as they do. But if we travel some distance from them, particularly when leaving earth then our "time" relationship changes. Under such circumstances due to gravitation and velocity/acceleration effects which can **slow** our timeline relative to those left behind on earth; on return, there are major effects on aging during the journey, such that on our return we might be lucky to find our friends and family alive. For this reason "time" travel is theoretically possible but rather impractical in our physical reality, because even if we spacially travel in a spaceship towards or away the location of "The Big Bang", to the past or future, if we return from sufficient distance to where we started, no one will recognise us.

In understanding this, finally a number of surprising conclusions follow:.

While in a space ship, travelling to different planets, clearly since our space ship and bodies move to different locations via differing directions, speed, and acceleration: differing gravitations are encountered. This variation will therefore ensure that the effect of "time" on our body and spaceship is relative, and subject to Einstein's equations and mathematics. In contrast, subatomic particles being quantum, do not experience time. Likewise, since our consciousness/soul is also quantum, it is unaffected by spacial movements in our universe and can travel anywhere in an instant (i.e. as a holographic quantum property).

This then exhibits the duality so often encountered, namely that in physical reality, spacial movement appears to create causality, with entropic deterioration effects whenever movement is involved (which is of course is continuous since we are still hurtling outward from the origin point of the Big Bang). It is therefore valid as a concept to talk about "time" lines, as this convention does assist complete understanding. But for non-physical reality, entities such as subatomic particles and our consciousness/souls, acausality applies i.e. events **can** happen without cause and there is no such thing as a time line, just an event line.

If therefore on a reincarnational basis, we regard non-physical reality, **our true reality**; then we must therefore regard events in such an afterlife reality to occur (as previously) - also as a sequence of continuous "nows". This would be likely a very different experience for us though - as though still a spacious present, space would also not exist in our terms. Both space and events though, would still occur continuously as a result of solely our individual and collective thoughts and ideas creating our reality. But in such a fully quantum environment we would expect thoughts and ideas to create reality instantaneously, rather than slowly.

It seems inevitability this leads us to the following conclusions, that not only is non-physical reality prime, but also quantum physics - as it is the base-line physics for non-physical reality. Noteworthy though, it must also embrace our current home environment on earth of classical physical reality, so this suggests it contains, (yet to be fully discovered), the physics of everything i.e. appropriate to the elusive TOE - "The Theory of Everything".

Quantum physics, as Paul Davies tells us (in his book *God and The New Physics*), allows **for a likely Universe which I personally find seems very much like that**

described in this book - in so far as its observable properties are concerned, and seems to fit all the facts. To accept his ideas, we have to accept the fact that in particular, not only are our ideas of elementary particles wrong but, "there are no **elementary particles at all**". Instead he postulates that, every particle (at least every nuclear particle) is made up of every other. But no particle is **elementary or primitive**; but each contains something of an **identity** of all the others". (Note: Davies is not saying this applies to **atom**s, but rather one or a single elementary particle).

If I read him correctly, Davies is suggesting an atom can comprise particles, fundamentally the same but having the flexibility of exhibiting any of properties of the others. His point of saying that "Each contains something of the identity of all the others we would perhaps identify as the Buddhist spark of God in each of us i.e. the **true** "*God particle*" inherent in everything (rather than the Higgs Boson which decays).

This Davies calls "The Bootstrap Theory"[11]

(Currently though, it is just a theory and awaits solid replicable science validation.)

Davies then explains that, with such a Universe though, and every event being contingent and dependent for its explanation on some other event, **it most likely follows a causal loop with no beginning or end**. (Perhaps therefore our "Big Bang" may after all, be a Big Stretch/bounce cycle with no end, energy conserved, and still somehow continuously habitable after a singularity/reversal?) Wheeler apparently has this view with the possibility of the reversal being "an opportunity for re-processing the Cosmos".)

At the moment of creation of this universe therefore, following esoteric tradition; a creator/God could easily both be exterior to and have entered his own Creation. As Davies suggests this defeats instantly the famous theological conundrum unanswered previously of: *How could a God as the simplest (but infinitely powerful and knowledgeable, but simplest being that one could possibly imagine, create an increasingly complicated Universe which continually creates its own life and actualises all possibilities?*

The answer is obviously for our creator/God to have replicated himself within it, at the act of creation.

In this way Davies points out that: "It is very unlikely that that a Universe would exist uncaused, but rather more likely that God would exist uncaused."

Finally, if this was our Universe and was arranged as **an endless spiral forming a loop**, one can easily see that in any quantum reality, the future and past would be readily accessible

This above "Bootstrap Universe Theory", known apparently to many physicists, if valid, has a key consequences for our understanding of our **"time"** reality.

Assuming this is the case, and in my words:

All things are ever "present" and proceeding together in step as a series of consecutive "now's". Therefore, ourselves, all other entities and together with our creator/God, we are all engaged in a never ending thrilling journey of exploration with all life and entities creating always a fresh new reality for ourselves and others, based on all our individual ideas and imagination from our collective present. It is unending, and since its creation it will never stop. All realities and possibilities will be actuated, limited only by our imagination.

Further development of these concepts, but tied specifically to **knowledge and information issues**, are covered in Annex 1 to the last Chapter, Chapter 9.

Note: References within this Annex are to be found immediately below "Chapter 4 References".

SECTION TWO

CHAPTER FIVE

Reasons for Reincarnation

The previous four Chapters have established the evidence for a creator/God and the science behind reincarnation. At this point in the book, I therefore felt that this Chapter should logically follow, to show that reincarnational belief itself - as a belief system for our existence, exhibits rationality and logical consistency beyond all others. As a belief system it is also one of the most widely accepted belief systems throughout the world.

This Chapter additionally covers possible **reasons** for reincarnation…and for death!

Surprising for some, it also includes **some reincarnational texts within the bible**, but also others within other conventional religious texts, and those of some mystics.

Definition of Reincarnation (Oxford Dictionary):

"Rebirth of the soul in another body."

5.1   POSSIBLE REASONS FOR RE-INCARNATION

"Work is futile if we cannot utilise the experience we collect in one life, in the next."

Henry Ford [1]

Before considering possible reasons for re-incarnation, we need to first consider why death should occur at all. Also whether immortality is a likely (or even desirable) end point for our development and progression as a species.

Biologists would be quick to point out that deterioration of all living cells is inevitable, since normal cell replacement over time is always accompanied with DNA coding errors which lead to degenerative disorders. In addition, our oxygen rich atmosphere is highly 'corrosive' and a major cause of free radicals - cited as a prime cause of ageing. In the future, with doubtless scientific breakthroughs, a very prolonged life may be possible. However, due to the above, immortality in **physical** form would appear impracticable.

Reincarnation, or a permanent existence in a **non-physical** form would clearly present a better option!

Surprisingly death actually seems a good idea - at least from a biological viewpoint - as it aids genetic diversity and opportunity i.e. progeny have improved opportunities to mate, and with biologically fitter partners. Also, without old timers to compete with, they have better access to resources.

John D. Barrow points out in his book *Between Inner Space and Outer Space* that:

"Death promotes genetic diversity and periodic extinctions have played a vital role in promoting the spread of life". [2]

There is also the issue that, if tomorrow we were to awake on earth as immortals, obviously our attitudes would be very much different from those today. We would probably be more orientated towards accumulation of wealth, power and resources; and far more conservative and less inclined to take risks. Most would agree that with an immortal life on earth it would be almost impossible not to eventually get bored with the same friends, family and associates as well as with all experiences and earth environments - since satiation would follow incessant repetition. (If you think this is incorrect, remember eternity is a rather long time!).

It is interesting to speculate what future each of us would plan for ourselves - assuming firstly we were immortal, and secondly that we had infinite power to choose.

Immortality would surely instantly fulfil our greatest wish, namely to escape the fear that we all share - that having gained the wonderful gift of life, and without choice, the preciousness of our life is fated to end in death. An ignominious end to all our endeavours, and an unwished parting from those we love.

Our speculative joy in imagining ourselves immortal though, would soon be surely dashed when one considers eon upon eon of unending life - as simply a continuation of the life we know. Dependant on our current age, we might perhaps have already savoured life pretty fully. Also immortality is no guarantee of health - so if our body became a burden, we may well wish vainly for death.

Even visualisation of a personal heavenly future of unparalleled wealth, fame and fortune over incalculable eons would be unlikely to enthuse us greatly. This is because as we are only too aware that those particularly wealthy around us now, already so privileged, do not as a group seem ecstatically happy. In fact we surely note that those that seem the most fulfilled, happy and driven, are those who are helping others, or involved in creative work beneficial to their fellow man, or to other life forms (e.g. animals).

It is therefore difficult to ignore that given a choice, the future we would choose for ourselves, would probably be along re-incarnational lines, comprising a cycle of rebirths with an infinity of choices of lifetimes, historical periods and environments. We would probably wish to make our own choice prior to each re-incarnational cycle of broad goals specifically suited for ourselves, which we would think likely to maximise self-fulfilment and assist our personal development. At a stretch, we might even choose amnesia from past re-incarnational cycles, to ensure an appropriate focus and concentration on the cycle in question. **Interestingly these logical choices align completely with the generally accepted beliefs and theories associated with re-incarnation.**

All must have felt at some time in their lives that there is a logical consistency in all things and in life around us. Also that the one thing that makes an older person different from others is clearly - **experience**. This is all that each of us have uniquely savoured over the many years and all that is left when the body has deteriorated to the point where it can no longer support life. Often experience has been gained at considerable expense, pain and heartache; and in some cases where we have learned the hard way, it might even be said that some wisdom has been gained. Given we see logical consistency in nature all around us, it would seem inconsistent and therefore almost ridiculous to contemplate that the experience and wisdom of each person and all other living things following a lifecycle is lost at death.

Re-incarnation must therefore be regarded, if nothing else, as a reasonable hypothesis for a way in which experience and wisdom could be retained beyond death.

As many are aware, the hypothesis of re-incarnation has more than retention of experience and wisdom going for it. It can help to explain many otherwise inexplicable situations that exist in the world such as early deaths, and inequalities of life such as the prosperity of the wicked, the misery of the virtuous, etc.

With multiple existences, not only can the joys of life be experienced, but the downsides as well, all of which could be seen as enrichment of experience by savouring all life has to offer - and as part of different families, clans, tribes, cultures, genders, races, and species.

John Dryden (d. 1711) wrote:

"Virtue in distress and vice in triumph make atheists of mankind". The theory of reincarnation, completely exonerates God from the charge of injustice, favouritism, malice, cruelty or caprice." [3]

Adding to the inevitable deterioration of an aged physical body mentioned above, Professor Geddes MacGregor points out that as we age, we lose our ability to be open to radically new ideas and our minds become cluttered with memories. In addition we also often become burdened with guilt and remorse, which can impede our growth. He considers re-incarnation can give a needed fresh start to continue growth.

Death is often the release from intensely limiting and painful conditions. As Mahatma Gandhi wrote on rebirth:

"……It is nature's kindness that we do not remember past births. Where is the good either of knowing in detail the numberless births, we have gone through? Life would be a burden if we carried such a tremendous load of memories. A wise man deliberately forgets many things, even as a lawyer forgets the cases and their details as soon as they are disposed of."[4]

Logic would certainly suggest the prime reason for re-incarnation is that suggested by Professor MacGregor above, namely to achieve **growth** - otherwise there would be no point to the baggage of experiences accumulated over multiple lifetimes. This received strong support from Elisabeth Kubler-Ross, originally an atheist, who as a doctor/researcher spent a life time studying and relating to thousands of patients approaching death. She baldly stated: "Our only purpose in life is growth." [5]

Further on in this Chapter a "multidimensional personality" called "Seth" channelled by Jane Roberts, is discussed in some detail. On reincarnation, even if not believed, he has some interesting things to say. He expands considerably on the above. Not only does he support the concept that the purpose of re-incarnation is to grow and learn, but also to *create*. In this respect he points out we each have multidimensional selves and are continually involved on a co-operative basis with all other life forms at an unconscious level and also in dreams - to collectively and individually create our physical and non-physical reality. Also that the re-incarnational experiences of every individual provides a rich source of experience from which all others can unconsciously draw.[6]

He states that other reasons for re-incarnation are:

"To generate activity throughout time's framework, to reinforce structures of knowledge, to transmit information, and perhaps most of all to reinforce relationships involving love, brotherhood and co-operation between generations of men and woman that would otherwise be quite separate and apart from each other".

He also speaks of the essential need for value fulfilment both as individuals and as a species.[7]

5.2 VIEWS OF MYSTICS

"You are as dead now as you will ever be"

Seth[8]

To ensure credibility, care has been taken in this book, to present the views of experts in their field. Most of these are world renowned scientists, some of whom are professors at leading universities.

It is therefore only after initial reluctance and considerable thought, that I have included below re-incarnational comment and beliefs of two 20th Century "mystics" on mind/ consciousness. Normally testimony or assertions of mystics or seers would be inappropriate when presenting evidence of a standard aimed at being acceptable in a scientific book. However I believe exceptionally, the quality of the material below justifies inclusion in this book as important background, as I found it provides remarkable and striking correlation with the scientific evidence presented in earlier Chapters. In addition, the views and teachings, adds some interesting possibilities to the concept that mind survives death, and to re-incarnation itself.

It should be mentioned that although some of the views of two particular mystics are given below, there are numerous other mystics or religious figures, who could also have been included. They have expressed similar views supportive of non-physical reality, the primacy of mind, the immortality of the consciousness/soul, and reincarnation. It will be noted that, certain teachings from both mystics **below** (as covered under comments in each case), exhibit a multitude of correlations with the science covered in previous Chapters, but also between them. It will be noted later, that this continues for remaining Chapters in this book.

For one scientific correlation to occur could easily occur by chance, but with many correlations i.e. "hits", and "few" if any misses, the odds favoring **all** their "ideas/ teachings" to be fundamental truths are obviously scientifically statistically high and compelling.

Observations which exhibit the predicted properties from a theory and which can receive correlation from science, is really what science is all about - namely to allow us to understand and make sense our universe.

The two 'mystics' are Edgar Cayce - often referred to as America's most famous prophet and - 'Seth', a claimed multidimensional entity channeled by Jane Roberts.

5.2.1 **Edgar Cayce:**

Background – Edgar Cayce was born in 1877 on a farm in Kentucky, U.S.A. He died in 1945 heralded as the most famous religious seer of the century and is often referred to as "the sleeping prophet". Even when young, he exhibited unusual 'psychic' gifts and when six years old, told his parents he was able to see and talk to relatives long since dead. He was not believed at the time, but later found he could sleep on a textbook and awaken with a photographic memory of its contents, without once having opened the book. As proof, he astonished his peers and teachers by rapid advancement through the grades at school. After leaving school early to become a salesman, Cayce developed a serious throat ailment involving gradual paralysis of the throat muscles. Doctors were unable to find a physical cause for this condition and he even tried hypnosis without effect. Desperate to find a cure for his illness, he asked a friend to make appropriate verbal suggestions to assist him reach a similar trance/sleeping state he had previously used when sleeping on his books. This was so successful that in a trance he amazingly spoke aloud a proposed remedy involving medication and manipulative therapy which completely cleared up all problems with his throat.

Later on physicians from Hopkinsville and Bowling Green, Kentucky, took advantage of his unique talent to diagnose their own patients. They discovered that while in a trance state, Cayce only needed to be given the name and address of a patient (as a cue), to be able to tune in telepathically on that individual's mind and body as easily as if they were both in the same room. Although he only required a patient's name and address, his suggested remedies were invariably successful. On awakening from trance he was never able to recall what he had previously said. He was deeply religious and for some time strongly argued against re-incarnational comments he made to others while in trance. In was only later in life that he came to accept his trance view of re-incarnation as correct.

One of the young doctors, Dr. Wesley Ketchum, submitted a report on this unorthodox procedure to a clinical research society in Boston. On October 9, 1910, *The New* York Times carried two pages of headlines and pictures. From that day on, many of the the sick from all over America sought his help.

In view of the incredible accuracy of his suggested remedies to patients, his close associates (including doctors), documented his trance state answers to their many questions on a range of medical and other subjects throughout his lifetime (including life after death). These became known as the "Cayce readings". When he died in Virginia Beach, Virginia, he left well over fourteen thousand documented records of these trance statements he had given for more than six thousand different people over a period of forty-three years.

5.2.2   His teachings

Cayce claimed his ability to gain information from what he called a "universal subconscious" was unremarkable, and something anyone could do in the same way that he did. He emphasised that he had learned that all knowledge is within and available via the subconscious. Also that every cell in your body has its portion of mind, and the mind has an infinite capacity to know the world, because 'mind' created it.

The following are some of his other propositions regarding mind/consciousness.
(Apart from the conscious and unconscious minds, well known to all of us, he

also introduced - as outlined below - the concept of the 'transpersonal' mind, termed by Jung, the "super self"):

> Mind is not exclusively the personal property of any one individual. Although we all have our unique experiences and sequences of thoughts about daily life, on the deeper level, all of us share in a universal mental activity.
>
> This deeper and universal reservoir of mind remembers everything that the human race has experienced.
>
> The conscious mind is functional and analytic, and of necessity focussed on physical life. In contrast, the subconscious is free of the restrictions and boundaries that characterise our usual everyday thought processes. It is at the subconscious level that all minds are in contact with each other - including the minds of the 'living' and the 'dead'. Each level of mind is a distinctive information channel - as follows:
>
> | | |
> |---|---|
> | Conscious | Sensory information from the external world |
> | Subconscious | Telepathic information from the subconscious minds of others (Jung called this the *'collective unconscious'*). |
> | Transpersonal | Universal information from the oneness of all life.[9] |

We can certainly identify with this as a rather non-scientific explanation of what we learned in Chapter 2, namely that - as he said above concerning 'mind creates the world' i.e. **consciousness creates reality, and the subconscious has access to non-physical reality i.e. all memory (personal and collective), and all universe information/knowledge.**

A useful analogy or metaphor to what Cayce is saying, is that suggested by Henry Reed [11], where universal mind can be regarded as a star. The central portion represents the collective mind of all (i.e. the transpersonal), whereas infinite arms and points surrounding the star comprise the conscious individual minds of each living being. Each subconscious mind is at the base of each arm, and can therefore link with the subconscious mind of all others. The mind you usually think of as "your mind" is but one of the points on the star. It is your conscious mind. The sharp points on each arm can be likened to the strong focus we all share while in a conscious state with physical reality and the separation of each arm from another, the separateness of each of our conscious minds.

Edgar Cayce also spoke of thoughts as tangible **things**, a finer form of matter and, when he was in trance, repeatedly told his clients that their thoughts created their destiny and that *"thought is the builder."* In his view, the thinking process is like a spider constantly spinning, constantly adding to its web. "**Every moment of our lives we are creating the images and patterns that give our future energy and shape**, *said Cayce"*.[10]

Reed has summarized Cayce's position as follows:

> "When a person dies the personal conscious mind dies with the body, but the subconscious mind remains unaffected... our dream images, or subconscious desires and fears, continue their existence after the death of the body. Cayce makes an important distinction about this continued life. There are the continued effects, which arise from the permanent records of all thoughts and experiences... and those thoughts live on in eternity. There is also the continued activity, which is the soul's journey in other dimensions of being".

Harmon Hartzell Bro, a minister of religion who for his doctoral thesis lived with Cayce and his family for a year, also pointed out that Cayce's readings stressed that a key re-incarnational role was **co-creation** (you will note this similarity with the views of "Seth" below). Eventually the goal was, together with the source of all life, **to share in the creation of worlds themselves**. Also in Harmon Bro's words, there was constant affirmation in the readings for:

> "Oneness, oneness, oneness." "All reality had not only one original source in the divine, but also one presence. Events were far more connected than we realised, resonating to each other so intimately that they could instantly be found by a consciousness with the right perspective."[12]

5.2.3   **Comment:**

It would seem reasonable that the credibility of Cayce's teachings on re-incarnation should be looked at in the light of his incredible and proven accuracy on healing thousands of patients. All this provision of correct diagnoses plus successful remedies - while in a trance state. Where patients could not visit in person (and almost universally in later life), he linked with patients mentally in a trance state merely by being provided with their address. For most of his life he was in the constant company of doctors - who were unwittingly also the expert witnesses necessary to constantly judge his efficacy in assisting the ill. Apart from this, his "readings" on other matters have been found unerringly accurate. For example, he pinpointed the location and described the historical role of the Essene community at Qumran eleven years before the discovery of the Dead Sea scrolls in the caves above Qumran.

Dealing with the content of Cayce's teachings, the degree of agreement with scientific research outlined in Chapters 2 and 3 is amazing - even to the concept that every cell in your body has its portion of mind. It is obviously unlikely that a relatively uneducated person such as Cayce would have had access to or would have been interested in David Bohm's little publicised Holographic Universe Theory, his observation of the conscious behaviour of electrons, and the experiments carried by Penfield and Pilbram. All these vindicate belief in the holographic nature of the mind, referred to in Chapter 2.

That *"Events.......resonate to each other ...."* etc. quoted above, is in complete agreement with Rupert Sheldrake's concept of morphic resonance vindicated by Walter Schempp's supporting scientific and mathematical discoveries. It is noteworthy that in trance, Cayce necessitated in all cases at least a patient's address (if the patient was unable to attend in person), in order to permit a medical diagnosis. As outlined in Chapter 3, this aligns with the Schempp's PCAR perception minimum communication requirement to obtain a returned reference wave to allow resonance and standing waves to occur for decoding and processing of clairvoyant information from a remote target. There is also a correlation with Chapter 2's position on the primacy of mind (Cayce said (above) that "**mind has an infinite capacity to know the world, because 'mind' created it**"). And, survival of mind after death, together with Chapter 3's retention of memory in an afterlife (i.e. within the zero point field) - where he talks of "the personal conscious mind dies with the body, but the subconscious mind remains unaffected" and "There are the continued effects, which arise from the permanent records of all thoughts and experiences... and those thoughts live on in eternity".

The alignment above with quantum physics holographic properties of **interconnectedness**, the memory concepts of the zero point field and the PCAR system involving resonance and frequency matching, is surely difficult to ignore.

5.2.4   Jane Robert's – "Seth":

Jane Roberts was an American medium who, in September 1963, channeled a direct voice entity called "Seth". As an author, she decided to try her hand at investigating ESP as a possible source of writing material, by experimenting with an Ouija board. Her success was very limited at first, but as she related in her first book, she quickly made contact with an entity who claimed he was a multidimensional personality. "Seth" explained he had completed his re-incarnational cycles on earth and was currently achieving fulfilment as a teacher. He indicated his intent was to produce, through her, a series of books which would be helpful in overcoming what he considered were distortions in the world view of physical and non-physical reality. The books were later published and resulted from "Seth" using Jane Robert's voice to dictate them word by word, while in trance, to her husband who faithfully recorded them. In many cases the trance readings by "Seth", were witnessed by a large number of people over some five years. Many were tape recorded and are freely available on the internet.

All of this might sound somewhat amusing and farfetched if it were not for a number of issues. The most surprising and enduring aspect (the books were written some 50 years ago), is the quality and content of the teachings - made even more remarkable in that they were spoken at a regular pace before witnesses **without a correction ever being required**.

Also the structure of each book together with the Chapter titles were given even **before** dictation commenced!!

Often scientific matters were presented far beyond the expected knowledge and abilities of Jane Roberts. Also Jane Roberts herself, initially sceptical, carried out tests with "Seth" on precognition, etc. She often invited the comments of scientists/engineers and in many cases invited them as guests to the twice weekly sessions to question "Seth" directly. She did this as a measure to satisfy herself as to the likely validity of "Seth's" statements and whether she should publish the material. As far as is known, there has never been adverse comment by any of these experts on Seth's teachings. In fact many aspects of the teachings have recently been supported independently by the development of new cosmological/biological theories, such as Lovelock's Gaia Hypothesis and Sheldrake's writings on his theory of morphic resonance.

5.2.5   His teachings:

As with Cayce, "Seth" teaches that consciousness is present in every electron and cell. However he expands this view further by asserting that consciousness is made up of individual units of consciousness (CU's), and portions of a particular organism's consciousness are everywhere at once. Also that "the self that you are aware of, represents only one "position" in which the invisible particles happen to intersect, gain mass, and build up form". He considers that consciousness is a way of perceiving the various dimensions of reality but to some extent, our physical senses inhibit the perception of equally other valid dimensions in which we unconsciously participate. He calls the conscious mind the "outer ego" - and the portion of mind which is aware, alert and focussed in physical reality. The "inner ego" is that portion of the subconscious mind which directs inner activities and carries with it the memory of all re-incarnational past existences. It is also natively clairvoyant and telepathic, so that warnings are received of disasters before they occur, whether or not the message is consciously accepted. He says there is a deeper identity (Jung's "super self"?) who forms both the inner ego and the outer ego, and who decides to be a physical being in this place and in this time i.e. "when you are (in terms of re-incarnational progression), determines where you are." As stated previously above, he advised that a person's re-incarnational experiences are used unconsciously by each individual and are also available to the species as a rich source of experience and knowledge. But he also indicated that dreams additionally provide communication between people or nations and a continuation of information flow from one part of a species to another. [13]

5.2.6 **Comment:**

The degree of correlation with the scientific evidence presented in Chapter 2 on consciousness, and the views of Cayce is very evident. As will be observed "Seth's" assertion that "*consciousness is everywhere at once*" is in total conformance with the non-locality and holographic aspect of quantum physics (this is certainly a scientific matter unlikely to be known or of interest to Jane Roberts). It also supports the view that the mind is separate from the brain. Of particular interest is "Seth's" view that the super self chooses the when and where of re-incarnation. It also confirms succinctly the concept of free-will continuously throughout reincarnation

During her lifetime Jane Roberts (1929–1984) produced 27 Books! containing "Seth's" teachings and information.[14]

Although it would be of considerable interest to continue to mention correlations with present day science, this is impractical due to the sheer volume of "Seth" information. Instead therefore, I have chosen to provide a few further relevant "Seth" concepts and correlation instances as merely background material, in Section 3 of the book, where relevant under each Chapter.

I have also added an Annex, Annex1 to this Chapter which contains a written record of some information provided by Seth in December 1968 and written down directly by Jane Robert's husband while she was in trance - soon after she began acting as a direct voice medium. Its purpose is to illustrate the high quality of channeled thoughts and content delivered at a somewhat measured conversation pace, but without ever requiring correction (as mentioned above). This, anyone can easily verify for themselves who wishes to listen to tape recordings taken at the many "Seth" classes run by Jane Roberts over a number of years, available on the internet.

Annex 2 to this Chapter contains some further selected quotes from a number of Jane Robert's books for those interested. There is also a wide source of internet information concerning the teachings of "Seth".

An example of "Seth's" quotes which has been strikingly vindicated **only recently** by scientific developments. It is taken from her book "Seth Speaks" written more than 40 years ago:

"Almost any cell has the capacity for growing into any organ, or forming any part of the body." [15]

Notably, knowledge of **adult** stem cell differentiation (by genetic reprogramming) providing the ability to form organs from almost **any** cell (as stated by "Seth") was discovered only a few years ago.

5.3 RELIGIOUS RE-INCARNATIONAL VIEWS

It is important at this juncture to make the point that reincarnation is not a religion as many might think, but simply a belief system. In support of this, there is no reincarnational biblical document such as the "Bible" or "Koran", which professes to be the word of God advocating what one might do or not. Nor is there any concept of sin or the Devil. Merely a belief in our immortality and a striving for self-improvement with a purpose of eventually perhaps uniting with God.

On a population basis, over a quarter of the world's population is considered to accept reincarnational belief. It is a key belief within both Buddhism and Hinduism. But other religions with belief in reincarnation include Jains, Sikhs, Rosicrucians, Theosophists, Spiritualists, and Wiccans. Reincarnation is also a belief described in Kabbalistic Judaism as gilgul neshamot (Reincarnation of Souls)). It is also embodied in most other ancient religions including the traditions of preliterate and primitive peoples in tropical Africa, in New Guinea, in the Pacific Islands, in Indonesia, Malaysia and amongst many Australian aboriginal tribes. Re-birth was also a belief of many American tribes including the Incas, Eskimos, Aleuts and Tlingit Indians. This belief also applied in Europe by the Persians, Egyptians, Tibetans, the Druids, early Greeks and the Jews (Judaism).[16]

Importantly though and not generally well known, is the fact that reincarnation was an accepted belief by many early Christian groups, and **within the Bible itself are a number of references which strongly support reincarnation**. In addition, many "books" regarded as parts of the original Bible (including those known as the "Apocrypha") were excised by the "Council of Trent" aimed at removing those which gave references to reincarnation. Reincarnation was also declared an "anathema" - a formal curse by a pope or a council of the Roman Catholic Church, denouncing a doctrine against pre-existence. This effectively banned re-incarnation as a belief for Christian churches and was passed in the Fifth Ecumenical Council (also called the Second Council of Constantinople), in A.D. 553. The Anathema stated "If anyone asserts the fabulous pre-existence of souls, and shall assert the monstrous restoration which follows from it: let him be anathema."

This was followed by persecution, torture and death of all who refused to surrender their convictions. Despite this there was strong resistance by Cathars and other groups, but by the thirteenth century, the concept of re-incarnation was largely extinguished in the West. It was retained however by mystical groups such as the alchemists and the Rosicrucians who ensured the belief was carried forward to modem times.

There is evidence that certain biblical texts supportive of re-incarnation were deleted from early versions of the bible. The Gnostic gospel *Pistis Sophia* quotes Jesus as saying that:

"Souls are poured from one into another of different bodies of the world."[17]

Also, in the apocryphal "*Wisdom of Solomon*":

"As a child, I was born to excellence, and a noble soul fell to my lot: or rather I myself was noble, and I entered into an unblemished body." (8. 19-20)

From the bible itself:

1. "Jesus answered and said unto him, Verily, verily, I say unto thee, Except a man be born again, he cannot see the kingdom of God". John 3:3 (KJV)

2. "Marvel not that I said unto thee, Ye must be born again". John 3:7 (KJV)

3. "At that time Herod the tetrarch heard of the fame of Jesus, and said unto his servants this is John the Baptist; he is risen from the dead; and therefore mighty works do shew forth themselves in him. Matthew 14 (KJV) [18]

It is surprising that despite the Roman Catholic church declaring an "anathema" against the doctrine of reincarnation in AD 553 , (as mentioned above) and executing any found to hold such views e.g. the Cathars; that these passages above from the bible (and others) were overlooked and remain to this day.

Also from the Muslim's "Koran" (Koran 2.28):

"How can you make denial of Allah, who made you live again when you died, will make you dead again, and then alive again until you finally return to him"

The above are only a few references from The Bible, Koran, and other religious texts including the "Apocrypha". Others can be readily found on the internet. We have covered above the possible reasons and logic behind a belief in reincarnation. It is therefore only reasonable that we should look now at possible reasons why many may have difficulty believing in reincarnation.

5.4 DIFFICULTIES IN BELIEF OF REINCARNATION

Perhaps the main difficulty in reincarnational belief by the large number of practising Christians throughout the world today, is the lack of support for reincarnation by the priests and ministers of all Christian religions such as Catholic, Anglican, Methodist, Baptist and Presbyterian etc. - despite the reincarnation texts mentioned above in the Bible. Given the repression, terror, torture and death handed out to adherents by the Roman Catholic Church in past years, this is hardly surprising. The concept of reincarnation where ultimately everyone gains perfection by their own actions over multiple lives - without the intercession of priests demanding payment of indulgences for release from sins - obviously had little attraction for the ministry of early Christian churches. It is also hardly surprising in today's world, that even protestant ministers would break ranks to overturn centuries of religious dogma up until today, to highlight to their flock the many passages within the bible supporting reincarnation belief.

5.4.1 Comment

Despite this though, today belief in reincarnation is growing very rapidly amongst all predominately Christian nations. This is doubtless largely due to the advent in recent years of large numbers of television programmes and books which provide observational evidence which continually supports reincarnation, such as case studies of NDE's (near death experiences), the television series "I Survived: *Beyond and Back*" and a number of television series involving mediums channelling supposedly dead relatives (e.g. John Edward, James van Praagh) etc.), covered in more detail in Section 3. Also it is becoming increasingly and surprisingly common today for people when a loved one dies to speak as if their soul still exists, by making such statements as *"Ted has now gone to a far better place"*. Perhaps because people are becoming better educated and informed, it seems illogical for all life's achievements, growth and wisdom to vanish at death.

Another likely main reason for doubting reincarnation, is the perception that such beliefs are too fanciful to be credible. Particularly with the reincarnation belief of the death experience, where immediately after death it is said that one first passes through what is described as a tunnel and continues on towards an incredibly strong light. Soon after, one meets welcoming "guides/teachers" and relatives or friends who long since have passed over. Later a personal life review is conducted by advanced entities accompanied by one's guide.

Also in this "in between-lives environment", 'thought' is considered to not only allow one to travel instantly to another location, but to create virtually anything instantly by mind alone including a dwelling, furnishing, etc. to suit one's choice.

It is certainly not surprising that on first encountering these concepts, that credulity is stretched to the limits. In fact it could be said that this not only has all the hall marks of a fairy story, but could most likely be regarded as unsophisticated and medieval rubbish, suggestive of an idea dreamed up as wish fulfilment to avoid confronting the inevitability of death.

The catch concerning disbelief of any these above reincarnation beliefs is that they **match exactly** the observational evidence of thousands of cases of NDE's (near death experiences) plus accounts of post death experiences related by mediums and professional regression hypnotists over many years (as will be covered in detail in Section 3). It is therefore difficult to refute this overwhelming statistical correlation, particularly when there are many cases cited where (for example), the person hypnotically regressed **had no previous knowledge of reincarnation beliefs** yet still described the above same death experience repeated at the conclusion of their many previous lives. Just because an account of some experience may appear fanciful, does not always mean that it is false - as with my earlier example in Chapter 1 of the once mainstream belief in a flat earth, which vanished overnight after circumnavigation of the globe. Who would have thought we could live upside down on a globe hanging in space whirling around a hot gaseous mass (the sun) at approximately 67,000 mph! It is also not often realised that the probability of a reality of many lives is exactly the same as the probability of one life!

It should also be recognised from the Chapter 3, that the reincarnational concept mentioned above - that while in-between-lives, thought - creates one's reality instantly. This aligns with a fully quantum non-physical dimension - unlike ours, where consciousness creates reality but only somewhat feebly, rather than instantaneously. Also, the concept mentioned above of travelling in a tunnel immediately after death is considered by quantum physicist and research chemist, William Bray to be a very good description of what one would likely see in travelling through a "traversable wormhole" to another location in the universe, or between dimensions.[19]

One of the remaining major reasons for difficulty in acceptance of reincarnation beliefs, is no doubt the strong atheistic beliefs held by many, who instead believe that everything occurs by chance. There is also many who believe in a form of creator/God (or God of nature), but in this case a God who does not choose to provide any form of afterlife whatsoever. In other words, "When you are dead, you are dead – permanently".

As somewhat exhaustingly dealt with in Chapter 1, the probability of the universe appearing by chance or life itself, is so statistically improbable that it is difficult to think that chance occurrence of our existence could ever be considered as a possibility. However to be fair to those who hold the atheistic view that we do not survive death; it certainly **appears** to be supported by observational evidence - as everyone we have ever met eventually dies, seemingly never to return. It also is a simple concept - which many might falsely consider makes it more likely to be valid (i.e. conforming to Occam's razor) - as compared with complex reincarnation concepts.

We are not dealing here though, with testing the validity for a specific scientific theory, but rather an all-encompassing reason for our existence together with whether an afterlife is likely, and what this is like. If our existence cannot be caused by chance then it must inevitably be attributable to a creator/God - who would be expected obviously to have justification and a plan for our creation. Reasonably too we would expect such a plan to be somewhat complex.

Also, if possible we would surely wish longevity for any of our own creations in art, literature, our work achievements, our breakthroughs in medicine and science, etc., but particularly our **human creations** - our own children, grandchildren, etc. Likewise we would expect a creator/God to wish and choose a continuance of life for all his created life forms. Therefore, it is difficult to believe that He would wish to quickly dispense with us, His creation, after a single lifetime (as thought by those who believe in a God of nature).

Instead, we surely would predict a creator/God to provide us with an interesting, brilliant, logical and coherent life plan. This would be a plan that allows us continual enrichment and maximising our opportunities for growth and experience over a multiplicities of lifetimes - which is exactly what is offered by reincarnation.

Having covered both reasons for and against belief in reincarnation; to attain logical consistency and credibility, we now need to examine whether there are possible reasons and purpose for a creator/God to create the universe, life itself and reincarnation cycles.

5.5 REASONS FOR A CREATOR/GOD'S CREATION, PARTICULARLY REINCARNATION

Almost by definition, our expectations of an infinitely intelligent creator/God's reasons and a plan for our very existence, would be very high indeed. Not only should the plan be logical and make perfect sense, but optimal for us by meeting both His and our visualisation of an ideal shared immortal life. If reincarnation is to be taken seriously as a fundamental truth, we would also expect that immortality, rebirth and multiple lives would be included in His plan.

Obviously any viewpoints in this area can only be speculative, as it is impossible to know the mind of a creator/God. For a possible source of information on His plan though, one might wish to look for written texts of ancient wisdom and revelationary or inspirational knowledge that may have been handed down as records of "truths" by mystics, holy men and religious leaders. Also one would hope that research in this area might find a commonality amongst such records in terms of a creator/God's purpose for us all. Fortunately there are such written records of strong esoteric traditions of reasons and purpose of a creator/God's plan, worthy of discussion.

Reincarnational beliefs themselves have a very long and distant history dating back to the Iron Age (around 1200 BCE). Discussion of the subject appears in the philosophical traditions of India (including the Indus Valley) and Greece (including Asia Minor) from about the 6th century BCE. Also during the Iron Age, the Greek Pre-Socratics discussed reincarnation. The Celtic Druids are also reported to have taught a doctrine of reincarnation.[19]

Key aspects and a useful summary of all religious beliefs and esoteric traditions are encapsulated in a book written in 1945 by one of the pre-eminent intellectuals of his time, an English writer, Aldous Huxley. He called his book "The Perennial Philosophy". As stated in the original cover text, his book is specifically intended to cover **commonality** amongst *"all theologies by assembling passages from the writings of those saints and prophets who have approached a direct spiritual knowledge of the Divine. Mr. Huxley quotes from the Chinese Taoist philosophers, from followers of Buddha and Mohammed, from the Brahmin scriptures and from Christian mystics ranging from St John of the Cross to William Law"*

Physicist Erwin Schrödinger (whom we met in Chapter 2), who developed the famous equation covering the collapse of the quantum wave function), has this to say about Huxley's book:

> "You are struck (within the book) by the **miraculous agreement** between humans of different race, different religion, knowing nothing about each other's existence, separated by centuries and millennia, and by the greatest distances that there are on the globe.[21]

Astrophysicist Bernard Haisch in his recent books *The God Theory* and *The Purpose-Guided Universe: Believing In Einstein, Darwin, and God* and has gone much further by providing a helpful synopsis of the key points within Huxley's book including universal principals underlying the world's different religions, as follows :

"Three essentials tenets

1. The physical universe of matter is not the sole reality. Other non-physical realities exist which may contain other life-forms. Thus the material world is a shadow of a greater reality not directly perceivable by the physical senses.
2. Our human nature has both a material side subject to physical laws, birth, and death; as well as a non-material immortal spirit and soul, which is actually the more essential side because it is made of the same stuff as the ultimate source, which is God.

3. All humans possess a capacity to intuitively perceive the true multifaceted nature of ourselves and the greater reality.[22]

Universal Principles

There is a creator/God who has infinite potential and intelligence and whose ideas become the laws and physics of our universe and others, and whose purpose in so doing is the transformation of potential into experience. His ideas and abilities become His experience in the life of every sentient being".

What greater purpose could there be for each of us humans than that of creating God's experience. God experiences the richness of his potential through us because we are the incarnations of him in the physical realm."

As Haisch points out, it is one thing to theorise but another to practise; therefore it not only makes perfect sense, but there is no substitute for a creator/God than to experience all his potentiality and possibilities through us, and all other life:

"Our experience is his experience, because ultimately we are him; that is immortal spiritual beings, offsprings of him, temporarily living in the realm of matter."

The statement above indicates not only our immortality, but the critical concept unique to reincarnation - namely that immortality applies to **us all**, not just the belief common to most Christian religions that after a single lifetime only the worthy few go to heaven, with the rest going to the other place. It is also a common belief in Buddhism and many other religions, that we each contain a 'spark' of God.

Scientific evidence in previous Chapters supports the concept that consciousness creates reality. Therefore the only consciousness that existed before ""The Big Bang" i.e. the consciousness/mind of a creator/God, is the only way in which the aftermath - all physical reality, could have occurred. This surely must add to a belief in a creator/God, but also suggests that just as our children contain a spark of ourselves, in line with Buddhist belief, we must likely also contain a spark of a creator/God.

Esoteric wisdom also contains the central concept of the idea of the physical world as, "**a great thought**" - also stated by an early leader of modern astrophysics, Sir James Jeans, as long ago as the 1930's:

"The concepts which now prove to be fundamental to our understanding of nature, seem to my mind to be structures of pure thought ..... The universe begins to look more like a great thought than like a great machine."

Theologian, John Haught suggests that, as one would expect, a creator/God; rather than a coercively directive power or an annihilating presence, voluntarily relinquishes control to its creatures so that new and autonomous things may arise. This provision of free will enhances creation by "bringing forth novelty by allowing the unplanned and the unscripted".

We note that all life forms doubtless have free will in terms of their ability to choose between any opportunities for action or thought at each and every moment. However, the unpredictability of quantum physics itself (as covered in Chapter 2), destroys any belief in a solely deterministic universe much loved by materialist physicists. It also seems to be the cause in allowing free will to participate in our continuous process of creating our own reality, by our unconscious choosing between probabilistic alternative physical realities.

To complete Bernard Haisch's summary of esoteric wisdom, a core element of "The Perennial Philosophy" is that:

> **"Humans have a dualistic nature - a material body and a non-material consciousness. . . Our physical world is a kind of school, created for development and evolution of spiritual beings. Through this process, you rise to ever-higher levels of moral development and wisdom. Through a series of material incarnations you ultimately attain perfection and are united with the creator of all. Thus, the One who became many, is becoming one again."** [23]

Noteworthy, the phrase "**series of material incarnations**" above, underlines that the reincarnation concepts of multiple rebirths and immortality are a fundamental part of esoteric wisdom.

Finally:

> "All individuals remember their source, and now dream of All That Is, as It once dreamed of them. And they yearn toward that immense source... and yearn to give it actuality through their own creations."
>
> Seth [24]

5.5.1 Comment

In reading "*The Perennial Philosophy*" by Aldous Huxley for myself, I feel that Bernard Haisch's "Universal Principles" highlighted above are an excellent and inevitable synopsis of Huxley's work. I personally find they certainly meet my expectations of a coherent, sensible and believable creator/ God's purpose and plan. I note that - as covered in **"Religious Re-incarnational Views"** above, some reincarnation elements aligning with these principles are also contained within the Christian Bible, the Koran, and texts from many other religions freely available today. In other words, when one looks for a commonality of religious views in available religious texts both in today's world and in ancient texts, the same result occurs. This is that the outcome of collectively joining all of them together, inevitably (and perhaps significantly) results in creating a synopsis of core reincarnation beliefs. **Also in contrast, no religion or religious belief on its own can make the same claim of commonality amongst many.**

It will be found that the inevitability of encountering evidence for the same commonality of reincarnational beliefs will also be universally evident in the next Section of this book - Section 3, which covers further scientific evidence for reincarnation under specific areas such as telepathy, direct recall of previous lives by children, regressive hypnosis, near death experiences, etc. However, rather than the inevitable relevationary/inspirational nature of information contained in earlier paragraphs within this Chapter; as with previous Chapters, **scientific experimental and observational evidence** will again be presented as the norm in the next Chapter and for remainder of this Chapter and book.

5.6 CLOSING CHAPTER COMMENTS

It is acknowledged that the provision in this Chapter of suggested reasons for re-incarnation has rapidly moved away from the high quality of scientific evidence submitted in previous Chapters. However it must be accepted (as covered in Chapter 2) that since 'inspiration' alone (as claimed by scientists in many instants in the past), has led to many scientific breakthroughs, **the ability of a number of ancient mystics to attain valid fundamental truths in a trance state should not be dismissed.** This is exemplified particularly in the case with the "Cayce" and "Seth" accounts described above concerning channelled information obtained while in a trance state. In the case of "Cayce", it led to countless verifiable cures of patients, yet impossible to explain with Cayce's ignorance of medical matters. In the case of "Seth", similarly credible information on a vast array of subjects was received and thought scientifically far beyond the capacity of the medium Jane Roberts to even comprehend. Both, on some occasions, have also provided a predictive capability (as covered earlier), which later has been verified as correct.

Further, accuracy of information is fundamental, accepted, and provable in the case of another trance state - remote viewing (used extensively in WW2 successfully for espionage – as mentioned in Chapter 4), but also in cases involving hypnotic regression - where it is essential for the professional hypnotherapist to locate the exact cause and instance of trauma to effect a cure. Recent experiments independently replicated and expanded have also scientifically validated that information provided by professional mediums supposedly from discarnates, has been found to be statistically extremely accurate, often as accurate as 100%.

These claims are critical to support belief in an afterlife and reincarnation and are covered in detail in the subsequent Section 3 Chapters which follow. A few individual case studies are provided as examples of the wealth of observational evidence readily available to support the experimental evidence.

Chapter Five Annex 1

"Seth's" Introduction to Jane Roberts

(Ref: *The Seth Material*, Page 304, by Jane Roberts (Appendix, Session 452, Dec 2, 1968 - unedited))

"Now: Children build houses of cards and knock them down. You do not worry about the child's development, for you realise that he will learn better.

You may smile at the child's utter sense of desolation until he finally connects the motion of his own hand with the destruction of the paper cardboard house that has now gone, and in his own eyes, gone beyond repair.

Now mankind builds civilisations. He has gone beyond the child's game. The toys are real, and yet basically the analogy holds. I am not condoning those violences that occur. The fact is they can never be condoned, and yet they must be understood for what they are: man, learning through his own errors. He also learns by his own successes, and there are times when he holds his hand, moments of deliberation, periods of creativity. Identities take many roles in many lives.

There are periods, cycles if you prefer, through which identities live and learn again within your system. To some extent they are taught by others - practice teaches if you prefer.

The race of man is far more than the physical race, however. You see him in but one stage of development. When an individual leaves your system, it is for other systems. He has learned his ABCs, but that is all. There are exceptions - identities who choose to return and teach. They are not in the same league, so to speak, as those whose reincarnation cycles are not complete. They may return, even enduring violence, as a man set up a school amid a jungle of savages.

Yet with all of this, there are advances made within your system itself. A nuclear weapon in the hands of the inhabitants of Middle - Age Europe would have been used almost immediately, and with nary a qualm, to wipe out all but Christendom. Christendom may well have perished along with the rest of the world, but this possibility would not have been considered, so narrow and evilly self-righteous were the governing powers at the time.

In those days neither did a sane, reasonable man give thought to sharing his wealth, or even consider the plight of the poorer classes. Not only was charity not given, its practical nature was not even considered. The archaic concept of God (at that time) nicely covered such matters. The poor were obviously sinful. Poverty was their penance, and it was considered a sacrilege to try to help those whom God had cursed. Animals were tortured in sport. Compassion for living things in males was considered a weakness to be plucked out. Women were scarcely thought of as human, except in select circles.

The progression through the centuries would be far more noticeable if you knew all the facts. There is one aspect here that I have not previously mentioned: Man was not able to play with the more dangerous toys until certain evidence was given that he had gained some control. This does not mean that he would not have destroyed the world he knew. It simply meant that such destruction was not inevitable. You do not give a child a loaded gun if you are certain he is going to shoot himself or his neighbor.

Now: the weapons and destruction are the obvious things that you see. The counterparts are not so evident, and yet it is the counterparts that are important: the self-discipline learned, the control, the compassion that finally is aroused, and the final and last lesson learned - the positive desire for creativity and love over destruction and hatred. When this is learned, the reincarnation cycle is finished."

From the book *Seth Speaks* - Page 201, by Jane Roberts,

"Some individuals are being born at this time simply to help you understand. They are forcing the issue, and forcing the crisis, for you still have time to change your ways. You are working on two main problems, but both involve the sacredness of the individual, and the individual's relationship with others and with **all** physically oriented consciousness.

The problem with war will sooner or later teach you that when you kill another man, basically you will end up killing yourself. The over-population problem will teach you that if you do not have a loving concern for the environment in which you dwell, it will no longer sustain you - you will not be worthy of it. You will not be destroying the planet, you see. You will not be destroying the birds or the flowers, or the grain or the animals. You are not worthy of them and they will be destroying you.

You have set up the problem for yourselves within the framework of your reference. You will not understand your part in the framework of nature until you actually see yourselves in danger of tearing it apart. You will not destroy consciousness. You will not destroy consciousness of even one leaf, but in your context, if the problem were not solved, these would fade from your experience.

The crisis is a kind of therapy, however. It is a teaching method that you have set up for yourselves because you need it. And you need it **now,** before your race embarks upon journeys to other physical realities. You must learn your lessons now in your own backyard before you travel to other worlds. So you have brought this upon yourself for that purpose and you will learn."

Chapter Five Annex 2

A Selection of Seth Quotes

GENERAL

I have been sent to help you, and others have been sent through the centuries of your time, for as you develop you form new dimensions, and you will help others.

Using your free will, you have made physical reality into something quite different than what was intended. You have allowed the ego to become overly developed and specialized. You were here to work out problems and challenges, but you were always to be aware of your own inner reality, and of your non-physical existence. To a large extent you have lost contact with this. You have focused so strongly upon physical reality that it become the only reality that you know.

You are like children with a game, and you think that the game is played by everyone. Physical life is not the rule. Identity and consciousness existed long before your earth was formed. You suppose that any personality must appear in physical terms. Consciousness is the force behind matter, and it forms many other realities besides the physical one. It is, again, your own viewpoint that is presently so limited that it seems to you that physical reality is the rule and mode of existence.

The human race is a stage through which various forms of consciousness travel... Yours is a training system for emerging consciousness. Before you can be allowed into systems of reality that are more extensive and open, you must first learn to handle energy and see through physical materialisation, the concrete result of thought and emotion.

When you leave the physical system after reincarnations, you have learned the lesson and you are literally no longer a member of the human race, for you elect to leave it. Only the conscious self dwells within it in any case, and other portions of your identity dwell simultaneously within other training systems. In more advanced systems, thoughts and emotions are automatically and immediately translated into action, into whatever approximation of matter there exists. Therefore, the lessons must be taught and learned well.

It is wrong to curse a flower and wrong to curse a man. It is wrong not to hold any man in honour, and it is wrong to ridicule any man. You must honour yourselves and see within yourselves the spirit of eternal validity. You must honour all other individuals, because within each is the spark of this validity. When you curse another, you curse yourselves, and the curse returns to you. When you are violent, the violence returns.

There is no man who hates but that hatred is reflected outward and made physical, and there is no man who loves but that love is reflected outward and made physical.

(The above are Seth quotes taken from "Experiences, Insights, and Stories from Jane Roberts's original ESP class participants": ,http://www.spiritual-endeavors.org/seth/Andy.htm)

Within the selves that you know is the prime identity. The whole inner self. This whole self has seen many lives. It has adopted many personalities. It is an energy essence personality.

Seth Speaks, *Page 231*

IMMORTALITY

You are as dead now as you will ever be.

Seth Speaks, *Page 472,*

You have lived before and will live again, and when you are done with physical existence, you will still live.

The Seth Material, *Page 2*

TRANCE

A trance state is merely a condition of increased concentration. It is harmless and can be most beneficial …… It is a state where your concentration is focused freely inward, in which you experience time as it actually exists.

The Coming of Seth, *Page 98*

TELEPATHY AND CLAIRVOYANCE

Telepathy operates constantly…..You must agree the subconscious is telepathic and clairvoyant….

Seth Speaks, *Page 178. Page 231.*

(Clairvoyance) is a natural method of protecting the individual through an inner knowledge of events. Without constant clairvoyance on the part of every man and woman, existence on your plane would involve such inner psychological insecurity that it would be completely unbearable. Individuals are always warned of disasters, so that the organism can prepare itself ahead of time. As telepathy operates continuously at a subconscious level as a basis for all communication, so clairvoyance operates continually so that the physical organism can prepare itself to meet its challenges.

The Coming of Seth. *Page 71*

CONSCIOUSNESS

All atoms and molecules have a condensed consciousness; so do even smaller particles. The atoms and molecules that make up all physical matter and cells are basically bound by your time. They act within the framework of your time, but the condensed knowledge that they contain contains within it its own peculiar and unique consciousness, that is not bound by physical laws.

When the physical origin of your universe is finally discovered, your scientists will be no better off than they are now. They will be up against the problem that they have avoided for so long, that of origin behind origin. The physical universe and everything in it is the result of consciousness. It did not evolve consciousness. To the contrary, consciousness not only created the physical universe but continues to do so.

Your physical reality is created in perfect replica of your inner desires and thoughts……. We form our reality.

Seth Speaks, Page 29

You are made basically of the same ingredients of a chair, a stone, a head of lettuce, a bird. In a gigantic cooperative endeavour, all consciousness joins together to make the forms that you perceive.

Seth Speaks, Page 47

Your environment is not simply the world about you, as you know it, but also consists of past life environments upon which you are not now focussing. You real environment is composed of your thoughts and emotions, for from these you form not only this reality, but each reality in which you take part. Your real environment is innocent of space and time as you know them. In your real environment, you have no need for words, for communication is instantaneous. In your real environment you form the physical world that you know.

Seth Speaks, Page 48

As the outer ego manipulates within the physical environment, so the inner ego or self organises and manipulates with an inner reality The inner ego creates that physical reality with which the outer ego then deals.

Seth Speaks, Page 328

THE THEORY OF EVOLUTION

(Charles Darwin) spent his last years proving it, and yet it has no real validity. It has validity within very limited perspectives only; for consciousness does, indeed, evolve form. Form does not evolve consciousness. All consciousness does, indeed, exist at once, and therefore did not evolve in those terms…….. It is more the other way around in that evolved consciousness forms itself into different patterns and rains down upon reality.

….. At the risk of repeating myself, let me state that time as you know it does not exist basically, and that all creations are simultaneous.… Some life forms are being developed in what you think of as present time. They will not appear physically until you reach your future time.

Seth Speaks, Page 350, 351

SECTION THREE

CHAPTER SIX

ESP, "Remote viewing" and Non Ordinary States of Consciousness

(Telepathy, clairvoyance, OOB and NDE states)

"The Paranormal - is normal" - *author*

In this first Chapter of Section 3, we cover scientific evidence associated with case studies for a number of areas, currently regarded as paranormal. Care has been taken to choose cases which have very strong observational and/or experimental scientific evidence, but which are also considered particularly important. The reasons why each particular phenomena is considered important, is given early in the text just prior to their presentation.

6.1   TELEPATHY

Importance to Reincarnational belief: Strong scientific evidence for the existence of telepathy is necessary, as without a form of telepathy, communication between entities in a non-physical state obviously would not be possible i.e. an afterlife. The scientific explanation for telepathy is of course the PCAR communication system.

6.1.1   History

There is evidence to suggest that telepathy and also clairvoyance may have been widespread in so-called primitive cultures. There are many cited cases where Shamans using various techniques to gain an altered state of consciousness (such as fasting, chanting, dancing and the use of psychedelic herbs), seem able to communicate telepathically. Whole tribes, in the case of Australian aborigines, are said to have had strong telepathic capabilities and have been reported to have had the ability to instantly determine death, birth or problems relating to the welfare of other distant members of their tribe. Some Australian aborigines are quoted as being able to detect underground water without even the aid of a dowsing rod. Another example, cited by Professor Hornell Hart, relate to a Zulu witch doctor, who accurately was able to describe exactly what was happening to eight Kaffirs who were on a hunting expedition two hundred miles away. Also Hart described a similar incident where a Commander R. Jukes Hughes, serving in the Transkei, received an accurate running commentary from local natives on a battle that was taking place three hundred miles away[1].

6.1.2 Evidence

Although there is fairly widespread acceptance among the public that telepathy occurs, this by no means includes the whole of the scientific community.

Serious scientific investigation into telepathy is generally accepted as first being carried out by Professor J.B. Rhine at the Duke University in the 1930's. Over many years Professor Rhine used university students for card and dice guessing experiments and applied statistical analysis to determine whether the results aligned with those which could be expected from pure chance. Results provided favorable evidence of telepathy - albeit a small but nevertheless statistically significant indication with most people tested. Critics have suggested explanations in terms of hidden sensory clues, machine bias, cheating by subjects and experimental error or incompetence. However, irrefutable results confirming transfer of information telepathically between people have been obtained in recent more sophisticated experiments, where rigorous experimental controls have been used with physicists and psychologists involved in designing the tests. Among them are tests carried out by Russell Targ and Harold Putoff of the Stanford Research Institute in the 1970's. These involved simply subjecting a sender to a series of regular light flashes and looking for responses in the electroencephalograph (EEG readings - 'brainwaves') of a receiver who was placed in an opaque, electrically shielded chamber some distance away. It was found that EEG readings for the sender, exhibited rhythmic patterns accompanying the flashes, and after a brief interval the same rhythmic patterns similarly appeared in the EEG of the receiver. More recently Jacobo Grinberg-Zylerbaum at the University of Mexico performed 50 similar experiments using flashes of light, sounds and electric shocks applied to a sender at random intervals. In 25% of cases, correlations were **consistently** observed in the EEG of the receiver. These experiments have been matched by hundreds of others in recent years, where identifiable and consistent electrical signals are found to occur in the brain of a receiver when the sender is provided with sensory stimulation, or attempts to communicate with the subject intentionally. The effects are found to be stronger if participants are closely related or emotionally linked, and particularly between twins.[2]

Experiments have also shown that if a person in one room is given an electric shock, it will register in polygraph readings taken of a person in another room[3].

Furthermore, amazingly if a sender reads a list of names, when a name known to a receiver is read, the blood volume of the test receiver's finger changes (as measured by a plethysmograph - a sensitive indicator of autonomic nervous system functioning) [4].

In Russia, experiments have found strong telepathic abilities amongst twins, the blind, persons with hearing difficulties, and young emotionally attached couples. In 65 percent of cases tested, mothers in a gynecological clinic in Moscow were found to show nervousness when their baby cried in a distant room out of earshot and the babies were found to cry when their mother experienced pain[5].

Interestingly, experiments have shown that it is extremely important for the receiver to be in a relaxed state, free of involuntary motion and distracting thought. With training this was found attainable, but otherwise this was normally difficult. Soviets have also claimed success in developing a coding system which can be used to send not only individual words but phrases and entire sentences with a recorded 70% accuracy involving transfer of 1,766 messages[6].

As Dean Radin, PhD points out in his book *The Conscious Universe*[7], results of recent experiments (in which he participated, in Scotland) and at a total of ten different laboratories throughout the world, using a consistent "Ganzfield Method"*, produced a meta-analysis hit rate of 37 percent. (As a useful comparison, this exceeds by a factor of ten times the well accepted experimental results showing aspirin to be effective in reducing the probability of a heart attack!). Sets of later replication experiments at the University of Scotland from 1993 through 1996 and all other tests at Universities in Holland, America, and Sweden produced an overall meta-analysis hit rate of 33.2 percent with odds against chance beyond a million billion to one!

These results are even more impressive when it is realized that with this "Ganzfield" method, **a specific and random target** is sent from the sender to the receiver comprising a video or picture. The outcome is therefore simply a "hit" or a "miss". (The target is randomly chosen by computer).

In 1995, the American Institutes for Research reviewed formerly classified government-sponsored psi research (primarily "remote viewing") for the CIA at the request of the **U.S. Congress**. Statistician Jessica Utts of the University of California, Davis, one of the two principal reviewers, concluded that:

"The statistical results of the studies examined are far beyond what is expected by chance. Arguments that these results could be due to methodological flaws

---

*   The Ganzield method, simply involves a very specific experimental procedure aimed at sensory deprivation to assist in eliminating distractions. While in a comfortable chair, receivers wear halved ping-pong balls worn over their eyes and headphones through which static noise is played.

in the experiments are soundly refuted. Effects of similar magnitude to those found in government-sponsored research . . . have been replicated at a number of laboratories across the world. Such consistency cannot be readily explained by claims of flaws or fraud.... it is recommended that future experiments focus on understanding how this phenomenon works, and on how to make it as useful as possible. There is little benefit to continuing experiments designed to offer proof."[8]

The results of the Ganzfield studies showed that we are fully justified in having a high confidence that all people do sometimes get telepathically small amounts of specific information from a distance without the use of ordinary senses.

This perhaps can account for cases of simultaneous culture development in history such as almost identical clay pot designs arising in the 5th and 6th centuries BC in Egypt, Persia, India and China. Simultaneous pyramid development in ancient Egypt and pre-columbian America. Also celebrated cases of simultaneous discoveries and inventions such the independent discovery of the calculus by both Newton and Leibniz, adaption to one's environment by Darwin and Wallace, and the concurrent invention of the telephone by Bell and Gray[9]

Another outcome of the Ganzfield studies, was that contrary to popular folklore, results indicated no star performers, but rather that telepathy was a widespread ability distributed throughout the population. No decline in effects as a result of distance was observable, despite many experiments where participants were thousands of miles apart, nor was there any effect when deliberate delay was introduced so that the receiver **had to pre-cognitively determine the target** before it was actually sent!

Primitive human cultures, together with animals seem to have stronger telepathic capabilities than ourselves. This raises the question as to whether our conscious awareness or normally well-developed cognitive reasoning ability may on most occasions block out the perhaps more direct or primitive perceptions provided by telepathy. There seems support for this by the Shamans' use of psychedelic herbs, and repetitive chanting, dancing etc. to subdue their conscious reasoning and so bring their subconscious mind (or alternatively more intuitive right brain) more to the fore. Such concepts have led to further Ganzfield type research using hypnosis to place suggestions aimed at achieving an enhanced psi - conductive state. The results of many experiments along these lines indicated there was statistically significant evidence to support the view that by bypassing conscious awareness, telepathy can be improved[10].

As mentioned in Chapter 5, our use of a highly developed language seems to have put us at a disadvantage with regards to telepathy, compared with other life-forms. Frederic William Henry Myers (1843 - 1901) was a founder of the Society for Psychical Research. In his book *Human Personality and its Survival of Bodily Death*[11] he considered that telepathy is stronger amongst primitive tribes and life-forms such as animals, insects etc. because they tend to use cognitive reasoning less than ourselves. He also even suggested with the publishing of his book, that telepathy seemed universally used amongst all life-forms and **may even transcend life itself**. This is of course the same conclusion we reached in Chapter 5. In our case though, due to the discovery of the science behind it - the PCAR system - which obviously would provide a non-verbal communication capability in an afterlife (as with all senses).

6.2   CLAIRVOYANCE

Clairvoyance is generally seen as quite different from telepathy since it is the *"faculty of seeing mentally what is happening or exists out of sight"*, whereas telepathy is *"communication from one mind to another at a distance ..."* (the Concise Oxford Dictionary).

It will therefore be seen that the key criteria with telepathy is that two minds are always involved, whereas clairvoyance requires only the single mind of the recipient to "see" what is happening elsewhere. The two South African instances quoted above concerning a Zulu witch doctor remotely reporting on his "viewing" of a hunting expedition and the instance where Transkei natives reported on a battle taking place 300 miles away, are good examples of clairvoyance rather than just solely telepathy.

6.2.1   Importance of Clairvoyance to Reincarnational belief:

The importance is critical, as without sight (and senses i.e. perception), a reincarnation life would be impossible and there would be no point in writing this book. The background science though is clearly the PCAR communication system, which as covered in Chapter 3, caters for all perception/senses required in a reincarnational environment.

Examples of clairvoyance below, provides observational evidence that not just sight is associated with clairvoyance. It also embraces the concept of "remote viewing" - i.e. sight including senses, but also the ability to obtain **information** at a distance (see below).

Quantum properties we have encountered previously, can easily provide the background science, in that the PCAR system - linked to our quantum consciousness, obviously provides the communication system function. The key characteristic of the PCAR system, uniquely and unlike any classical physical communication system, is that it can on resonance, extract information from its focussed object. It is thought that in the majority of clairvoyance cases, information is obtained by frequency range matching and resonance with the target object via the zero point field. However, there is strong evidence (in the examples given below) that, in some cases and if desired, one's consciousness can actually travel to the distant site to gain information. This then becomes an example of an OOB state as well as clairvoyance. As will be seen below, in some instances there will also be seen cases of precognition, where information is gained if desired from a probable future, as explained in the Annex, Time and Space section of Chapter 4. (Note: the science background to OOB states will be discussed under OOB states below)

6.2.2 History

Anecdotal cases involving clairvoyance are common, with the most celebrated cases attributable to Emmanual Swedenberg. He was born in 1688, the son of a Lutheran Bishop, a mining specialist, geologist, astronomer and a gifted tutor of mathematics. During his childhood he described having a number of visions and claimed daily rapport with spirits. This would not have singled him out particularly if it were not for hundreds of others receiving through him, convincing messages from their dead relatives. Many attesting to being able to see the ghosts themselves while he participated in his daily chats. Two notable instances of clairvoyance in his lifetime were his accurate and detailed commentary of the great fire in Stockholm in 1759 from 200 miles away, (verified by eyewitnesses some days later) and his similarly accurate remote description of the assassination of Tsar Peter III of Russia[12].

6.2.3 Evidence

There has been intensive laboratory research in recent years into clairvoyance, because of its obvious military applications i.e. the desire to remotely view what an enemy is doing. This has meant that clairvoyance type research called "remote viewing" particularly by the military has been particularly well funded. Research has not only covered verification of the phenomenon and assessments of accuracy using different participants, but also techniques aimed at improving performance.

The best-known remote-viewing research in modern times began in the early 1970's, when various U.S. government agencies initiated a program at Stanford Research Institute. Physicist Harold Puthoff founded the SRI program. He was joined soon after by physicist Russell Targ, and a few years later by another physicist, Edwin May. In 1990, the entire program moved to a think tank called Science Applications International Corporation (SAIC), a major defence contractor. That program finally wound down in 1994, after **twenty-four years** of support and expenditure of about $20 million in funding from U.S. government agencies such as the CIA, the Defence Intelligence Agency, the Army, the Navy, and NASA.

In the initial remote viewing research SRI programme, a system of rank-order judging was used which involved the following:

Five targets were assigned to each experiment, with four used as decoys, and one the real target, selected randomly. A "receiver" experimenter, first remote-viewed a randomly selected target (usually a geographic site such as a satellite earth station, thousands of miles away). A judge then ranked the receiver's response (a sketch and written paragraph) against photographs or videos of the five possible targets using a system, where a rank of 1 meant that the possible target matched the response most closely, and a rank of 5 meant that it matched it the least.

Progressively tighter methods were implemented over the years prompted by criticisms and suggestions which followed publication of results in 'Nature' and the 'Proceedings of the IEEE'.

Independent analysis of the results took place in 1988 by Edwin May and his colleagues of all such psi experiments conducted at SRI over the sixteen years from 1973. The analysis involved 154 different experiments, consisting of 26,000 separate trials of which just over 1000 trials were remote viewing tests. The analysis confirmed that the overall results of all these remote viewing experiments provided a hit rate of in excess of 54% with odds against chance of more than a billion, billion to one!

These experiments were replicated in 1978 by further trials performed by the Princeton Engineering Anomalies Research (PEAR) Laboratory at Princeton University. Their chosen method however differed from the rank-order method used by SRI/SAIC, e.g. in this case the judge visited the actual site in the field after remote viewing had taken place to aid his assessment. Despite the differences, qualitatively, the results were found to be essentially the same as those reported by the SRI/SAIC program.

As mentioned previously, in 1995, **the USA Congress** commissioned a review of the CIA sponsored psi experiments led by Dr Jessica Utts, a statistics professor at the University of California. This review also included remote-viewing research at SRI but additionally some further six government-sponsored remote-viewing experiments were conducted by the Science Applications International Corporation (SAIC). These experiments were rigorously controlled and overseen by a distinguished committee of experts from a variety of scientific disciplines. The committee included a Nobel laureate physicist, internationally known experts in statistics, psychology, neuroscience, and astronomy, and a retired U. S. Army major general who was also a physician.

These remote viewing experiments were **not** conducted as "proof-oriented" studies, since this had been accomplished by the earlier SRI experiments, but rather at learning more about how remote-viewing could be enhanced.

Their main findings were that about one percent of tested volunteers had exceptional ability, but neither practice nor training appeared to improve performance. Also, that neither distance nor electromagnetic shielding had any effect whatsoever on results[13]

Adding to this, SRI experiments had also found earlier, that remote viewing was able to provide **detail concerning a scene which may simply not be observable to an experimenter at the actual location**. For example, an experimenter at the remote location standing in front of a house, might not see a tree *behind* the house, which was blocked from his view. But the receiver might well report it, apparently by vision which has a 360 degree 3D capability. This suggests that clairvoyance/remote viewing works by using a different process to telepathy by suggesting that a portion of conscious actually travels to the site. This is in fact supported by different figures between them derived for accuracy and methods found successful for improving performance[14].

As mentioned earlier, SRI experiments at Menlo Park, California had previously shown that remote-viewing /clairvoyance, (as with telepathy) is completely independent of time. By this it was meant that incredibly test subjects were found able to describe locations experimenters would be visiting in the **future**, *before* the locations had even been decided. To relate a typical experiment of this type - Hella Hammid, a particularly talented remote viewer was asked to describe the location where Puthoff (as the judge), would later visit for confirmation as part of the experiment. She spoke of a black iron triangle bigger than a man, and a persistent rhythmic squeaking sound. Later, after a random number generator was used to choose the target from ten others, Puthoff visited the target site and found a lone child's swing with a black triangle structure. When he sat in the swing, it squeaked rhythmically as it swung back and forth.

In case it is thought these are spurious results, on the contrary, Puthoff and Targ's precognitive remote-viewing findings have been duplicated by numerous laboratories around the world, including Jahn and Dunne's research facility at Princeton University. In 334 formal trials Jahn and Dunne found that volunteers achieved an accurate precognitive hit rate as high as **62 percent**.[15]

Apart from laboratory results, there are countless examples of remote viewing being used in the field. Reports of successful instances of pre-World War II remote viewing are legion. One such case was in 1925 in an action against the Hungarian republic when Czechoslovak soldiers stationed at Prandoff were engaged in the battle over Levice, Dekyse, and Almase. A private, Karel Hejbalik, formed a remote viewing intelligence unit from two "sensitives" and used these to spy on the enemy. Amazingly, using techniques later re-discovered by the US Army, their remote viewing abilities were strengthened by his first hypnotising them and then by using one soldier as a control to check out the information obtained by the other.

There are reports on how remote viewing was used during the uprising in India between the two wars. The rebels were reportedly constantly able to find out the positions of the British Army, much to their amazement. Also the well-known Polish clairvoyant, Engineer Stefan Ossowiecki, is known to have aided scores of people during the war in Poland, the siege of Warsaw and the Nazi occupation, by locating missing persons and following the activities of army officers during battles. He reportedly even located specific individuals buried deep in mass graves[16].

There are many excellent accounts of remote viewing used intensively for intelligence gathering in World War II, among them the following books: Joseph Moneagle – *Mind Trek: Exploring consciousness, Time, and Space Through Remote Viewing*, and David Moorehouse – *Psychic Warrior, Inside the CIA's Stargate Program*".

Imagine a typical day during the last world war where a sergeant kisses his wife and family goodbye after breakfast, then drives to a Nissan hut in a forested area in Virginia to start work for the day. In this instance "work" involves, as on countless previous days, simply lying on a bed in a completely relaxed state with headphones on. Alongside him is another staff member (a monitor) sitting in a chair with a note pad at the ready. Others in the same Nissan hut and elsewhere, are doing the same. They are all involved in "remote viewing" of targets assigned to them.

A typical case was when a talented US army remote viewer, Joe Moneagle, was asked to check out a target comprising an unusual building in Northern USSR. He found inside the building, was housed the largest submarine in the world - which was later found to be the first of the new Typhoon class of Russian submarines. Remote viewing could provide any desired level of detail. For example he was able to describe details including how torpedo tubes were mounted and could even gain access to papers etc. within filing cabinets and drawers. For this and other remote viewing work for the US Army, he later received the Legion of Merit award for excellence in intelligence with a citation calling his data "critical and crucial for the highest echelons of military and government"[17].

Another more recent instance cited by David Moorhouse was where, as a Major in the US Army, he obtained details about the Lockerbie disaster. These included descriptions of the terrorists, their names, sketches of houses they lived in, and meeting places together with details of the bomb which had been concealed in a tape recorder and radio[18].

It is noteworthy that in this case, remote viewing took place **after** the event. Indicating that not only can remote viewing provide great detail remotely from the object, but can operate on past events (and future) equally well as existing events. We immediately would recognise this as exhibiting the consciousness characteristics of quantum independence from time and space, as covered in previous Chapters.

Further research found that efficiency was vastly improved by using all possible techniques to distance the conscious mind as much as possible from the remote viewing activity itself and give free reign to the subconscious. Among them, the use of an assistance "monitor" (mentioned above) soon became routine in every case. The monitor's role was to direct, guide the remote viewer and to take notes and draw diagrams to record information as necessary. The use of a monitor was found to be critical in relieving the remote viewer's attention from being distracted. Use of detailed target information was soon scrapped, and initially replaced with just geographical co-ordinates. Surprisingly limiting information in this way, had no effect whatsoever on the remote viewer being able to instantly identify the target. This led to a universal approach now used where even the use of geographic co-ordinates has been abandoned. Instead, all the remote viewer is given, is a randomly generated four-digit number assigned to the target. This has no correlation with geographic co-ordinates whatsoever, but, miraculously, the subconscious always instantly seems to know the desired target! Protocols currently used are complex but well described in Dr Courtenay Brown's book, *Cosmic Voyage*[19].

Since the use and details of remote viewing for espionage still remains as classified information by all countries' defence forces, it is of little surprise that its use is not widely known nor reported greatly by the news media. However, despite this, in 1995, President Carter revealed publicly that the CIA used psi during his presidency. He was particularly impressed when "distant viewing" techniques located a military plane carrying secret technology that had crashed in Zaire[19]. Also in 1995, a Congressional report on the SRI/Princeton review mentioned above, was released as part of a CIA housecleaning effort. It provided details of the more than 20 year history of US Government's top secret experimentation with psychic and paranormal phenomena. In 1995, David Moorhouse, the US Army Major (mentioned above in association with the Lockerbie disaster) decided to leave the military remote viewing program and go public. Despite the prospect of facing a court martial, dishonourable discharge from the military and threat of CIA surveillance of himself and his family, he revealed the story of his espionage in his book, *Psychic Warrior - Inside the CIA's Stargate Program*.

The CIA "officially" abandoned remote viewing operations in 1996 as a sequel to the Oliver North scandal when the Pentagon began reviewing operations that could be potentially embarrassing to the US Government. One of the concerns which had dogged issues of funding in the past, regardless of the success of all remote viewing during World War II, was called the "**giggle" factor**. This was simply the fact that many people such as US Senators who had little education, interest and belief in this area (despite previous Congressional investigations overwhelmingly scientifically finding it valid), would not support its continuation. It is thought that even those who supported it, might have felt the public were likely to respond to any further post war funding with scepticism, incredulity and mirth. Regardless though, military programmes still continued albeit using private industry companies, many of which were established by a number of early military remote viewers who continued working for the intelligence community and military through contractual arrangements.

As a result of practical experience in the field and scientific developments, accuracy and techniques used for the military changed markedly from the days of the laboratory experiments described above at the Stanford and Princeton Universities. Accuracy attainable today is claimed to be very high - up to 85%, and where accuracy is important, teams of remote viewers are allocated - each comprised of a remote viewer and monitor to view the same target.

Terms often used to describe some observed paranormal behaviour are confusing. This is evident from the above where "clairvoyance" has meanings of 'seeing afar', but also as we learned from psychic capabilities in Chapter 4, can have the characteristics of precognition (i.e. independence from time) - where information can be obtained from the past or the future. Additionally "dowsing" very much has characteristic of obtaining 'information from afar'. To add to the confusion, where "remote viewing" evidence suggests that consciousness in some form **actually travels to the remote site**; then reasonably as mentioned above, this must also be a case of clairvoyance involving an out-of-body situation (i.e. an OOB state.).

6.3   OOB STATES (OUT-OF-BODY OR OBE, OUT-OF–BODY EXPERIENCES)

Definition: is an experience that typically involves a sensation of floating outside one's body and, in some cases, perceiving one's physical *body* from a place outside one's body. –

Wikipedia

The term is generally applied to experiences in which an individual's conscious awareness appears to detach itself from the physical body **and travel** to some other location. A typical non-intended OOB experience, is said to be spontaneous and occurs often in association with sleep. It has also been reported to occur during meditation, anaesthesia, illness, and instances of traumatic pain. The sensation is widely reported as being pleasurable and often commences suddenly with the person sensing separation from the body, floating and then viewing one's physical body from above. Travelling to other locations while experiencing a sense of movement then occurs, just as if one were flying. This contrasts with remote viewing, where **instantaneous** arrival at the desired target is claimed - perhaps because in remote viewing cases a particular target is intended.

6.3.1   Importance to Reincarnational Belief:

Just as "clairvoyance" is considered critical for reincarnational belief, so is a capability for a discarnate to be able to move from place to place in a life-between-life environment. As will be found below, the science based **observational** evidence for this is exceptionally strong, even in classical physical reality. This, together with hypnotic regression examples given later in this book, tend to make arguments in favour of its validity as real, and very credible. With regard to science behind the phenomena; it seems the ability to achieve successful laboratory experiments to replicate the OOB phenomena is indisputable - as the phenomenon is clearly that described as "teleportation", and quantum teleportation of subatomic particles was recently achieved (May 2014) in milestone experiments.[20]

Obviously, it is one thing to transfer a few atoms to a specified place, and yet another to be able to explain how "intent" can transfer ones consciousness or part consciousness to a desired location progressively or instantaneously. However, the May 2014 experiments have demonstrated the scientific validity of teleportation as a possible quantum process which can explain at least the possible transport science. It would however seem conclusive that for consciousness to perceive, interact and return information from a distant object, that the PCAR system must inevitably be involved as well. Also, in Chapter 4's Annex, a possible explanation is given for how motion could readily take place in a fully or partial quantum reality.

There is much to learn about this PCAR system - in reacting to conscious intent which hopefully will be researched more intensively in years to come. However the experimental and observational evidence given below certainly give impressive credence to its validity. So also, does its science background (even though in this instance the scientific detail for interfacing with consciousness is not yet complete). OOB states - from the evidence given below seems to affect us all, as Monroe's research determined indicators (e.g. polarity reversal) which suggests we all engage in OOB states involuntary at some point during our nightly sleep. If one accepts OOB states as real, this in itself inescapably must confirm a non-physical existence and life-after-death, as otherwise OOB states would have no other apparent function or purpose in classical physical reality.

Apart from this, as is covered below, proficient trained adepts at achieving OOB states such as researchers or professionals, claim to continually encounter and interrelate with discarnates at will, including their own friends and relatives who had previously passed over. Although this might conflict with one's belief system, to deny this, anyone would have to also deny the outstanding and undeniable success and accuracy of military remote viewing during the last World War and in history down the ages.

6.3.2 History

The term has a long history of anecdotal accounts of shamans, and mystic claims of being able to travel outside their body to other locations.

6.3.3 Evidence

There are many striking anecdotal instances which support belief that a portion of psyche/consciousness can actually travel to a distant location, many involving patients under anaesthetic, in coma or experiencing a heart attack. Dr Michael B. Sabom, a cardiologist and professor of medicine at Emory University and a staff physician at the Atlanta Veterans' Administration Medical Centre, was a sceptic of the OOB phenomena. He changed his viewpoint completely after carrying out analysis of a trial group of 57 patients, all of whom had to be resuscitated at his hospital while suffering a heart attack. He found those who claimed OOB experiences (about half) were able to describe the resuscitation techniques actually employed on them in unbelievable detail compared with a control group who did not experience an OOB but were nevertheless asked to describe what they thought may have occurred.[21]

Perhaps the most well-known OOB case which was related by Stanislov Grof, concerns a patient, Marie, in a hospital in Seattle, Washington who, in April 1976, was resuscitated following a cardiac arrest. Her social worker nurse, Kimberly Clark Sharp (who later became a clinical professor), although anxious to go home after her shift, found that the patient Marie was disturbed by an experience she had during her heart attack where she claimed she found herself floating near the ceiling of the ward. She said she then inadvertently floated outside the building and found herself eyeballing a sandshoe on an outside window ledge on the third floor. Amongst other details she noted – the shoe was old, the little toe had worn a hole right through, and the lace was stuck under the heel. It all seemed so odd that she couldn't rest until her nurse had checked it out. Amazingly, after some difficulty Sharp found the shoe, was able to recover it and found everything Marie said was true. Marie had not given the colour, but when asked later, correctly described it as blue. Sharp had found the shoe was not visible from outside and even the ledge could not be seen properly from any windows except one, where by pressing her head against the window she finally was just able to see the tennis shoe, but no details. It wasn't until she retrieved the shoe that she was able to confirm Marie's various observations. "The only way she would have had such a perspective was if she had been floating right outside and at very close range to the tennis shoe," stated Sharp, who has since become a believer in OOB. "It was very concrete evidence for me."[22] The sequel to the story is interesting in that the well-known author Ian Wilson, a noted debunker of paranormal stories, relates in his book *The After Death Experience* that he decided to check the story out for himself. To his credit, after interviewing all concerned, he admits the story is true and that he remains perplexed[23].

There are also cases quoted where not only has an OOB been experienced, but the person who experienced the OOB was seen as an apparition by an independent witness. In the following often quoted case, the person was seen by two witnesses and interacted consciously with one of them. This is known as the "Wilmot" case and was reported in Volume 12 of the Proceedings of the Society for Psychical Research. It relates the story of Mr S. R. Wilmot who, while travelling on the ship "The City of Limerick" from Liverpool to New York, felt he was dreaming when visited by his wife in her night dress and kissed by her in his cabin in front of his fellow cabin passenger. When his wife left, the fellow passenger complimented him on being visited by such a pretty lady. Mrs Wilmot at this time was residing in Connecticut! When her husband returned to Connecticut, before he had a chance to relate his experience to her, she described having an OOB experience where she remembered travelling across the water to the ship, entering the cabin, noticing and describing accurately the fellow cabin passenger being in the top bunk and being observed by him while kissing her husband. She was also able to accurately describe the cabin and the fact that the upper bunk was displaced further back than the lower (an odd and distinguishing characteristic, since for that vessel, the cabin was located close to the stern).

A large number of polls taken over many years indicates an average of one in five people claim at least one such OOB experience during their lifetime.[24]

Since these experiences are erratic and infrequent, experimentation to investigate the veracity of OOB states is difficult. However some laboratory investigations have taken place with a few rare subjects who have claimed an ability to enter an OOB state at will.

Obviously, if a person claims they can physically leave their body, float near the ceiling, and see clearly anything around them, it is desirable to derive an experiment to test this capability. In 1968, C. Tart reported in an article "States of Consciousness and State Specific Sciences", published in Science, June 16, 1972; 1203-10, that he had achieved this with a "Miss Z" who claimed the ability to induce an OOB in her sleep. While connected to an EEG machine and other instrumentation in an OOB state, she was able to correctly identify a random five digit number placed on a shelf above her bed on countless occasions. This work was later replicated successfully in more complex experiments performed by Dr Karlis Osis. He used optical devices and mirrors, to avoid any question of ordinary ESP, and ensure "vision" was involved. He carried out these experiments at the American Society for Psychical Research in New York in association with psychologist Janet Lee Mitchell. After some initial difficulty in finding suitable subjects, they found several gifted subjects who were able to "fly in" from various locations around the country and correctly describe a wide range of target images. These included objects placed on a table, coloured geometric patterns placed on a free-floating shelf near the ceiling, and optical illusions that could only be seen when an observer peered through a small window in a special device.[25]

One of these experiments was also modified to see whether the OOB subject "flying in" could also be seen by someone else while physically present at the target. A psychic, Christine Whiting was chosen and succeeded in accurately being able to describe in detail the OOB subject's appearance and clothes - and at the correct time. There was also evidence to suggest that loss of electrical activity and a speed up of the brain waves in the visual, occipital regions of the brain was also found to accompany an OOB state.[26]

A separate series of experiments was performed in 1973 by Dr Robert Morris at the Psychical Research Foundation in Durham. These were aimed specifically at verifying under laboratory conditions, that it is possible on occasions to view the OOB subject at the actual target. These tests were successful as frequently PRF staff located at the target sensed, saw sparkling lights or claimed to see an apparition of the OOB subject at the actual target and at the correct time. Dr Morris extended his tests to include some animals, and encountered considerable success with a kitten which belonged to the OOB subject. The cat stopped meowing and started purring on **every** occasion when his owner was invisibly present.[27]

Further experiments suggested that the OOB subject could "travel" in a variety of ways, as an apparition, a ball, or shaft of light, or merely as a point of consciousness.[28]

The fact that expenditure of millions of dollars has been spent on research and practise into clairvoyance/remote viewing by the CIA, plus tens of thousands of hours spent by US Army staff actively involved in remote viewing (one of whom received a Legion of Merit award) - overwhelmingly proves the reality of remote viewing, and therefore the ability to be able to see and gather information independent of distance or time and without the necessity for being physically present. There is therefore conclusive evidence, that functions such as being able to see and communicate, do and can take place independently of the body and are an ability we all unconsciously share. Their independence from distance or time indicates these attributes are part of non-physical reality and **are therefore likely to be able survive death**.

Interestingly, Carl Jung came to the same conclusion following study of Dr Rhine's telepathy laboratory experiments in the 1930's at Duke University, which vindicated belief in telepathy to Jung's satisfaction. He was particularly taken by telepathy exhibiting "non-local" characteristics i.e. independence from distance or time. In his writings he goes even further than the above and with impeccable logic, argued that since abilities such as telepathy, which exhibits independence of space or time must be an attribute of each person's psyche, therefore the "**psyche, in its deepest reaches, must participate in a form of existence beyond space and time**". In addition, he points out that "*such an existence beyond space and time, would by* **definition therefore be 'eternal'**"! [29]

This is extremely convincing and, for those convinced of the power of logic, this may well be sufficient evidence for them to believe in life after death.

However, there is other supporting evidence for life after death which should be considered and in any case we also need to consider evidence for reincarnation, as this is not necessary implicit by proof of life after death.

First, it is helpful to consider more closely whether during remote viewing/ clairvoyance, the remote viewing on occasions is not so remote after all - whether there is evidence supportive of some field or portion of consciousness actually being able to travel to a 'target' and exhibit consciousness and intelligence. If this is the case, then clearly we can exist independently from physical reality and we will gain further evidence for survival after death. For this we must return to discuss further the work of Robert Monroe, the inventor of the Hemi-Sync" process first mentioned in Chapter 4.

It would in any case be totally inappropriate to leave the subject of OOB states without returning to discuss further Monroe's outstanding OOB research work. His importance to this book is not just for his experimental success in assisting in the acceptance and relevance of OOB phenomena to a case for reincarnation, but also for the **information** he and all his researchers and members of the public obtained from using the facilities he invented.

Robert A Monroe who died in 1995, spent some 30 years commencing in 1956 researching OOB phenomena. He studied engineering, science, pre-medicine and journalism. In 1937 he graduated with a Bachelor of English Degree from Ohio State University. He then worked as a writer and directorate for two radio stations. Two years later he moved to New York and expanded his broadcasting career, producing and directing weekly radio programs and eventually producing his own radio production company. During the 1950's his company was producing 28 radio shows per month. He served as vice-president and member of the board of directors for the Mutual Broadcasting System network. Building on this success, Monroe's production company acquired several radio stations in North Carolina and Virginia and later moved into developing cable television systems.

During the early 1950's his focus on his business interests to some extent fell apart when while sleeping, on at least two occasions a week, he was shocked to experience an involuntary and conscious awareness and a vivid sensation of his consciousness leaving his body. Thinking that he might have a brain tumour, or some other serious health issue, he submitted himself to intensive medical tests among top medical experts in their field. To his relief, their eventual conclusions were that there was no evidence whatsoever that he had any medical or psychiatric based problems, and was in good health.

In view of his extensive contacts amongst scientists, engineers etc., since his OOB problems continued, he decided in 1956 to set up his own self-funded research and development division company using the expertise of these scientists, others and himself to research OOB phenomena. His research and that of his team led to the fact that if anyone could be considered an expert on the practise of remote viewing/ clairvoyance and OOB states, then he would be it - as he spent most of the remainder of his life (some 40 years) experimenting on the subject, and running and participating to some extent personally in practical OOB courses attended by thousands of members of the public at courses run by his "Monroe Institute".

He considered all people move into an OOB state during sleep and that the process of dropping off to sleep is simply "where one moves out of phase with physical reality and space/time constraints". When deep sleep is reached (the "delta" state), separation becomes complete and the physical body simply remains in a standby mode to revert to physical reality and consciousness if needed.[30]

"In sleep and dream states you are involved in the same dimension of existence in which you will have your after-death experiences" [31]

Seth

There is experimental evidence to support this, as by using hypnosis, Salter (1963) was able to make a number of subjects immune to gunshots within five feet, indicated by a complete absence of rise in blood pressure. Also Barber (1970) found that by making hypnotic suggestion of blindness to subjects, this completely eliminated an involuntary physiological response which normally follows visual stimulation, as demonstrated by EEG alpha blocking. These examples suggest that hypnotism may have actually created an OOB condition where consciousness had temporarily left the body.[32]

As mentioned above, there are occasional reports of evidence and an observed variation in the appearance of a person seen in an OOB state. Monroe agreed with this concept and has asserted that it is our "thought habits that create our OOB forms and that because we are habituated to being in a body, we have tendency to produce the same form in the OOB state. Also that stripped of disguises, we are in essence a "vibrational pattern (comprised) of many interacting and resonating frequencies".[33]

The major research success in OOB phenomena by Robert Monroe, was the discovery of the use of special sounds passed through headphones to facilitate coherent brain activity and allow the OOB states to occur at will. It was developed by Robert A. Monroe himself and involves sending slightly different sound frequencies to each ear (termed the "Hemi - Sync" process, as mentioned previously). This has the effect of resonating left and right brains to a desired beat frequency and focusing both hemispheres to an identical state of awareness and consciousness at the same time. The purpose is to access and make dominant a part of the mind that is not normally utilised during normal waking consciousness. Experimentation has found that different states can be obtained, some of which correspond to the familiar Alpha, Beta and Theta states. Different blends of frequencies (known as "Focus 1, 2, 3, etc.) were found useful for different purposes e.g. Focus 12 was found to facilitate telepathic communication. Electronic equipment is also used to indicate when the remote viewer achieves **a 180-degree polarity reversal shift in body voltage, which usually indicates that the altered state has been achieved**.[34]

During his lifetime Monroe produced three books covering his research and experience in OOB states: *Far Journeys, Journey Out of the Body* and *Ultimate Journey*.

In much of his books he relates his OOB experience in visiting other realities (from his early experiences), as he kept a daily diary. When in an OOB state, he claimed that he could pass through solid objects and travel virtually anywhere in the Universe or to different realities in an instant by just thinking he was there. His early visits included visits to his friends where he mentioned that people were seldom aware of his presence. His friends though quickly became believers, when he accurately described their dress and activity at the time of his out-of-body visit.

During visits to other realities he claims and relates many instances where he communicated with other entities by a form of telepathy (covered in further detail below). By "entities", he indicated this included on occasions deceased friends, members and relatives of his own family and non-physical beings.[35]

While all of this might seem fanciful at best, it must be said that none of these experiences he claimed is different from those experienced by people who have written books on what they encountered in remote viewing while working for the USDF during World War II. The point here is that Monroe was a pioneer in developing the technology and later assisting with many others (particularly training military remote viewers) to optimise the methodology in achieving OOB states at will. In fact complete agreement between reports by all others using the Hemi-Sync process, which includes the thousands of attendees at Monroe Institute courses and the training of professional remote viewing practitioners for the military. This in itself, adds to its acceptance as valid, real and credible.

To deny the reality of Monroe's lifetime 40 years of experience researching OOB states, the integrity of his researchers and the some 4-5000 members of the public who have attended the Monroe Institute workshops over the years to date and used the Hemi-Sync facilities is one thing. However the same experiences are shared by those who have or will be trained as professional remote viewers, so such denial must also mean denial of the scientifically expert committee assigned by the US Congress in1995. This was led by Dr Jessica Utts (covered above), who overwhelmingly accepted the validity of OOB experiences and remote viewing. She not only advised that validity was no longer an issue, but rather that future research should concentrate on learning more about how remote-viewing could be enhanced.

There is much to learn on reading Monroe's books, but a summary of some of the main points which have relevance to our earlier chapters covering science aspects associated with his experiences in OOB states, is useful here.

Monroe claims that for anyone travelling in an OOB state, that:

- "You find yourself fully conscious and act as if you were functioning physically - with several exceptions. You can move through space (and time) slowly or apparently somewhere **beyond the speed of light**. You can observe, participate in events, and make wilful decisions based upon what you perceive. You can move through physical matter such as walls, steel plates, concrete, earth, oceans, air, and even atomic radiation without effort or effect."

From what we have learned in previous Chapters, none of the above should be too surprising, except we should note that it follows the physics expected of quantum non-physical reality. Even to the point (as has been mentioned previously), that one's consciousness, expected to be similar in size to subatomic particles, would have a wavelength less than walls etc. It therefore would be expected to easily pass through much larger masses without any effect.

- He goes on to say that, "This is not all, as you go virtually anywhere you wish, including the moon, solar system and the galaxy. But even to other reality systems only dimly perceived or theorised." [36]

- His reports on his experiences and interrelationship with these entities were particularly interesting, but in all cases there were some commonalities. For example he found all entities were friendly, engaging, benevolent and helpful. Many assisted in explaining and answering questions (non-verbally i.e. telepathically), and some assisted in taking him to wherever he wanted to go in his OOB state.

- Even during early OOB experiments, Monroe mentioned that, as the OOB state progressed, subjects universally reported within their perception a pinpoint of light. "When the subject learned to move in the direction of light until it became larger and larger, and then move through it, the OOB state was achieved. In slow motion, it felt as if one were going through a tunnel to get to the light." As noted by Monroe, this is a classic description of what has often being described as a NDE (a near death experience).

From a science point of few, even obviously assuming quantum physics is involved and envisaging a form of teleportation (as mentioned above), we have no understanding whatsoever of the physics associated with intent causing motion. We might though expect intense light to be associated with a non-physical largely photon-type realm. As mentioned earlier, quantum physicist William Bray (who also as with Robert Monroe, suffered from spontaneous OOB experiences for most of his life), suggests this phenomena gives every appearance of a wormhole. (Near Death Experiences (NDE's), will be covered later in this Chapter).

- Monroe claims that "anyone even mildly proficient (e.g. researchers or those who have attended many of his courses) soon become fully aware of the survival of physical death - not just having faith, or believing, but **knowing**. In addition, such survival takes place whether we like it or not, and without any consideration as to what we do, or are, in a physical life. Survival of self beyond physical existence is a natural and automatic process."

The R&D division of Monroe's company intended for OOB research, was set up initially as he puts it with "….the motive - personal and selfish; not profound, idealistic or noble", it was simply to see if he could determine the cause of his involuntary OOB experiences which he found frightening. After an initial period of researching the R&D section of his company, it was detached and established as a non-profit organisation known as the "Monroe Institute". Its aims were to continue research and allow the public to experience the phenomena for themselves, by attending in-house courses on the subject.

Since its establishment, as mentioned previously, thousands of the public have attended courses there and participated in OOB experiences. Some have even written books on this, one of whom is a particularly credible author, Dr Courtenay Brown. As an Associate Professor of political science at Emory University he put himself out on a limb by describing his own experiences in remote viewing, while employing the services of a former member of the US Army remote viewing unit as his "monitor". Brown initially gained OOB training at the Monroe Institute in Faber, Virginia via their one week 'Gateway Voyage Program' (For some years, these courses were a necessary prerequisite by military remote viewer trainees).

In a matter of fact way, Dr Courtenay Brown relates in his book many instances where he has used "Focus 21" to gain access to non-physical reality. He explains that non-physical reality is the realm easily accessible via the "Hemi - Sync" process, where one can encounter **us all in our non-physical form** (he claims this occurs when we are asleep or when dead). Those who no longer exist in our physical reality, he says, "live" there and although we would regard them as dead, he claims they are very much alive and can be contacted and communicated with by anyone practised in remote viewing techniques.[37]

Brown is a reputable academic whose forte is non-linear mathematic modelling.

Following his experiences, he published a book entitled *Cosmic Explorers* (1999), which provides coverage of his most recent remote viewing and non-physical research.

Of particular significance is the fact that, apart from Dr Courtenay Brown; **all involved in operational remote viewing**, claim they continually and all others practised in remote viewing, continually and **routinely encounter non-physical entities either accidently or at will**, and many cite instances of communicating with dead relatives or other dead and recently terminally injured people. These include all of the following who have written books on the subject, namely, Robert Monroe (*Far Journeys, Journey Out of the Body*, and *Ultimate Journey*), David Moorehouse (*Psychic Warrior - Inside the CIA's Stargate Program*), Joseph Moneagle (*Mind Trek: Exploring consciousness, Time, and Space Through Remote Viewing*). David Moorhouse for example claims a team colleague, Lyn Buchanan found it very upsetting to meet and communicate with recently dead crew and passengers, particularly children, while remote viewing Pan Am Flight 103 associated with the Lockerbie disaster.[38]

Before we leave the subject of OOB states, as mentioned in Chapter 4, Monroe, referred in two of his books to the ability to communicate in a non-verbal fashion by thought alone. He described that on many occasions entities "...threw him a "Rote" (his abbreviation for **R**elated **O**rganised **T**hought **E**nergy). He explained this as "a thought ball" which provided knowledge, information, experience and history, and was more than just telepathy i.e. non-verbal communication.[39]

He described it as a quantum jump beyond a talking moving colour picture, a direct experience and immediate **knowing,** transmitted from one intelligent energy system and received by another. One of the main problems he claimed in communicating with non-physical entities encountered in OOB states, was both his and other researcher's inadequate and one-sided lack of mastery of the non-verbal communicating system.[39]

An amazing but similar and perhaps an even better description of this communicating facility was given by Swedish mystic Swedenborg, born in 1688 (mentioned earlier in this Chapter). He described entities he encountered during his trances communicated using thought balls and described these telepathic bursts of knowledge as "a picture language so dense with information that each image contains a thousand ideas". He mentioned that a communicated series of these portrayals can be "quite lengthy" and "last up to several hours, in such a sequential arrangement that one can only marvel".[40]

The author of the somewhat dated, but excellent book *The Holographic Universe*, - the late Michael Talbot; points out that as a **psychic himself**, he often had this experience when meeting a stranger, (or even hearing a name) where a ball of information about that person would instantly flash into his awareness. This described this thought ball could include important facts about the person's psychological and emotional makeup, their health, and even scenes from the past.

He also mentioned in the literature describing Near Death Experiences (NDE's) that there are many similar accounts, "NDE er's often say the information arrives in 'chunks' that register instantly in one's thoughts, rather than being strung out in a linear fashion like words in a sentence or scenes in a movie".[41]

We would also recognize these descriptions as absolutely the same as those described by psychics as described in the New Zealand television programme mentioned above called "Sensing Murder"- where merely touching a photo upside down of a murder victim immediately gave the psychic astonishing details of the victim and often details of the murder as if in a movie.

The point of course in mentioning all these cases of instances of psychics, people in OOB states and people near death experiencing NDE's is two-fold.

- First, it is obvious from a science point of view, that the system described can only be Walter Schemppt's incredible PCAR communication system, as covered previously. As confirmed above, it clearly also has a capability far beyond being just a non-verbal telepathy system. Noteworthy also is the fact that we even use this system in normal physical reality, continuously, routinely and unconsciously, to daily faithfully mimic our perception of reality by presenting to our consciousness following brain processing, a **complete** simulation of what is received from our senses, in full color, motion and 3D in a continuous motion, historical manner.

- Second, the remarkable correlation over a time scale, from Swedenborg's account in the 17th Century, to virtually the present day, describing completely identical accounts of known scientific properties of the PCAR system, surely must vindicate OOB, NDE and psychic capabilities as being completely real and valid. (This is not dissimilar for example to classical physical reality science (again) in the case of Newton, who got bonked on the head from one apple then later went away and developed his gravitational theory and mathematics, as a result.) Here we have highly qualified researchers, together with psychics etc. having faithfully recorded observational science phenomena over centuries, all of which correlates perfectly and even has supporting science and mathematics already, and yet it is largely ignored by mainstream science.

6.4 NDE'S (NEAR DEATH EXPERIENCES)

6.4.1 Definition:

"NDE's", refers to a personal experience associated with impending death, encompassing multiple possible sensations including detachment from the body, feelings of levitation, total serenity, security, warmth, the experience of absolute dissolution, and the presence of a light. These phenomena are usually reported after an individual has been pronounced clinically dead or has been very close to death. -Wikipedia

The key point about NDE's, is that the reported occurrences are almost **identical with descriptions of OOB states indicated above** - except mainly that the experiences are reported by a significant number of individuals only when close to death, and are always non-voluntary. The occurrence also occurs **regardless of the belief or nationality of those concerned**. Description of experiences is also universally regarded by participants as a life-between-life experience. This is because it usually includes, being greeted by dead relatives and friends, encountering entities often described "beings of light", receiving a life review, (commonly referred to as "seeing one's life flash before one's eyes"), receiving knowledge about one's life and the nature of the universe, offered a choice to return or stay, making a decision to return and suddenly finding oneself back inside one's body.

6.4.2 Importance to Reincarnational Belief:

NDE experiences are obviously critical (as with OOB experiences) – since, if valid, they provide advance knowledge to us all as to what will befall us all at death, and what a life-between-life could be like. From a science point of view correlations between accounts is particularly important as, if reports exhibit conformity, they assist in acceptance of its validity. This also must apply to correlation with properties expected of the underlying science e.g. PCAR type non-verbal communication, and other non-physical quantum like characteristics, e.g. time and space independence, instantaneous motion resulting by teleportation, etc. That these experiences even occur at all, that they are involuntary and in such numbers - all deserve explanation.

6.4.3 **History**

The sheer quantity of historical accounts of NDE's over past centuries is staggering. Like OOB's, NDE's are obviously a universal phenomenon. They are described at length in the 8th Century Tibetan Book of the Dead, the 2,500-year old Egyptian Book of the Dead, in Plato's *The Republic*, an 8th Century account of the Venerable Bede etc. Medieval literature is filled with accounts of NDE's.[42]

6.4.4 **Evidence**

As related by Michael Talbot, in his book, *The Holographic Universe*, there are many astonishing aspects of agreement among the NDEs reported by various cultures throughout history. For instance, the life review, a feature that crops up again and again in modern-day NDE's, is also described in the *Tibetan Book of the Dead*, the *Egyptian Book of the Dead*, in Plato's account of what Er experienced during his sojourn in the hereafter, and in the 2,000 –year old yogic writings of the Indian sage Patanjali. These and many other cross-cultural similarities between NDEs have also been confirmed in formal study.

In 1977, Osis and Haraldsson compared nearly nine hundred deathbed visions reported by patients to doctors and other medical personnel in both India and the United States. They found that although there were various cultural differences. For example, Americans tended to view the "being of light" as a Christian religious personage, wheras Indians perceived it to be a Hindu one. Nevertheless the "core" of the experience was substantially the same.

Skeptics, including many psychiatrists and without any evidence, continuously suggest all reports of NDE's amount to nothing but hallucinations. However there are many cases of NDE's where the patient later fully recovered and yet exhibited a "flat-line" EEG for extensive periods during an operation. EEG flat-lining indicates no brain activity whatsoever. This means theoretically no conscious awareness which can account for the ability for them to later relate astonishing details of previous efforts to save their lives by others while in an OOB/NDE state. Yet this is exactly what has happened in case after case as testified by expert medical practitioners (in some cases neurosurgeons), and recorded as occurring in recent years in operating theatres throughout the world.

Critics (as mentioned above), continually attempt to explain the above by making unsubstantiated assertions that this can easily be explained by hallucinations. However this simply does not fit the facts. Instead, it would be more reasonable, logical and scientific surely, to suggest that such occurrences were more likely to be examples of one's consciousness temporarily leaving the body. After all, the section above on OOB experiences indicates that using Monroe's Hemi-Sync facilities, anyone can (and do) easily achieve OOB states every day at the Monroe's Institute in Virginia, USA, while attending one of their public courses. Also the evidence above suggests that OOB states are a normal occurrence for all of us during sleep, and many (as with Monroe and quantum physicist William Bray), even experience involuntary instances of OOB states while awake.

One particularly interesting example of the many available real life cases in the literature which exhibits most of the range of NDE experiences, concerned a woman named Pam Reynolds. In 1991, she underwent a basilar artery aneurysm in her brain that threatened her life. The size and location of the aneurysm, however, precluded its safe removal using the standard neuro-surgical techniques. She was referred to a doctor who had pioneered a daring surgical procedure known as hypothermic cardiac arrest.

The operation (nicknamed "standstill" by doctors who perform it), required that Pam's body temperature be lowered to 60 degrees, her heartbeat and breathing stopped, her brain waves flattened, and the blood drained from her head. In colloquial terminology, she was put to death.

After removing the aneurysm, she was restored to life. During the time that Pam was in "standstill", she experienced a NDE. Her remarkably detailed OBE observations during her surgery were later verified by the operating staff and surgeon to be true. Her case is considered to be one of the strongest cases of verified evidence in NDE research. What shocked the medical staff present was that following the operation, she was able to describe in detail the unique surgical instruments and the surgical procedures used on her - but with no blood to stimulate the brain, nor brain waves registering - she was technically and clinically brain dead. She also described as if she were floating above the operating table but claimed that her vision:

"…was not like normal vision. It was brighter and more focused and clearer than normal vision. There was a sensation like being pulled, but not against your will. I was going on my own accord because I wanted to go. I have different metaphors to try to explain this. The feeling was like going up in an elevator real fast. And there was a sensation, but it wasn't a bodily, physical sensation. It was like a tunnel but it wasn't a tunnel. At some point very early in the tunnel vortex I became aware of my grandmother calling me. But I didn't hear her call me with my ears. It was a clearer hearing than with my ears. I trust that sense more than I trust my own ears. The feeling was that she wanted me to come to her, so I continued down a dark shaft that I went through, and at the very end there was this very little tiny pinpoint of light that kept getting bigger and bigger. The light was incredibly bright. It was so bright that I put my hands in front of my face. I noticed that as I began to discern different figures they were all covered with light, they were light, and had light permeating all around them - they began to form shapes I could recognize and understand. I could see that one of them was my grandmother. Everyone I saw, looking back on it, fit perfectly into my understanding of what that person looked like at their best during their lives. They would not permit me to go further … It was communicated to me - that's the best way I know how to say it, because they didn't speak like I'm speaking - that if I went all the way into the light, something would happen to me physically. They would be unable to put this me back into the body me, like I had gone too far and they couldn't reconnect.

Dr. Peter Fenwick, a neuropsychiatrist and considered a leading authority in Britain concerning NDEs, understands that the state of the brain during a NDE, is that:

"The brain isn't functioning. It's not there. It's destroyed. It's abnormal. But, yet, it can produce these very clear experiences ... an unconscious state is when the brain ceases to function. For example, if you faint, you fall to the floor, you don't know what's happening and the brain isn't working. The memory systems are particularly sensitive to unconsciousness. So, you won't remember anything. But, yet, after one of these experiences a NDE, you come out with clear, lucid memories."[43]

Some NDE researchers have found that **even patients who are blind**, and have had no light perception for years, can see and accurately describe what is going on around them when they have left their bodies during an NDE. Dr Kubler-Ross, related in her book, *On Children and Death*, that she had encountered several such individuals and interviewed them at length to determine their accuracy. "To our amazement, they were even able to describe the colour and design of clothing and jewellery the people present wore," she states.

(Note: Dr Kubler-Ross, was famous for her definitive and valuable medical research over many years into commonality of psychological experiences as terminal patients approached death. She was a 2007 inductee into the American National Women's Hall of Fame and the recipient of twenty honorary degrees. Her credibility is therefore beyond question.) [44]

Another group of NDEs and deathbed visions involves two or more individuals. One case, related by Kenneth Ring in his book *Life at Death*, concerns a female NDE'er who found herself moving through the tunnel and approaching the realm of light, when she saw a friend of hers coming back! As they passed, the friend telepathically communicated to her that he had died, but was being "sent back." The woman, too, was eventually "sent back", and after she recovered, she discovered that her friend had suffered a cardiac arrest at approximately the same time as her own experience.[45]

A very popular US television program dealing solely with NDE's, commenced in 2011, and still going strong. It is called "I Survived... Beyond and Back". It covers re-enactments by the actual people themselves claiming to not only have had an NDE, but were declared clinically dead and yet later recovered to describe their experience in person on television. Their accounts are also particularly compelling and credible, because not only were first-person detailed accounts given, but also live television testimony from the medical personnel and family members who were actually present at the time.

After watching a number of episodes, it would be difficult for anyone not to notice that every person who related their particular NDE experience, gave absolutely similar accounts of their experiences. In addition, all indicated their experiences had changed their outlook and belief in favour of an afterlife after death. Most indicated they were reluctant to return to their life on earth and now did not fear death. Reluctance amongst people experiencing NDE's is of course understandable as all would be faced with returning to a sick and often pain racked body. Understandably most would feel a commitment and obligation to return to care for their family. Their desire to stay though (as indicated by many), was the obvious attraction of being able to unite again and be with friends and family who had passed over.

In this, it is interesting to note that the USA National Pollster, George Gallup wrote in 1981[46], that a recent survey indicated about 35 % of Americans polled reported an NDE. If only 20% of these claimed re-uniting with friends and family, this would amount to some **46 Million in America alone** who would then claim if asked, that they were absolutely convinced they had identified and readily communicated with relatives and friends while in an OOB state when near to death. I am sure all of us would agree that we could never be fooled or mistaken in recognising accurately a friend or close relative, if we had an opportunity to meet and communicate with them again after their physical death. It is also noteworthy that recent polls conducted by USA researchers indicated that approximately 98% of all those who have experienced NDE's, since responded that they now had an unshakable belief in an afterlife.[47]

The wealth of documented and well authenticated NDE accounts twenty to thirty years ago in the literature is so vast, it is daunting for any researcher. This evidence also includes researched articles appearing in many respected publications such as those of the International Association for Near-Death Studies (IANDS) and annals of the various Societies for Psychic research in many countries etc. Since then, and today, NDE reports and research have accelerated - probably due to the scientific medical developments in recent years and use of trauma teams which have been instrumental in saving many more patients near death than previously possible. Television programmes such as the above "I Survived…Beyond and Back", and perhaps the experiences of many cardiologists and doctors encountering many NDE cases for themselves, seems to have changed things. In recent years, there are so many cases so evidential in suggesting an afterlife, that funding as well, now seems to being made available for more high quality research than was the case previously.

For example, recent results of NDE research at the University of Southampton were heralded in newspapers recently throughout the world, using the following caption:

"There May Be A Small Amount of Life After Death, Scientists Believe" ("The Dominion Post", Oct 8th 2014). The research was claimed to be the largest undertaken to date, taking four years, and examining more than 2000 people who suffered cardiac arrests at 15 hospitals in the UK, US and Austria. Of the 2060 cardiac arrest patients studied, 330 survived and 140 said they had experienced some kind of awareness while being resuscitated. One in five said they had an unusual feeling of peacefulness, while nearly one-third said time had slowed down or sped up. 13 percent said they felt separated from their bodies and one recalled leaving his body completely while watching his resuscitation from the corner of the room. Dr Sam Parnia, a research fellow who led the team, pointed out that in this case, the patient had been clinically dead for three minutes during which the heart was not beating - even though the brain typically shuts down within 20-30 seconds after the heart is stopped. He said the man described everything in the room that happened, but importantly he heard two bleeps from the machine that makes a noise at three minute intervals. "So we could time how long the experience lasted for."

Dr Parnia also said that "A higher proportion of people may have similar vivid experiences, but do not recall them, due to the effects of brain injury or sedative drugs used in the process of resuscitation". Dr David Wilde, a research psychologist at Nottingham Trent University compiling data about OOB experiences, said, "There is some very good evidence here that these experiences are actually happening after people have died."

In case we have become wedded to regarding ourselves only as a physical form, it is noteworthy that all the cells in our body replace themselves approximately every five years, and yet our behaviour, our memories, our sense of integral existence as an individual are all unaffected and still retain their unique pattern. The fact that the physical material used to express the pattern disappears but the pattern still continues to exist surely suggests **there is a non-physical dominant self**. Also if this pattern survives death of all cells during life, what is to stop it continuing after complete physical death?

6.5   CLOSING CHAPTER COMMENTS

To anyone researching this material such as myself, it is immediately evident that the wealth of information available on reported cases of telepathy, clairvoyance, OOB, and NDE states is immense. It is also in many instances the result of high quality experimental scientific research carried out by medical professionals and highly qualified scientists. Recently it has also included increased sample sizes and meta-analysis of results used to test validity over large time scales.

Such has been the effort, time and resources expended into analysis of case studies and research that it would be difficult to think of any other area - except medical research, which could compare. Moreover these investigations and research are scarcely the work of primitive savages filled with superstitious views, poorly educated and ill-equipped with modern day equipment and facilities. Instead the quality of research cannot be other than impressive in most cases covered in this Chapter as it has been undertaken and funded as formal research projects by many prestigious universities around the world.

Obviously the purpose of the research into the areas covered: telepathy, clairvoyance, OOB, and NDE, is to test their validity. As pointed out earlier in the Chapter, some authors in the literature (in their books or research papers), have proposed a possible link between properties of quantum physics and the paranormal, but few have suggested a link between the observed properties of quantum physics and those one reasonably would possibly expect in an afterlife - such as a timeless/spaceless environment.

Following scientific principles therefore, (and to comply with the purpose of this book), the following would seem to be a reasonable statement of the theory we are looking to validate:: "That the quantum physics properties covered in earlier Chapters, provides the science which supports an afterlife, but also reincarnation, meaning not just afterlife, but rebirths."

Referring this therefore specifically just to the areas of telepathy, clairvoyance, OOB and NDE covered above, the following may assist in your evaluation of this Chapter:

It is noted that none of these phenomena discussed are inconsistent amongst themselves. In fact they are all interrelated. Taking a typical example from the data above. A psychic who successfully solved a murder case (as covered in the "Sensing Murder" TV programme case) did so on live television by contacting the victim telepathically, obtained information via clairvoyance **independent of time**, from a victim who was technically dead (but according to reincarnational theory - very much alive in an afterlife).

The science aspects are relatively simple and support very well the observed data, since the PCAR system is the quantum communication system which allows non-verbal communication for telepathy, but also provides the inherent capability to retrieve information from the murder victim or associated events.

Similarly we note also from the data above that OOB and NDE states are both trance type situations where even in sleep, consciousness can leave the body - just as in Robert Monroe's experiments or professional remote viewers involved in spying. In either of the cases above concerning OOB or NDE states - dead relatives, friends or other non-physical entities are reported as being able to be encountered at will. Communication with all discarnates is universally described as non-verbal communication and information (plus **knowing**) is repetitively said to be able to be obtained from any time-frame – which is again characteristic of a quantum PCAR system. All entities met in OOB or NDE states, are said in every case to appear universally as photon type light-forms. Photons, as covered earlier, have a theoretically almost infinite life. We would therefore expect entities in a timeless/spaceless quantum environment to exhibit the same characteristics – which is what is observed. When consciousness leaves a body, movement is reported on occasions to exceed light speed - but this again is characteristic of quantum non-locality interconnectness. Vision is also reported as being 360 degrees, in 3D and in full colour - which again completely conforms to the unique characteristics of the quantum PCAR communication system.

Although this demonstrates complete consistency of all data across the four areas covered in this Chapter - telepathy, clairvoyance, OOB and NDE states, it is obviously necessary that all the descriptions of events described by all data should be consistent amongst themselves, regardless of location or whether recorded long ago or recently.

On a metadata analysis basis, both horizontal correlation and vertical correlation of data must apply. As can be seen from the above, this is a particularly strong feature of the evidence provided. There are no exceptions - either in the descriptions of events as stated, or compliance with the same quantum science properties.

In conclusion to this Chapter, perhaps one final point is worth noting: If one travels in an OOB state every night during sleep (as covered experimentally above), surely at death this is not only likely, but routine.

CHAPTER SEVEN

Past Life Recall - Spontaneous and via Hypnosis

"Our birth is but a sleep and a forgetting…"

William Wordsworth

This Chapter deals with the two main areas of past life recall, involving:

1. People claiming cases of spontaneous recall of alleged previous lives, by mainly children aged typically 3–5 years old, and

2. Claims of cases where using hypnotic regression on almost all people, they can recall alleged details of their previous lives.

7.1 SPONTANEOUS PAST LIFE RECALL OF CHILDREN

This covers reports of spontaneous cases of alleged recall of past lives concerning children. These cases by far outweigh the relatively few available spontaneous cases concerning adults. Since a large sample size is more likely to give accurate scientific results, the larger group concerning children is obviously chosen for reincarnational research.

Apart from this though, individual anecdotal reports claimed by adults although they may well be true, are more likely to be attacked by skeptics or naysayers as being attributable to exaggeration, distortion or even fraud. In contrast, children, particularly very young children, tend to be completely unsophisticated and innocent. Importantly this means, they have not yet developed a belief system nor been subject to cultural conditioning. Therefore they are more likely to give an honest account of any recollection suggestive of remembrance of a past life. For this reason, to ensure validity, only cases concerning very young children are included below.

7.1.1 **History**

Reports of adults claiming spontaneous remembrance of one or a number of past lives as mentioned above seem relatively rare. A few reports though are available in recent years stretching back to perhaps the fifteenth century when successive reincarnations of the Dalai Lama were first recognized and documented[1].

In many Eastern countries and elsewhere there is a tradition of reincarnational belief and many Tibetan monks have claimed they can recall their previous lives at will. By far though, the greatest number of reports of spontaneous recall of a previous life or lives, are associated with mainly children aged typically 3-5 years old. Once most children become older than 5 years old, and perhaps as a consequence of interrelating with others and their development of language skills; they tend to not only to lose their ability to recall fresh details of a previous life, but generally forget completely their earlier comments or recollections.[2]

7.1.2 **Importance to Reincarnational Belief:**

This is extremely important, as there are extensive claims by many, that detailed recollections of past lives have in many cases been found (as a result of intensive and thorough investigations by independent researchers) to be most likely true.

As stated by the eminent psychologist and philosopher, William James, M.D.:

"In order to disprove the law that all crows are black, it is enough to find one white crow."

A similar argument is therefore said to be applicable to reincarnation - in that a single documented and proven case of multiple re-births is all that is necessary to establish that reincarnation is a fact. Absolute proof though, even for a single case, is always likely to be difficult to prove. However, if multiple lives can be verified independently for a large number of cases in different countries and over large time frames, then this would provide extremely strong evidence, not just for life after death, but obviously also for reincarnation.

7.1.3 **Evidence:**

Cases credibly researched, range from just a simple case to complex cases. Taking a simple case first:

A 4 year old girl named Abby Swanson from Ohio, USA, after having her bath one night, completely shocked her mother by saying. "*Mommy, I used to give you baths when you were a baby*". Abby explained that she bathed her mother when she also was once her mother. When asked for the name she was given then, Abby responded with two names - "*Lucy...Ruthie...Ruthie*". On this final attempt, incredibly she got her grandmother's name right. This was particularly impressive, as Abby's grandmother died some nine years before Abby was even born.

It will be seen that in this case two correct statements were identified by Abbey. Her grandmother did give her mother baths, therefore one can count one correct statement for this, and one for identifying her grandmother had the unusual name of "Ruthie", even if the response was a little hesitant.

Is this evidence of reincarnation? Absolutely not. As clearly her mother could have made the whole story up, or the girl could have been fantasizing somewhat and by coincidence came up with the idea that she once gave her mother baths occasionally. She could also have got the name right from listening to her mother using Abby's grandmother's name at some earlier point - despite Abby's mother insisting that she never used her grandmother's name in front of Abby[3].

This exemplifies the difficulty in acceptance of simple cases of anyone relating anecdotal stories of children who spontaneously recall past lives, as the case actually documented above could be true or false, we just do not know.

The reported incidence of such spontaneous child past lives recollection cases is so large that there are fortuitously many cases reported (unlike the simple case above), where not just two, but the number of matching characteristics able to be verified are considerable. In many of these, both independent witnesses happened to be present at the time and were able to testify to a particular child's recollections. Later these were found to match almost identically with a particular cited deceased person (they generally were found to previously belong to the same family, or lived in the neighborhood). Regarding personal recollections found to be accurate. These range in some cases from the name of the deceased cited, plus matching characteristic such as scars, birthmarks - to unique personality characteristics. In addition, often a wealth of matching but important detail including the names of the deceased family members and friends, where they lived, what their house looked like, what they did for a living, how they died, and even obscure information, such as in one case where the deceased hid money before death (found as a result of information provided by the child) and, in a number of cases involving murder; sometimes even the name was given of who killed them.

From a statistical point of view, if a large number of correlations are found to be accurate in one case, but also the number of such accurate cases is also large, then evidence for previous lives could be vindicated by simply applying mathematical probability theory. If on the other hand the number of successful matching cases found over time is vast then statistically the case for reincarnation could then be expected to overwhelming.

It is no doubt for this reason that Dr. Ian Stevenson (1918–2007), a professor of psychiatry at the University of Virginia Medical School first became attracted to carrying out what later became his world famous research into such cases. His research commenced in 1958, and continued for some 40 years until his death in 2007[4].

His international recognition for his research into reincarnation, resulted from his discovering evidence suggesting that memories and physical injuries can be transferred from one lifetime to another. He traveled extensively over this period of 40 years, investigating 3,000 cases of children around the world who recalled having past lives. His meticulous research presented evidence that many of these children had unusual abilities, illnesses and, phobias which could not be explained by the environment or heredity. He authored around 300 papers and 14 books on the subject of reincarnation, among them his 1966 book, *Twenty Cases Suggestive of Reincarnation*. This became a classic in the annals of reincarnational research. In 1997 he published his third book *Reincarnation and Biology: A Contribution to the Etiology of Birthmarks and Birth Defects* which focused on 200 cases of children who had birthmarks and memories which corresponded remarkably with the lives and wounds of deceased people whom these children recalled as themselves living in a past life[5].

Before discussing further Dr. Stevenson's work, it is important to note that as a meticulous researcher, although there was no shortage of cases of children remembering past lives to investigate, he felt it necessary to establish a credibility classification system. This was aimed at reasonably quickly eliminating any which were possibly doubtful. To this end, his immediate goal was to obtain a "solved case" worthy of recording but warranting further investigation. These were cases where he alone (or an assistant) were able to match the child's memories with a single cited deceased person. Such cases then only became "verified" when he was satisfied, after vigorous investigation, that the child had no possible opportunity by any alternative means to learn about the previous personality (even by telepathy or possession). To date he and his colleagues have collected more than 2,600 cases throughout the world, of which there are now more than 800 "verified" cases on file! [6]

The issue of the correspondence of birthmarks is particularly interesting from an evidential point of view, particularly as the visual correlation of scars/birthmarks between the child and the cited deceased person is usually dramatic and obvious. In many cases correlations comprised two or even three different instances of visual scars/birthmarks. In some cases medical records and testimonials were able to be made available for the use of Dr. Stevenson or his assistants by medical practitioners. These were those that had been recorded and photographed soon after the time when the scars and wounds had occurred, or available from autopsy records following the children's death. Since Dr. Stevenson was himself qualified as a medical doctor, he was well placed himself to professionally analyze their comparability. He did this by himself or jointly in liaison with the doctors who had supplied the medical records.

The birthmarks in most of Dr. Stevenson's cases (meticulously taken photos are available in his books and on the internet) - really look like scars and wounds. Not the common mole like birthmarks that appear in most adults. Those birthmarks in Stevenson's cases are typically puckered and scar like, sometimes puckered a little below the surrounding skin, areas of markedly diminished pigmentation, or port-wine stains[7].

Amazingly, the belief that comparability between a child presenting with scars/birthmarks that match those of a previously deceased person, provides proof of reincarnation; has a long history amongst many races today. Jim B. Tucker, child psychiatrist at the University of Virginia and Medical director of the child & family Psychiatry Clinic, a previous assistant to Dr. Stevenson is continuing Stevenson's work since his death. He has written a book, *Life before Life, Children's Memories of Past Lives*. In this book he cites the Tlingits, a tribe in Alaska who have a tradition of making predictions about rebirth. He mentions cases where they expect their particular body scars to be duplicated on their death on a future child born to a favored parent within their tribe. For example in a case investigated:

"A man named Victor Vincent told his niece that he was going to come back as her son. He showed her two scars he had from minor surgery and predicted that he would carry those marks to his next life. Eighteen months after he died, she gave birth to a boy who had birth marks in the same spots. One of them even had small round marks lined up beside the main linear mark, giving the appearance of stitch wounds from a surgical scar. The boy later said that he was the previous personality, and he seemed to recognize several people from Victor's life".

Stevenson's work records that the Igbos of Nigeria have a similar belief[8].

Tucker also points out that in several Asian countries, a family member or friend may mark i.e. scar the body of a dying or deceased individual, in the hope that when that person is reborn, the baby will have a birthmark that matches the marking[9].

This was found also to apply to various tribes of West Africa[10].

It is astonishing that the Tlingits Indian tribes of Alaska, Igbos of Nigeria and those of several Asian countries (all from disparate countries around the world) have independently come to the conclusion that children's birthmarks are often likely to signify a given child's rebirth as that of an earlier deceased member of their tribe. This suggests that this conclusion could only have been reached by them because they must have found incidents of this kind common over many years. Also the matching of scars/wounds on a body with child birthmarks, must have been relatively easy and obvious.

Dr. Stevenson's research gives complete support to these tribal expectations for rebirth being able to be easily identified by birthmarks in children. Of Stevenson's **all "verified"** cases of children reporting memories of past lives, he found 35 % (309 of 895), of children had birthmarks or defects that matched wounds from a previous personality. This is an astonishingly large percentage and difficult (in fact, to date, impossible) to reconcile, **unless one accepts it is both a natural phenomenon and indicative of the validity of reincarnation.**

Many of Stevenson's cases involved extreme violence encountered by the deceased. An Indian boy remembered being killed by a shotgun blast to his chest. On the boy's chest was an array of birthmarks that matched the pattern and location (verified by the autopsy report) of the fatal wounds. Another shotgun victim was hit at point-blank range in the right side of his head. One woman had three separate linear scarlike birthmarks on her back. As a child in this current life, she remembered her death as a woman who was killed by three blows to her back with an axe.

This case involves three matching birthmarks! However, a significant number of Stevenson's birthmark cases involved two or more birthmarks such as in this case. In fact, of 210 such cases amongst all his books, eighteen cases are of double birthmarks. Nine of these involve bullet wounds, where not only do the marks match the exact site of entry and exit, but the mark corresponding to the entry wound is small and round, and the mark corresponding to the exit wound is large and irregular. This conforms perfectly with forensic ballistic science, where the exit wound from a bullet is always larger than the hole where the bullet entered the body.

We are now in a position to consider mathematically the probability of these occurrences happening by chance. In considering a single case of two birthmarks corresponding with two wounds occurring by chance, Stevenson determined the odds against were 1 in 25,600. However, his research found eighteen such cases already in the relatively small sample of 210 cases. The odds against chance, taking all eighteen cases into consideration, are therefore astronomical[11].

As mentioned above, Dr. Tucker is now continuing Dr. Stevenson's work using his same meticulous criteria. The figures above and for other correlations likely to arise from his research and by others entering this field can only be expected to rise substantially even further.

Nevertheless, with Dr. Stevenson's work already achieved, whether or not one accepts the validity of rebirth, there is even now a credible science based explanation for the relatively high occurrence of his cases of matches between scars/wounds of a deceased person with that of birthmarks in a child born in a later life. Unsurprisingly, testimony from the children concerned in Stevenson's cases indicated that a large proportion of the scars/wounds identified, caused their death in an earlier life. Earlier Chapters indicate that as determined by repeated experimental evidence, we unconsciously all individually or collectively create our reality. This includes all physical reality including the shape and features of our body. At birth therefore, apart from genetic and DNA programming influences, we would therefore expect if reincarnation is correct, that the trauma and remembrance of a violent death and immediate bodily effects just prior to this death would have a major effect on our consciousness. This therefore would be likely in some instances to trigger the fetus consciousness to create a reasonable facsimile replication of scars/wounds as a birthmark from the memory of the earlier body at death. After all, in normal life there are many examples where strong emotion or even hypnosis can cause physiological changes such as a facsimile of burn marks appearing on the wrists of a person recollecting being bound; or in cases of stigmata occurring on religious devotees. This would also explain the fact that normally children do not present at birth with multiple birthmarks which unmistakably mimic scars/wounds - since the majority of people lead a full life without encountering an early, violent and unexpected death.

The fact that this fulfils reasonable expectations consistent with reincarnational belief in itself is strong support for reincarnation, **but also the normality of rebirth**. Likewise without a rebirth explanation for these cases, it would seem impossible to explain them – which again is yet another argument in favor of reincarnation.

Dr. Stevenson himself considered correlation of child birthmarks the most evidential of his cases. No doubt due to the fact that it eliminates entirely any suspicion of fraud, distortion or exaggeration by the child, parents or any others in relating or recording details of the case (including himself). But his research is perhaps best remembered for, the fact that, throughout his whole life, the majority of cases he investigated and documented, though less dramatic than these; are memorable for their amazing correlations. Such an example is the case of an Indian girl called Swarnlata which began when she was three:

While travelling as a three year old with her father about 100 miles beyond her home just past the town of Katni, she pointed and asked the driver to turn down a road to *"my house"*. Although her father ignored this, soon after, when returning home she related to him further details of a supposed previous life, which he wrote down. She claimed she was called "Biya" then, and said she had had two sons, died of a "pain in her throat" and gave the name of the doctor who treated her. She said she had lived in this house previously, then described in detail where the house was located and the layout of each room in the house.

Later when Swarnlata was 10 years old, the case came to the attention of Dr. Stevenson. He then sent an assistant, a Professor Banerjee to research the case. Banerjee then travelled to the house successfully, but solely using Swarnlata's descriptions. He then met the owners who knew nothing of Swarnlata, nevertheless they amazingly were able to corroborate to Banerjee **every** recollection she earlier had made to her father.

Some months later, following Banerjee's visit, a number of Katni villagers, arrived at Swarnlata's house unannounced to confront her. This included a group of those whom she had claimed when only three years old were her relatives and had lived in this "Biya" house. Amongst the group, importantly were a supposed son of hers, and a supposed brother. In addition, the group included the most significant person of all who had travelled to Swarnlata's house to confront her - it was her supposed previous husband, who was still alive.

When ushered into the house, Swarnlata immediately recognized her brother and even called him by his pet name. In short she recognized everyone she remotely could have been expected to identify, if she had lived in a previous reincarnation as Biya. Apart from villagers, some of whom she accurately identified, she correctly identified a brother of Biya, despite his attempts to mislead her with continual claims for the rest of the day that he was someone else. When she came to Biya's husband, she lowered her eyes and acted bashfully as Hindu wives do in the presence of their husbands, and correctly spoke his name. Then to his shock, she reminded him correctly (which he quickly admitted) that he had purloined 1200 rupees from Biya before she died and that the money had been kept in a box.

The sequel to this account, continues with further remarkable correlations. A few weeks later, Swarnlata's father took her to Katni to visit the home and town where Biya had lived and died, Swarnlata related correctly all changes to the house subsequent to her death. She identified Biya's room correctly where she had lived and died, correctly identified more than two dozen people Biya had known, reacting to each with emotions appropriate for Biya's relationship to each of them.

In the years that followed, Swarnlata visited her supposed previous family at the house in Katni regularly, and developed a close relationship with many of them. Significantly all accepted her as Biya reborn. Obviously with such a long and close relationship with this family they would have a continual ability to test her validity as Biya - yet their unwavering support for her authenticity has continued, as they still continue in having complete acceptance of Swarnlata as a reincarnated version of Biya. Dr. Stevenson himself visited and corresponded with Swarnlata throughout the years following the investigation.

(The above is an abbreviated version of this case suitable for inclusion in this book, rather than in a research paper. For those wishing full details of the case, these are readily available on the internet (via this referenced link)[12]

In the detailed version of the story, 60 correlations are claimed by Stephenson. Such a number of unlikely correlations occurred which unquestionably identified Biya that the probability of chance occurrence is not just remote; but statistically impossible to have occurred by chance. This is no doubt why, in review of one of Stevenson's works, the prestigious Journal of the American Medical Association stated that "Dr. Stevenson painstakingly and unemotionally collected a detailed series of cases in which the evidence for reincarnation is difficult to understand on any other grounds"...."He has placed on record a large amount of data that cannot be ignored"[13].

The case of Swarnlata/Biya is one thing, but it must be remembered that Dr. Stevenson documented painstaking evidence for at least 800 such "verified" cases - very much the same as this case.

Perhaps this is a case of a "white crow" mentioned earlier above. However with Dr. Stevenson's and his successor Dr. Jim Tucker's "solved" and "verified" cases to date, there is likely to be many such "white crows".

Dr Stevenson's and Dr. Jim Tucker's industry, dedication to accuracy and meticulous research; is a heritage for us all, of many such "white crows" amongst their painstaking documentation.

Meryle Secrest in publishing a 1988 Omni Magazine interview with Dr. Ian Stevenson, introduced the subject by back-grounding his career to date indicating that his (then) recently published book, *Twenty Cases Suggestive of Reincarnation*, had been translated into seven languages and sold more than 50,000 copies. He responded by expressing disappointment that more were purchased by the public, than by scientists.

I must say that I feel I have some understanding why this is so; as scientists, more than most, have spent a lifetime on complex issues developing their scientific belief structure very carefully. Being time poor - from a quick and superficial critique of Stevenson's amazing "solved" results, it is very easy to conclude that his results are simply too good to be true.

As pointed out by Merle Secrest in her Omni article: "The idea that some children of ages 3-5 not only remember a previous existence, but can identify loved ones from it, strikes some Westerners as so bizarre that it compels disbelief".

We have all become rather accustomed to an expectation today that major scientific breakthroughs can only result from the use of complex technical equipment, almost incomprehensible mathematics, repetitive experiments and analysis by scientists with typically the intellect of a physicist such as Stephen Hawkings. The thought that a relatively unknown psychiatrist/doctor such as Dr. Stevenson and assistants, were able to achieve a breakthrough discovery and provide watertight evidence for an afterlife - simply by interviewing children without experimentation and complex equipment – might easily be thought surely ridiculous, and not worthy of further interest.

On this subject, another (earlier) interview with Dr. Stevenson in a BBC programme interview in 1976, is rather illuminating. Professors Cohen and Taylor regarded a notion by Dr Stevenson (while attempting to suggest that a child's ability to remember past lives) might well be explained by extra-cerebral memories, as totally absurd. Dr. Stevenson vehemently disagreed. "Memories may exist in the brain," he said, "and exist elsewhere also. The best evidence that they may exist elsewhere", Stevenson continued, "comes from his own reincarnation research". On the question of the "storage" of memories, he remarked that there "might be a nonphysical process of storage." The memories "might be in some dimension...which cannot be understood in terms of current physical concepts[14]."

As we are now aware from earlier Chapters in this book, some 40 years later; evidence suggests that Dr Stevenson's statements are both correct and fully compatible with modern quantum research. PCAR quantum non-physical processing is undoubtedly the mechanism that all life-forms use for memory storage, and memory is believed to be extra-cerebral and stored in the zero point field - the internet of the universe. Also few are aware of Dr. Stevenson's meticulous, skeptical and even pedantic approach to a new case. His first premise was to believe that all involved in each case were fraudulent and that all other explanations had to be examined minutely before a case was worthy of being classified as "solved" and recorded, let alone given a "verified" classification. As stated by Carol Bowman, Stevenson's approach is also "extremely academic, and in researching them she "had to struggle to follow his categorical reasoning, and to sift through the pedantic verbiage and long discourses on methodology."

Before we leave these milestone cases and the efforts of Dr. Stevenson in support of reincarnation, we also need to consider some other remarkable correlations which occur as patterns in a number of his cases. Among them are such factors as the young age at which children recall previous lives, i.e. typically between 2 to 5. This is found to be universal, occurring in every country and culture. Such a universal pattern obviously has statistical significance, since not only in this case is it readily explainable (as covered above) as being attributable to reincarnation, but has no other explanation. There are many other factors such as behavior traits, special skills, phobias, preferences and cultural or social characteristics, which themselves provide matching "hits" which often add further impressive support in some cases to a case. A particularly key pattern-overarching issue, is whether the results of other researchers in the same field have identical correlations. Some of these pattern correlations are worthy of a brief discussion.

Cultural matching was very evident in Swarnlata's case above where her bashful deference to her husband could rightfully be expected of a Hindu wife. This was and as seen was completely vindicated, adding to the validity of the case.

As pointed out by Carol Bowman, past life researcher and practicing past life regression therapist for more than 25 years, in one of her two books dealing with children's recall of past lives, called *Children's Past Lives*:

"Dr. Stevenson admits that a lone example of unusual behavior in a child means nothing: the trait could be explained in many ways. **But when many characteristics, all unusual and seemingly unrelated, form a syndrome of behavior that corresponds perfectly to the life of the previous personality, then that offers convincing evidence for reincarnation**. Dr. Stevenson documents clear correspondence of behavior in almost all of his solved cases[15]".

Phobias are so common amongst Dr. Stephenson's cases, that as with the universality of the young age when children are first likely to speak of past lives, phobias are a flag likely signifying the case is likely to end up on further investigation as a "verified" case. But they are also a classic characteristic of reincarnation for both young and old alike. As is explained below:

Phobia are often present in a multitude of ways - such as a fear of water, fire, noises reminiscent of gunfire etc. Although many seem inexplicable; all make perfect sense when the child, amongst his or her recollections, actually happens to state the reason for their death. This is because the reason given invariably relates to its cause. Such cases are even more common if the death was violent, e.g. a strong obsessive fear of any noise reminiscent of a gunshot, can be identified directly by the child's description of their earlier death, as the child invariably gives the most likely rational reason (i.e. they were shot), as the cause of death; but without the sophistication of ever logically relating this to the phobia.

As stated by Stevenson himself during the Omni magazine interview above:

"Violent death is a factor in our cases. In more than 700 cases in six different cultures, 61% remembered having died violently.........Children also tend to remember the final years of a previous life. Almost 75% of our children appear to recall the way they died, and if death was violent, they remember it in vivid detail.[16]"

Another repetitive characteristic of such phobias in children is that - if the parent (or a therapist) is able to successfully encourage the child to fully relive the experience, such recall aided with reassurance is usually successful in overcoming the child's phobia permanently. Again, expectations and fulfilment that phobias are likely, especially in cases of violent death which invariably credibly matches the child's recollection of death, is also itself strong support for reincarnation. The fact that there is no reasonable alternative explanation for this linkage **in every such case**, and the fact that Dr. Stephenson has many such verified cases; further vindicates belief in reincarnation[17].

In this group of pattern type matching correlation cases, the last but most important issue is the issue of whether Dr. Stevenson's research results were and are being replicated and verified by researchers elsewhere in the world and today. There is of course continuation of Dr. Stevenson's work following his death in 2007 at the University of Virginia by Dr. Jim B. Tucker MD together with his assistants around the world. Carol Bowman M.S. mentioned above has considerable personal experience with her own two children, both of whom spontaneously recalled a past life sparking her interest in the subject. Based on her experience with her own children (and that of many others over the years) as a fully qualified and practicing therapist, she later has written two bestselling books on the subject with details of many case studies. Norman Inge, whom acted as her mentor and tutor together with another pioneer of this subject in the late 1990's, Dr. Roger Woolger (who wrote the best seller book), *Other Lives, Other Selves*, trained her in regression techniques[18].

Other authors such as Joel Whitton and Dr. Raymond Moody have also written books which have included case studies and information on children who remember past lives. Although none use such a sophisticated and meticulous methodology as Dr. Stevenson, all have case studies included in their books. These completely support his findings by exhibiting a similar number of identical type and pattern of correlations found by Dr. Stevenson and his colleagues. In fact, the stimulus of Dr. Stevenson's work and that of other pioneers of the past life research at the time, may well have subsequently caused exponential growth in hypnotic regression therapy by psychiatrists on patients. This almost without exception has proved successful in remedying their phobias. It is noteworthy, that since there is no other explanation, that each case vindicates reincarnation. This is covered in the next section of this Chapter.

7.2 HYPNOSIS AND PAST LIFE REGRESSION

7.2.1 Hypnosis

Before dealing with hypnotic regression i.e. regressing a hypnotized subject back to an earlier date (e.g. childhood) or to a supposed previous life, we first need to learn a little more about hypnotism and its properties.

Definition

Hypnosis is a state of consciousness involving focused attention and reduced peripheral awareness characterized by an enhanced capacity for response to suggestion. – Wikipedia.

History

Hypnosis has been used extensively by stage hypnotists and hypnotherapists since its discovery in the mid 1800's by Mesmer.

As evident with stage demonstrations of hypnosis, the person being hypnotised, voluntary subjugates his normal belief system in favour of the hypnotist - as reported in *Scientific American* Article, July 2001 (see "The Truth and the Hype of Hypnosis" by Michael R Nash). **The hypnotist, in effect, replaces the conscious mind, ego and belief system of the subject and communicates directly with the unconscious mind.**

Notably for hypnosis, remote viewing and Monroe's OOB research - all are importantly aimed at ensuring the subject enters a relaxed slight trance type state. In the case of remote viewing (described in Chapter 4), the remote viewer relaxes with his eyes shut lying on a bed while a monitor offers guidance and suggestions taking notes to ensure the remote viewer is not otherwise distracted from his task. This also mimics the similar role of a technician in the case of Monroe's use of his Hemi-Sync process for research and experiments in OOB states at the Monroe Institute in Virginia, as covered in the previous Chapter.

A light trance reduces the influence of distractions and ensures the subject is attentive and responsive to what the hypnotist is saying. However the most important characteristic of hypnotism has nothing to do with this, but instead it is the trance state itself. The commonality and inevitable result of invoking a slight trance state (as covered in previous Chapters and perhaps unknown generally to hypnotists themselves), is that with the conscious mind suppressed, our unconsciousness, and right brain processing comes to the fore where we inevitably access non-physical reality. This was described by the Russian quantum Physicist Mensky (see Chapter 2), Therefore quantum holographic property of interconnectedness applies, and as we would expect, we then have the possibility of gaining unlimited access not just to our classical current life physical memory, but also our **non-physical memory** via the zero point field. It therefore follows, that from what has already been covered in this book, a hypnotist's ability to enable subjects to accurately recall instances from their earlier life, **or previous lives**, is not magical, nor an enigma – but instead it would be expected from the underlying science.

The Importance to Reincarnational Belief:

Children's spontaneous recall of previous lives, which formed the first section of this Chapter, is by its very nature random and unpredictable. Knowledge gained in this way concerning reincarnation and the reincarnational process is therefore **largely**

opportunistic and minimal. In contrast, with hypnotic regression, the hypnotist has an unparallelled opportunity to seek responses from a subject directly and continuously to gain vital information **interactively** from previous lives and the reincarnational process.

7.2.2 Past Life Regression

History

Hypnotic regression has become a useful tool for hypnotherapists and psychiatrists ever since the days of Freud, when he found hypnotic regression an excellent method of seeking out earlier traumatic incidents which may have caused the patient's current phobias **or illness**. It was found that *reliving* such experiences under hypnosis generally effects a permanent cure. The reliving aspect is critical in achieving catharsis of symptoms as it seems phobias can remain problematical until the conscious mind identifies the cause. By reliving the experience again fully when relaxed in an unconscious state, it is thought that this enables the subject to cope and find resolution with what was previously such a frightening issue, that it had earlier became buried almost irretrievably in the unconscious. Hypnotic regression has also led to successful cures by therapists in dealing with problems such as smoking, bed wetting, and many psychiatric illnesses such as compulsions, unexplained and unreasonable fears, and traumas. Hypnosis has also been shown to be effective in removing persistent pain issues and muscle cramp when thorough medical and specialist clinical examinations detect no physiological cause.

Evidence

Scores of books have been written by professional hypnotherapists/ researchers containing hundreds of cases of regressions of subjects/clients back to supposed previous lives. It seems self-evident when reading any of these books, that the purpose of author's in writing is unlikely to be for commercial gain (few write for a living, and most are relatively well-off professionals). Instead they are all most likely to be primarily written altruistically by author's wishing to share their experiences which led to their personal reincarnational belief (importantly it follows that this ensures they are likely to be truthful accounts). While some case studies are often fascinating, their repetition scientifically does little to augment their case. In fact there is a real danger that portrayal of case after case as evidence, or provision of copious detail, could unintentionally become repetitive, and boring. Thus becoming counterproductive to the point where it succeeds in readers either *"not being able to see the woods for the trees"*, or concluding that *"the whole multiple lives thing seems too fanciful to be true"*.

Structure of Evidence Presentation

Accordingly, what follows in the Chapter, is a desirably science based evidential approach, structured as follows:

- First presented below is an analysis of speculative criticisms often made by critics, suggesting that the regression process itself is flawed by being susceptible to fraud, misconception, acting by subjects, and hypnotists leading the subjects. These criticisms are then compared with actual regressional practices adopted by professionals together with the methodologies they take to completely avoid any of these issues.

- This is then followed by presentation in some detail of a unique and milestone research 10 year study by a Dr Helen Wambach, who, for her research, used a scientific statistical approach to a very large initial sample number of subjects (1088) she personally regressed. Her aim was to determine whether there was comparability between all results of her subject's regressions, and whether these results support reincarnation. Scientifically therefore, if successful, this would amount to vertical correlation of her cases in favour of reincarnation.

- Next, a number of key evidential supportive findings with reincarnational theory documented by other hypnotherapists/researchers are compared with each other and with the massive findings of Dr Wambach. This approach is aimed at vindicating or otherwise her findings, as well as their own (scientifically, if comparability is achieved - this amounts to horizontal correlation).

- Finally the remainder of the Chapter is concerned with the essential test of whether or not a supposed regressed subject's recollections are found to truly agree with historical records. This is of course a critical issue. It is also an important facet of Dr Wambach's statistical evidence and results. However, scientifically one should never accept results from a single source such as Wambach's, so it is necessary to seek correlation from other findings. In this respect there is no shortage of cases cited elsewhere of successful historical matching with subjects recollections. There are countless instances in the literature of claimed successful historical validation by professional hypnotherapists/ researchers (and others). To avoid repetition and guard against the unlikely event of falsification by these authors themselves, two cases are included where the regression itself and subsequent historical verification of the regressions were not just (as is typical) reported by the hypnotist/researcher concerned, but were witnessed by a producer, and film crew as part of an Australian Channel Seven documentary. Thousands of members of the public who watched the subsequent screening, could rightly also be regarded as witnesses to the regressions and their historical validation.

The following therefore is this evidence presented in this structured manner:

First dealing with an analysis of speculative criticisms often made by critics:

Measures Taken by Hypnotherapists/Researchers to Avoid Data Contamination

As mentioned previously, children's recall of previous lives is unlikely to be coloured by exaggeration, imagination or even fraud. However, such innocence is **not** the case with hypnotic regression of adults. Therefore we all need to be personally satisfied that procedures used in any regression research experiments either must remove completely, or minimise the effect of any such tainted data affecting the results.

The most common criticism, is that the suggestibility aspect of hypnotism leads to subjects simply fulfilling the hypnotist's expectation, by fantasising or acting. Fairly, at first sight, there certainly seems some justification for such a view - as evidenced by the flamboyant behaviour of those subjected to stage hypnotism. There have also been successful experiments aimed at creating fantasy personalities with hypnotised subjects and then seeking their responses with pseudo life recall. While it is possible by suggestion to create a fantasy personality; in real life circumstances involving a **professional hypnotherapist or researcher**, this is simply not the case. Nor is it particularly likely that a regression subject seeking a cure, will claim under hypnosis a previous life as a well-known historical figure. Instead, as in everyday life, and as would be expected, professionally regressed subjects constantly report normal, rather uneventful and mundane lives.

Happily, (although not often appreciated), there is though a major difference between the training, expertise and intent of stage entertainment hypnotists, and those of professional hypnotherapists or researchers. In the latter case, professionals are often university qualified doctors and psychologists who have specialised in psychotherapy. None are likely to be other than highly qualified and trained for their vocation. In today's world, hypnotherapy is a growth industry of particular value to practitioners, and for many members of the public. This is because regressive hypnosis has a **prime commercial purpose and medical benefit**. It is a valuable tool to effect a cure, for practising hypnotherapists to identify the cause of phobias, traumas, illness and unexplainable pain. As mentioned previously, a cure is fairly readily and simply attained, since once the incident which has caused the problem is re-visited and brought to the attention of the patient, the problem usually disappears. **Significantly, whether the incident occurred earlier in the patient's existing life or during a previous life, is irrelevant, as the cure occurs just as easily**. The fact that this itself is impossible to explain away without an after-life explanation, is itself the reason why psychotherapists themselves come to believe in reincarnation, even if they did not before. The secondary professional purpose for regression, is a fairly recent growing demand by the public (as we will learn more later in this book), to learn details about their individual past lives. This usually covers information about their most recent past life, their reincarnational progress, and their wish for identification of their **current life purpose** (covered more fully later).

For these reasons, professional regressive hypnotists and researchers have studied intensively in their training those characteristics that will allow them to quickly identify any patents who are only in a superficial trance (or none at all). Plus any patient's state and position in various stages of trance or consciousness at any time throughout the session. On occasions there are patients who are unable to be hypnotised initially or at all, and they **might** try to fake their responses and provide fantasies instead, often too embarrassed to admit that they are not really recalling past lives. Such instances though seem unlikely, as patients are paying for their therapy or past life information, and would be expected to bring any difficulty they might have with the process to the attention of the hypnotist. Professional hypnotists in any case would be expected to mention the issue of fantasising or acting particularly to their patients before commencing a session.

Regardless of this, in the literature, professional hypnotists, contrary to many critics' claims - that all cases of regressive hypnosis, are subject to fraud and fantasies; are adamant that this is not the case. They stress that fantasies and deceptions, if they occur, are easily identified and dealt with. Moreover, in the case of past life scientific research using hypnotic regression; adopting a large sample size when looking solely at statistical correlations, swamps any possible small number of spurious or perhaps fanciful results.

Because any suggestion of fantasy, acting, or the hypnotist leading the subject, could be severely detrimental to reincarnation research verification, it is worthwhile including here some technical detail on the way in which fantasies and other regressional issues can be identified by professional hypnotists. They report that fantasies can easily be distinguished from true past life regression, primarily by the **absence** of emotion while unconscious. In contrast, with true hypnotic recall, subjects vividly **relive** experiences in the regressed state, and exhibit **intense** emotion and often physiological responses. One such physiological response for example, is that a person regressed to early childhood often adopts the foetal position, the sucking reflex and even the fan-like extension of the toes that occurs in infants when the lateral part of the sole is stimulated by a sharp object.[19]

Some hypnotherapists use EEG (electroencephalograph) techniques, where waveforms detected of 8.3 cycles per second have been found to indicate a genuine altered state of consciousness where past life recall occurs[20].

Dr Helen Wambach, in her book, *Reliving Past Lives* reported that true reliving of experiences (whether in the same life or past lives), as with the depth of hypnosis; can also easily be identified. This is shown by the presence of rapid eye movement, by lifting limbs to check on muscle tension and by a characteristic ability by clients under deep hypnosis **to recall any desired degree of detail**. Also valid recall is evident **by subjects universally being resistant to being led**. Contrary to critics who might claim suggestibility, Dr Wambach said "they stick stubbornly and literally to whatever it is they are experiencing." She also relates that when deeply hypnotised, subjects have difficulty in articulating, and their voices become almost inaudible. [21]

Of significant interest is the fact that as reported by her, regressed subjects simply do not recall events as just visual images, but are able to describe feelings they had at the time, as well as **all** sensory impressions such as hearing, touch, taste and smell [22].

(It will be appreciated that this is as we would expect, as when consciousness is focussed on non-physical reality via the right brain, unconscious state - as in a light trance; the PCAR communication system comes to the fore.) Regression often deepens into a strange state termed "identification" by many hypnotherapists, where awareness of the present completely vanishes, and the subject is so focussed in the past that they feel and think as they did then. In many cases continually challenging the hypnotist as to "Who is he? Why doesn't he have slaves of his own? etc. [23]

Many readers will note that this seems little different from remote viewing except that rather than geographical sites, buildings, or installations, etc. being the target, in this case the target is the subject themselves in a previous incarnation.

Voice changes are said to be common - such as a girl reliving an experience as a male, speaks in a deeper voice. Not only are speech patterns changed, but also handwriting. Faces of those who recalled old age can become haggard and drawn, while creases in the faces of the elderly become smoothed out when recalling a previous youth. Muscular spasms in the faces of former stroke victims has also been observed [24]

The breathing rhythm and posture often changes and in some instances physical changes are extreme, such as red stripes appearing on the skin while the subject describes being whipped.[25]

Detail of Regressional Researches – Wambach's Statistical Approach

Dr Helen Wambach, as a practising psychologist at Monmouth Medical Centre in Long Branch, New Jersey and teacher at the local community college, first became interested in telepathy and hypnotic regressional theory when applying psychotherapy to a severely autistic child Linda at the Monmouth Medical Centre. To her consternation she became convinced that the reason for her rapid progress with Linda was attributable to her becoming telepathically linked with Linda. Linda had never spoken and yet after some weeks of therapy, she seemed to constantly respond to Dr Wambach's thoughts. Dr Wambach's confusion was attributable to the fact that up until then, she had maintained the same disbelief in the paranormal as her university college teachers. Her experience with Linda then sparked her interest to the point where she, somewhat reluctantly but then successfully tried out hypnotic regression on a number of patients with phobias. Gradually over some years she became both a proficient practising hypnotherapist, and also a lecturer at the university college. There, as part of her Introductory Psychology course, she taught parapsychology. Then in the late 1960s, wishing to "…want to know more. I wanted to apply what I had learned about the scientific method to the areas (such as the paranormal and hypnotic regression), that most people shove aside as being of no importance"[26].

She then began what became a 10-year survey and research of past life recollections - which amounted to unquestionably the most comprehensive statistical and scientific investigation of the validity and basis for hypnotic past life regression ever undertaken.

For anyone interested in the details of the research which is both detailed and very well set out with accompanying graphs and charts, they are all contained in the latter part of her book *Reliving Past Lives*, which claims *Startling new evidence of reincarnation* as a subtitle.

Essentially her research provided the results and analysis of her regressions of eventually over 2000 adults from which she gained responses to very specific questions about the time periods in which people lived, their clothing, footwear, utensils, money, housing, etc. which they used or came in contact with. In addition, how they looked, what they wore and ate, and questions about their supposed daily lives. Her intention was therefore then to match their answers against known available historical data.

The plan was simple but ingenious. The answers would either align regularly with known historical data, or there would be very few such alignments. Given the large sample size, a few alignments could happen by chance. This would support the skeptics. On the other hand, if the answers almost always align with known facts and time periods, then both regression and reincarnation would be completely validated.

The results as they say, are now history - in that matching was verified in all but 1% of the total sheets submitted by all 1088 adult subjects in the largest of Wambach's samples. As described by Dr. Wambach in her book *Reliving Past Lives*, all eleven sheets rejected as a match, were based on a just single time displacement on a sheet despite many other correlations which were found accurate, and not very far off from the event described. She also stated "It could be that in these cases, my subjects' awareness of the time period was in error, rather than the past life recall". She concluded that she found peoples' recollections to be amazingly accurate and wrote that ''fantasy and genetic memory could not account for the patterns that emerged in the results".

As summarised by Carol Bowman (above), "the final result was an amazing correlation point by point between the composite of the subject's past life recalls and historical fact".

It is interesting to note that with regard to the few instances where Dr Wambach encountered time displacement in a subjects data, a number of other hypnotherapists have also mentioned that with regression, subjects usually have extreme difficulty in recalling dates and their past life "names". This is particularly frustrating, as some researchers wish on occasions to use official birth records to investigate a subject's account against available historical records of their lives including birth/death certificates. The reason for this difficulty is not known, but it might well be that in the case of dates, since non-physical reality is timeless (and spaceless); while in a trance state, particular dates have little significance for us, since reincarnation belief suggests we spend the majority of our existence between lives. "*Names*" for one life, amongst a very large number* of existences would likewise have little significance. Alternatively, it would seem possible that the storage structure of our seemingly unlimited non-physical memory in the zero point field might well be different from that of our limited memory in this classical physical life. (* Note: in some cases, over 1000 reincarnational cycles have been reported).

In the case of Dr Wambach's research though, she was not in the least bit interested in her subjects names in previous existences, but she was critically interested in whether they lived during the time frames she had chosen (eight intervals of 500 years each, four before and four after the birth of Christ) for her graphs. A match was only successful if the subject was able to record accurately the correct historical time **period** (not particular date) for the event recalled (e.g. first wearing of armour in battle in England). An important aspect of Dr Wambach's methodology, was that to speed up the regressions and reduce her work load, she made all her subjects fill in appropriate questionnaires immediately after a particular regression (a number of samples of these questionnaires recorded during her research are included in her book). This was achieved by her giving her subjects a suggestion that they would vividly remember what they had experienced, and that they would fill out their data sheets easily upon wakening. She also said to them "You will not share your experience with others until you have completed your data sheet." The questionnaires thus formed replicable and documented evidence created by the subjects themselves rather than by Dr Wambach. In addition, they form a replicable record of results which could therefore be examined by others if desired.

During all the sessions, interestingly, Dr Wambach mentions she became conscious of forming the same telepathic link with a number of her subjects which first started her on her career and later research into past life regression. During one-on-one regressions earlier in her career, she had encountered subjects responding often to her questions before she had even asked them. During these non-verbal sessions, when some of her subjects were experiencing any physical or emotional difficulty with regression or the written questions, she immediately became aware of this and was able later to intervene without their even verbalising an issue[27].

A quick summary of the results follows:

- In excess of 90% subjects reported previous lives, with the remainder unable to be hypnotized due to fear of encountering a particular unpleasant death experienced. *This nevertheless means that all who were regressed, experienced past lives* (i.e. Some 980 subjects, which obviously is an extremely high statistical result, which gives a high degree of confidence of only the chance of a few percent possibility of error.)

- 50.3 % of the past lives reported were male and 49.7 % were female - this is exactly in accordance with biological fact.

- The number of people reporting upper class or comfortable lives was in exactly the same proportion to the estimates of historians of the class distribution of the period.

- The recall by subjects of clothing, footwear, type of food and utensils used was better than that in popular history books. She found over and over again that her subjects knew better than most historians – as when she went to obscure experts to check historical facts more accurately her subjects were invariably correct[28].

Dealing specifically with some of the most interesting areas covered:

Gender: Despite the fact that 78% of the subjects chosen for the experiments were woman, they switched their gender seemingly randomly between past lifetimes. Nevertheless the overall average result of all regressions, subjects and time periods, indicated the classical factual uniform statistical population split of 50.3 percent male to 49.7 percent female! (The slight bias toward males is generally considered nature's way of compensating for the greater number of male infant deaths).

Rich and Poor: Contrary to expectations claimed by many sceptics of regressions, not one subject claimed a previous life as someone famous. Instead most subjects reported past lives which were mundane, ordinary and hard, with the normal occupation farming and gathering food in almost all time periods. Most wore homespun garments, living in crude huts and eating cereals with their fingers from wooden bowls. For all time periods, the results indicated a consistent ratio of rich to poor lives over all time periods with the rich never less than 10 percent. In contrast, the lower classes (defined as peasants, natives, and slaves) were never less than 60 percent. During bleak periods of history, the proportion rose to as high as 80 percent. All of which aligned accurately with statistical expectations.

Food: Most reported food as bland foods, such a gruel made with cereal grains, roots and berries gathered by natives, and some tree fruits or vegetables. Meat was rare, with beef not even mentioned at all until 1500. Many subjects reported they only often tasted spoiled food and that wild game was small animals that tasted greasy. Dr Wambach was even able through the subject's sheets to trace the evolution of eating utensils. From crude spoons and scoopers first reported, these transitioned to a three-pronged fork which first appeared in 1500 and then finally to today's modern four pronged fork which appeared first around 1800. Unsurprisingly, the majority of her subjects reported eating with their fingers.

Clothing and Footwear: The subject's description of their clothing worn during former lifetimes invariably corresponded correctly with historical records amongst all time periods. Even dealing accurately with the different clothing worn by upper and lower classes in Egypt where upper classes wore either a half-length or full-length white cotton robe. The lower classes wore something like an exotic-looking type of pants that was wrapped downwards from the waist. Regarding footwear, to gain a satisfactory response to what a subject was wearing on their feet, Dr Wambach often found it easiest to ask her subjects to look down and describe what they saw. On one occasion a female subject related that as an Italian knight in AD 1200, she was surprised when she lowered her head to look at her feet and saw a pair of triangle headed boots on her feet instead of her expectations of round headed armoured footwear, as she had seen in a museum. She was later to discover in an encyclopaedia, that her recollections of a past life were more accurate than her current life beliefs, as this was the type of boots worn in Italy by knights within her previous life's timeframe.

Death Experiences: Dr Wambach specifically asked all subjects the nature of the death and emotion they individually experienced following their death. The commonest experience described was identical to those reported in NDE (i.e. Near Death Experience) research, as almost invariably and reassuringly as "like being released, going home again". An average of 40 percent experienced feelings of calm and peace. Also an average of 20 percent experienced seeing their dead bodies after death, and floating above the body while watching activity around it. After the sessions Dr Wambach's subjects commented "again and again" (contrary to popular belief)" that how pleasant it was to die, and what a sense of relief they had after they left their bodies".

Naturally as would be expected, a number, about 10 percent of Dr Wambach's subjects reported feeling upset or emotions of sorrow at death. This was said to be due to a number of factors, such as leaving children behind together with other close family members, and concern due to others' grief for their death. Additionally the cause of death, if violent, was often reported as a major reason for an unpleasant association with death. Dr Wambach was surprised to find that some of her subjects advised her some weeks after the group regressions that their lifelong phobias had disappeared. The strength of emotion experienced at death particularly that of fear, seemed the main factor. A sudden and unexpected death also caused disorientation, as it took a while for some to become aware that they were dead. It was evident though that these phobias were always related to the mode of death the subjects had experienced in a particular past life. For example a fear of water disappeared when the subject remembered drowning, etc. This repeatedly indicated logical consistency, a key scientific parameter of credibility in results. It is noteworthy that many of Dr Wambach's subjects were cured of phobias without any guidance or intervention by a therapist - and without any preconception by them that by just remembering their past lives, their phobias could vanish. This tangible and yet unexpected result surely must provide further support for belief in validity of multiple lives and reincarnation.

Unquestionably Dr Helen Wambach's statistical and thorough research approach to past life regression is unsurpassed to date. Apart from the statistical approach, it is perhaps unique for three main reasons:

- The large size of the sample – over 1088 subjects which is suitably large enough to provide a high statistical confidence in the results.

- The statistical methodology adopted of using time periods completely overcomes difficulties researchers normally experience in checking individual dates for **historical validation**. As mentioned previously, regressed subjects often encounter memory issues with trying to provide an exact birth/death dates (also names). In addition, historical information is often unreliable or non-existent when the subject's lives pre-date national birth/death records and also for names of small towns or street names.

- Results indicate 90% of subjects were able to recall previous lives with only the remaining 10% unable to be hypnotised initially. Wambach, determined to succeed, tried again, and this time was successful on a second attempt with a further two. In these cases and by asking them the reason while under hypnosis, she found their initial resistance was due to fear of encountering a particular unpleasant past life death experience. She felt this vindicated that all subjects, even those initially resistant, could eventually be successfully regressed to recall multiple lives. Therefore there was no need to bother those remaining further. With such a large statistical sample, and with many subjects having previously no particular belief in an afterlife, this result by itself must surely provide incredible compelling evidence that we all likewise experience multiple lives. (To be certain scientifically though it does require correlation with other independent researcher's results – as is covered below)[29].

It is difficult to envisage Dr Wambach's approach ever being repeated due to two reasons. The first is the sheer size, scope and the calibre of the research which took 10 years of dedication she put into it herself, aided by many volunteer university students. The second reason is that the results largely make any major investigations irrelevant as they overwhelmingly indicate the reality that **all of us experience multiple lives**; therefore vindicating belief in reincarnation.

From a scientific point of view though, it is necessary to ensure that Dr Helen Wambach has not fabricated or distorted all the results herself (however unlikely). We need therefore to ensure that independent research into the same subject has been both been carried out by other similarly qualified professional researchers and that their results align exactly with hers. The irony in this case is that not only are there numerous researchers in the field, but when looking at each documented case where professionals are involved in regression research and/or therapy, one finds outcomes which correlate exactly with the findings of Wambach. By this I don't mean that others have used Wambach's statistical approach using a massive sample, as Wambach's work is unique. But simply that in the context of individual professionally initiated regressions carried out either for research or for hypnotherapy (where worldwide typically regressions occur hour after hour, every hour of the day, day after day); all the critical hallmarks encountered by interrelating with regressed subjects when analysed are found to correlate with those determined by Wambach **without exception**. Most importantly of all, they universally suggest a genuine recall of a past life. These are the hallmarks expressed by physiological or emotional behaviour during a regression together with the commonality of experiences contained within actual verbal accounts. A complete list would be formidable, so instead I have provided ten of them chosen to cover a range of areas associated with regressional practise, and to make the point of universal correlations.

Some of these have been taken from Hans TenDam's book *Exploring Reincarnation*, with the subtitle *The Classic Guide to the Evidence for Past-Life Experiences* These ten cases are but a fraction of correlations of TenDam's own experiences and results covered in his book compared with those of other authors - all detailed in his book with page references of the other referenced authors. His book is formidable (it comprises 425 pages) and unique in that it contains this verification comparison research. Hans TenDam was a pioneer in Dutch hypnotic regression and the excellent credentials as a graduate of the University of Amsterdam in psychology and pedagogy. He is currently an independent consultant and researcher, a Board member of The International Association of Regression Research and Therapies in California, and he trains psychotherapists in past-life therapy.

Comparision of Findings of Other Hypnotherapists/Researchers with those of Dr Helen Wambach on Key Reincarnational Beliefs

A number of **areas** below are covered as necessary evidence to demonstrate comparability of findings amongst a number of different hypnotherapists/researchers i.e. horizontal correlations. Importantly though, I have chosen them as fundamental issues which by themselves may assist one to decide whether the case has already been made for reincarnation.

1. **The most basic tenet of reincarnational belief is that all subjects would be expected to have multiple lives.**

    Therefore it would be expected that if reincarnation is true, than regression would find that all of us are capable of remembering past lives. As indicated above, in effect this is exactly what Wambach found. Her results also align completely with those of James Parejko, a professor of philosophy at Chicago State University, who revealed similar results to those of Wambach i.e. he found that 93 out of his 100 hypnotized volunteers were able to be regressed to a previous life.[30] Scientifically this by itself fundamentally indicated that reincarnation for all of us is vindicated i.e. *if we are hypnotically regressed, statistics overwhelmingly indicate we all will likewise experience past lives, and that reincarnation is true.*

As just an interesting aside, there is a striking aspect found by Professor Joel Whitton in his book *Life Between Life*. He mentioned that not only did his subjects remember previous lives, but the interesting point that some remembered as many as twenty to twenty-five. Although a practical limit was reached when Whitton regressed them to what he calls their "caveman existences," when one lifetime became indistinguishable from the next.[31]

2. **Another core reincarnational belief is that we all frequently reincarnate as a member of a different sex.**

Within most accepted viewpoints of reincarnation, is the concept that to gain experience each person reincarnates on occasions in a different sex. As above, Wambach with a very large sample found her subjects met the statistical population index of 50.3 percent male to 49.7 percent female[32].

Statistical population surveys are reported as indicating that, given a choice, the average person would prefer life as a male. However in marked contrast to this, there is no known researched case of regression of multiple lives where at least one sex change has not been encountered. This is supported and covered extensively in TenDam's book *Exploring Reincarnation*[33].

3. **Physiological indications during regression should be the same for the existing or previous lives**

As mentioned above, hypnotherapists/researchers constantly report all the common characteristics of regression are identical whether involving **same life regression or regression to an alleged past life**. Amongst these are the two main indicators of deep regression - fluttering of eyelids and the unique ability to solicit any desired level of detail. Variations or difficulty in breathing, change in facial expressions, adoption of foetal position appropriate to an infant and different voice expressions are also invariant[34].

4. **Subjects should be able to be regressed equally as well for past lives as for the current life":**

There is also no discernible difference in the ease with which subjects are able to be regressed either within their existing life or to an alleged past life. Additionally, as stated by Hans TenDam "Reliving and regression are the same for our present life, with the same possibilities and difficulties"[35].

The distinction seems in fact so arbitrary that there have been many cases of spontaneous and unexpected regression to a past life during hypnosis. Hypnotherapists intending regression only to **childhood**, have found that **past** life recall has occurred instead. A psychiatrist, Dr Brian Weiss, even wrote a book, *Many Lives, Many Masters*[36], which was triggered by such an incident involving a patient. Spontaneous past life recall has in fact occurred so often during regressions, that the psychiatry textbook *Trauma, Trance and Transformation* warns fledgling hypnotherapists "not to be surprised if such memories surface spontaneously in their hypnotized patients".[37]

Apart from Weiss, Dr Michael Newton has mentioned the same experience of accidental regression to a past life in his *Journey of Souls*, Michael Newton (1994), Kindle Book, but in this case, a life between lives.

5. **Cures of phobias likewise should equally be successful in either the current or past lives.**

Hypnotherapists' livelihoods depends on their ability to cure patients from traumas and other issues arising from phobias. A number have reported in their books that they have had equal success in using regression to cure phobia symptoms involving an incident in an earlier life, as well as in past lives. Wambach in her book *Reliving Past Lives* mentions a case early in her career of improving the symptom of a severe trauma when regressing a subject "John" in an existing life. She reported this was instrumental in setting her onto the path of regularly using hypnosis to successfully cure subject's phobias. She did this by regressing them to past lives - if this was found necessary in order to find the source of a trauma. Unintentionally she even found that a cure can be obtained so readily, that as an unexpected result of her statistical research group regressions work, as mentioned earlier, some of her subjects mentioned to her after the sessions, that their previous phobia symptoms had disappeared as a result of their regression[38].

6. **Revisiting a past life at another session should give the same result. In addition, reports by practitioners of the results of regressions for all subjects should exhibit logical consistency in depiction of a past life:**

We would expect that repeated regression of the same subject to the same time frames should consistently give the same and similar data to that obtained in previous regressions. Hypnotherapists constantly affirm that this is always the case. The ability to repeat past life experiences without change has also been tested by getting the subject to go through their alleged different past lives in varying order during different sessions. This was documented by TenDam referencing the hypnotherapist De Rochas who said "he had some of his subjects go back ten lifetimes. However often the experiments were repeated, the descriptions and even the different handwritings remained identical"[39].

Carol Bowman, the physiologist mentioned above, notable for her research and interest in children's alleged past lives, reported that children re-tell a past life experience repeatedly over a period of days, weeks, months, or years without making significant changes to the story or details. Also that details may be added as their use of language improves, or as things they experience remind them of the past. Further, all cases of hypnotic regression are characterised by an amazing logical consistency in a given subjects recollections of a past life. This, together with the ability to revisit the past life recollection again and again, and in a different order to corroborate and attain further detail, defeats critics who often suggest that past life regression is indistinguishable from dreaming, particularly lucid dreaming, or simply fantasy spoken aloud[40].

7. **When regressed, all subjects should exhibit an almost infinite memory.**

A fairly unique and demanding expectation of reincarnation, is that a person would need in some way to have a memory capability virtually without limit, as it would have to cope with an infinity of lifetimes. Remarkably (but as mentioned earlier in Chapter 2 as a holographic quantum property with memory externally stored in the zero point field), it is very easy to demonstrate both for existing life recall as well as past life recall, that the subconscious mind of subjects fulfils this requirement. In fact it can be shown to provide virtually any desired level of detail. As an example, Elizabeth Loftus, Professor of Psychology at the University of Washington in her book *Memory* relates a typical story of crime solving using hypnotic regression. A busload of twenty-six children and their driver were kidnapped and buried in a container by three masked men in the California town of Chowchilla in 1976. They managed to escape the next day, but none was able to provide much information to the FBI concerning the kidnappers. The Bureau used a hypnotist who was successfully able to get the driver to recall all but one digit of the licence plate of the kidnapper's van.[41]

There are countless other examples which demonstrate the prodigious and unusual aspects of subconscious memory available during hypnotic regression. Among them instances where patients have been able to recall complete details of earlier surgery, despite being unconscious. A brick layer who could provide an exact description of defects on bricks he laid on any past day and their location - which was subsequently verified. Memory is said to be often so complete, that a regressed person can hear sounds, smell scents and even experience thoughts, moods and feelings that occurred at the time. Emotional intensity and recall are so strong that streaks have appeared on hands and face while recalling a thrashing within an existing life and rope marks and other symptoms have appeared during alleged past life regressions[42].

Probably the most impressive scientific evidence for the notion of subconscious permanent memory comes from the work of Wilder Penfield who in the 1940's was operating on epileptic patients to remove damaged areas in their brains in order to cure their epilepsy. He stimulated the surface of the brain with a weak electric current in the hope of discovering in each patient, an area in the brain that was related to the epileptic attacks. He discovered that when he moved his probe near a portion of the brain called the hippocampus, some patients re-experienced events from their **existing** life, some from an alleged **past** life! He recorded in his notes: "It is clear that the neuronal action that accompanies each succeeding state of consciousness leaves its permanent imprint on the brain. The imprint, or record, is a trail of facilitation of neuronal connections that can be followed again by an electric current many years later **with no loss of detail**, as though a tape recorder had been receiving it all".[43]

Although the evidence above indicates these memories are permanent, they are not normally accessible. This conundrum therefore is very suggestive of the reality of past lives, as otherwise such an unlimited memory would serve no other known purpose.

8. **Occasional instances should be encountered of subjects slipping into a different language from their native language in their current life.**

Perhaps one of the most amazing feats exhibited in about 10% of cases encountered during regression, is xenoglossy - the ability to speak in a forgotten or earlier language. There are cases involving xenoglossy within the same life, such as that related by Hans TenDam, the Dutch hypnotherapist in his book *Exploring Reincarnation*. He describes a 17 year old French girl who was regressed back year by year to her life as a 5 year old child. Suddenly she spoke in "Gascon", the language she was familiar with as a child. This well indicates the unerring accuracy of true **same** life recall - now largely undisputed by practitioners such as psychiatrists and hypnotherapists.

Recall of a language learned in one's lifetime is one thing, but surprisingly to those unfamiliar with it, there are countless cases of xenoglossy associated with **past** life recall, where subjects speak fluently in **a completely unfamiliar language unknown to them and unlearned in this life**. Hans TenDam, mentions a case where a Swedish woman impulsively interjected and asked questions in Swedish at a session where an English hypnotherapist was not getting any response from an English girl being regressed. She was rewarded by the girl responding to all the questions in fluent Swedish, a language completely unknown to her.[44]

Joe Fisher in his book *The Case for Reincarnation* mentions a tape recording taken of an 11 year old boy hypnotically regressed to a past life, who spoke for eleven minutes in a Chinese dialect. A Chinese professor later identified this as an ancient and forbidden Chinese language. Also an American psychiatrist regressed to a supposed life in Mesopotamia (part of Persia) in AD 625, wrote in a childlike spidery writing, the written language of the day (This strictly speaking is xenography rather than xenoglossy). A Dr Idrahim Pourhadi of the Near East Section of the Washington Library of Congress later confirmed that the writing was "Sassanid Pahlvi" - a form of writing that has not been used since A.D. 651 and bears no relation to the present day Iranian language[45].

9. **Subjects should be able to instantly provide their specific appropriate life purpose for any past life recalled.**

In a later series of regressions carried out by Dr Helen Wambach detailed in another 750 regressions in her second book *Life Before Life*, she sought from subjects their specific purposes which led to their rebirth in their past lives. Some examples are "I wanted to expose myself to a weak and indulgent life and to overcome this", "I knew my parents needed me because they had just lost an 18 month old girl in a fire", "I wanted to come back because I had just died young", "I had to tie together and round off all the loose ends from the life just before"[46]. Also in her book *Reliving Past Lives* a single recorded case:

"That the purpose of this life was to demonstrate that single minded devotion to work and high ambition could result in high achievement"[47].

10. **Regressed subject's death experience reported by hypnotherapists/researchers should be generally consistent.**

It will be recalled that Wambach reported her subjects death experiences were identical to those reported in NDE (i.e. Near Death Experience) research, as almost invariably and reassuringly as "like being released, going home again". An average of 40 percent experienced feelings of calm and peace. Also an average of 20 percent experienced seeing their dead bodies after death, and floating above the body while watching activity around it. This conforms with results of other researchers such as Whitton, Dr Fiore and NDE's as reported by Dr Raymond Moody, as stated by Carol Bowman in her book *Children's Past Lives*:

"The reports of death are amazingly consistent with each other, with the reports of Dr Wambach's regression subjects and with reports of near death experiences in Dr Raymond Moody's *Life After Life*. Everyone who remembered dying describe a continuation of consciousness after death; their awareness didn't cease when their heart stopped beating. Their perceptions remained viable. They could still see, hear, and sense what was happening to them and around them. Any physical or emotional pain they had been feeling at death was gone, hunger was satisfied, thirst was quenched. They felt whole again."[48]

Finally Historical Validation:

7.2.3   Detail of Historical Regressional Researches – A Few Cases

There are thousands of individual documented cases of subjects hypnotically regressed in the literature, where professional hypnotists have claimed that **historical** verification has been obtained. This may well be valid **in most or all cases**, particularly if written in books written by a professional psychologist/hypnotherapist. However without witnesses, critics can rightly suggest that they could easily be fabricated or falsified in some way. There are however documented cases **where witnesses were present,** and the following two cases as samples, are summarised below. These were screened in a television programme called "The Reincarnation Experiments" by Australia's Channel Seven Television Network and first screened in 1982, (I well remember seeing the programme myself and being impressed when it was screened later in New Zealand). Videos of the regressions were first carried out in Australia using Australian subjects, but the television network carried out historical checking on the validity of the two subject's recollections by taking one to France and the other to England - the countries where each had regressed to a (supposed) earlier life. The producers had hoped that by taking the subjects to the sites in these countries where they claimed earlier lives, they might find landmarks mentioned in their Sydney regressions and find corroborative evidence of a past life. This was more than just a single hypnotist witness (an author) documenting a regression in a book, as in the case of this television documentary programme, not only were all who were involved in creating the programme witnesses, but obviously the millions of viewers who have watched the documentary. In fact at the time of writing, the complete TV documentary is still available on "YouTube" for any to see for themselves[49].

The regressional hypnotist was Peter Ramster, a Sydney psychologist who had specialised in reincarnational research and has written a book on it *The Truth About Reincarnation,* 1980

Case 1 - The French Chateau:

While in trance, a Sydney woman Cynthia Henderson recalled having lived during the French Revolution. Not only did she speak in English but also in fluent French, a language she had never learned in her current life. A Sydney academic who studied the tapes taken during her regression considered she was speaking in an eighteenth century dialect. Cynthia's recollections in the TV documentary film included descriptions of her life in an old French chateau and, while still hypnotised in Sydney, she drew very detailed exterior and interior sketches of the building and its gardens. Next Cynthia and Peter Ramsey, the hypnotist, together with the producer, presenters and film crew were flown to France to check on the issue of historical verification. She had claimed she had never visited France previously, so before leaving Australia, her Passport was checked to confirm this.

On arrival in France (and as shown in the TV documentary), using antique maps (which were the only source that contained the needed old street names), she directed the film crew to the chateau of her recollections. She and all witnesses, found this to be an identical match with earlier exterior drawings she sketched during trance. Previously, when more than a mile away from the chateau itself, she even correctly described the ornamentation which was later found to be exactly as she had sketched in Sydney before she left.

Case 2 – The Artist and the Excavated Floor

Although Cynthia Henderson had travelled previously outside Australia, this was not the case with Gwen MacDonald, as she had never before even travelled out of Australia. Although she had no belief in reincarnation, she nevertheless while hypnotically regressed was able to remember a life in Somerset between 1765 -1782. She was also able to draw sketches of what she had '*seen*' there. On arrival in Somerset, she was immediately able to point out the directions leading to three villages she had known. She then directed the film crew to a waterfall she had described while regressed, and pointed to a place where she claimed there had earlier been stepping stones. Locals later confirmed that the stones had existed but they had been removed 40 years earlier. With equal accuracy she pin-pointed another long vanished landmark, a cider house which had stood among four other houses at what now was an intersection. Obscure people she claimed to have known were proved to have existed. One was an officer listed in the regiment's ancient records. She also displayed a detailed knowledge of old Somerset legends, some of which were in verbal form only.

But her most astonishing insight occurred when in trance earlier in Sydney, when she described a house she had known in eighteenth century Somerset. It was close to a stream, and about 2.5 kilometres from Glastonbury Abbey. On the floor she mentioned what for her she said, was a memorable and intricate design - which on request from Peter Ramster she then drew. In Somerset she was prompted to find the house and its decorated floor. Using her recollections she led the team inexplicably to a chicken shed, which turned out to be used earlier as a cottage. On the floor inside, there was no trace of her promised swirl of pictures.

Peter Ramster requested the current owner's permission to excavate a small corner of the cottage floor, and sure enough, buried beneath centuries of dirt was the old stone floor that Gwen had described. It was identical to the design she had drawn for the TV cameras in Sydney, three months before[50].

7.3   CLOSING CHAPTER COMMENTS

Both Dr. Stevenson and Dr. Helen Wambach were obviously very much aware that to attain a high and necessary degree of scientific credibility for their research results, that they had to use a large sample size. In both cases, their effort for which I feel we should be grateful, occupied a large amount of dedicated effort by them, but also their working lives.

It is not often realized that in pure science, acceptance of a so called breakthrough -instrumental in changing the belief structure of scientists (and consequently most of the rest of us) - is often based on little evidence. A good example, is the recent apparent success in discovering what is considered to be evidential decay in a particle thought to be the theoretical Higg's boson, using the CERN Hadron Collider, in March 2013. The Higg's boson particle is thought to be responsible for mass. This conclusion was based on just one single observational result (one hit) which met expectations, despite the fact that before verification can be considered scientifically valid, independent replication is still required. More amazingly a Nobel Prize has already been awarded to the theorist Higgs, in anticipation of subsequent confirmation.

It is interesting to compare this with just one (the first in the list) of my "*Comparision of Findings of Other Hypnotherapists/Researchers with those of Dr Helen Wambach on Key Reincarnational Beliefs* above". You will recall that this examined Wambach's finding, that more than 90% of her subjects (i.e. all who were found could be regressed, equating in this case to 980 subjects and therefore hits!), were able to recall past lives.

This applied to all who could be regressed (the remaining 10% resisted hypnosis, due to fear of an unpleasant death experience). Unlike the single indication in support of the discovery of the theoretical Higg's boson mentioned above. The number of hits is actually far greater, as many subjects reported more than one past life. Critically also, is the fact that James Parejko, a professor of philosophy at Chicago State University, was able to independently replicate Wamback's findings, in that he found that 93 out of his 100 hypnotized volunteers were also able to be regressed to a previous life. In fact none of this should be of any surprise to any of us, as hypnotherapists would be out of business if they could not regress subjects to past lives. Unless past lives and therefore reincarnation is true, the fact that regression works at all makes no sense whatsoever, since there is no other possible explanation for it.

The only logical conclusion that one could make from this, is that if virtually all of Wambach's and Professor Pareiko's experimental subjects, when regressed, inevitably experience previous lives, **then so must all of us, including you and I**.

Not only that, but regression to an event in one's own lifetime has been shown repeatedly to be historically accurate, with virtually unlimited recollection detail available when required. Likewise regression before one's present lifetime and birth to past lives, has also been found virtually unlimited and unerringly accurate - whether intentional or accidental. Additionally the memory capability and ability to detect and cure phobias resulting from existing or previous lives is the same. Therefore since there is no discernable difference in the ability to regress anyone to either within their existing current life or a past life, this further validates reincarnation.

Again, all these issues have been experimentally and successfully confirmed and align not with just one researcher's results, but with all other researchers who have carried out similar experimental regressions. One could go on and on discussing further available correlations and substantiations of Wambach's findings listed earlier in this Chapter. The fact remains that all Wambach's findings where comparisons can or have been made (not just the ten samples of which have been analyzed for correlations above), would appear to have identical correlations with those of hers.

While we are at present only looking at Dr. Wambach's results, the same sort of comparisons can of course be carried out with Dr. Stevenson's work covered earlier in the Chapter, with children who spontaneously remember past lives. In the case of just one of his subjects, "Swarnlata"; there were 60 correlations recorded by Stevenson. Actually we know there must really be hundreds more, as these 60 correlations applied only at the time the case was documented. Since then, as mentioned in Stevenson's book, Swarnlata's husband (in a previous life), family and their friends continued to associate with each other and doubtless still enjoy discussing their previous life they spent with her. So hundreds more unrecorded correlations would be expected. This though, is of course just one of Stevenson's *"800 verified cases on file"*.

Therefore, Swarnlata's case, is just one of many more which Stevenson meticulously documented. No doubt some of these cases exhibit just as many or more correlations than Swarnlata's. Many other researchers concerning children's past life recollections have separately vindicated Stephenson's results including of course his successor Dr Jim B. Tucker, and Carol Bowman. Carol in her book, although commending Stevenson for his well-earned reputation for painstaking meticulous research over a lifetime, also indicated that she was irritated by his reluctance to commit himself publically to belief in reincarnation. One way or another he instead tended always to use the phraseology that his work was "suggestive of *belief in reincarnation*". Carol Bowman though, in contrast deliberately stated in her book, "I'm not going to be so circumspect", and also, that she "believed from Dr. Stevenson's empirical evidence, Dr. Woolger's clinical results, and my own experiences, that these memories derive from past lives." [51]

Only quite recently due to the above argument, I reached the point that I cannot help but agree - *scientifically the evidence is not just overwhelming, but overpowering*.

Since this is the case, how can we possibly reconcile the attitude of the majority of world's mainstream scientists who are largely ignoring the evidence in the literature - or such caution, exemplified by Dr. Stevenson, when Carol Bowman says with incredulity concerning Stevenson "that he is steeped in evidence for it every day?.

To some extent it might be thought that critics are responsible for his excessive professional modesty, as it sometimes seems that critics seize with ridicule upon almost every opportunity suggestive of the paranormal, However, I feel this is unfair to most critics (apart from naysayers), as many critics understandably and rightly provide a public service by challenging issues they genuinely consider absurd. In fact there are a number of cases in paranormal studies where critics have proved helpful in pointing out the need for further experimental controls. Although there may be some concern that by committing oneself, one is likely to invite unwelcome attacks by critics, I feel the reason is more fundamental than this. On reflection, I myself have been reluctance and somewhat obdurate to accept the evidence until only recently.

In the case of scientists, I believe a major issue is that, concerning the paranormal and also reincarnation; the background supporting science was simply not there until only recently. This is no longer the case, but currently known to perhaps just a few. This is because quantum physics is a minority interest for most scientists even many physicists, who are unaware of any relationship subatomic particle science could possibly have to their classical macro physical world. Nor could most really care, as the majority consider the paranormal is nothing but fantasy, and that reincarnation is also a nonsense idea, perpetrated by some ancient beliefs such as Buddhism.

The problem though, is that on analysis, we all inevitably very much depend upon scientists views to form our own personal belief system. If scientists show no interest in something, and declare it rubbish, then it is difficult for us to believe we know better. It is though a trap, as once our world view (and that held by scientists at the time) was that the earth was flat. Another earlier view, was that it was not only flat (but as mentioned earlier in this book) stood on turtles all the way down. Perhaps this though is close to the core of the whole problem, namely that the main constraint is the fixation we have developed for each of our personal belief systems. It must therefore take overwhelming evidence to justify a change.

Within our personal belief system, usually we each have developed a particular religious belief which our friends and family may well have favoured and endorsed to us from birth. There is also a mistaken view held by many that reincarnation is a religion, which it is not. Rather than a religion, it is instead a belief system in itself, of not just one life, but many, also that immortal life is not just for a few, but for all of us. Core reincarnational facets therefore conflict with the doctrine of most religions - which most certainly could cause major difficulty in reconciling one's existing belief system in favour of reincarnation.

Another major factor in accepting reincarnational belief, is the issue which we encountered before with remote viewing, namely *"the giggle factor"*. In essence, it is the difficulty anyone might have when they encounter something which stretches their credulity beyond limits. The result is, it is simply not believed.

CHAPTER EIGHT

Psychics and Mediums

"We are not human beings having a spiritual experience. We are spiritual beings having a human experience"

Teilhard de Chardin

In this Chapter we will first review some research and case studies by psychics and mediums, as a continuation of our evidential science treatment of life-after-death.

There are first two milestone (but largely unknown) comprehensive research studies involving exceptional mediums, followed by two psychic/medium case studies. These case studies are included as just two examples of the hundreds of such case studies available which provide strong observational mediumistic evidence for reincarnation. They also supplement the experimental evidence preceding them.

8.1 PSYCHICS AND MEDIUMS

The words "**Psychics**" and "**Medium**s" are somewhat synonymous (as covered by the Oxford dictionary definitions). However, a "psychic" is usually accepted as a generic term relating to anyone with paranormal abilities of some kind, e.g. telepathy, clairvoyance etc. Whereas, a "medium", claims to have the specific ability to contact the dead in order to source information. A "medium" may or may not also have other psychic capabilities. Obviously for this Chapter we are more concerned with an afterlife, therefore our focus is on "mediums". There are however a number of different types of mediums, including psychics who claim medium capabilities. The more unusual mediums are those who claim to be: "direct voice mediums". These claim to be able to attain a trance state and to be taken over by a discarnate who provides information/knowledge while speaking through them. They can respond to questions (examples encountered earlier, were the late Jane Roberts who channeled "Seth", and also Edgar Cayce known as "the sleeping prophet"). Others claim to be able to receive only "automatic writing" from discarnates, A particularly large group are known as "trance mediums" - as they claim to be able to contact those who have passed over, by falling into trance or while they are asleep. But by far the largest group, are those who usually provide services to the public on a paid basis by providing messages supposedly from friends and family who have passed over. This is usually in the form of messages to the client(s) of reassurance, comfort and of their survival post death. This group of mediums claim the ability to communicate with discarnates directly and at will, while they are apparently in a conscious state without any evidence of trance. Some of the ablest of this group of mediums appear on stage or on television and a number have a regular television series. Examples are John Edward, James Van Praagh, etc. The majority prefer to be known as "psychics", as a number appear to use many other paranormal abilities such as clairvoyance and psychometry to assist in their liaison with discarnates. Examples are Nancy Weber on the American Television series "Psychic Detective" and Deb Webber on the New Zealand Television series "Sensing Murders".

8.1.1 History

Probably the earliest historical record of a "psychic" was that of the Greek "Oracle of Delphi". A tradition of a seer/prophetess in ancient Greece which commenced about 1600 B.C. The prophetess was always a woman and spoke for the god Apollo answering questions for the Greeks and foreign inquirers about colonization, religion and power. By her statements the city of Delphi was made a wealthy and powerful city-state.[1]

8.1.2 Importance to Reincarnational Belief

Generally psychics and mediums are of lesser importance to reincarnational belief than the cases dealt with in the last Chapter which covered the spontaneous recall of children's past lives or hypnotic regression. With regard to children's spontaneous recall of past lives, their recollections are innocent and therefore unlikely to be falsified. Hypnotic regression allows any subject's recollections of past lives to be explored at random solely by live recording what each of them individually describe under hypnosis. Therefore both of these sources are less likely to be subject to assertions of possible fraud than cases involving mediums, where all the information supposedly received from a discarnate, is inevitably and exclusively sourced to the subject via the single medium concerned. In the 19th Century, fraud and deception by mediums was common, leading to general disbelief of the whole concept of so called "mediums" being able to contact those who have since passed over. There nevertheless are still some amazing instances reported of mediums in this era, such as Daniel D. Home, Elizabeth Garrett and Leonora Piper. In the case of Piper, detectives were even employed without ever being able to determine any hint of fraud. All three died at the end of an astonishing but unblemished career of mediumship.

Today, some credibility has been regained by the fact that many children are now known as "indigo" children. These spontaneously claim to have the ability to "see" and hear dead people from an early age, in complete contradiction in many instances with their parents beliefs. Depictions of their independent investigations of haunting, as shown on the television programme series, "Psychic Kids: Children of the Paranormal" exhibit remarkable agreement amongst each other in their descriptions of spirits/ghosts they claim to "see".[2]

In addition, there are now a number of professional psychics who, with their own television series, constantly provide what seems like credible messages from the dead to living relatives and friends present in audiences in mediums' TV shows, tours or at private sittings. These messages often comprise a stream of correct validation information, in some cases information known only to the recipient and the dead person contacted. For example the recipient's pet name, wearing of a gifted object such as a watch or necklace, etc. Such psychics include the Americans, John Edward, and his television series "Crossing Over", and "John Edward, Cross Country", also, James Van Praage with his television series, "Living with the Dead ". There are many others, including British psychic Lisa Williams, with the television programmes; "Lisa Williams: Life Amongst the Dead", and "Lisa Williams: Voices from the Other Side. " Lisa Williams is particularly gifted and will receive further mention later in the Chapter.

8.1.3 Evidence

One might well think that with all these world famous mediums available, all that would be necessary to determine validity is to set up a series of scientific laboratory experiments with a number of these mediums and test for their accuracy using appropriate statistical and chance probability analysis. In fact this is exactly what happened in February 1998, when Dr Gary Schwartz commenced what became known as "The Afterlife Experiments" – described in his book by the same name. These experiments were so successful that Schwartz wrote this book with a subtitle *Breakthrough Scientific Evidence of Life After Death*.[3]

Dr Schwartz's credentials were ideal for the purpose. He is currently a professor of psychology, medicine, neurology, psychiatry, and surgery at the University of Arizona and the Director of its Laboratory for Advances in Consciousness and Health. He received his doctorate from Harvard University and was a professor of psychiatry and psychology at Yale University as well as Director of the Yale Psychophysiology Centre and Co-director of the Yale Behavioral Medicine Clinic from 1976-1988. In his early career he wrote on biofeedback research and health psychology.[4]

Dr Schwartz, having obtained the all-important funding had just started some preliminary research, when word got out about this to the television network HBO company, "Lucky Duck Productions". This was a prominent television production company started by the award winning former network journalist, Linda Ellerbee. Their television producer, Lisa Jackson planned to do a serious documentary for HBO on the survival of consciousness. She rang Schwartz indicating that not only did they wish him to carry out the research as a segment to be filmed live on the documentary programme, but they had already approached the popular American mediums, George Anderson, John Edward, Rev. Anne Gehman, Suzane Northrop and James Van Praagh, about participating in the show. [5]

Despite the endeavors of Dr Schwartz and his team to convince James Van Praagh to appear on the documentary television show, he was adamant in refusing. His reluctance was well justified, as he was mocked unfairly on TV on one occasion when he incorrectly diagnosed an ailment of Barbara Walters. There are a number of such cases where the media, or skeptics, thrive on pouncing on any instant where a professional medium makes an error in receipt of a "message". Rather than accepting the obvious conclusion that a medium may for many reasons (e.g. difficulty in interpreting a discarnate) get a number of messages wrong, they may then instead assert publically that the psychic a fraud.

John Edward and Suzane Northrop were similarly nervous about HBO, but finally agreed after much persuasion by Dr Schwartz and others. Schwartz - concerned himself of possible HBO biased editing, did in fact gain HBO agreement "That the portion of the documentary that presented the science - our (Schwartz's) laboratory -would have to be previewed and approved by us for accuracy and clarity". This later took three attempts before approval was given by Schwartz for screening.

The first HBO series of experiments was planned to keep to an absolute minimum, contact between mediums and subjects (i.e. those for whom messages were intended from close relatives or friends who had already passed over). The aim was to ensure a vanishingly low opportunity for "cold reading".

This is defined in Wikipedia as follows: "Cold reading is where a person (i.e. a psychic or medium) can quickly gain a great deal of information about a subject simply by analyzing the person's body language, age, clothing or fashion, hairstyle, gender, sexual orientation, religion, race or ethnicity, level of education, manner of speech, place of origin, etc. Cold readings commonly employ high-probability guesses, quickly picking up on signals as to whether their guesses are in the right direction or not, then emphasizing and reinforcing chance connections and quickly moving on from missed guesses". [6]

(Note: The concept of elimination of any chance for *"cold reading"* to occur is essential in carrying out any serious laboratory research into the validity of mediums being able to contact the dead. Unless measures are taken to avoid this, skeptic's delight in asserting all mediums information is gained by means of "cold reading".)

To eliminate the possibility of cold reading entirely, Dr Schwartz and his research team's plan for this first series of experiments was to arrange the seating and laboratory rooms in such a manner that it was absolutely impossible for the subject and medium to be visible at all to each other before, during, or after the experiment. The subjects entered the laboratory and were seated before the mediums were permitted to take up their seats. Also both the medium and subject had their seats screened from each by sheets even though their seats were arranged roughly physically alongside each other - so that if required and under the direction of the experimenters, they could communicate verbally. Otherwise at all times they were to remain silent. At no time were the mediums allowed to liaise with each other or the subjects, and they were under constant surveillance in rest periods to ensure that this was observed. [7]

For the initial experiment, the mediums, George Anderson, John Edward, Rev. Anne Gehman, and Suzane Northrop were chosen with another medium added - Laurie Campbell, to replace the earlier desired James Van Praagh. To ensure a reasonable response from discarnates, the criteria included a desired two subjects for all the experiments, that anyone was suitable, but arbitrarily they each should know and be familiar with at least six closely related people who had died within the last ten years. Two subjects for each experiment were desired, as it was critical for scientific acceptability that the experiments be replicated. HBO supplied a volunteer subject, Patricia Price and Dr Schwartz provided another, Ronnie Nathanson. Both gave their assurances that they had never had any contact with the selected mediums. They were also requested to fill out a detailed questionnaire asking for exact information on the history and death of each person they expected or hoped might visit during the experiment. These were sealed and stored. However none of those involved in any manner with the experiments, were permitted access to the documents. The intention was presumably for these records to be used if required as verification of a subject's responses during statistical and rating evaluation after the sessions had concluded.

Experiment 1 – Medium Suzane Northrop with subject Patricia Price.

Special Arrangements: Only yes/no questions were allowed by any medium (to minimize any risk of cold reading/cueing).

Reading: Suzane only asked five questions during the whole session. The initial question concerned Patricia's father, who Suzane had confirmed from Patricia had passed over.

A sample of this - the start of all the sessions; was as follows:

"Father's been gone some time, they tell me, Patricia. And I don't know why, but your father gave me your name, cause he says, I gave, I gave her my name, I gave her my name. Or, I gave her a name connected to me. Feels like he's been gone a long time, feels like your father passed very fast".

Your father also wore hats. He's got a hat on today. He's actually quite a cute man, and your father smoked. I don't know if that's what he passed from, but he shows the center of his chest".

All this information her father had given her - his name, he wore hats and he smoked, was later found, as with much of the session, completely accurate. The "Yes" responses were almost continuous throughout the session. This is of course remarkable, but not unusual today with the caliber of mediums available.

The readings continued with the remaining four mediums and with the same subject Patricia Price, and then continued with the second subject Ronnie Nathanson - but in this case with only two of the mediums Suzane Nortrop and John Edward. This was because as filming took seven hours since starting at 8 am, and the allotted time ran out.

Results: The average accuracy for all 5 mediums was 88%. Incredibly with two mediums, John Edward and Laurie Campbell, their accuracy was rated as 100% for each. As a rough estimate. Schwartz, an expert statistician himself, determined the probability in just a single event concerning the suicide of Patricia's son and details of his dog "PeeWee" who had passed over. The analysis of the mediums accuracy gave the probability of this being a chance occurrence of less than 1 in 2.5 billion! With a second subject on the second day, accuracy overall for just the two mediums available was 77%. For the first medium it was 64%, and for the second it was 90%.

Unsurprisingly Dr Schwartz concluded that the data suggested the mediums were receiving (and providing to the subjects) accurate information from discarnates.

With screening of mediums from subjects using a cloth covered screen, cold reading was impossible. Similarly "fishing for information" by the mediums could be ruled out as only yes/no answers were permitted.

Experiment 1A

A variation of the first experiment was carried out at a later date using even tighter controls on mediums to eliminate any possibility of bias or fraud. Regardless of this, the experiment gained similar results as is seen below. Four of the five previous mediums were able to participate.

Special Arrangements: (1) A different selection of subjects was made by using a wide group of subjects from various parts of the country who varied in age, sex, history of number of personal losses, belief in the plausibility of after-death communication, and depth of love for the departed. (2) A test was added where for the first 10 minutes of a mediums reading, no verbal communication whatsoever was allowed between the medium and the subject. After this the mediums were allowed to ask questions, but the subjects were only allowed to respond with yes/no answers – as for the first Experiment, Experiment 1.

Results: The average accuracy for the silent periods was 77% and for the questioning period 85%. The difference between the silent and questioning experiments in percentage accuracy can be seen as not statistically significant. It is noteworthy also that the difference from the first experiment is not only relatively small, but since it is replicated at a different time and with different subjects, it supports Schwartz's earlier experimental finding that mediums can receive accurate information from discarnates.

A further two experiments were conducted to explore other possibilities. The first followed intensive discussion with advisers on cold reading aimed at making any **communication** whatsoever between the medium and subject completely impossible. Resulting from this, the experiment commenced with an initial silent period of 10 minutes where the subject was not permitted to speak. During the second part of the experiment the subject was told to continue to remain silent, but was allowed to respond solely by nodding or shaking their head in response to information provided by the medium. A professional experimenter would then speak and provide feedback on behalf of the subject by advising the medium over a phone of the subject's intended yes/no answer. The experiment resulted in a dismal average percentage accuracy of about 40%, with one subject failing completely in the readings and appropriately assigned a zero score. This seriously affected the overall averaging of results. Another medium complained that he was receiving continued information concerning his previous subject, instead of the information being applicable to his current subject. From what we now know about the PCAR system, it is not surprising that such a poor result was obtained, as it is obvious that the necessary PCAR communication system resonance with a given subject would be extremely difficult without some means whatsoever (i.e. a cue) of identifying the intended subject. This was vindicated by information given to the wrong subject, a complete failure by one medium, and an uncharacteristically low score.

For the second and final experiment, fortunately, a characteristically high score was regained ranging from 80-100% for mediums in double-blind experiments comprising three parts. The experiment involved using what is known as the "Russek" procedure.

This was where subjects and mediums were separated at completely different locations (in one case over a thousand kilometers apart, but with communication linked with a particular subject and a particular medium via phone **at all times** regardless as to whether it was in use or not. In this respect it was also muted, unless the medium's reading was desired to be spoken out loud to the subject, or feedback to the medium via the telephone was required. The first part of the experiment was particularly interesting, as it successfully tested and vindicated the claim that precognition was possible. The test involved a single medium (Laurie Campbell) meditating for 30 minutes before the session commenced. During meditation, she wrote down impressions gained purely mentally in advance of the commencement of the session. Only after this phase, was telephone contact established with the subject (George Dalzell). The medium then read out loud to the subject her pre-reading impressions written down earlier, seeking the subject to respond to these by confirming, questioning or contradicting the information. The accuracy as determined by later independent and professional subject review and analysis, was 90%.

In this case, it appears the later establishment of the telephone link after the pre-reading, provided a sufficient but necessary methodology by which PCAR communication could be established without difficulty by a medium to a specific subject. It also exhibits the time independence of the PCAR communication system, as the order of events did not appear at all affect the high success rate of the experiment.

Across all experiments Dr Schwartz stated statistical analysis of results indicated for all mediums an accuracy which gave a chance probability of less than 1 in a billion![8]

Commenting on the issue of accuracy, in case one might consider that the results of all Schwartz's experiments are exceptional; perhaps the only exceptional character of them is that they were scientific experiments. Importantly, they were also carried out under unbelievably stringent conditions aimed at removing any possibly of fraud, cold reading or cueing. This is because audiences at public appearances where readings are carried out by any of today's most acclaimed world mediums/psychics, expect accuracies of 90 -100% of continuous hits. Otherwise, few would be bothered to attend, and such psychic celebrities would rapidly lose their credibility and livelihood.

In contrast, there are skeptics such as James Randi and Michael Shermer, whose celebrity and livelihood depends perversely on denial and ridicule of psychics/mediums and even the existence of the paranormal. They naturally fulfil expectations by continuing their skeptical assertions - even in the face of such pristine evidence as Schwartz's three-year rigidly controlled scientific experiments.

Schwartz himself puts it very aptly in his book on these experiments, by expressing the view that many skeptics instinctively dismiss data on the basis of reflecting a perceived "bias so strong that it begins to border on the pathological".[9]

This is in fact what occurred with both the skeptics, Randi and Shermer mentioned above, following publication of Schwartz's experiments. As stated by Schwartz "they were the most skeptical reviewers of the manuscript; and despite the data and safeguards, persisted in their personal belief that fraud must somehow be involved in medium research of this kind."

Another celebrated skeptic Dr Ray Hyman, at least took the trouble to analyse the design of Dr Schwartz's experiments before attacking the methodology with fanciful assertions, e.g. that mirrors **might** be involved. His critical assertions are readily available on the internet together with detailed rebuttals of his analysis by two others, Journalist Craig Wailer and Victor Zammit. Gary Schwartz has also provided his own rebuttal and review of Ray Hyman's critique.[10]

It is interesting to note that once the results were finalized, initially Dr.Schwartz himself was momentarily guilty of the very criticism that he aimed at skeptics. As stated in his book he was taken to task by his associate research assistant, clinical psychologist, Dr. Linda Russek, concerning their experiments by asking him one day "how could he see all these data and still not believe."[11]

This jolted Schwartz out of his momentary skepticism to see that his doubt "in the presence of all the data, was frankly irrational". He explained in his book, that he was brought up as a scientist, to be biased towards thinking that **full belief** had to be withheld until certainty had been obtained by scientific verification. He then reviewed all his experiments again plus results and (no doubt with some embarrassment) indicated that certainty for himself now existed, as the evidence was exhibited by the results. He stated that earlier he had been guilty of "sceptimania" and stated in celebration of the results of the experiment: "That we celebrate the existence of living souls in a living and evolving universe". I must say I have considerable sympathy with Dr Gary Schwartz, as I myself struggled with certainty of belief over many years until my recent review of Dr Stevenson's lifetime research on children's remembrance of past lives. This demonstrates unfortunately how many of us including myself, rather than claiming an open mind, can ourselves be victims of an entrenched belief system we develop from an early age (as I mentioned earlier in the last Chapter).

Another area worthy of some short discussion in this context, is the subject of professional and world acclaimed psychics/mediums. In Dr Schwartz's experiments, John Edward is probably the most world famous. The others though are well known as being similarly talented and accurate. They therefore obviously would wish to retain their support and credibility amongst their clients, friends and family. In participating in Dr Schwartz's experiments it is clear that they were putting their reputation on the line if the experiments were a failure. Should this have occurred, there would inevitably be attendant consequences for these psychics/mediums, such as loss of livelihood and public ridicule. Yet they were so confident of their success, that with some persuasion by Schwartz and others, they agreed to participate. By comparison, skeptics take no such risk - as failure by psychics/mediums, would likely lead to an increase in skeptics' reputation and acclaim. The courage of these psychics/mediums in taking such a risk is not just commendable, but suggests that they have so much confidence in their abilities to perform under any degree of stringency which could possibly be contrived, that fraud and any complicity for deception by them would be extremely difficult to believe.

The names of purchasers of tickets to any mediums' public performances, even via the internet, do not appear on tickets. There is therefore no way whatsoever of normally identifying attendees to mediums at their performances. Skeptics however assert continuously that the accuracy of all mediums' readings results from fraud of some kind. A moment's reflection of the skeptics continuous claims of fraud, suggests that for a single public viewing by a medium; without the identity of subject for a reading, teams of private detectives working in advance would be necessary to determine both an appropriate system and to carry out the necessary research to identify a group who intend to be present at the performance. For the later readings, they would also have to research and provide an incredible detail of background data concerning passed family and friends for this chosen group of subjects. The medium also would have to memorise before the performance, all this data intended for all the planned readings. Great care would be essential during the performance to somehow allow the medium to identify visually or in some other way each of the intended subjects in the audience, despite glare from the floodlights making it almost impossible for anyone in the audience to be identified from the stage. Alternatively a system of arranging "plants" amongst the audience to acquiesce to false data provided by the medium would be necessary. The same almost impossible problem of identifying accurately the "plants" in the glare of floodlights would also occur. Whatever system adopted, it would then have to be repeated continuously for every appearance/performance by the particular medium. For a celebrated medium this would entail venues throughout various countries and cities throughout the world. Despite critics' suggestions of fraud, the fact is that such public performances occur today somewhere in the world almost daily, yet there has never been a single case reported to the media of even a hint of fraud, or any evidence supplied of a "plant" or complicit assistant. It also needs to be remembered that the majority of mediums work is not public performances, but private readings, with just one or two subjects and no opportunity for "plants" to be present at these readings. Also psychics/mediums seeking to identify murderers for the police, simply use clairvoyance and psychometry by handling photographs of victims, and/or handle items belonging to the victim. In such cases there are not even subjects, let alone "plants", just operation of the PCAR communication system.

It is therefore clear from the above, that such claims of skeptics are unbelievable and absurd.

Summing up therefore, (and with regard to Occam's razor – which suggests the simplest explanation is most likely), **we are left with the only logical conclusion, namely that psychics/ mediums are actually able to receive valid and accurate information from discarnates.**

It is also appropriate at this point to quickly dispense with another fallacy - namely armchair skeptics suggesting that mediums are gaining information not from discarnates, but by telepathy from the subjects themselves. To anyone who has researched the issue, this is also apparent as fiction. This is because both mediums and discarnates are naturally fixated on providing validation indicating that those who have passed over are really still alive, well and not dead. The end result is that discarnates aim at providing information which is not only extremely personal **but not even in the subject's mind at the time**, such as detail of some shared holiday, the fact that the subject is wearing a necklace given to them by the discarnate etc. To assist validation, the medium is also likely to relay character information such as how the discarnate appears to them, that he/she smokes, is domineering, abrupt etc. Again since none of this is in the subject's mind at the time, how can it be telepathy with the subject? It is nonsensical.

Thanks to the internet, we are also able to easily verify apparent accuracy of famous mediums for ourselves, as a number of their public and private readings are available as "YouTube" videos. I chose Lisa Williams as an outstanding popular and celebrated medium for a quick analysis of some available readings. Simply by carefully recording hits, one can easily determine that her likely average accuracy is typically near 100%. Taking a random choice of four video clips of private sessions - those for Anna and Laura, Pamela and William, Paige, and finally Erin, these averaged 20 hits (typically from readings lasting a mere 3 minutes each, but obviously unedited sessions). Considerably more hits would result from public performances lasting about one hour). The average probability result was calculated as less than one chance in 2^{20} or approx. 1 in 1,050,000 i.e. just over a million. An amazing verification result. (Note: It is stressed I am not suggesting for a moment that such a check is scientific, but merely just an **indication** of validity). It is of course completely without appropriate experimental controls. Nevertheless, even with a superficial examination of such recorded sessions, which are routine daily occurrences for many mediums, it is difficult to imagine how fraud could possibly be involved and maintained.

Noteworthy, I also found a skeptic's webpage by Jon Donnis entitled "Bad Psychics"[12] which gave hopeless results by Lisa Williams where she rushed readings for a few quick spot readings in a TV audience breakfast type show. It is well known that, just with most of us, psychics/mediums sometime react badly to pressure, and, in their case and in such circumstances, cannot get into the "zone". Characteristically the author of the skeptic webpage has cherry picked the worst performances of not just Lisa Williams, but a number of other psychics/mediums to provide a completely false and uncharacteristic indication of their expertise and talent. Sadly, this is readily apparent by comparing other more typical performances of celebrated psychics/mediums which are available in the adjacent listed "YouTube" videos. As Dr Schwartz had said, "skeptics typically dismiss positive results",[13]

In this respect they are using deception to further their cause - the very method they use to attack psychics/mediums, but, particularly in the case of Dr Schwartz's research, when science suggests truth and validity.

Before leaving coverage of experimental evidence of the validity of psychics/mediums, it is interesting to note that Dr Schwartz, as his pick of hypotheses for mediumistic ability and the success of his experiments, indicates the following scientific possibilities: (1) *telepathy with the physical living*" (e.g. discarnates with mediums), or (2) "*extended systemic memory resonance*".[14]

Combining these gives a hint perhaps of what we now know as the 'PCAR communication system'. The PCAR system though as we have learned previously gives not only a complete and scientifically validated explanation for the psychics/mediums ability described, but is most likely the non-verbal communication system for all life.

Obviously as part of the 'scientific method', it is necessary to correlate any finding with at least one other independent scientific experiment. Fortuitously, following Professor Schwartz's milestone successful work, this was accomplished by Dr Julie Beischel in 2007, as outlined in her 2013 Amazon/Kindle book, *Among Mediums: A Scientist's Quest for Answers*.

Dr Beischel is Co-Founder and Director of Research at the Windbridge Institute and received her doctorate in Pharmacology and Toxicology from the University of Arizona in 2003. She is a full member of the Parapsychological Association and the Society for Scientific Exploration, and serves on the scientific advisory boards of the Rhine Research Center and the Forever Family Foundation. Dr. Beischel is Adjunct Faculty in the School of Psychology and Interdisciplinary Inquiry at Saybrook University. She is also Director of the Survival and Life After Death research department at the World Institute for Scientific Exploration.

In her book, she describes her experimentation work (together with other members of the WindBridge Institute) into the validity of expert mediums to source accurate information from discarnates (as with that carried out formerly and described above by G. Schwartz). Dr Beischel's work was similarly very successful and involved an experiment which comprised 21 readings. This particular project is now complete.

Both the methodology adopted by The Windbridge Institute for the selection of mediums and that methodology/protocol for the experiments was remarkable for its scientific rigor and professionalism:

Medium selection: To select mediums of an outstanding calibre, Beischel used a demanding test procedure to test volunteer mediums for acceptable accuracy. This can even take up to a year to complete. As an analogy she says, *"If we wanted to study the phenomenon of high jumping, we would find some good high jumpers"*.

Successful mediums chosen for such experiments, are granted certification of the Institute and are termed "Windbridge Certified Research Mediums" (WCRMs)". There are now nearly 20 such qualified WCRM's, which is considered sufficient for current and immediate Institute work. The protocol designed for the experiments, is a compliment to Beischel and her Institution, as it probably cannot be surpassed in being designed to avoid any possibility of fraud, cold reading, cuing, or rater bias. (Rater bias is where the subject/sitter provides a biased inaccurate rating of a reading).

Experimental Methodology/protocols: To avoid cold reading, cuing or fraud, Beischel's experimental approach is to ensure that the medium and subject/sitter **never** meet or communicate in any way. Further, the methodology used to avoid cold reading **generalisations** by mediums, is the protocol's use of a fixed set of questions for all readings. This standard list of questions is used by the experimenter to seek answers from the medium regarding the discarnate's physical appearance, personality, hobbies, cause of death, but also includes a question inviting the discarnate to provide any desired specific message(s) for the sitter they wish. The subject/sitters (i.e. the persons who receive readings from the medium) are unpaid volunteers, as with the mediums. Some 1000 volunteers have currently been accepted by the Institute for this work.

For a typical experiment, arrangements are made for two readings (a pair) for each experiment. This involves two different mediums chosen randomly, one for each reading. With regard to sitters, the software is programmed to match discarnates chosen for the two readings on the basis of selecting complete opposite discarnate (and thus sitter) matches. The selection is based on the discarnate physical and personality characteristics, their interests and their causes of death. Following readings, each of the sitter pair then scores for both readings (i.e. for the intended discarnate plus the decoy). As it would be most **unlikely** scores could be close, this enables checks to be made for rater bias. Although preparation arrangements to select sitters/mediums etc. are made jointly for two readings at the same time, the actual two readings comprising each experiment are separated (often) by one week.

Importantly, only the experimenter has any association whatsoever with the medium and this is restricted to the reading itself when he/she contacts the medium by telephone at the appointed time for the reading. The experimenter then provides just the first name of the discarnate and supervises and records the reading – but without any participation of the sitter. The sitter therefore only sees the results of readings (but of both mediums) later when scoring. In other words the sitter is completely blind to either medium at all times and must score both mediums readings on the basis of which is most likely to apply to his (or her) chosen discarnate. As a measure aimed at increasing the likelihood of success, the experimenter requests at any time prior to the readings, that the sitter should attempt to mentally advise their chosen discarnate of the scheduled time for the sitting and to request them to then link with the correct medium at the sitting.

Further details of the standard protocols used for each experiment, the rating and analysis is summarised to some extend in Beischel's book, but complete details are available from research papers available via the Windbridge Institute's website (http://www.windbridge.org/). As can be seen from the above, the experimental protocols used are rather complex, but justifiably brilliantly devised to defeat any suggestion of fraud or complicity. The outcome is that rather than the usually encountered normal "double blinded" experiments for such work, these are "quintuple - blinded" experiments!

After detailing above, a somewhat lengthy but necessary explanation of most of the experimental protocol precautions taken to avoid fraud, or deception in the results, the outcome (covered below) may seem somewhat brief and unimpressive.

Such a judgement though is invalid, as despite the incredibly rigid conditions which are obviously likely to adversely affect to some extent the mediums performance, the results below nevertheless can be seen to affirm the ability of expert mediums to gain valid information from discarnates - and at a level beyond chance.

Results: of 21 readings: Sitters scored more of **their** items in their readings as accurate, versus the number of items they considered accurate in readings intended for **other** sitters, and this difference was statistically significant. In fact 16 out of 21 (76%) of sitters chose correctly their own target readings as the one intended for them This is highly statistically significant as compared with a 50/50 result - as would be expected by chance, as this is statistically identical when compared with flipping a coin, and getting 16 heads out of 21.

The overall outcome, in the words of Dr Beischel is that "Skilled mediums can report accurate and specific information about the deceased loved one, termed discarnates, of living people termed sitters, without any prior knowledge about the discarnates or the sitters and in the complete absence of any sensory feedback."

Dr Beischel scientifically correctly claims that the above series of experiments cannot by itself be taken of evidence of an afterlife, as the information gained by mediums from discarnates might possibly be sourced instead by considering an alternative explanation - as suggested by some disbelievers in an afterlife. This is that mediums' valid information for sitters is not obtained from discarnates, because there is no survival of life, or consciousness whatsoever after death. Instead, the suggestion claims that valid information concerned with previous lives could be obtained by mediums using "super-psi", and the information is sourced from the "Akashic Field".

This is of course just an assertion but without evidence. Also, "super-psi", has no formal definition (and is therefore unscientific). In contrast though, the Akashic Field has a form of definition, as at least a theory (see Wikipedia), and is perhaps best described as "the memory source of the whole universe of all that has happened". It is also often referenced in esoteric literature (of a Sanskrit Indian source). Readers will probably recognize the above definition/description of the "Akashic Field" as a aligning completely for what we in this book have come to know (probably more correctly) as "the Zero Point Field".

This whole idea that mediums solely gain information from such a memory source using an unspecified "super-psi capability, is apparently thought to have arisen by some parapsychologists. Though accepting that telepathy has been experimentally proved, are nevertheless said to have a perceptual bias against the possibility of an afterlife, and are obdurately blind to any evidence whatsoever for it.

Arguing against this concept, Dr Beischel, mentions that occasionally there are instances where, the information provided by a medium has been corrected by a "discarnate" during readings, and that there are also instances where the medium has been surprised and disconcerted by the information received. This clearly does not suggest information is being derived by the medium from the zero point field, but rather directly **from** a discarnate. To support this further, it is self-evident for anyone who as actually taken the time to attend a public or private reading by professional mediums, that the content of the information they provide for the sitter, is specifically and carefully chosen and targeted by the discarnate to validate their survival. Typically this information concerns a very personal message describing a holiday shared, a teasing, joke etc. only known to the sitter and the deceased. Also it makes sense that a discarnate's goal would be aimed at validating their existence, and the medium would simply wish and strive to act as a conduit; not a seeker for the information. Finally, to suggest that discarnates are neither involved, nor the source of the information, would therefore imply that every medium on earth is deluded - even those mediums who have claimed a lifetime of contact with discarnates (including their own dead relatives), and in many cases from an early age, with the innocence of a child.

It can be seen from this, that any such suggestion that mediums source this information themselves without a discarnate, simply does not align with observational evidence of the practice of mediumship.

Nevertheless, to Dr Beischel's credit, despite this, she designed and carried out a further series of experiments with the Institutes' pool of mediums and sitters. These experiments successfully refute the belief that mediums **normally** gain their past life information from the zero point field. The first of this series of experiments involved gaining questionnaire responses from mediums. The aim was to determine whether more negative emotions were experienced in their reading for a discarnate, compared with their results arising from a control reading using the telephone to communicate with a very much alive human. As expected, the experiment was successful, as results were able to distinguish cases of readings with a discarnate. This was found to be due to an expected higher level of negative emotion reported as resulting from mediums inevitably being adversely affected by grief, loss, anger, remorse, regret etc. These emotions are known to be typically encountered when associated with a valid communication and reading with a discarnate.

A similar second successful experiment was aimed at determining if psychics/mediums could detect a difference in their experience when seeking information **psychically** via a reading with a live human, as compared with a reading of a discarnate by a medium. The desired ability to discriminate between the two, was found could be detected by the medium being only **aware** of a human's emotions during a psychic reading, but in the case of a medium reading of a discarnate, the medium actually **experienced** the emotions of the discarnate. (There were also other distinguishing correlates). Dr Beischel's final experiment in the series used a fully blinded protocol, by which the mediums were given only the cue of a randomly assigned first name at the commencement of each experiment, each of which either applied to a live or deceased target for the reading. The result again was highly successful, in that from analysis of questionnaires completed by the mediums following the readings, it was able to be determined that mediums could identify whether the person communicated via the reading was living, or dead; 83% of the time.

There is another argument (theoretical) which supports further Dr Beischel's results. It will be recalled from earlier Chapters that the PCAR quantum communication system is most likely that used for the following communication purposes between **all** lifeforms/consciousness for non-verbal communication with each other:

- for all consciousness communication including that in an afterlife,
- interface with the environment to detect epigenic change etc.,
- consciousness/memory access to and from the zero point field (or the synonym "Akashic Field").

It therefore does appear that some **psychics**/mediums might obtain **some** information concerning discarnates by use of the PCAR system access and interaction with the zero point field. However, we also learned earlier from observational evidence that **discarnates** in a non-physical fully quantum environment would be expected to have a vastly superior capability in the use of the PCAR system compared with a human's comparative feeble expertise (Monroe). Therefore, the logical direction of communication of information would be expected from the more adept discarnates to mediums, rather than from mediums accessing memory contained within the zero point field - as is confirmed by Dr Beischel's experiments. In other words Dr Beischel's findings follow theoretical expectations.

Within these experimental results, but also following observation and theory, there most certainly does seem vindication for at least **psychics** to gain a degree of information on all subjects from the zero point field. Importantly also, Dean Radin's experimental findings (covered earlier) demonstrates that ability seems dependent on attention and intent. Ability also seems dependent on the Mensky's concept of altering one's conscious focus towards the unconscious state or non-physical reality. With mediums, their focus of attention and intent would obviously be on discarnates.

Summing up therefore, it can reasonably said that the desired independent corroboration of Professor G. Schwartz's earlier afterlife experiments has been achieved (and even added to) by the above plethora of excellent hard experimental and pristine science by Dr Beischel and the Windbridge Institute.

Based on the experimental and theoretical evidence above, it would therefore be difficult to believe otherwise that, **not only do discarnates provide valid information to mediums, but that this itself now provides almost overwhelming evidence in favor of an afterlife.**

As far as I am aware, the Windbridge is the only institute in the world dedicated and focused to research specifically in this area. It is also self-funded. The primary institute focus is said to be "*on applied research with the goal of developing and distributing information, services, and technologies that allow people to reach their full potential so that they can live happier, healthier, and more fulfilling lives*".

Since establishment in 2007, the research outlined above has now been completed. In just the two years since publication of Dr Beischel's book in 2013, many additional experiments have also been completed, planned, or are already under way by Dr Beischel and her team, aimed at further experiment led exploration/discovery research. Another institute goal as stated by Dr Beischel is to: "*investigate the capabilities of our bodies, minds, and spirits and attempts to determine how that information can best serve all living things*".

Apart from these successful validation experiments of the ability of mediums to obtain factual information from discarnates, within the detail of the Institutes overarching aims are also applications research projects, aimed if possible at gaining practical benefits and applications which might benefit mankind arising from furthering and enhancing contact with those in an afterlife. A key concept is to use mediums or any other (e.g. mechanical/technological) means to source from those deceased, wisdom or knowledge that could benefit scientific, technological or social progress.

Amongst the following are just a few of those already planned or under action (further details are available on the Windbridge website):

Operational and application research studies - on determining how psychics/mediums could be more effective in aiding the police to source information to solve crimes and locate missing people. Investigating the potential for using after-death-communication (ADC) aimed at therapeutically reducing grief. A similar project aimed at reducing the fear of impending death, particularly for those in hospices etc. or palliative care. Use of ADC to derive information on overall better applicability in the use of pharmaceutical medication and medicines etc.

(Note: as an aside, it is interesting to note (as mentioned in Chapter 5), that Edgar Cayce in the early 1900's, with no medical knowledge whatsoever, demonstrated, albeit on an individual person basis, that this approach could very successful. He spend most of his life deriving from an apparently discarnate German doctor, information which purportedly always effected a cure to those who sought his mediumistic ability.)

Exploration of traditional parapsychological topics (i.e., telepathy, precognition, clairvoyance, and mind-matter interactions), as well as experimenter effects, alternative healing, intention, our holistic interconnection with each other, and conscious mind-mind, mind-matter potential that exists within each of us. Also, allied work investigating technologies that may be useful in enhancing interaction and communication with the deceased including, electronic voice phenomena (EVP) and instrumental trans-communication (ITC), addressing reports of haunting and apparition phenomena, and exploring afterlife cosmology. Finally, non-human animal consciousness research investigating a variety of phenomena including animal psi, the human-animal bond, and survival of animal consciousness after physical death.

In view of work already accomplished and planned by Dr Beischel and her team, the day that Dr Beischel chose to forsake her earlier planned (more remunerative) career as a normal pharmacist - rather than commence her present pioneer research in this area, I cannot help but feel, was a day we should all celebrate; as it is likely that her work and that of the Windbridge Institute, today and in the future, could be of incalculable benefit to all mankind.

The remainder of this first section of the Chapter gives two case studies involving mediums, to add to the experimental evidence (covered above) by present compelling observational evidence for an afterlife and reincarnation.

8.1.4 Case 1 - The Mystery of the Buried Crosses

In the early 1930's, a man by the name of Gregory Parent of Redlands, California, wrote to Pulitzer Prize winning author Hamlin Garland, concerning his wife "Violet's" experiences as a trance medium. Garland was not just a celebrated author, but also he was an investigator for the American Society for Psychical Research. In view of this, Parent thought that Garland might be interested in writing a book about his wife's Violet's experiences.

Parent mentioned in his letter that his wife was "strangely gifted from birth, and after an illness, she developed the facility of going into trance and communicating with dead people". These included in particular, the famous California missionary Father Serra, and other deceased missionaries and Indians associated with them in their missions. **The missionaries said they were anxious to provide evidence of life after death, and "would therefore reveal information that no one living knew or could have known"**.

This then led the "Parents" over a period of 10 years, to more than 50 widely separated locations across a region of 600 miles long by 300 miles wide, **where under direction from "spirits"**, they together with friends and family found 1,500 Indian artefacts - mostly metallic crosses and miscellaneous other relics. Although of interest as artefacts, these had no real monetary value. The crosses had been buried by the Indians when the missions were threatened by the Mexicans. Many of the crosses were encased in balls of adobe to look like common rocks. In addition to the crosses, the Parents were also directed to finds of gold and silver coins as well as currency and other treasures in tin cans, rotted pocketbooks and various containers. The recovery of these valuables were explained by the deceased missionaries as being aimed at assisting the Parents in their searches. Although initially desperately poor, the Parents soon were able to buy a car to assist them in their travels and searches (up until then neighbours and friends provided their transport). They eventually accumulated so much wealth from their finds, that they were able to buy their own house! Numerous affidavits were available signed by people who assisted on one or more of the expeditions searching for crosses, certifying that they found crosses precisely where the spirits predicted.

At the time that Garland received Parents letter, he was busy completing a book. When later in 1936, he attempted to re-contact Parent, he found both he and his wife had since died. Following further inquiries, Garland eventually was able to contact Parent's half-sister Louise Stack of Moorpark, California, who had inherited Parent's collections of manuscripts of 22 journals and artefacts. Gregory Parent was found to have kept the dates and times of every excursion, and listed every item in every find. To Garland's surprise, Mrs Stack willingly turned over custody of Parents collection of not only his manuscripts, but all 1500 relics to him, which were all arranged neatly in 17 glass-topped cases.

Garland was so impressed with the Parent's evidence that he decided to try and substantiate it further. He therefore decided to see if he could replicate it himself by carrying out his own investigations. He even went to the extent of seeing if he could find further crosses by locating his own suitable medium to see whether Violet, Parent's wife (now in spirit) could lead him to find more crosses.

He first set out to see if he could find friends and neighbours in Redlands, who had assisted the Parents in their searches and discoveries. While many had moved away, he did successfully locate 15 people and found them all to be credible witnesses. One of these, who operated a business, recalled being very sceptical when Mrs Parent told him there were crosses under a large boulder. Using crowbars, two men he related had moved the boulder under which they had found three crosses.

Garland chose as a proficient and recommended medium, a direct voice medium called Sophia Williams to assist in 'contacting' Parent's wife. Rather than contacting Violet Parent, the medium was able to directly contact Father Serra himself and other missionaries. Over a period of **six months,** they directed Garland and his medium, Williams over hundreds of miles through Southern and central California and Mexico searching for more artefacts. They found 16 artefacts similar in substance and design to those collected by the Parents, in 10 widely separated locations almost as a replay of the experiences related by Gregory Parent in his original journals. Some were in deep gullies, others on high cactus-covered hills far from the highway. One was hidden in a ledge of sandstone behind a wall of cactus plants which Garland had to chop away before finding it. Some were buried more than two feet deep and had not been disturbed for many years. An ethnologist George Parker Winship when consulted, explained some of the crosses originated from Central America, also from Yucatan and Guatemala, and preceded Christianity. In case these crosses might be considered common, Garland's researches found the opposite. He could only find a mere two references in a single footnote in an obscure padre's journal. One quoted an explorer saying that in 1604 (150 years before the establishment of the first mission) he had come across a tribe that wore crosses in their hair. The other was a picture in the book *Handbook of the American Indian*, of a similar cross dug from a mound in Wisconsin. As for the crosses and artefacts, Garland found little interest by Museums, however a dozen were donated by a granddaughter, Victoria Jones to the West Salam Historical Society housed in Garland's old home in Wisconsin.

The location of the rest is now unknown. For anyone interested, the full detailed account is available in the last of Hamlin Garlands Book's *The Mystery of the Buried Crosses*.

This case is obviously extremely evidential due to the large number of apparently very rare crosses discovered - in a manner that leaves no explanation other than for the existence of life after death. The search for the crosses credibly appears to have been achieved solely by the help of discarnate clergy, with the aim of assisting belief in an afterlife. Many witnesses are available with testimonials to vindicate Gregory Parent's incredibly detailed journals. Unerringly the crosses were found despite the extremely difficult terrain, the vastness of the search area and the fact that most were disguised to look like rocks. The account is remarkable in itself, but a successful replication of the Parent's investigations, by no less than an investigator for the American Society for Psychical Research, and famous author, Hamlin Garland; surely places this case as one of the most evidential in the literature of afterlife research. It seems Father Serra and his colleague missionaries wishes to provide evidence of life after death has been successful.[15]

Scientifically a detailed statistical analysis would score highly due to the number of hits of successfully found crosses and artefacts, and the replication of results by Hamlin Garland. A detailed chance probability analysis though could only be approximate, as although one would be justified in assuming a high hit rate, no indication is given of misses i.e. instances where the padres indicated a site for a cross/artefact would be found, but where the search was unsuccessful. Also statistics cannot account for the extreme rarity of the crosses which would dramatically increase the probability against chance. Indications though would suggest a probability against chance of possibly billions to one.

Significantly there are no adverse reports on the internet on this case by sceptics – as is often the case.

8.1.5   Case 2 - The Cause of the British R101 Airship Disaster

This particular case in October 1930, concerns the famous crash in France of the hydrogen filled British Airship R101, the world's largest flying craft during its first maiden overseas voyage. It effectively ended airship development in the United Kingdom. The crash spectacularly filmed, killed 48 of the 54 people on board.[16]

Two days later, on 7th October, at 3pm, a séance was held at 13 Roland Gardens in London, the home of the National Laboratory of Psychical Research. Present were Harry Price, a keen investigator of psychic phenomena with a reputation for exposing fraudulent mediums, a secretary, a stenographer and of course the medium. The medium, Eileen Garrett, was a famous **direct voice** medium, and possibly the most distinguished and respected medium of the 20th Century. While carrying out an experiment aimed at contacting the recently deceased famous author, Sir Arthur Conan Doyle, those present found that they instead heard the agitated voice of a different discarnate who gave his name as "Flight Lieutenant H. Carmichael Irwin." Although his name was not known to those present at the time, it was later found to be the correct name of the Commanding Officer of the R101 flight. In a trembling voice heard shaken with anxiety and speaking through Eileen Garrett, the stenographer recorded Commander Irwin's voice saying:

> "The whole bulk of the dirigible was entirely and absolutely too much for her engine's capacity. Engines too heavy. Engines too heavy. It was this that made me on five occasions have to scuttle to safety. Useful lift too small. Useful lift too small... Gross lift computed badly - inform control panel. And this idea of new elevators totally mad. Oil pipe plugged... Flying too low altitude and never could rise. Disposable lift could not be utilized. Load too great for long flight... Load too great for long flight".

Several of Irwin's statements - such as the ship being too heavy for its engines - were public assumptions, or could reasonably have been guessed. But many were technical, confidential, or simply unknown to anyone at the time. Here are three examples:

Commander Irwin in a continuation of the dialogue recorded above, said: "Load too great for long flight. Same with SL-8, tell Eckener"

No one at the séance knew the meaning of "SL-8" or recognised the name Eckener". British experts who later reviewed transcripts of the session, determined that Dr Eckener was the designer of the Graf Zeppelin, but they even had to search through records of the German airships to discover that "SL-8" was the identifier for a dirigible built by Schutte-Lanz Company of Mannheim, Germany.

Irwin said: "Starboard Strakes started."

"Strakes", is a term foreign to all at the session, but was originally a naval expression that was adopted by airship designers. "Strakes", are parallel layers of longitudinal plates that form the sides of a ship. Irwin, was formally a navy man, so it was a term that he would be expected to use.

None of those listening to this knew much about lighter-than-air flight. But, of course, they listened most intensely to the next few words which then broke off momentarily.

> "Cruising - bad and ship badly swinging. Severe tension on the fabric which is chafing... Engines wrong - too heavy - cannot rise. Never reached cruising altitude. Same in trials. Too short trials. No one knew the ship properly. Weather bad for long flight. Fabric all water-logged and ship's nose is down. Impossible to rise. Cannot trim. Almost scraped the roofs of **Archy**. Kept to railway".

The following next very last words of Commanding Officer Irwin proved to be exceptionally important and prophetic:

> "At enquiry to be held later, it will be found that the superstructure of the envelope held no resilience and had far too much weight in envelope... The added middle section was entirely wrong... too heavy, too much overweighted for the capacity of the engines".

And then - silence.

The R101 catastrophe was alarming. It proved to be one of the failures that destroyed much of the confidence in such airships. Naturally, and, because of this, an official inquiry was launched.

The results though took six months of expert investigation. They confirmed in detail, all information given by Commander Irwin channeled by Eileen Garrett. The details conveyed through Garrett were too numerous and specific to have been a matter of guesswork and coincidence. For example **Archy** is a tiny railway station that does not even appear on most maps including the authoritative Michelin Guide to France. In 1930, it did not appear either in the equally reputable Baedeker's Northern France (5th edition), or in a variety of other detailed London commercial maps consulted by investigators following the séance. Eventually they found it on a large railway map used only by professional railway and some military people. They therefore considered that it was such a map that Commander Irwin must have had to identify the small village between Amim and Beauvais. The information provided through Garrett (in the name and voice of Irwin), was at that moment unknown to anybody except Irwin, and yet his observations two days after the crash were later amply confirmed by a team of experts. Witnesses near the town of Archy testified at the hearing that the airship had passed over very low.

But even more evidence for an afterlife came later, as Major Oliver Villiers of the British Ministry of Civil Aviation asked Garrett to attempt further communication with those aboard the doomed airship. She agreed, and the Major became not only a witness but an active participant. Major Villiers heard testimony from several other (deceased) people who had been aboard R101.

The following is an excerpt from Villier's conversation at a later séance with a deceased crew member by the name of Scott, who had died in the crash:

Villers: "What was the trouble? Irwin mentioned the nose.

Scott: Yes. Girder trouble and engine.

Villers: I must get this right. Can you describe exactly where? We have the long struts numbered from A to G.

Scott: The top one is 0, and then A, B, C and so on downward. Look at your drawing. It was the starboard of 5C. On our second flight after we had finished, we found the girder had been strained, not cracked, and this caused trouble to the cover... it split the outer cover... The bad rent in the cover on the starboard side of 5C brought about an unnatural pressure, forced us into our first dive. The second was even worse. The pressure on the gas bags was terrific; and the gusts of wind were tremendous. This external pressure, coupled with the fact that the valve was weak, blew the valve right off, and at the same time the released gas was ignited by a backfire from the engine".

These and other statements taken by Major Villiers through Garrett's trance communications were verified by the subsequent official investigation of the R101 disaster. An officer of the Royal Airship Works where the airship had been built asked for a copy of the séance transcript, as did an airship pilot who had been a friend of Irwin. These two experts discovered forty! detailed technical references in the transcript that would not have been known by or comprehensible to anybody other than an airship specialist acquainted with the project. Furthermore, the pilot who had been Irwin's friend, was impressed by the peculiar manner of speech that came through Irwin/Garrett. In life, Irwin had a quick and jerky speech pattern (Garrett did not).

The case is probably unique in reincarnational literature, in that a medium was able to source highly technical information ostensibly from a dead person who died in the crash. Later a committee of inquiry, using engineering airship experts to testify, found the information provided by the medium while in trance to be sufficiently accurate and credible that they accepted them as the likely causes of the crash. [17]

8.2   CLOSING CHAPTER COMMENTS

The two above case studies, although exceptional, credible and with many supporting witnesses, are just two of no doubt thousands of other exceptional examples suggestive of an afterlife in the literature. They are also brilliant examples of excellent observation science - yet the science aspect, of course, continues to be completely ignored by mainstream science. The bulk of this Chapter deservedly covered in some detail, the fairly recent milestone work by both Professor G. Schwartz and Dr Beischel and their research teams. Their high quality, replicated successful experimental evidence for both an afterlife and reincarnation, should surely speak for itself. It is hoped Dr Beischel's ongoing imaginative and exciting investigative, and applications research work will continue to be fruitful, supported, expanded and joined by many others to the benefit of us all. Sadly to date, as far as I am aware, there appears little media coverage of the Windbridge Institute's work, so this work is relatively unknown.

I have left the coverage of some regression recall of "life-between-lives" to the next Chapter (the last), to the point where, hopefully readers who have read this far - will have a strong and inviolate belief in reincarnation. In this last Chapter, we will encounter the concept of guides, ghosts and other things we may find hard to believe, but are nevertheless well supported evidentially. Also it seems reasonable as stated earlier in Chapter 5, that just as then, for reincarnational and afterlife belief we should take the same approach as Dr Jessica Utts, a statistics professor at the University of California and chairperson of a USA Congress review of the CIA sponsored psi experiments in 1995. This is where (as mentioned previously) she reported back to Congress "that future experiments should focus on understanding how this phenomenon works, and on how to make it as useful as possible. There is little benefit to continuing experiments designed to offer proof."

Along with concluding comments on this book, the next Chapter provides a summary of regressional knowledge indicating how our life-between-life is likely to be like, gained from high quality and credible replicated regressions. The nature of life-between-life is perhaps a fitting end as the sole concluding subject for the last Chapter and the book.

CHAPTER NINE

Life-between-Lives and Concluding Book Comments

Also - in an Annex, Ideas and thoughts. Information and knowledge

9.1 LIFE-BETWEEN-LIFE

"There is an infinite storehouse of knowledge which is placed at the disposal of all who desire to have it, but it must be earned by growth and struggle, by evolution and progress"

Channeled by medium Maurice Barbanell[1]

This Chapter (apart from closing comments on the book and a supplementary Annex concerned with Information and Knowledge), is solely concerned with the provision of a selection of information currently available in the literature on what life-between-life is like. It has been obtained by methods indicated in Chapter 6, as a result of qualified psychiatrists using hypnotic regression techniques. It is supplemented by information provided by a few mediums (mainly "Seth" readings). This brief coverage of regressed type information is included in this book, as it is thought this information/knowledge might be particularly helpful for readers.

Moving now to the issue of the likely credibility of the actual information summarized below. Validation and credibility for an afterlife - as documented by both hypnotherapists and mediums - has already been exhaustively covered scientifically earlier in the last two Chapters. Earlier Chapters have also provided examples validating NDE (Near Death Experience) research evidence for an afterlife. In addition, the milestone lifetime research on OOB and remote viewing experiences by Robert Monroe (where discarnates are routinely encountered), and also Helen Wambach's successful statistical research validating the accuracy of regressions.

It therefore has to be said, that if expert and respected regressionists and mediums are found to be able to source valid information from discarnates - as has been found experimentally earlier in this book, **then why we would not expect life-between-life information derived by this same method likewise be completely the truth**.

With regard to the hypnotherapists mentioned responsible for the bulk of the content, they all have academic qualifications for this work and are therefore highly trained. They also have reputations to protect, have relatively high incomes without the need to write research books on their subject. Finally they have no reason whatsoever to fabricate their regression findings.

For those (once they have read the summary below), who may still have doubts concerning this regressional material, extensive validation research covering a very large sample including this and other afterlife material is available on a website, called: "AfterlifeData", http://www.afterlifedata.com/afterlife_analysis.php. This includes a massive and expanding database, which includes a resource of a large number of quotes on various areas from afterlife book material available from down the ages to the present date. Critically though, this website uses its database to provide a detailed statistical analysis comparative study to determine the correlation of these afterlife statements - but fully adaptable to cater for further material yet to be researched. This is covered under a "statistics" section on the database, which includes **both mediumistic and regressive type material**.

Noteworthy also, is that all the relevant quotations under each topic, are flagged as accepted or rejected, so that readers can check these classification findings for themselves. With such transparency indicating the correlation assessment in each case, there would seem no point or purpose in replication of this work by others.

Currently the overall percentage correlation calculated result, across all afterlife topics and quotes is 94.3 % - which is an amazing result for such a large sample size of 1090, over the wide afterlife area described. This statistic, surely to just about anyone, must itself provide overwhelming evidence that we all not only have an afterlife, but will experience there an afterlife existence along the lines of the "affirmative" corroborated statements, as determined in the research results. Can one imagine (say) books on gardening or any subject attaining a 94.3 % correlation on all aspects, or for that matter books on any other subject e.g. car maintenance, cat breeding and so on! Probably not. So whether we accept it or not - documented evidence on our likely life-between-life when we die, from both all available mediumistic or regressional material is strongly in agreement on just about everything!

I have inserted this above reminder of experimental evidence validating belief in reincarnation, i.e. an afterlife with multiple lives - as I feel it definitely necessary before we embark on reviewing what regression subjects have to say in their descriptions of between life experiences. This is because I believe otherwise most might regard what follows as fanciful, wishful and idealist rubbish.

For anyone who believes or is interested in reincarnation, they would naturally be interested in learning about what is likely to be their life-between-life experiences. Even if still somewhat sceptical, they perhaps would wish to examine some detail to determine whether it makes sense, is rational, coherent and whether the information source is likely to be credible. The following are what is considered the most likely initial questions:

If we really have a soul, where does it go after death, is there really some form of heaven full of not only people like us, but advanced intelligent souls? What do we look like as souls? Where is it, is it outside our physical universe? What does it look like, what do we do when we get there, and is there a supreme being in charge of this universe? Do we still have free will to do as we please, and are we judged in any way for misdeeds in this life and others?

I myself in searching seriously for such information some two years ago, found a principal source of this information fairly readily, as I was able to find quickly a treasure house of credible information provided by a Dr Michael Newton, available in his four books. The first two include his own personal case studies and the third book is intended to train hypnotherapists in his methods and discoveries. These are: *Journey of Souls: Case Studies of Life Between Lives* (1994), *Destiny of Souls: New Case Studies of Life Between Lives* (2000) and *Life Between Lives, Hypnotherapy* (2004). Following publication of these, he published and edited with footnotes, his final (and fourth) book to date *Memories of the Afterlife* (2008). Although edited by him, it comprises solely case studies written by 32 **other** hypnotherapists on life-between-lives experiences by certified hypnotherapist members of "The Newton Institute" (see below).

Dr Michael Newton, now retired; is particularly well qualified for this research as he holds a doctorate in Counselling Psychology, is a certified Master Hypnotherapist and a member of the American Counselling Association. He has been on the faculty of higher educational institutions as a teacher and counsellor and been a practising hypnotherapist for over 50 years.

Early in his career, and at that time an avowed skeptic of past lives, he initially chose orthodox hypnosis and clinical age-regression techniques to assist client's trauma conditions and symptoms - but solely within their **existing** life experience. Later in his career, while seeking the cause of a particular client's unknown cause of physical pain, he accidently regressed him to a supposed past-life death experience where he described being bayoneted as a World War I soldier in France. As this quickly led Dr Newton to a cure for the client, he then began his lifelong treatment of subjects using regression to **eithe**r an existing or supposed **past** life - wherever this might lead to effect a cure. Uniquely though in Newton's case, this led to his historic discovery of a methodology which allowed himself and others to gain information as to what actually happens in a life-between-life scenario.

Newton's breakthrough discovery occurred (by yet another accidental discovery) where he was sympathising with a client about her feelings of loneliness and isolation while she was describing the end of her most recent past life. He suggested "she go to the source of her loss of companionship", and then used what turned out to be a "trigger word" association, by asking if she had a specific **group** of friends whom she missed. As we will learn later, as far as is known and as indicated by Michael Newton, all those who pass over join a *"cluster group"* of souls of similar progression to learn, bond and advance while in a life-between-lives (some of whom often apparently share many lives together as relatives or close friends). These cluster groups and life in this environment, they regard as their permanent "home". As Newton described, this trigger word association caused his client to slip into "a higher state of consciousness". He calls this a "superconscious" state which reveals one's true identity, and is the highest level of self with complete and detailed access to all past lives – particularly to experiences between lives. After considerable effort involving trial and error, Newton claimed he developed a skill in being able to phrase questions so that he was reliably able to gain life-between-lives information.

Dr Michael Newton's three books have become best sellers and translated into 10 languages. They are essentially research works, as in order to write his case study books, he ceased his normal clinical regression practise of patients to concentrate specifically on life-between-life work. Following publication of his first two books, due to encouragement and pressure from other psychiatrists, he wrote the text book *Life Between Life Hypnotherapy* (2008). This was aimed at assisting fellow psychiatrist hypnotherapists, and outlines the successful methodology he discovered to regress subjects to a life-between-life state. He also founded "The Newton Institute", where he taught his techniques for many years and which now provides certification for those qualified hypnotherapists who have attended his courses to learn his techniques. This is so that they can then successfully apply his methods to clients who wish to regress to a life-between-life stage and learn detail of their experiences there for themselves. A search facility is available on the Institute web page so those interested can seek the trained and certified Michael Newton Institute hypnotherapist nearest to where they live, in just about any developed country in the world [2]. With regard to credibility, Dr Newton books comprise exact transcriptions of tape recordings "case studies" with clients, aimed at covering features of their life-between-life experiences. The tape recordings are indexed and can presumably be made available if desired. The same approach was made for the book *Memories of the Afterlife* edited by him, but similarly containing transcripts of clients regressions - but in this case conducted by different qualified and professional hypnotherapists. Unsurprisingly, information detailed in these different hypnotherapists case studies align identically with the two case study books of Dr Newton - which is what one would scientifically expect as verification of the validity of the information.

What follows is a synopsis of what I consider key points concerning information both he and his colleague hypnotherapists relate as their hypnotic regression case studies about life-between-life. These researched experiences are documented in the three books above. Space constraints mean that this is but a short summary. For further detail, one should naturally consult these books. Critically, Newton mentions himself from his 50 years of personal hypnotherapy experience, that "Once subjects were regressed back into their soul state, they all displayed remarkable consistency in relating their experiences". He also stated that **"I found the place where we go after death to be one of order and direction, and I have come to appreciate that there is a grand design to life and afterlife"**. [3]

At this point I feel it needs to be emphasised that many hypnotherapists who specialise in past life regressions such as Dr Michael Newton, claim that when subjects are regressed to a level where they can provide past life experiences, **that in contrast to ill-informed assertions by critics, they cannot and do not lie**. It will be recalled from earlier coverage, that Helen Wambach's comments supports this, as well as her experimental and milestone regression statistical research. It will also be recalled that Dr Wambach and other hypnotherapists find that with regressions repeated at any later date, that clients **always unerringly relate without variation, the same regression experience**. In addition, I myself certainly support Dr Newton's claims above, as, after researching numerous accounts of case studies of recent life-between-life experiences by different authors, the correlation amongst them all appears remarkable and strikingly consistent - even at a detailed level.

To assist readers or for possible future research, I have added a list to this Chapter "References", of all the books I have personally consulted for correlations with Dr Newton's works. Incredibly I cannot find any differences whatsoever, and the additions I have added in the summary below are simply supplementary to add further detail from that particular source which I consider might be helpful to readers.

Emphasising again the issue of credibility, it must be appreciated that in the "Summary" that follows, the content has nothing whatsoever to do with the personal views of Dr Newton or the 32 professional hypnotherapists who documented their own independent results of regressions for Dr Newton's book *Memories of the Afterlife* (2008)". Instead, rather than these being the views of all the hypnotherapists involved, all of Dr Newton's books used to compile my "Summary" below are taken from records of the independent regressions of no doubt hundreds of ordinary people just like you and I, with the same uniqueness discovered by Wambach earlier - namely that **they report exactly the same descriptions as each other in their life-between-lives**

experiences! It therefore follows, if you or I were similarly regressed by a professional hypnotherapist trained at the Michael Newton Institute, that our accounts of life-between-life experience would most likely be exactly the same.

In what follows, I have chosen to use the word "Home" rather than "Heaven", and "soul" for "spirit", and "advanced soul" instead of "Angel". Also the choice of other words appropriate to a non-physical realm. I have noted other authors have used a similar approach and feel, no doubt like them, that this ensures less of a religious connotation, which I feel is more appropriate since this is not a religious book. In addition, I feel this better suits a modern science notion of a completely different sphere of existence, incredibly more advanced than our own, from which we came and will return.

In the following "Summary" of Dr Newton's findings, it is intended to skip fairly briefly over Near Death Experiences (NDE's), as they have been mentioned earlier.

Note: In what follows, where sources are obtained elsewhere from Dr Newton's books, the source is indicated in the text and referenced accordingly:

9.1.1 **Summary**

"Earth Is a schoolroom, and the soul is the student".

James Van Praagh[4]

In Jane Robert's book, *The Seth Material,* Seth advises that at death we choose the time and manner of our death.[5] The literature (Newton's books and others) also describe that at death, our consciousness/soul experiences an ability to rise above its body. The experience is described in many sources as obviously disturbing, as it is often unexpected and therefore somewhat frightening, but said otherwise to be quite pleasant. Invariably a brilliant light is seen accompanied with a slight tug in its direction, which if desired can easily be ignored. If the discarnate chooses to ignore this tug and remain in this state; then, if contact with living humans is desired, the soul can and does often present visibly as a "Ghost". Some discarnates remain in this "halfway" state (commonly referred to as 'ghosts') for lengthy periods for various reasons e.g. they are unaware they are dead, or do not wish to proceed into the tunnel (as mentioned usually in NDE experiences). This may be due to disorientation/shock of a sudden death, or where they have taken their own life and wrongly think they will suffer retribution, etc. Most stay temporarily to observe their funeral. At any time, going towards what is described as an intense light source, enables the non-physical entity to enter a tunnel like entrance (as mentioned in Chapter 6) that appears to be a wormhole to another realm.

On arrival in the "home" environment, friends and/or family are normally present to greet and welcome any who have passed over. This usually includes those who have acted as a guide or guides in a just completed life. "Guides" are usually advanced entities who are sufficiently advanced to have completed their earth cycles and aspire to this work. However, discarnate friends/family members often assist in guidance where they can throughout one's life. To facilitate adaption back in the "home" realm and overcome any dislocation, trauma etc., and to enable complete restoration to full health, a period of recovery is prioritised. So that this appears natural and reassuring to arrivals, this often appears to look like a hospital with those assisting, wearing appropriate clothing, e.g. doctors and nurses seemingly to be wearing uniforms that meet expectations.

Any pain associated with death cannot be remembered. If not a violent death, then, as mentioned earlier, the death experience and transfer to a life-between-life could be (surprisingly) quite pleasant, but also painless. Although understandably somewhat frightening. None of this should be particularly surprisingly, since it has scientifically been shown, as mentioned earlier (Monroe), that we unconsciously experience OOB states with consciousness leaving our bodies **routinely** for a period every night! **Additionally, consciousness is programmed to leave our bodies instantly when either trauma, or death occurs**. All this is also constantly reaffirmed by reports of people who have experienced NDE's. Some at death (fortunately rarely) during regressions claim a temporary encounter with what they describe as "the Devil". However information gained from regressions overwhelmingly indicates the concept of "the Devil" is simply an invalid fanciful human erroneous belief and myth. (There is historical scholar support for this, as there is no mention of "the Devil" in the Old Testament, nor the concept in Judaism. In the New Testament, references are considered merely allegorical, not personal **and refer instead to sin.**)[6]

Reports of so called encounters with "the Devil" immediately following death, are therefore said to be an occasional mind construct of a person at death. In other words the person's consciousness/soul at death is momentarily, but brilliantly, exhibiting an expected strong ability in non-physical reality - to create a temporary facsimile aligning with mistaken fears and expectations of punishment for perceived sin.

Following death it is also said that at "home", there is never any pain, nor fear.

The important point which must be stressed which follows from all this, is that there is simply no reason whatsoever to fear death. This fact alone suggests at least one reason why those who return following a near death experience (NDE), are often unwilling to return.

One soon finds that in a life-between life, not just the environment, but oneself is very different from any experienced on earth. All entities/souls appear in a natural state as radiating somewhat transparent pin-points of light (i.e. which we of course would now recognise as a fully quantum state). Souls/consciousness, habitually though, often appear to each other in **a simulated physical appearance** chosen as that preferred and regarded as optimum from any previous incarnation. Since one experiences different sexes throughout various reincarnational life-cycles, the soul's preference for a particular gender is normally reflected. However such a preference disappears as the soul advances. In circumstances where a guide may wish to overcome fear and relax a young soul who has just passed over, to meet expectations the guide may temporarily appear on arrival to a new soul as the Buddha etc. (Seth). It is apparent from this, that all souls (and of course guides) in non-physical reality have the ability to telepathically induce in any others' minds whatever image of themselves they wish. Proficiency to achieve this does though seem to take considerable training and this also applies to an ability to instantly create any degree of actual reality desired in one's immediate surroundings (with this, we would recognise consciousness creating reality, although instantaneous in non-physical reality). For example wherever surrounding buildings are required for meetings, or for public purposes or one's home, they are instantly created mentally - presumably jointly or individually as required. Some buildings e.g. Libraries etc. seem to be mentally and consciously retained as permanent structures due to their usefulness for all (a default condition of permanence would be expected, as entropy i.e. disorder over time would be impossible in a quantum timeless environment). This applies also to such things as for example creation of delightful fields of wildflowers, castle towers, rainbows etc. and other vistas of great beauty, created solely by the consciousness and imagination of the souls. An example Dr Newton gives, relates to possibly only a temporary structure - where a discussion between a guide and a new arrival took place in what appeared to be an exact copy of his own familiar local pub. The guide created the pub to provide a pleasant and relaxing environment for discussion on the soul's immediate past life. Entities in this environment also experience, a feeling of weightlessness, with nothing comprising an obstacle or solid mass. There is cloudy brightness with layering of light, warmth and quietness with the feeling of being surrounded by thought, concern, companionship and empathy plus a feeling of well-being. All senses appear intact including scent and taste. A low level very pleasant tranquil sound with a constant echo of music vibrations/resonance like wind chimes is said to be heard at all times, which becomes modulated with movement.

Unsurprisingly, communication is solely telepathic and instantaneous, but also one normally can read "minds". If though two entities desire privacy, this is regarded as "*touch*" where - by moving so close to each they are conjoined, they are said to then rotate together around each other. This enables private thoughts to be conveyed by intermingling of "electrical sound impulses". The experience is said to both exceed and provide a substitute for a physical "sex" experience. It is emphasised however that, as said by Dr Newton due to telepathy, "No subterfuge or deception exists in a telepathic world." The advancement of souls to a higher spiritual level is indicated by a progression in colour appearance one emits as a light being, From white, a new soul - through light to dark shades of yellow then blue and finally to a purple – signifying a very advanced soul. The location of this realm is reported as being close but just beyond earth – to a point that Robert Monroe says via his OOB experience – to be just beyond the clamour and noise of emotion and thought emanating from earth's inhabitants.

Contrary to the view held by some, that souls might immediately on passing over attain a "spiritual" character; this is not the case, and they arrive very much as we know them before their death. They do however, on arrival, soon regain remembrance of their previous lives and become very much aware of any failings to meet their intended and agreed goals in their just completed life. This is often devastating and hugely disappointing to a soul. This is also despite the fact that they know that returning souls will never be judged by higher entities or punished for any failings or misdemeanours (this obviously contradicts popular religious belief). Instead all higher entities (such as guides, teachers or "members of the council of elders") have themselves during their advancement over many past lifetimes, failed to meet their own, and their guide's expectations of them. Guides and higher entities therefore are non-judgemental and continually respect and love all others regardless; and merely guide, counsel and do everything they can do to help those whom they assist. The point also is that since all souls exist in a timeless realm and are therefore immortal, the only pressure for a soul to progress and advance is the pressure they impose on themselves and the desire not to lose the respect of their guides and friends. There is the concept though of "Karma" or its meaning - which is the inevitability of achieving a balance in all things, if advancement is to be achieved and maintained. This, therefore, together with the encouragement, advice of guides and elders, does motivate a soul to do better and try again by means of another life-cycle. Thus, in this realm there is no such thing as Hell (just something approaching that perhaps on occasions during our human existence on earth). Nor as mentioned above is there any such thing as the Devil, or identification of failings as "sins". By this there is no suggestion that 'wrong actions' are acceptable and in this event, particularly when serious issues are involved, intense counselling is inevitable plus the necessity to encounter similar situations in a next incarnation and subsequent cycles of reincarnation until the lesson is learned, the weakness overcome, and karma resolved.

In such an environment where everyone cares for each other, those generally of like advancement are assigned to the same cluster group (of some 3 -15 souls), where they work together to gain knowledge and discuss their previous lives and plans for the next. Discussion with one's guide and advice on one's past life takes place soon after arrival, but later, a full review takes place before a Council of Elders accompanied by one's guide for support. No criticism or penalties for failings are ever issued by the Council, merely advice and encouragement on how to do better with the next round of challenges - usually on earth, but it could be in another existence, planet, etc. alien to our earth experience. The Council arrange a later meeting prior to the next incarnation to discuss this in depth, to meet the soul's wishes and gain the soul's full and willing agreement to various available options for a future life. At all times free-will is paramount and respected, with a slower or faster progression at the discretion of the soul concerned. Regressions commonly make the point that souls choose their parents in the next life and some members of a cluster group often reincarnate to share a life experience with a soul as their child, a relative or a friend - to assist them in their life, and share in their experience.

Many choices are involved by the soul in planning for a future life. In many cases a soul might wish to accelerate resolving an inability to overcome a particular weakness exhibited in many earlier reincarnations - by themselves choosing a disability. This could mimic the effects of violence and anger meted out by them to others in a previous life. A high degree of suffering is obviously likely to be more effective in experiencing what a victim might have suffered and obviously vastly superior to any reprimand or imagining the consequences of one's actions ("There is a difference between being told things and knowing them" – Seth[7]). This then can explain why so many on earth may suffer pain and hardship seemingly without reason.

Cases of children who die young can also have one of many explanations. For example, one case quoted was where a fellow cluster group friend, chose to assist in creating an agreed test experience, but did not wish stay for a full earth cycle. Some souls are said to find themselves unsuitable for incarnation on earth; in which case they are able to choose another life in a different part of the universe or realm. Those who commit suicide are encouraged to return to complete their agreement with the Council of Elders. On their return though, they are expected to again encounter the same events and the same challenge which led to their suicide, but on this occasion cope with it successfully without again resorting to suicide.

Those regressed often speak of a continuous sense of the infinite i.e. God. From what we have read earlier in this book, it also seems rather obvious scientifically from quantum interconnectedness of everything, that we are irrevocably linked with God forever in a holographic existence. Esoteric literature interestingly (Buddhist belief) puts this another way by saying we each contain a spark of God. It also indicates we will each eventually advance to unite and become one with God. Regressions of clients via Dr Newton supports not only all this, but indicates that we will still retain and never lose our personal individuality.

While in a life-between-state though, we mentally need only to think of a question and the answer is usually available (dependant on the level of the soul). When reborn on earth though such knowledge is said to disappear (this of course suggests the brain "filter/resonant frequency" concept we encountered earlier in this book). Guides are said to instantly respond to prayer during a soul's life on earth. The exception is where the guide decides that to do so, would not meet the soul's intended plan for their life. Guides are often said to respond to prayers by placing thoughts covering their recommended solutions in the minds of those seeking help. These suggestions though are often ignored despite the guides' wishes.

Contrary to popular belief, a soul decides when to enter the mind of a new-born and stay permanently (during sleep or at other times, cellular consciousness is said to maintain life and basic subconscious functions). Transition of souls is said to occur often before birth (temporally, usually not before six months and at other times), to achieve compatibly with brain function. It usually becomes more frequent close to the birth and at longer intervals thereafter, but not at all if an abortion is foreseen. (Seth & Wambach[8])

A rather difficult but perhaps necessary area to cover, is the concept that the energy of a super-self soul while in a life-between-life existence, is vastly higher than that of a soul while on earth, since a much lesser proportion only can cope with an incarnated state. Apparently, while in a life-between-life existence in this much higher energy state, we exist as the totality of all personalities in any other lives - regardless of our incorrect assumption that each of our reincarnational selves have existences at different times. Although difficult for us to accept, since no time exists in non-physical reality, all personality fragments of our soul (i.e. reincarnational selves), can be regarded as existing simultaneously. Even in our time sense while on earth (as covered previously), this does in fact align with our correct concept in classical physical reality that there is really no **absolute** past or future, merely a spacious present.

It is necessary and important to mention this here, since it explains how we can still telepathically and in sleep interrelate with our friends and family in their life-between-life state regardless of them experiencing a number of simultaneous reincarnations at once. In essence therefore, it is said that we all are multi-dimensional personalities. ("Seth", provides the analogy of each of our reincarnational personalities being different leaves on a tree, with the tree trunk being our "super-soul" which permanently resides in our life-between-lives). The above hopefully also clarifies the concept that our real "home", and the principal part of our entity is always in non-physical reality.

Attainment of reaching the goal of no longer needing reincarnations is sought after by all souls - as this point is reached when challenges are all met satisfactorily and higher responsibilities are then both deserved, and can be assigned. The first level of these, is as a guide for others. When even more advanced, guides are assigned as a member of a Council of Elders. Some very advanced and progressed souls (level VI and above), are also said to eventually become co-creators in the universe or in other spheres. In such a role they may be given all sorts of responsibilities which may even include populating new planets, changing environments to favour life (in physical or non-physical realms), but only if they show acceptable capability and then carried out satisfactorily intensive and appropriate training.

9.1.2   Comment on the Summary of Life-Between-Experiences Above

The concept of very advanced souls being assigned such duties as populating and manipulating planets to favour life, suggests this would include the creation of entirely new species and assisting in ensuring their ongoing survival. Importantly, this would overcome the conundrum mentioned in the first Chapter as to how new species were formed. You will recall in Chapter 1, that this was where, although subspecies variation of all earth life was shown explainable scientifically by one's DNA code influenced environmentally by epigenic adaptions; no cause whatsoever could be found to explain the appearance of entirely new species, or even life itself. However, the following Seth quote (See Annex 2 of Chapter 5) infers as one might expect, **that highly advanced souls are responsible for populating planets with new species**:

> "…. Some life forms are being developed in what you think of as present time. They will not appear physically until you reach your future time."[9]

Little is reported in life-between-life regressions to date on the science aspects of afterlife technology, although there is mention in Dr Newton's books of recent arrivals using a form of book which, via video and sound, enable us at will, to relive for review purposes any moment of one's previous life. Also Newton's books describe particularly advanced technology associated with reviews of the next possible life, where full size 3D colour and sensory replication of possible lives is simulated - even to the extent of allowing full emersion by the soul temporarily into the simulation as desired using mental control.

An almost unbelievably advanced science and technology though must be associated with the ability of extremely advanced elders to arrange soul personality reincarnational re-births on earth as desired, and also a soul/consciousness return to an afterlife following death. This really should not be too surprising as in just the last few centuries mankind has made almost unbelievable scientific advancement. But for highly advanced non-physical beings - souls, they would have considerable important advantages over us as humans. Among these is the fact that since conscious creates its own reality, all souls - presumably as long as they have the knowledge sufficient to imagine an object - could in a non-physical environment, manipulate matter to instantly create anything they wish. Presumably also, very advanced souls could access the zero point field instantly to source all available technical and scientific information and knowledge without hindrance of the "filter" mentioned in previous Chapters, but appropriate to their advancement. However, it seems reasonable that information would still have to be assimilated and experience gained before new and complicated technology could be implemented. With some 13.8 billion years since our Big Bang heralding the birth of our universe, it would seem that there would have been ample time to develop the afterlife technology (as mentioned in the life-between-life summary covered above) to suit human reincarnational cycles and progression. However, it is probable that other physical species in the same way may use the same or similar technology, and each have their form of afterlife "home" and collective consciousness. Since non-physical realities must predate our universe, it is envisaged that highly advanced entities may not only have also preceded the birth of this universe, but may well have been assigned eons ago to develop and nurture our universe including our earth planet.

With regard to Dr Newton's view expressed above that - "I found the place where we go after death to be one of order and direction, and I have come to appreciate that there is a grand design to life and afterlife", - it certainly seems that the afterlife structure described and summarised above with regards to order, direction and design; would perfectly meet all we could possibly wish. This would seem to apply - even with the horrendous initial reaction to the thought of eternal life - where ultimately one feels, boredom and satiation would inevitably follow. Reincarnational theory therefore appears to cover all angles.

Boredom seems solved in part by the simple expedient of our memory loss during each reincarnational cycle - as each life seems new, fresh and full of challenges. But boredom is no doubt completely solved by being rewarded increased responsibility as we prove we are competent enough to perform and are therefore assigned more challenging, interesting and diverse tasks.

Each of us now, no doubt the living result of umpteen incarnations - could certainly not claim boredom. By our earth concept of time, most of all those alive today including you, the reader; are no doubt millions of years old! We also get to choose the next "life" and every life, plus all our assignments. It is said we can even choose to have a rest and accept as a life-cycle (for example) the life of a giant tree, if we wish (Seth).

Notably, we never lose our friends and family as we can always remain in contact. We are always in contact as well with caring guides and higher entities who always have our welfare in mind, and guide and assist us in our progress to advancement.

Conflict, argument, anger, hate, and wars - in a life-between-life state, is seen to be impossible, as not only can we read each other's thoughts, but in any case every soul is concerned only with harmoniously getting along with, and helping others. Planning, progressing, exploring and assisting each other, and all entities in a co-operative way, is easily seen as the optimum method of learning and increasing knowledge for all. (A lesson we never seem to learn while on earth).

It seems inherent in our nature to be happiest and sense the greatest feeling of self-worth when we are working to help others. Therefore the afterlife structure seems amazingly organised to ensure that our future will always be aimed at maximising this desire. From a scientific point of view, the future of all life is seemingly also planned to embrace all potentialities possible. This is because, as we see in just our own universe, new galaxies and presumably new life is being formed continuously. Clearly from Bob Monroe's remote viewing adventures in non-physical reality, we must conclude that an almost infinity of existences, universes and life are probable. We also must conclude, that although we all would hope fervently that mankind, as we currently exist on earth, will eventually go to the stars. But as non-physical immortal souls, we are nevertheless assured of doing just that. On this basis each of us would seem to be able, like Captain Kirk of 'Startrek' fame, one day, *"to go where no one has gone before" (*perhaps to even an 'Avatar' type planet with hanging islands and, vines if that is your wish*)*.

9.2 CLOSING CHAPTER COMMENTS

In these closing comments for this Chapter and close to the end of this book, (an Annex follows) I hope you have found the experimental evidence and validity for both hypnotic regression and the ability of mediums to source accurate information (from those who have passed over), both surprising and compelling. In my research for this book I am very much like yourselves, in that all that I have written, is the result of following the evidence wherever it has led. I thought it reasonable therefore to document the order of my investigation into the possibility of a science base for reincarnation, largely in the sequence of my arrangement of Chapters.

It has to be said that with the totality of all the evidence in the whole book, I am also surprised at both the quality and volume of the scientific evidence available which I was able to include - to support not only belief in reincarnation and an afterlife, but strikingly and unexpectedly for myself, also immortality for us all. Not for a moment did I believe when re-commencing research for this book a few years ago, that such scientific evidence was already available.

Unfortunately though, in the foreseeable future, I cannot see much in the way of change in the present attitude of mainstream science; to be dismissive to the importance of non-physical reality, quantum physics and the paranormal. In recent years, quantum processing has been discovered as a critical facet of brain processing with Walter Schempp's PCAR system identified as the likely form of non-verbal communication for all life. Also, much of the paranormal is now fully able to be explained by science. Yet mainstream scientists are unmoved. Despite also the fact that telepathy,(as covered in this book) has been fully scientifically vindicated and replicated by experiment - even with modest and relatively inexpensive equipment, certainly not the cost and complexity of the Large Hadron Collider.

I believe the main reason, as I have mentioned earlier, is that science overall has lost the wonderful sense of inquiry of the ancients - in that rather than being open-minded, it is just the opposite and instead wedded to rigid materialism. Largely ignoring quantum physics seems like only exploring one side of a coin, but non-material reality consciousness and quantum scientific experiments such as the double-slit experiment, have shown that material reality itself arises from non-material reality. It is therefore prime. Because of this, clearly logic suggests that quantum physics is not only the most important, but also the most likely to be able to provide the TOE (the theory of everything as covered in the introduction to Chapter 2), and elusively sought after by physicists over the last 50 years.

Wholehearted and enthusiastic research into non-material quantum physics therefore would surely provide a mountain of possible new developments and breakthroughs yet to be discovered - with no doubt unimaginable benefits to humanity. As mentioned in Chapter 3, investigations into methods of extracting energy from the zero point field, if successful, could provide the whole world with an unlimited energy source, but available anywhere, since it ubiquitously surrounds everything. Also Walter Schempp's fMRi successful scanning research to produce 3D colour images, suggests that further development of such a system resonating to specific frequency ranges of an object may enable video images of past events currently claimed by psychics via psychometry, to even be possible. After all, Kirlian still photography can already show past leaf structure of a cut leaf. Perhaps then, **the past history** of all objects and their surrounds in visual, and colour 3D video is within our grasp.

Unquestionably, naysayers and some skeptics have been particularly unhelpful for paranormal research, as was shown earlier in this Chapter on research into the validity of mediums contacting the dead. This is because the negativity of naysayers, and those skeptics who only have the aim of egotistically and publicly throwing scorn at genuine research into the paranormal with merely assertions, or cherry picking evidence which suits their cause, is destructive, harmful to reputations and ultimately destructive to science. It may well be that when their current life ends, they may be very surprised to learn the paranormal is normal and so also is reincarnation.

Perhaps though none of this really matters, as there is some suggestion in the literature that if correct, means that mankind was never intended to stray as far as it has currently reached in lack of belief in its true origins. There is also evidence outlined below that the situation is currently being changed to remedy this issue. While I have noted four references to this below, there may be many more.

The first is towards the end of Dr Michael Newton's first book *Journey of Souls: Case Studies of Life Between Lives*, where he indicates there a number of particularly advanced souls who have indicated in his regressions that there are changes intended:

"....to permit more information and understanding of who we are and why we are here".

An earlier indication of this was documented some 45 years ago by the medium Jane Roberts channelling the supposed multidimensional entity "Seth" in the book *The Seth Material*.

"You were to work out problems and challenges, but you were always to be aware of your own inner reality and your non-physical existence. To a large extent you have lost contact with this. You have focused so wrongly upon physical reality that it becomes the only reality that you know." [10]

Further mention is made in a relatively recent book (written in 2010) by Robert Schwartz (no relation to Dr Gary Schwartz). His book is entitled *Your Soul's Plan: Discovering the Real Meaning of the Life You Planned Before You Were Born*.[11]

This recent book compiles information on this subject - provided by arranging a number of well-known mediums, to channel discarnates to provide details of how and what were the reasons for them arranging **their plans for a future life**. These mediums are: Deb DeBari, Glenna Dietrich, Corbie Mitleid and Staci Wells.

In his book Schwartz, says that in one case, a soul speaking through a medium says that when returning to earth, as part of his "life's plan", it was expected of him to affirm an afterlife existence. Schwartz also says, the arrival and presence recently of "indigo" children being born (mentioned earlier in this Chapter) was highlighted by the soul as a deliberate change and indication that psychic abilities are currently being increased (i.e. aimed at presumably remedying the world's current lack of belief in our true origins). This has further strong correlation from a 1980 book *Messages from Michael*, by Chelsea Quinn Yarbro, purportedly resulting from the channeling of 'Michael' by a group including a medium Jessica, for some 11 years! 'Michael' spoke of a "Psychic Revolution" which had then already been initiated which would eventually change the belief system of those governing throughout the world.[12]

The validity of at least a "psychic revolution" to me seems self-evident, in that since July 2000, the number of psychics and mediums has exploded, assisting in solving previously unsolvable crime/murder cases or primarily supposedly contacting passed family and friends – all of which must have fostered markedly belief in an afterlife and reincarnation.

In recent years we also have seen many books published by mediums on their life (many of which have been best sellers). There are also many others on reincarnation, psychics and the afterlife. I have chosen July 2000 (above), as the date from which the medium John Edward was the first to be uniquely accepted in the world, for a psychic/medium television series ("Crossing Over").[13] He was successful in this, as he convinced the previously skeptical producer with information concerning the producers' parents, which was only known to him. Following Edward's breakthrough, as the first medium to achieve a successful television series; today, psychic and medium television programmes are extremely popular throughout the world, with many mediums travelling to major cities around the world constantly to present live performances.

To some extent the fact that mainstream science discredits psychics and mediums, may well eventually count for little, as most shows are packed out with believers in an afterlife - exhibiting at least, that they do not share the moribund belief system of conventional materialistic science. This seems likely to continue. As we have shown earlier in this Chapter, the high hit rate of most professional mediums strongly advocates that the public, not the mainstream scientists are right.

We now even have "ghost buster" type organisations in cities and towns in developed countries throughout the world offering free investigations and often staffed by researchers including university students and graduates. All in defiance of popular scientific belief that ghosts do not exist.

Hopefully it will not be long before a tipping point is reached and all our world's people and eventually all religions will re-embrace belief in multiple lives and immortality for all. Also the quantum holographic interconnectedness of all things highlights the nonsense of wars, religious differences etc. and instead affirms that we should treat all others as ourselves.

The brilliant systems theorist and world renowned scientist Ervin Laszlo (mentioned earlier in Chapter 3), in his excellent latest (2014) book *The Immortal Mind: Science and the Continuity of Consciousness Beyond the Brain*, envisages we are close to the birth on earth of a new and wonderful era which will follow such a tipping point. This is an era he calls "An Era of Conscious Immortality", where we would no longer live in fear of death. This he believes would lead to a major change in our relationship with each other, and a more responsible life, caring for the well-being of others and our environment.

He goes on further to say:

"We would know that when our body dies, we do not leave this world, but only transit into another phase of our existence. Realizing that our consciousness is immortal would give us the assurance we need to experience joy in living and tranquility in dying. It would give us the enduring satisfaction of being able to contribute to a world we can experience and enjoy over and over again, in this life and in lives to come." [14]

In addition, many may feel in our twilight years there is simply no purpose in persisting with art, music, literary, educational and other interests. However with complete belief in our immortality, we would be surely be reinvigorated with a new sense of purpose to continue our current interests unceasingly, since it would be evident that none of these, or knowledge gained would be wasted or lost at death.

Obviously such a change to complete belief in our immortality can only occur by a change in the existing fundamental belief system of the majority of people on earth. To me, the trigger for change is for science to now pick up the ball dropped many years ago when the relationship of quantum physics to consciousness, the paranormal, our immortality and an afterlife was either ignored or overlooked by mainstream scientists. Their skepticism - an antithesis of an open minded approach, has been a major impediment to progress, as the general public obviously tend to be strongly and inevitably influenced by scientists' view.

Since non-physical reality is prime but scientifically neglected, there would seem an inexhaustible opportunity for new discoveries in quantum physics as mentioned above. Successful research in quantum physics with benefits to mankind would naturally spark interest further in quantum physics and perhaps for beneficial further and major scientific investigation of the paranormal. A rather simple and immediate research project that comes to mind which might be worthy of investigation. Robert Schwartz's has had the novel idea (in his book referred to above) of using mediums to source information on obtaining details of life purposes from discarnates - in this case advanced guides. Instead, it seems this concept could easily be expanded to similarly use mediums to in the same way seek other new information from advanced guides but in this case, beneficial information for us all specifically on science matters. Appropriate to science though, controlled laboratory conditions should be used and a number of proven talented mediums.

It would not be expected that knowledge would freely be given to scientists beyond our level of advancement and responsibility, but this would surely not apply to some areas such as medicine, agriculture and our environment. Also, the method would be able to be interactive, and therefore have to be vastly superior than just thoughts impressed in a scientists' mind occasionally by an advanced entity. Obviously apart from mediums, hypnotherapists could be used to regress subjects to derive useful scientific information from high level souls in the same way. Perhaps the Windbridge Institute may be the research institution that might pave the way for all this work?

Leaving science reluctantly but momentarily for a final word to this Chapter. In researching whether science could support an after-life, I inevitably have been led to study reincarnational belief. What I have found is that conventional religions tend to exhort somewhat complex, different and contentious demands on their followers as to how they must live their lives and avoid "sin". In many cases these religious differences themselves have fostered alienation, to the extent that any idea of our true commonality (and interconnectedness) has been lost, with conflict and war the result.

In contrast, reincarnational demand on its followers, is so simple, that it is worth sharing with you.

This is best encapsulated by the current Dalai Lama in a single word:

"My religion is very simple. My religion is **kindness**."

Dalai Lama XIV

Also that:

"Our prime purpose in this life is to help others". [15]

Dalai Lama XIV

To end this Chapter and book, the following is a poem supposedly provided by a higher entity via a "rote" included in the book *Far Journeys,* written by the landmark and iconic researcher/explorer of non-physical reality, fellow professional engineer Robert Monroe:

"For those who would die, there is life
For those who would dream, there is reality.
For those who would hope, there is knowledge.
For those who would grow, there is eternity." [16]

And a final Chapter comment from Seth:

"You always were, and you always will be." [17]

END

CHAPTER NINE ANNEX

Reincarnation/Recycling, Our True Reality, Ideas and thoughts. Information and knowledge

Also the Culmination of the concepts in this book

(Note: As I consider this a culmination of some key concepts in the book, I feel it rightly should be regarded as an Annex to the whole book.)

Ideas lead us to the future and to the benefit of all mankind - *author*.

PREAMBLE

Entrenched belief systems (including formally that of my own), I consider a major issue in limiting currently mankind's progress (as is covered in this book and the following Annex). Due to credibility issues, it was not intended initially to include this Annex in this book - as I considered that it could be a "bridge too far" for some (particularly scientists) at first reading. My concerns were that this might unfairly lead to them rejecting my book completely, based on their doubts concerning the validity of ideas presented in this Annex. However, I finally decided to include it for two reasons, as follows:

> Without this Annex there would be no explanation as to how sages, savants, dowsers, or psychics using psychometry or precognition (or other paranormal means), gain access and source previously unknown information/knowledge. In addition, likewise how scientists have on occasions gained inspirational knowledge. And finally how primitive humans and other lifeforms on occasions have inexplicably gained new knowledge which has assisted their development and survival (e.g. such as a novel hunting strategy).

Importantly I also wished to describe the methodology needed to gain such knowledge (alluded to by researchers Tart and others) by including it in this Annex in the hope that it would allow inspirational knowledge breakthroughs to be achieved more readily by scientists and others. (Many years ago I had a minor inspirational breakthrough concerning an important 'work' science/engineering matter, but clearly beyond my intellectual/knowledge capability then or now. At the time I had no idea of how this happened. However, following research for this book, the cause to me is now apparent and therefore I consider this worthy of its inclusion for the benefit of others).

INTRODUCTION

Since (hopefully) the issues of afterlife and reincarnational belief are no longer in doubt for any who have read this far in the book; all of us and future science researchers should be focussed on gaining knowledge, a better understanding of reincarnation reality, and perhaps also if possible, learn of our collective destiny as a species.

The issue of gaining new knowledge is surely of critical and practical interest to scientists.

To this end, the last and remaining but important issues covered in this book are information and knowledge. Knowledge leads to a betterment of all our futures, and from what we have learned, it is clearly readily accessible almost as a gift (e.g. savants, psychic's etc.) via the non-physical realm - using regressions, psychics/mediums, and remote viewing.

Paul Davies considers that organised information is an essential ingredient and **pattern** of mind [1], but both information and knowledge seem also **a prime fundamental pattern designed and orchestrated into the structure of the universe, by a creator/God.** An essential component of this must also comprise the **universe internet highway** for the transfer of all information/knowledge. Evidence provided earlier this book, suggests it is the "zero point field" and that access to all universe memory and information/knowledge is via the inner, subconscious mind. As we will see in later in this Annex, there is also evidence to suggest that almost unlimited "free" information/knowledge seems readily available to those ethical enough to be trusted with it, but limited to those insufficiently advanced.

Hopefully it will have been remembered that in the Foreword to this book, the following headings were used to identify how knowledge is gained by science.

Knowledge is gained from:

1. Science (includes experiment, observation and discoveries),
2. Inspiration, and
3. Revelation.

The tools of science were presented and then expanded on in some detail under the various headings, as these were the tools which were then applied for the remainder of the book. Rigid independent replicated experiments ('solid' science), as the ideal method of science application has been applied throughout this book **wherever possible**; but where impracticable, statistical probability analysis has been used.

I believe rightly, that despite my love of science and great respect I have for all scientists, in this book I have criticised the lack of use of observational science in recent years. This is because it is a method that seems to have now been abandoned completely when wishing to achieve new discoveries. Instead the norm is for independent replicated laboratory experiments, many of which today are not even replicated as a means to avoid bias. This is despite the fact that observational science has been used repeatedly and extensively in the past to achieve major breakthroughs. Two significant examples are (of course) Newton – often called the father of science, who (as mentioned previously), discovered gravity simply by observing the effect of an apple falling on his head. Earlier, Archimedes discovered "density" and its method of measurement - again simply by using observational evidence while taking a bath. Neither of these used independent replicated experimental evidence. Some other of the world's greatest discoveries have also been made resulting from observational science, and/or even, inspiration. Examples are, Francis Crick's discovery of the DNA structure, and also the famous *'Periodic Table of Elements'* - which was discovered by the Russian chemist Dimitri Mendeleev while lying in bed day dreaming.

The science methodology described in this Annex (as with the earlier Annex to Chapter 4) - is the use primarily of independent replicated experimental science documented by researchers. This is also supplemented by some **observational** science of my own, checked with that of an **inspirational** source – the esoteric **mediumistic** 'writings' from "Seth". All **three** of these sources have been used to arrive at this Annex conclusions. They also arose from an open-minded approach to our reality, which seems very absent today. In fact even the word, 'Paranormal' or 'Reincarnation', is sadly so much of an anathema to most wedded materialist scientists today, that they would **be unlikely to bother lifting this book 'off a shelf, let alone read it.**

Although in these two Annexes, esoteric wisdom was used to assist my observation of our reality, it surely is a valid scientific approach to be used to reinforce or stimulate observational science and assist inspiration. But also the use of **logic and logical consistency** - another critical scientific tool. If one is serious about furthering science, it surely follows that every science tool in the armoury should be applied to benefit mankind.

Finally, I would respectfully suggest to readers of this Annex, not to quickly and superficially dismiss what follows, without reading on. This is because some observational instances discussed, might initially appear (to some), as seemingly obvious. However, simply assuming *'that it is obvious'*, could disguise the underlying cause - the very reason why I believe that important truths in this Annex have been previously overlooked. This applies also to my discussion in the Annex on "time" (in Chapter 4) - which allowed me to choose the most viable "universe" option, based on consciousness criteria and "Seth" esoteric wisdom from the likely universe options (based on Paul Davies brilliant work in his book, *God and The New Physics*).

(To provide a quick reference, the relevant esoteric wisdom quotes appropriate to this Annex taken from "'Seth" books published by medium Jane Roberts are appended immediately following this Annex. **It may be helpful for readers to read them first before continuing.**)

REINCARNATION/RECYCLING AND DO WE HAVE ANY TRUE REALITY, OR ARE WE JUST A SIMULATION?

The concept of reincarnation/rebirth/recycling seems a fundamental universal truth that applies not just to humans, but to all entities and life. All matter decays or deteriorates, including the cells of our bodies. Even rocks washed by rain and wind. The dust, which is all that is left, eventually re-unites with other particles in a form of rebirth - or perhaps, using a more appropriate word, "recycling". In the case of star dust, new planets are formed. Each minute particle has a degree of consciousness and continues its existence with intervals of recycling, so that all time/event lines continue forever. Therefore everything which is created, all lifeforms and consciousness - **are eternal!**

Professor Robert Lanza, the 'Einstein of biology', mentioned earlier, puts it another way: "the evidence lies in the idea that the concept of death is a mere figment of our consciousness. The concept of death as we know it, cannot exist in any real sense, as there are no true boundaries by which to define it. Essentially, the idea of dying is something we have long been taught to accept, but in reality it just exists in our minds." The concepts of space and time, he describes also as "simply tools of the mind".[2]

Virtual reality games mirror somewhat life itself, in that in a virtual reality computer game, we are ourselves the controller (as in life itself), and create our desired reality within that game in whatever manner we wish. Time is irrelevant, as we manipulate it by changing the speed of motion or acceleration as we wish. Space is easily changed at will, by moving within or beyond the initially presented background created by simple computer or micro-processor programs. Movement beyond a depicted background, then allows the instant appearance of new three dimensional space to occur as a fulfilment of our wishes.

All of this raises the question that because such a simulation is so lifelike, is all we perceive and feel (i.e. our reality) also a simulation? The similarity is strikingly similar to a modern virtual reality game in a number of ways. Firstly we have learned repeatedly (earlier in this book) that we create our own reality, but we note that in doing this **we are actually oddly within our own creation**. A virtual reality game surprisingly mirrors this, but also with the fact that in both cases time is irrelevant, just a series of spacial "nows". In addition, space is but a mental construct and a tool of the mind - as stated above by Professor Robert Lanza. Despairingly we are on the verge of jumping to the inevitable conclusion that in comparing ourselves with a virtual reality game, we are it seems, perhaps (correctly) - **but a dream in the mind of God**. But, when we realise that, as with the virtual reality game, in both cases there is one thing left which has eternal validity - it is our consciousness in everything we create. This includes our thoughts and ideas. Plus also our own consciousness - which itself must have been created by a creator/God. (This fits rather well with the famous Descartes dictum that, "I think, therefore I am".)

We therefore come to the inevitable conclusion that we are certainly **no** simulation, and are in fact co-creators with God. Also, that we have an **eternal ultimate valid reality - as with all consciousness and creations** - which must include our thoughts and ideas. **Clearly without consciousness, thoughts or ideas, nothing would exist.**

THOUGHTS AND IDEAS AND - HOW WE CREATE OUR REALITY

As humans; we seem particularly focussed in physical reality with little thought as to what goes on in our inner unconscious mind. Obviously our unconscious is our auto pilot, and handles all the functions we can satisfactorily hand over such as breathing, repairing cell damage etc. Importantly though, **since we have no conscious awareness of it**, it must additionally fulfil the critical (but normally unknown) function of collapsing the quantum probability wave function, to effect a single choice outcome for ourselves amongst all probable realities available. Then, at the next event point, to again choose similarly from probabilities, the next event which will add to our time line and experience; then the next and all subsequent ones, and so on - to fulfil our experiences in our physical life and beyond. (Noteworthy is the fact that in doing so, we all individually create our own unique time/event line).

Others though, when presented with the same range of possibilities at a subconscious level, obviously with free will, could and without question make different selections for collapse of the wave function, mirroring the fact that, happily we are all different. It also mirrors the fact that again and again (as described in detail below, based on mountains of observational evidence all around us), these different decisions that we make in life, **depend entirely on the beliefs and the overall belief structure we hold at the time**. If we change our beliefs, we change our experience for the **good or bad**, and we alone are responsible!

A simple example is - if we negatively believe we are accident prone, then we will perfectly exhibit that belief as long as we retain that belief.

Saints have on occasions exhibited for years, wounds on their wrists called stigmata, as a facsimile of the marks of Christ's crucifixion. Similarly, many under hypnosis have exhibited realistic but temporary indications of being thrashed or similar flesh indentations suggestive of being bound while relating past life experiences - all testifying as to the ability of their beliefs at that time of being capable of changing **even** their physical appearance while in trance. There are even credible accounts of levitation occurring with saints, Tibetan monks and psychics. This again testifies to our ability to be able to change our reality to whatever matches our beliefs. Not only are these all examples of our ability to create our reality, unconsciously and automatically based on our beliefs; **but also they demonstrate again and again, that the paranormal is normal!**

Moving away from events currently regarded as paranormal, to a seemingly prosaic everyday life example - that of driving a car. We assume we are the driver and a good driver most of the time. Therefore, most of the time we are likely to be on auto pilot, or more scientifically we would say that we are focussed more on non-physical reality i.e. using our **unconscious** mind. We also suppose we have somehow developed a false belief - that, in that particular town; many other drivers are particularly *terrible*. It is then not hard to imagine that we, the driver (based on probability alone), and with such a belief, may occasionally **unconsciously** select a particular one of all the probable events encountered during the drive through the town. The **very one** we assume, which exhibits the shocking driving we would naturally expect to encounter by our belief. You guessed it! Since we create our own reality in accordance with our expectations, such expectations are always likely to be fulfilled - such that the driver ahead could swerve in our path. (You guessed correctly, it was a recent experience of mine).

The outcome of my negative belief, was an approaching car which suddenly swerved directly towards my path and nearly killed both myself and my wife. Happily my belief did not encompass death at this stage, so I am alive to tell the tale.

In contrast, it is easy to imagine that the other drivers I encountered in the town on that particular day, had no such strong belief such as mine concerning the inadequacy of other drivers - so after I braked, we both passed each other unscathed.

It might be argued that my take on what happened was purely speculation and more a matter of chance. But if this is your belief, I guarantee that if you analyse **any** of your life experiences based on your current beliefs; you will find that you will, on a scientific observational evidence basis, encounter a reality such that your belief expectations **will always be fulfilled.** Therefore rather than chance, **this seems a fundamental truth of the universe, which embraces everything and all consciousness, including all life, and even ideas and thoughts which, (as above) demonstrate that they themselves have a form of consciousness.**

A really important issue here is that **due to our current belief system we have embraced since childhood**; most at this stage will regard the above example of a car swerving in my direction, as purely a common chance event. However quantum physics, rationality, and estoteric wisdom itself says otherwise (as covered in the quotes included at the end of this Chapter). If the reader stops here, in disbelief and disgust; it is possible that you will miss out on what appears to be a fundamental truth (covered below) which could change your life for the better. It also overwhelmingly seems an important, **essential,** orchestrated and a design feature of our reality by a creator/God.

Surprisingly, **the fact is,** that **"our expectations are always fulfilled based on our beliefs"** and this **happens at all times, without consciously being aware of it**. Not just when we are on auto pilot, but also when our thoughts are very much focussed in "awake" consciousness. **After all, we are not consciously aware of our unconscious mind carrying out other repetitive functions for us**, so why not also, the repetitive function of deciding from various possibilities offered to us via the Schrödinger wave function, as to **which one we will accept based on our beliefs?**

Not only this, but it gets particularly interesting if for example, one harbours **negative** thoughts about our ability to do anything, for example, painting an artistic likeness of anything or anyone. In this case it can be seen that our expectations again are most likely to be fulfilled, such that a poor result will be inevitable. On the other hand, if we have positive or open minded expectations, we obviously are more likely to have a better result.

Observational science therefore tells us that - "positivity is the way to go".

Negative thoughts seem particularly prone to fulfil undesirable expectations. Since one finds that this is **so observationally obvious**, then we could easily conclude that it might be a **designed bias (by a creator/God) aimed at favouring positivity and creativity over negativity - so that useful progress will be achieved for all, rather than stasis.**

Negativity for sport is continually **banished** by sports coaches and sports psychiatrists as being counter-productive to sports performances either individually or collectively as a team.

It works for the better, and achieves **peak** performances in sport, ballet, singing, art etc., **so why don't we adopt such an approach everywhere?**

The advantage of expelling negativity everywhere, is exemplified well by the quotes - in the vernacular, *"Negativity sucks"* **(mine) and** *"Fortune favours the brave"*.

A critical point is that while **both** quotes I consider correct, the second has for me some issues. The word "brave" - reminds me somewhat of the "Vikings" who were most certainly brave, no doubt equipped with a positive inclination and also received great wealth and fortune. As innocent victims, the recipients of their slaughter and mayhem would though no doubt argue, that they didn't particularly have a joyous association with them. Today we would agree, and also that fortunately things for most of us have since improved. Apart from the Vikings, gang members though; psychopaths, and others are often very brave and positive, including dictators and **some** CEO's, and remain so all their lives. But most of us would prefer to be without them. In passing, we may also note that Vikings no longer exist!

On reflection, it would be difficult surely to believe that all the above could have been orchestrated **other** than by a creator/God - as it most certainly is so technologically clever, that the mathematical probability of it all occurring by chance, would have to be zero.

However if this was our reality - "full stop", we would surely argue that it was hopelessly flawed, as rabid Vikings and dictators etc. are not exactly anyone's favourites. So there just has to be something more to ensure reality could be different than this **– for those who wish for a different reality.**

As we will soon find out below though, our universe appears brilliantly orchestrated by a creator/God to provide just this option. This is because those who do not want a life associating or encountering some of the undesirable people or experiences on this planet; **only have to change their beliefs, and their belief system strongly away from those which lead to misfortune, and their life and reality will change for the better**. Also we will find, that if these arguments are thought metaphysics or religion, they are not. Instead; although verified by replicated experimental science (as covered below) it seems overlooked, and undiscovered to date - presumably because observational evidence has been largely ignored by scientists and others for possibly more than a century. All of it though is rather obvious, when observational science is applied to our typical life experiences.

This is because observationally and importantly, it can always be found that if anyone changes their individual beliefs about **anything, then their reality will tend to experience that thought**. For example if a housewife thinks repeatedly that that she may get a burn while ironing clothes, then her reality is very likely to fulfil her expectation. Similarly if one feels lucky at almost **always** getting a car park, then this belief is almost inevitably likely to be successful **dependent on the strength of belief.**

I should know, as I have had fantastic success with this most of my life; but wrongly attributing this always to luck when it occurred (but strongly believing it).

Mirroring and fulfilment of beliefs can also be seen to apply to collective or **whole** belief systems. In such cases, the results are more likely to be deemed obvious than a random individual belief, such as discussed above. A disturbing example, is the case where a person has just become a gang member. His belief structure and system soon changes (usually) to own a motorbike, get tattoos, a patch and comply with others who have such a belief system in engaging in crime. His viewpoints and beliefs attract others who wish for this lifestyle, such that group mentality occurs, and the actions of the gang are endorsed and reinforced by association, to the point that their reality perfectly matches their collective thoughts. Those that have differing thoughts though, might attract different realities - one might **negatively** feel strongly that he will be caught and end up in jail, another might **positively** feel the opposite. Again their thoughts - depending on how strong they are believed, will mirror their reality. A former gang member I met, changed his views to eventually reject this gang group mentality, due to the harm it was doing to others and his wish for a different life. He is now employed usefully in working to help others very successfully by using his life experience. (Ironically he would be unlikely to ever understand that it was **his changed beliefs** which ended his misery, not the unhappy consequences associated with his former choices, which he finally found were unacceptable.)

Scientific replicable experimental validation for the above has been well documented by a number of paranormal researchers such as Professor Charles Tart (and by others, although not highlighted) in their books. What has been overlooked is that all simple paranormal experiments aimed at (for example), determining successful hits, are usually accompanied by misses. Many experimenters have been astonished though to find that on analysis an enigma invariably occurs, in that negative results always exhibit a statistically significant pattern similar to that for the positive results, but no explanation has been offered by researchers as to why misses should not be random, rather than exhibit order. The discussion above indicates that the likely explanation, is that the experiment satisfactorily exhibited reality, in that the subjects were simply expressing perfectly their differing belief systems. This result is even more evident in experiments on the effectiveness of placebos (as mentioned previously), where commonly about **35–40%** of participants obtain valid cures, from nothing but pills comprising simply sugar/chalk composition, etc., and the remainder receive no discernible improvement.[3] The result demonstrates, that belief creates perfectly what then becomes the reality for the subjects of any such experiment after taking a placebo, i.e. those who falsely and genuinely believe in the ability of the placebo to cure them get better, but those who don't believe, and cotton-on (perhaps telepathically) to the fact that they are fake, don't get better.

> Believe that life is worth living and your belief will help create the fact
> *William James*

ATTRACTION OF LIKE THOUGHTS AND BELIEFS, INFORMATION AND KNOWLEDGE

During the above discussion concerning gangs and group behaviour; inherently the concept of the attraction of both belief systems and thoughts to each other arises - suggestive of the saying "like attracts like". Again as above, the fact that it is obvious that association leads to shared beliefs, may well be due to observational experience reflecting an unknown scientific base which itself validates the common observation. We note that all masses are attracted to each other (via gravity), and since thoughts create masses themselves (i.e. physical objects) as part of our creation of reality; it seems not unreasonable to suggest that thoughts themselves must attract each other as well as entire belief systems. In fact this suggests that **this attraction is the unknown scientific base** which underlies a fundamental truth perhaps for our whole universe and all reality, that everything attracts everything – **even information and knowledge**. This is also supported by esoteric literature.

There is a shocking but inevitable downside to this which also seems a fundamental truth, but also an upside - **which if you believe, may well change your whole life for the better.**

If "like" information/knowledge anywhere, (as entities) attract each other, it follows that if one harbours **false** beliefs, then such beliefs are themselves likely to also attract other **false** information and knowledge which shockingly supports such beliefs. These additionally could be expected to attract like-minded associates, companions etc., who will likewise reinforce such false beliefs. Similarly, those whose belief system are focussed on **truth**) i.e. **valid** information; then they similarly would be expected to attract associates etc. plus ideas and information/knowledge **which reinforces and adds to their knowledge.**

Stressing further the upside, then if additionally, we have **caring and loving concern for all others and all life**, and a desire for allied type information/knowledge, plus association with others of like mind; then that will be our experience. If we have the opposite attitudes, then (from the above) our life could exhibit possible attendant miseries and misfortunes which might follow. The good news is that for those who are experiencing **anything** that they don't like in any aspect of their life, then they need only change their thoughts and belief structure. This will then change (over time) their life to meet their new expectations - such is the power of thought, and the ability we have to create our own reality. In a non-physical quantum reality, we would of course expect the effect would be most likely instantaneous, wheras results take some time in the physical world. (In the witch doctor example we gave earlier in this book, we would expect the effect of him pointing the bone at anyone is likely take a few days in physical reality to achieve his intended result).

Attitudes and beliefs currently perplexing and rightfully causing dismay to many scientists, include such examples as climate deniers of man-made global warming, and their call to do nothing. Some are known to be professors with good climate science credentials, others are even heads of state. On the basis of the above, if any have little regard for truth or honesty, they could inevitably attract information and knowledge which includes and supports falsity. Since they would believe it fully, they would naturally wish to perpetuate such falsehoods to others. Amazingly they still stick to such beliefs when it is obvious that we are already harming our planet in other ways, with our oceans choked with increasing rubbish and unchecked increasing populations. Regardless of their beliefs, therefore we must do something to remedy the damage we are all doing collectively to our environment, as there are inevitably and obviously limits to what our environment can withstand.

It follows also from all this, that science is at a crossroads currently. Particularly with the advent of the internet, since information now readily available there, whether true or false, allows anyone to cherry pick information to justify their personal belief systems. Those that **disregard** (or falsify), lifetime research by honest, truthful, reputable and dedicated scientists in any endeavour, could have attracted and derived false information from the internet. They then may use this information to rail against all sorts of valid and useful scientific developments. A good example is fluoridation of water supplies. If these detractors are listened to, and fluoridation is removed locally, they, their children and all others in the community may inevitably suffer misfortune of later experiencing serious tooth decay – as a consequence of this modern world being saturated in sugar products.

A similar situation applies with recycled water. Many believe this may be harmful, despite scientific data indicating purification levels are achieved far beyond those of natural rivers, lakes or reservoirs. Such a false obdurate attitude results in abandonment of recycling proposals which adversely encourages water waste and inadequate availability of drinking water during droughts throughout the world. And so on.

Far more serious than any of this; is the situation engulfing the world currently, where war rages continuously, based on fallacious perceived religious differences. In many cases there is not only antagonism, but an intention to kill horrifically those with, or even without, any opposing views. The fact is, that these religious views were not even different, **but commonly held** when first written into different biblical texts. In biblical days few would argue that this was an environment where, in many cases, one had to cope with the daily reality of "kill, or be killed". This though is simply no longer the case, nor acceptable today. The fact is that mankind has developed considerably since then, through lessons learned in many wars. Rather than a world of warring tribes, there is now also a need to relate more closely with each other, in our today's global village world of communication, trade between all nations, and undoubted **interconnectedness**.

"Seth" highlights this by saying that in biblical times when Christian or Muslim religious beliefs were documented in the Bible or Koran, **"....no man loved his neighbour, but distrusted him heartily"**[4]. In addition, **"you cannot hate yourself and love another"**. **"It is impossible."**[5] Little surprise then that many malcontent's and those that hate others, have flocked to wars since the dawn of time, happy to have a cause that gave them an opportunity to attempt to expunge their hate on others.

Time has moved on, but for some they have not. In the Bible and Koran there are passages, little known to many, that **both** exhort followers in biblical days to violence and appalling death to any who held differing views or belonged to other tribes. Links to details on these are included in this Chapter References.[6] Clearly we all have the right to choose which passages from religious texts that align with our beliefs, and of course this is exactly what people do.

Observational science above though, in terms of the attraction of like-information to views already held, indicates, that those who harbour such beliefs - such as wishing others harm or even death (as we see currently in the Middle East), will most likely themselves reap miseries and misfortune. Those who believe the opposite, will conversely be unlikely to be affected. Which is also supported by esoteric wisdom. i.e., **"You form your own reality. Those who think thoughts of peace will find themselves safe from war and dissention. They will be untouched by it. They will escape and indeed inherit the earth"** - Seth.[7]

Having established this, and returning to more conventionally accepted science aspects; many other experiences we might encounter normally or exceptionally in life, can easily be explained from the above concept that like-attracts-like information/knowledge.

Within the everyday and normal experience of laboratory experiments, from the above, it is obvious that any experimenters who are strongly negative about the outcome of their work are unlikely to have successful results - as their negative expectations are always likely to be fulfilled. Worse, any experimenters who are not open minded and whose belief system does not support the existence of what they consider, "the paranormal", would be most unlikely to find any results whatsoever supporting evidence for the paranormal. This is clearly indicated by most simple experiments concerning the paranormal, where **the public are involved as subjects**, such as telepathy tests using zener cards, and also the "REG experiments" mentioned earlier. Where favourable outcomes are found, although positive, they are invariably minute. This would be expected anyway, since - as we create our own reality, we would surely expect the effects of their differing belief systems of any number participating, to be averaged out. Strangely we seem somewhat blind to this, yet we would expect a very successful professional gambler or foreign exchange dealer to continue to beat the odds (at least until such time as they lost their confidence and therefore a belief system in their continued success).

Ironically, skeptics claim the possibility of rater bias must be removed for subjects assessing hits in all experiments aimed at validating mediumistic abilities (as was criticised in Professor Gary Schwartz's afterlife experiments). For them, any subjects in such experiments presumably must only be complete disbelievers. Common sense therefore indicates that the best way of proving paranormal events and attaining science **breakthroughs in any endeavour** is the opposite approach - namely to **fairly** select in all cases for these types of experiments, those subjects who profess to be open minded but always strongly and **positively** have a belief in the likelihood of success. There seems no point in selecting any with a negative view of the paranormal, as it is obvious their results would most likely fulfil their expectations.

In contrast to the above; rather than normal experiences, there are many experiences that one would classify as **exceptional, inexplicable or claimed to be "paranormal"**. In my view the most important of these with regards to science, is the case where receipt of new previously unknown information (but breakthrough type knowledge) seemingly arrives from nowhere. This is where scientists or others, claim inspiration or revelation for their discoveries. Evidence below suggests that such seemingly modest claims are not modesty, but instead, are well supported by recent scientific theory and mathematics. They are also supported by the observational science which follows from the above and by esoteric wisdom.

RECEIPT OF INSPIRATIONAL INFORMATION/KNOWLEDGE

Here, we are looking to see if we can determine the methodology mentioned above, where scientists since ancient times have occasionally achieved breakthrough discoveries which have often led to major improvements to mankind. To learn how to do this routinely, would itself be a monumental benefit to mankind. There are certainly issues with the advent of the internet in today's world (as mentioned above), that make even independent replicated laboratory experiments (previously considered to be the cornerstone of science), now difficult and problematical, due to bias and differing belief systems.

Inspirationally gained information/knowledge though, has no such issues and in fact usually does not normally even require physical experimental apparatus. Just one's own mind and intellect.

We learned earlier in this book (in Chapter 2) that from the Russian quantum physicist Mensky in his 2011 research paper (referenced), **theorises**, "That if consciousness equals a separation of the alternatives from each other, then the absence of consciousness equals the absence of separation. Therefore, turning off consciousness (in sleeping, trance or meditation) opens access to all **classical** alternatives.....Thus, when going over to the unconsciousness state, one obtains the information, or knowledge, which is in principle unavailable in the usual conscious state". Obviously from discussion in previous Chapters concerning consciousness it seems Mensky is correct. **In addition, mathematical detail in his research paper, logical consistency and its historical science base, well supports its validity**. (His theory is an extended "Everett's" (parallel universe) concept (EEC). Interestingly, his theory and mathematics supports even the concept of miracles, since he claims it describes that a very small probabilistic miraculous event - as long as it has a non-zero probability, can nevertheless be shown to be mathematically possible with sufficient intent.)

In studying this research paper (see Chapter 2 references), it seems though, that he has not realised that this can occur easily while wide awake, nor has he described satisfactorily the likely methodology as to how this can occur. In addition if his theory is true, one would wish to know the source of the information obtained via the subconscious inner mind, and why it should be freely available.

Surprisingly up until now, no one seems to have realised, that by simply using observational science and esoteric wisdom, **not only is validation of his theory easily obtained, but also the detail of the methodology, the source of knowledge and the cause**.

It seems, (as we will discover below), that this must also be method that sages, witchdoctors, savants (plus all other species and forms of life) must have also used in the past, to obtain information/knowledge which has assisted them in their future development. From this, it appears that our highly developed **conscious** mind (not apparently present in many less complex forms of life) would appear to be a major impediment to our species (mankind) not progressing more rapidly than otherwise would be the case.

Explanation

From the discussion earlier in this Chapter, and from personal experience – I believe one should mentally adopt a quiet questioning approach with focussed attention, intent, inquiry and belief in likely success - seeking answers and mulling over unknown issues. **"Belief"**, and **"Positivity"** is particularly important, in that the subject must have sufficient belief to feel that **rational mental inquiry** alone is very likely to prove successful in achieving the desired outcome. In a sense we are directing our mind to create our reality in that direction and enhance our current knowledge. Scientifically, there are in fact two factors that should assist our belief. The first is that we know others have undoubtedly been successful in the past with this approach, and secondly as theorised by Mensky, it is fully supported by quantum theory and mathematics.

For example in the case of a scientist, reinforcement of belief may have been aided by past success and a positive attitude to the point where the methodology of concentration and focussed attention with the expectation of success becomes somewhat habitual. This then leads to a breakthrough where the scientist will often claim that he is not responsible for the success, and instead felt that the knowledge which suddenly came to him, was of an inspirational/revelationary nature.

When a habitual and repetitive approach such as this is used, psychologically it seems reasonable to conclude that the subject is likely to be in a light trance like state - as there is little to differentiate this from any self-hypnotised person, or an externally hypnotised person who would also be considered to be in a light trance. Slight trance like states though, are common for us all in many instances during our daily life where we function using an unknown source and flow of continuous desired, but already known knowledge, e.g. in doing the dishes, driving a car etc. Notably this always involves our subconscious mind coming to the fore, with our conscious mind subdued but ready to protect us from harm if needed. (Noteworthy though is the fact that by using our unconscious when driving a car we are using **a continual stream of very useful and freely available subconscious – but correct, valid information.** Otherwise we would crash!)

Quelling conscious thought, in circumstances aimed specifically at seeking unknown information, is certainly different (though **similar** to driving a car unconsciously). With the **difference of focussed attention, intent, inquiry and belief** (i.e. **the positive expectation that a successful discovery may be achieved**). This seems to disable the normal brain filter restriction which normally impedes access to non-physical reality. It can be seen that this then is **little different, from "awake consciousness" either in the case of a practised psychic or a medium attempting to derive "new" valid knowledge or information.** In fact there are only two relatively small differences likely to be evident from that of mediums and psychics. The first difference, is that psychics and mediums' area of interest is **usually** solely confined to gaining information from discarnates. The second is the degree of proficiency. In the cases of mediums and psychics, this is exemplified by the observation that some are but novices, but others excel.

This large range of capability and proficiency is similar to the rest of us seeking new greater information/knowledge for use in our vocations, or for our general life - as in the example of a scientist above.

In these cases, we must look more deeply at the likely cause which can explain quoted instances of inspiration, the receipt of revelationary material and even claims of enlightenment in a given area of inquiry. In a typical case of determined but positive attempts to seek new knowledge, we will assume that a scientist seeking the answer to a problem, is open minded with (importantly) **an amenable expectation of success**. In some reported cases, the scientist might claim a feeling of being directed to source information from a book, and when opening the book randomly, is shocked to find text which provides what he might consider a complete and revelationary answer to his problem. In view of this he might identify this as a paranormal event. **Where focussed attention and intent, plus rational thought are applied with expectations of success in a habitual slight trance; the scientist often may find a continuous supply of such normally unattainable information arriving in his mind.** A simple example is a person involved in the practise of "dowsing", (mentioned by "Seth"), which if he believes is a valid practice, despite the views of most people believing that it is not, from the above we could predict that it is likely to provide valid and useful previously unknown information. Even those who believe it might work, consider it a paranormal function. A moment's reflection though, indicates that clearly this is not paranormal, but normal; as not only does our true reality (but generally **unknown** reality) always fulfil our beliefs and expectations, but the dowser most certainly could in the light of the research above, be predicted to provide valid new information continuously from beneath the soil. He would have course have no idea how this is achieved. Those that don't believe in dowsing and think this nonsense, can similarly be predicted of course, to be extremely unlikely to ever succeed.

This explains the operational method as to how scientists, mediums, psychics - and **anyone in any sphere and for any purpose can obtain valid new information and knowledge** – seemingly appropriate to their current level of advancement. But incredibly, **free** information/knowledge for all, from the Universe, Wow! And on any subject at all.

This ends the discussion on the methodology, but surely from a scientific point of view we would still wish a further explanation as to **how, or why this is?**

THE LIKELY SOURCE OF ALL INFORMATION/KNOWLEDGE

We are now (again, as with my previous Annex dealing with "Time") leaving what is considered to be acceptable science within our current reality. Hopefully this attitude will change, to encompass belief in what seems to me to be this "new" methodology which can gain information/knowledge on perhaps any subject, and which is seemingly unknown currently to science until now. Essentially what follows, provides validation of this different method of obtaining new information/knowledge independent of mediums or regression methods. It is able to be applied by scientists or virtually anyone - not just by using mediums or professional hypnotherapists for regressions. What follows is a description of this, validated by application of solely observational scientific evidence based on information provided earlier in the book, and by rationality. It is also supported by information obtained from a "Seth" book *The Nature of Personal Reality*, channelled by Jane Roberts.

Contrary to the expectation of many, that mediumistic information is rubbish, this book has shown **solid** replicable experimental evidence that demonstrates with **talented mediums**, the information they provide has a very high scientific probability of being true. Regarding the "Seth" information, Jane Roberts, the medium who channelled "Seth", unquestionably has been found to be one of the most exceptional mediums ever covered in the literature. Despite the large quantity of information she provided, to my knowledge, none has ever been shown to be false.

What follows, I therefore consider to be unquestionably correct.

Seth comments, emphatically indicate access to all knowledge/information is received via the **inner** mind, the subconscious. This aligns with previous coverage in this book of the filter concept which normally **in waking consciousness** restricts full access to information which otherwise can occur in sleep or trance states. This is said to be an earlier **collective** human species decision for species development, so that we are more focussed on our physical reality and responsive to any immediate danger. (This seems less important now that we have long since risen to the top of the food chain). Above, we learned of the **attractive effect** such that information gained elsewhere is linked, to other 'like' information/knowledge contained in our minds. It is therefore easy to imagine, that sought information/knowledge flows between our subconscious and conscious mind when there is deliberate attention and intent, **plus belief (endorsed by a positive attitude)** to receive this information/knowledge on any particular selected subject. Seth concepts indicate that, not only is there an attractive effect with information/knowledge, but once sourced and attracted, it becomes associated with one's consciousness -"*it becomes new and is reborn*", as consciousness "*units*" – becoming part of one's soul/consciousness.

There seems to be a few caveats we learned also from the above. If we honour truth, our endeavours are likely to be successful. If not, then the information received may well be false. Also since like-information attracts-like, then it helps if we have a degree of competence in a subject in order to advance our knowledge further. Finally we will only receive such information/knowledge if it is appropriate to our current species level of advancement.

On the arrival of information/knowledge thoughts or ideas, such information is said to appear as "beads of perception". Therefore there is a sense that we must be prepared to expect and carefully listen' to any new information/ideas which may **occur unheralded and appear as normal thoughts**. Since information is provided via the subconscious mind which has access to non-physical, quantum reality, the response is instantaneous.

But you might ask, what about the source of the information/knowledge itself. Where is it?

Esoteric literature often talks about a rather vague term, the Akashic Field, as the source and library of all universe information/knowledge stored since the dawn of time. The term Akashic Field seems to have an identical meaning to what has been described more meaningfully, accurately, scientifically and descriptively in this book, as the "Zero Point Field". However, while this describes the communication "pipeline", it does not tell us specifically where all memories, ideas, thoughts and all universe information/knowledge is actually physically stored. Seth's few comments on this seem eminently reasonable, by inferring that they are located at *the point where they arise*. This of course means **every particle which contains consciousness/ mind in the universe**. The fact that desired knowledge/information is distributed and associated with any consciousness in the realms of the universe, is in quantum reality completely irrelevant; as access anywhere to all points in the universe via the zero point field is instantaneous. As covered in previous Chapters, vibration of all objects creates quantum waves which allows transfer of information to and from the adjacent zero point field (which embraces and mingles with all objects). This effect applies to both physical and non-physical reality, so that (as covered previously) the zero point field itself must act as the "internet highway of the universe", for the transfer of all information/knowledge and memory of all events and experience, to or from anywhere in the universe. Noteworthy, is the fact that the source is independent of time, so it could be from the past or future.

As I was involved previously as a communications, computer systems and network professional design engineer, I cannot help but identify this in computer terms with modern computer networks, local and distributed processing/memory and internet access to distributed cloud storage. All of this provides a growing daily capability via the internet and Google's search engine/and processors to gain **free** current world information/knowledge at the click of a mouse. For convenience, If desired we can even instantly download (i.e. copy) any specific e.g. "Google" type information we wish to add to our existing local computer's hard drive storage.

This information and communication technology we now use on earth, does mirror fairly closely and simulate to some extent the above. It therefore assists in its understanding and validation. (With this, I cannot help but be reminded of the maxim of "as above, so below").

But again, a moment's thought indicates that the power of intellect of the creator/God who conceived and implemented his incredible mind blowing technological creation, is clearly beyond our comprehension. By comparison it makes our feeble information technology efforts although vaguely similar, but a toy. Who else but a creator/God could have envisaged that all He had to do to make everything above work, was to ensure that all information/knowledge is **attracted to each other.** If this was not the case, we can clearly see that kindness and caring for each other and for all life, is unlikely to be sustained. It probably would not even have arisen at all on earth (or elsewhere), except for one's immediate family. Instead, we would all tend to be **loveless self-serving** Vikings always hopelessly laying waste and creating mayhem everywhere. This action might lead inevitably to an ultimate destruction following purposeless perpetual recycling for all entities everywhere. Our only knowledge presumably would be that given to us at birth, as without the knowledge attraction capability, no "updating" could occur. We might then possibly be only automatons with intellects similar to that of an amoeba.

This above methodology, must surely also be the means by which all life-forms, from the most primitive to the most complex on this planet, gains new information/knowledge and in a regulated way.

In this respect, within our own human species, we cannot help but be reminded of the case mentioned previously of savant's abilities – **otherwise unexplainable**. This is where, without being mathematicians or even much schooling, many savants attain an enviable and incredible capability to carry out complex arithmetic calculations in their heads. Others can provide detail on major events in the world on any chosen past date. Since **no learning is involved in these feats whatsoever**, we most certainly must identify such cases as involving "free" information/knowledge. Likewise, the same comment must apply in the case of "dowsing", where professional and successful practitioners cannot claim years of university study of complex earth's geological structures to match their undoubted rewarding and proven capabilities. Natives of South America use "curare", a paralysing poison on their arrow heads to assist their hunting of birds and animals. In some areas to assist in their objective, the poison is augmented with parts of animals or worms to impede coagulation of blood. None of course are research chemists from Johnson and Johnson etc., yet the extraction of curare is a complex and resource intense process involving scrapings of bark, and takes some two days to prepare. It is therefore most unlikely to have been discovered by trial and error. One could go on and on with many other examples.

Accessing information/knowledge via ones unconscious inner mind and the attraction effect, also explains how new knowledge gained by one, is immediately available to another. A simple example mentioned earlier, is that of birds lifting milk tops off glass milk top bottles. (Other fascinating examples are covered in detail in Sheldrakes books). This also explains many other quoted simultaneous discoveries by scientists. For example, Wallace and Darwin, are both known to have discovered valid theories concerned with species adaption to the local environment, both at the same time.

The explanation above which explains how new information/knowledge has been made freely available to all lifeforms since the dawn of time, (but until now thought inexplicable or paranormal); covers so many other situations, that just **a list** of all of them, most likely could not even be contained within a book this size.

Surely, since the above **is** our observational reality we see all around us, one cannot help but note that it exhibits not a shred of randomness or chance. Rather it exhibits an incredibly and meticulously designed plan by the most brilliant, intelligent and loving creator/God one could ever imagine.

Finally, esoteric and Buddhist belief insists that the creator/God has distributed himself as a spark within all consciousness. This then if true, suggests a ready availability of infinite wisdom adjacent to us at all times, and also a creator/God who intends to experience his own creation. Putting it another way, we are perhaps all fragments of a creator/God experiencing with Him, His creation - in a similar way to that in which (as covered above) we ourselves can participate in a mere virtual reality game. **Except ours and God's is the experience of a valid, real, eternal life.**

Also importantly, as a concluding statement to this book; we have learned that the holographic interconnection of everything, means that at another level, **we are all dependent and linked to each other.**

Why therefore should there be hate amongst us, and why wars? When instead, we should (and could) resolve any problems we have with each other, by friendly negotiations aimed at achieving with truth and respect, a fair resolution.

So now that we are really at the end of this book, it is perhaps appropriate to reflect on this the end of the journey. I hope you, as I do, feel that **everything fits.**

If this is the case, then surely this validates the subjects contained within the title, namely reincarnation (recycling), the paranormal, and your immortality.

But importantly it must also vindicate, validate and honour truth and science.

Repeating here, the conclusion reached at Annex 1 of Chapter 4

All things are ever "present" and proceeding together in step as a series of consecutive "now's". Therefore, ourselves, all other entities and together with our

creator/God, we are all engaged in a never ending thrilling journey of exploration with all life and entities creating always a fresh new reality for ourselves and others, based on all our individual ideas and imagination from our collective present. It is unending, and since its creation it will never stop. All realities and possibilities will be actuated, limited only by our imagination.

THE END

Seth Quotations Applicable to this Chapter

Below are a few relevant quotations (including Page numbers) from "Seth" on the areas covered by this Chapter that might be helpful (these are not exhaustive, there are many others on this same subject):

Jane Roberts - *The Seth Material*, Pg. 4,

> **We form physical matter as effortlessly and unselfconsciously as we breathe.**

Selected Extracts from Jane Roberts book *The Nature of Personal Reality*, Pages xii to 64

> **Everything that you experience has consciousness (Pg. 4). .... all events and all manufactured objects appear from the inner mind or soul of mankind (Pg. 4).**
> **There is nothing in your exterior experience that did not originate within you. (Pg. 11). You create your experiences through your expectations. (Pg. 13)**
> **We create our personal reality through our conscious beliefs about ourselves, others and the world. (Pg. xii). You are a creator translating your expectations into physical form. (Pg. xxii)**
> **You must accept the idea completely, that your beliefs form your experience (Pg. 91). Your thoughts blossom into events (Pg.33). Each thought has a result (Pg. xix) ..... Even atoms, then, constantly seek to join in new organisation of structure and meaning. They do this "instinctively"**

> **Beliefs of a like nature attract each other (Pg. 121)....... Similar beliefs congregate (Pg. 46). You get what you concentrate on (Pg 53). Like attracts**

like, so similar ideas group about each other and you accept those that fit in with your particular "system" of ideas (Pg.43).

As soon as the need ....for information or knowledge – arises, then it is immediately forthcoming unless your own conscious beliefs cause a barrier (Pg. 95). ....Some of your knowledge is conscious knowledge and is instantly available. Some is unconscious... (Pg.4).

The conscious mind is basically curious, open...it is meant to receive and interpret important data that comes to it from the inner self (Pg. 33). ... If you use your conscious mind properly, you are also aware of intuitive ideas that come to you from within (Pg. 32).

Information does not exist by itself. Connected with it is the consciousness of all those who understand it, perceive it, or originate it. The information itself wants to move towards consciousness, so it gravitates towards those who seek it (Pg. 63).

Information, then, becomes new and is reborn as it is interpreted through a new consciousness.

....

APPENDICES

APPENDIX ONE

Darwinism and Atheism

A1.1 DARWINISM

Darwin depicted evolution of species and the **formation of new species** as a random chance occurrence attributable to three basic assumptions:

1. That all organisms descend from a common ancestor,
2. That new traits in species evolve by random mutation,
3. And that these traits persist only if they help the species to evolve ("natural selection") [1]

A1.1.1 Environmental Influences on Genes - Epigenics

A breakthrough in explaining subspecies variation (e.g. in man, skin/hair colouring etc., Mongolian eyelids [epicanthic fold] and minor changes to skeletal structure, e.g. jaws, skull etc.) occurred in 2001, when experiments were carried out on Agouti rats by Randy Jirtle a professor of oncology at Duke University together with Rob Waterland of Cornell University. They aimed to determine whether dietary change (i.e. an external environment factor) could overcome genetic defects. The experiment was successful and replicable. For the first time it showed that apart from gene shuffling caused by mating, the mechanism for observed subspecies variation, rather than random mutations, was instead directly attributable to certain exterior influences acting on genes. Vitamin B injections to female Agouti rats was found to cause switching off of the defective gene amongst a number of progeny i.e. this reversed genetic destiny. Surprisingly, later experiments found an amazing array of environmental gene switching triggers (particularly stressors). These even include what we eat, who we surround ourselves with and how we lead our lives. Effects were mainly beneficial and adaptive, but occasionally harmful. For example, it was found that despite no particular genetic weakness to breast cancer, that use of HRT drug therapy, as an external influence on genes, caused the statistical chance of contracting breast cancer to be beyond that of those who had a genetic pre-disposition for cancer. Other experiments showed that favorable outcomes could always be expected from certain external factors e.g. a good diet by a parent could improve the health for at least one or two generations and vice-versa. Amazingly, it was found that the cause of gene switching, was thousands of cell effector proteins on every cell membrane acting as gatekeepers to respond to external environmental molecule triggers to switch genes on or off. This process of gene switching caused by external triggers rather than gene shuffling became known as "epigenics".[2]

Appropriate to a simpler organism than man, in 1988, John Cairns a geneticist at Harvard's School of Public Health, found a remarkably ingenious mechanism within bacteria for survival under extreme stress conditions. Under such conditions a special enzyme is activated which initiates a fevered copying process of cell DNA. This provides a deliberate array of random mistakes (now called "*somatic* hypermutation"). Unlike gene shuffling caused by mating, epigenics or random mutations (e.g. caused by cosmic rays or mistakes in gene copying), is self-directed mutation of the bacteria's genome.

This process in bacteria therefore explains their observed eventual resistance to antibiotics.

In vertebrates such as man, this process is present solely in individual immune system cells as an attack mechanism (ironically) against bacteria, etc. Remarkably the immune system is able to both control the process (in an unknown way) by switching the process either on or off). Further, these mutations cannot be passed onto subsequent generations.[3] If this mechanism were present in all cells, it would lead to appalling mutants in a multicelled organism. In fact mistargeted somatic hypermutation in immune systems is considered a likely mechanism in the development of B-cell lymphomas (Ref. Wikipedia).

Interestingly, Darwin in his day actually observed and reported what we now know as the effect of epigenics - i.e. switching genes off or on as triggered by the environment. As he stated in his book *On the Origin of Species* published in 1859:

> "… some slight amount of change may, I think, be attributed to the direct action of the conditions of life - as, in some cases, increased size from the amount of food, colour from particular kinds of food and from light, and perhaps the thickness of fur from climate".[4]

AI.1.2 Subspecies Variation and Limitations

Apart from epigenics mentioned above, the other mechanism which causes micro variation, i.e. subspecies variation (as mentioned above), - is mating. The fertilisation process while providing a random shuffling of the genes available from both partners can obviously only provide a variation which is limited by the gene pool available.

Similarly epigenics while providing variation triggered by the environment, is similarly limited to the existing genome of the particular species.

Subspecies variation is evident in many areas around us, and can be seen in the amazing diversity obtained by selective mating in dogs to form breeds which can range from a large Great Dane to a tiny Chihuahua. But even different races of humans can range from dark coloured and small African pigmies to yellow coloured Mongolian races and white Europeans.

Despite such differences though, the genome particular to all such individual species is always the same and the genes and genetic sequence is still the same.

As mentioned above, epigenics is known to be the mechanism for an amazing diversity of variation present **within a particular species.** Birds of the same species often exhibit incredibly different and exotic plumage to attract mates. Pigeons have different colours, shapes and tail feathers, even the pouter pigeon looks almost deformed with a massive crop. Sex differences are also feature of many birds with the male peacock bearing a flamboyant tail - a huge contrast to the dull and uninteresting female peahen. Often these variants live in close proximity to each other but in other cases the variations have developed in distant environmental niches. It was in such cases of movement to another more remote geographical area, particularly where the population was cut off, that neo-Darwinists presumed that new species would occur. However we now know that epigenics is the explanation for such changes. Their assertions that this allows the formation of new species is just one of the many *'Just -so'* presumptive fantasy stories of neo-Darwinism, all without proof! In fact, it was well known (even in Darwin's day), that when small isolated populations breed, over time vigour is lost, and ultimately with in-breeding the population may become sterile.

Darwinian and neo-Darwinian concepts of small changes leading to entirely new species also leads to the absurdity that should this occur, the first single member of the new species would have no partners to mate with. Any attempt then to breed with earlier mating partners or other different species would be impossible - as in the only known cases where progeny occur as a result of species mating, the progeny is almost invariably sterile e.g. a mule (mules have 63 chromosomes a mixture of the horse's 64 and the donkey's 62). The different structure and number usually prevents the chromosomes from pairing up properly and creating successful embryos, rendering most mules infertile. There are no recorded cases of fertile mule stallions.

There seems good reason for nature ensuring cross-species mating cannot be successful - as shown by recent GM ("Genetic Modification") experiments. It has been shown that carrying out GM experiments without full knowledge of the consequences can lead to serious outcomes. For example, the disruption of a normal gene by insertion of a foreign DNA in a mouse, has shown to be the cause of a lack of eye development, lack of development of the semicircular canals of the inner ear, and anomalies of the olfactory epithelium - the tissue that mediates the sense of smell. Also germline introduction of an improperly regulated normal gene resulted in progeny with no obvious effects on development, but enhanced tumor development in later life. Such effects may not be recognised for a generation or more. Ref: Wikipedia.

A sense of rationality and intelligence seems very evident in these genetic limitations and many epigenic changes themselves support the concept of intelligence, purpose and design. For example, a case was recently reported where small damsel fish grew a bigger false "eye spot" near their tail and reduced the size of their real eyes. This was a way when constantly threatened, to distract predators and dramatically boost their chances of survival.[5]

Another examples of aided survival is the *"ink"* released by octopus while they make their escape using a jet propulsion method of swimming. These and many other examples surely defy any belief in **chance** 'evolution' and in the same way as the genetic limitations above prohibiting species mating, strongly denotes intelligence and planning.

Darwin was well aware in his travels and as a pigeon breeder of the variations which could be achieved by breeding. However, without knowledge of modern genetics and DNA, he could be fairly excused for mixing up subspecies/micro variation with macro variation. This is because DNA and genes were discovered after Darwin died by American biologist James Watson and English physicist Francis Crick who discovered DNA in 1953.

Although Darwin can be excused, the same does not apply in the case of many evolutionists today, as there is virtually no evidence whatsoever for the claim that entirely new species can be formed by small mutations over eons.

As indicated by Ian Wishart in his book *Eve's Bite*:

"Evolutionists often deliberately distort the two issues, using the evidence of change within a species (moth colourations/finch beak sizes/bacterial resistance to antibiotics) to argue that evolution as the wider public understands it (pond-slime to space traveler) is therefore true.

The problem with their argument is this. A moth that changes colour is still a.....?

A bird that has a bigger beak remains a .....? A bacteria that becomes resistant to an antibiotic remains a ....? A human who becomes immune to a bacteria remains a .....?

You know the answers."[6]

A1.1.3 Mutations

When sperm impregnates an ovum, a new cell is created by the DNA of the sperm cell replicating itself and passing on the genome to create with the ovum the new cell.

The process seems almost as if it has been designed remarkably well to avoid error and is almost mistake proof, but occasionally a mistake occurs and is called a mutation. Mutations can also occur due to cosmic rays and other forms of radiation of high energy particles. Typically the results of mutations are diabetes, club feet, hemophilia, mongolism, colour blindness, sickle cell anemia, calves with deformed jaws, seedless oranges etc., etc.

Sensibly, appropriate to the development of "the scientific method" since the time of Darwin, experiments have been carried out exhaustively to determine the effect of deliberately creating a high level of mutations. The hopelessness of mutations to produce 'evolution' has been confirmed by many classic experiments on fruit flies using high radiation levels e.g. 15,000 percent greater than background radiation (fruit flies are used universally as they breed rapidly). A typical experiment involving a huge number (25 million) of fruit flies resulted in an expected array of variation. However in all such experiments, all fruit flies stubbornly refused to turn into anything else i.e. a new species.

Results included stunted wings, lack of wings, yellow eyes, useless eyes, abnormal feet and bodies. There were grotesqueness and freaks, but they were still fruit fly wings and bodies, though deformed. Never was there the start of a new organ of a different species.

Most important of all, no matter how monstrous the offspring, it was able to breed with the parent stock (if it were capable of breeding at all). This meant that it still remained the same species.

Evolution's case has been based on a claim that there occasionally happens a "favorable mutation" preserved by natural selection, and that an accumulation of these provides new genetic information for a new species. When one considers, the appalling damage caused by mutations, but particularly the fact that there is no documented example ever recorded of a favorable mutation; then the concept of evolution caused by mutations is seen as not in accordance with the experimental evidence i.e. unscientific and nothing other than fanciful. Mutations are misfortunes, they simply cannot generate macro variation i.e. the development of a new species.[7]

Lynn Margulis (1938 - 2011) who held the position of Distinguished University Professor of Biology at the University of Massachusetts was a world - renowned biologist responsible for crucial work on mitochondria - the energy source for plant and animal cells. She gained considerable attention at a conference of molecular biologists where she challenged them to come up with one, single, unambiguous example of the formation of a new species by the mechanism of an accumulation of mutations to an original species. But none have been able to meet her challenge.[8]

She also held a view that history will ultimately judge Darwinists and neo - Darwinists as comprising: "a minor twentieth-century religious sect within the sprawling religious persuasion of Anglo-Saxon Biology." She also believed that proponents of the standard theory: "wallow in their zoological, capitalistic, competitive, cost-benefit interpretation of Darwin.

She also claimed that Neo-Darwinism, which insists on the slow accrual of mutations by gene-level natural selection, is in a complete funk": (Ref: Wikipedia).

Her strong views on the inability of mutations as a mechanism to achieve evolution are well justified, not only due to the complete absence of evidence of even a single instance of a favourable mutation, but also on probability estimates of the likely frequency of their occurrence.

Biophysicist Dr Lee Spetner in his 1996 book *Not By Chance*, uses science to debunk Darwinism, and foresaw "epigenics" as the main method of subspecies variation. He even mentioned results of diet - see above.

But his most devastating criticism of Darwinism is his mathematical probability argument. His calculations (based upon standard evolutionary mathematics of such authorities as Gaylord Simpson and Sir Ronald Fisher) give results that should a chance random favorable mutation actually occur, the odds for the mutation surviving against nature's odds are of the order of 1 in 10^{102738}. These odds would require earth to be 74 trillion years old before this could happen, which is 1500 times longer than the 4.5 billion years the earth has been in existence. And this is for just one chance random evolution relating to one species! [9]

Convergent 'evolution' (or parallel 'evolution'), where the same feature has appeared in the fossil record more than once in totally unrelated species e.g. birds and bats' wings, or sonar in bats and dolphins - is obviously even less likely to succeed and appear in the fossil record by a chance mutation, than its appearance on a single occasion.

Probability theory as mentioned previously, is a particularly useful mathematical tool to test the likely validity of a theory. The French mathematician Emile Borei, summed up the laws of probability in his Single Law of Chance where he says that, when the odds are 10^{15} against, then the chance of a single event happening are negligible on the terrestrial scale. When the odds get beyond 10^{50}, there is virtually no chance of it happening even on the cosmic scale.

Unsurprisingly Spetner's probability mathematics and his conclusions above have never been challenged, nor by atheists or academic biologists. Dr Lee Spetner is an impressive scientist well versed in mathematical statistics theory, information theory and biophysics. He has a Ph.D. in physics from MIT, and taught information and communication theory for years at Johns Hopkins University. In 1962 he accepted a fellowship in biophysics at that institution, where he worked on solving problems in signal/noise relationships in DNA electron micrographs. He subsequently became fascinated with evolutionary theory, and published papers concerning theoretical and mathematical biology in prestigious journals such as the "Journal of Theoretical

Biology, Nature", and the "Proceedings of the 2nd International Congress of Biophysics".

Apart from his probability analysis, his other devastating criticism of Darwinism and Neo-Darwinism is that, (as he explains in detail in his book), all mutations achieve a loss of information. Therefore mutations cannot provide the addition of new information necessary to create the macro changes appropriate to creating a new species. Further, grand scale evolution (i.e. bacteria to baboons) necessitates a massive gain in information over time. However mutations cannot achieve this, as an accumulation of mutations achieves the reverse i.e. it is an information losing process. As Spetner says: "Just like a fortune can't be made by losing money, evolution can't build up information by losing it. Moreover before you can lose money, or information, you first have to make it." Spetner also states that: "Despite the insistence of evolutionists that evolution is a fact, it is really no more than an improbable story. No one has ever shown that macroevolution can work. Most evolutionists assume that macroevolution is just a long sequence of micro evolutionary events, but no one has ever shown it to be so".[11]

Nobel prize- winning biologist Professor Christen Anfinsen has labelled Lee Spetner's book, *Not by Chance*, as "extremely thorough and compelling and one of the best anti - Darwin offerings".

AI.I.4   The Fossil Record

Darwinism has lost out completely on the basis of both theory and experimental evidence. We now need to look at the observed data to see if there is any evidence in the fossil record whatsoever for macro 'evolution' i.e. the formation of entirely new species.

There are only two known theoretical and experimentally proved methods of providing any variation in life forms as indicated above. These are the mechanisms of gene shuffling i.e. mating, and gene switching (epigenics) - none of which by theory or experiment can be shown to produce an entirely new species. However, there is a number of immediately observed conundrums evident from even a cursory inspection of the fossil record. Despite the fact that neither Darwinism nor science can come up with any explanation for how new species can occur, the most obvious observation is that new species are evident in the fossil record everywhere - and, in mind boggling numbers over eons - up until the Pleistocene era, when the most complex species of all occurred, man. Secondly, there was an explosion of new species arrivals during an unparalleled era in history during the so called "Cambrian explosion" (often called "Biology's Big Bang"). This was the relatively rapid appearance, around 530 million years ago, as demonstrated in the fossil record, of most major animal phyla.

All present phyla appeared within the first 20 million years of the period - a mere heart beat in the estimated 4.5 billion years age of the earth. At this stage the diversity of life began to resemble that of today (Ref Wikipedia).

Significantly none of these had any of the fossil ancestors required by Darwinism and also clearly contradicted the core principle of Darwinism, namely that evolution must have occurred by an almost imperceptible slow process of tiny changes performed over eons of years.

Before 580 million years ago, most organisms were simple, composed of individual cells occasionally organized into colonies. However the virtually instant appearance of new phyla, animal classes and species (e.g. birds, fish, amphibians, reptiles, mammals, spiders and insects etc.) in the Cambrian era were certainly not simple, but complex new life forms involving radically new body plans (a complete trilobite even appeared early in the Cambrian explosion). In 1859 Charles Darwin himself admitted the 'Cambrian Explosion' as one of the main objections that could be made against his theory of evolution by natural selection. As stated by Stephen Jay Gould: "The Cambrian explosion was the most remarkable and puzzling event in the history of life".[13]

Also in a scientific paper authored by Thomas, Shearman and Stewart on the subject:

"The Cambrian Explosion has long been an enigma for biology. The more we learn about the introduction of complex animals on earth, the more puzzling the Cambrian event becomes for evolutionary biologists. The authors of the reference identified 182 possible skeletal designs, and of these 182 possibilities, 146 appeared during the Cambrian Explosion. That is, over 80% of all possible skeletal designs appeared suddenly in less than 3 million years based on recent evidences. (The unrepresented skeletal designs include land animals and vertebrates which do not appear in the Cambrian layer.)"[14]

Since the Cambrian period about 600 million years ago, a large number of new species have formed through eras which include the Mesozoic era - where Dinosaurs roamed the earth, and to the recent Pleistocene epoch - when humanoids arrived.

The Darwinian concept of evolution relies upon the concept of life beginning with simple forms and steadily progressing upward into more and more complex creatures to culminate in man. The fossil record therefore should record the process step by step. If creatures evolved, they would have lived and died and have fossilised innumerable intermediate creatures, steadily bridging the transitions between one kind and the next kind. In fact, there would have been so many intermediates in successive stages of transition, that we would have difficulty in identifying the latest most perfected version amid the profusion of transitional stages.[15]

Paleontologists have now been digging for some 152 years, during which millions of fossils have been unearthed. But not one transitional fossil form has ever been found. During this time there have been numerous instances where claims have been made that a transitional fossil has been found, but in every case, later examination has found the claim to be incorrect. It could be said that both the arrival of completely formed new species as evident in the fossil record and the fact that no transitional forms occur is unsurprising. Nature always seems to go unerringly to its target e.g. the human eyelid exactly covers the human eye with the process that began the eyelid growing must also stop it growing when it reached the right size.

There is also no evidence in the fossil record for a key concept of Darwinism namely that that all organisms descend from a common ancestor and that the arrival of new species conform to the Darwinian supposed '*Tree of Life*'. Analysis of the genome of species who have survived today shows that each is a discrete species with different numbers of chromosomes. In the case of humans they have 46 chromosomes compared with monkeys with 48 chromosomes. In the case of man, with the so called different species of prehistoric man e.g. Neanderthals etc., most if not all are now thought instead to most likely be subspecies variation (Since soft tissue of fossils has long since disappeared, DNA cannot usually be recovered from fossils.) Further, the recent critical examination of brain cavities of adults reveals (despite large variations in skull shape), the actual brain size is little different from the brain size of modern humans today.

In summary, the Darwinian and the Neo-Darwinian supported concept of small chance mutations over long time scales - as the mechanism for macro variation (and even micro variation) - has been shown above to be nothing other than a false widely believed myth. **It is simply cannot be supported by scientific theory, experimental evidence or the observed data in the fossil record.**

The fossil record shows no evidence of evolution, just propagation and entirely new life forms arriving suddenly of increasing complexity up to the arrival of the most complex - man in the Pleistocene. There is no evidence of species being able to transform into other species, nor new species emerging today. It does though exhibit a simply amazing diversity of life forms of varying complexity, but with differing capabilities to flourish in different environments. Wherever life is even barely possible, we find the environment teaming with life. Since the majority of people believe in Darwinian type 'evolution', it would be nice to support such a view. However rather than evolution, what is seen is a propagation of an amazing variety of life forms in a multitude of environments, all exquisitely designed to experience life in those environments. Each could perhaps flourish to a point where they might maximise their opportunity to gain sentience and evolve themselves - as evident in man.

The reality though is that there are millions of species (each immutable by definition to be able to mate with other species) evident in fossil record. This, and the shock arrival during the Cambrian of massive changes in form characterised by the arrival of completely new phyla and animal classes - must have a cause.

The similarity, within family types, e.g. types such as birds, grasses, trees; together with animal class groupings such as cats, humanoids etc. - all with a similar DNA structure and varying complexity, does however surely suggest intelligence and planning i.e. a creator /God using a base design varied suitably to both populate the earth and culminating in the most complex species of all, man. However, the science behind the creation of a new species is simply a mystery. On a science basis, we don't know the critical original source of the new information fundamental to change genes appropriately to form a new species almost overnight, nor the mechanism.

Where therefore is the information for the creation of new species and how is it supplied?

Rather than evolution, what we see in the fossil record are fully formed species with different complexity all without apparent linkages. This seems more suggestive therefore of a system whereby a range of different blueprints for life are released sporadically (such as during the Cambrian era) - perhaps purposefully appropriate to conditions and time based on progress. There is also abundant evidence with some species that subspecies changes are common, whereas with others there are many species that have not changed in millions of years (lungfish, gingko trees, the New Zealand tuatara lizard, many shellfish such as scallops etc.).

Darwin therefore really got it wrong when he said in his *On the Origin of Species* - "any form that which does not become in some degree modified and improved, will be liable to be exterminated". [16]

Epigenetics shapes heredity (i.e. by acting on reproductive cells) by adaptive changes to the expression of genes without altering the DNA sequence. There are many other genetic changes discovered which solely effect bacteria or somatic non-reproductive cells, with therefore no ability for transmissibility of the induced genetic changes to future generations. Among them is a gene swapping process (triggered in a similar way by environmental pressures to epigenics), which has recently been discovered by James A Shapiro, Professor of Biochemistry and Molecular Biology at the University of Chicago. This and all other adaptive processes where cells re-organize their genomes in response to hundreds of kinds of environmental inputs, he calls 'Natural Genetic Engineering'. Many such processes he claims meet the description of having a form of "microprocessor" control and also that all cells themselves exhibit cognitive actions, since they are "knowledge-based" and involve decisions appropriate to acquired information". One fascinating example of a form of "guiding intelligence" he provides, is where bacteria preferentially first completely consume sugar (i,e, glucose) that provides the most rapid growth, before switching to the less efficiently digested one.[17]

He also mentions in his book *Evolution: A View from the 21st Century*, published in 2011, that a cell is not just a mere repository of genetic information (or "read only memory", as Shapiro puts it), but a full blown information processor - storing, manipulating, and creating new information. There are error-correction functions that actually repair strands of DNA in real time during replication, and strands of DNA can actually "double" to increase the amount of information that can be encoded, as new information is acquired by an organism to adapt to its environment.

Genetic biology is a complex area where clearly there is much to learn, with no explanation yet for how fully formed new species arrived without transitional stages.

A1.1.5 Natural Selection

Unquestionably Darwinian type natural selection occurs, and it has an effect in maintaining the genetic fitness of a population e.g. infants with birth defects without medical help are unlikely to survive to leave descendants. Losses of progeny are therefore inevitable in many instances. Amazingly a loss function capability seems built into all organisms as they seem innately aware of this, and generally produce more offspring to cater for losses.

Without any supporting evidence however, Darwinists stretch the very real aspect of the tautology *"survival of the fittest"* to suggest that small gradual changes improving fitness as a result of losses plus the nonsense of favorable mutations causes revolutionary changes in shape and form over eons. They also suggest that all new species were provided sequentially beginning with a bacterial cell, then trees, flowers, ants, etc., to finally culminate in man. Unfortunately for Darwinists, as shown above, there has never been a single instance found of a favorable mutation - either in the fossil record, experimentally or as a result of breeding i.e. selective or artificial breeding carried out by man. It has also been shown earlier that mutations cause loss of information, and probability mathematics shows the impossibility of the survival should a favorable chance mutation ever appear.

It is readily understandable that Darwin could make such a mistake to think that all variation he observed was attributable to natural selection. As an avid pigeon breeder himself, he was well used to employing selective breeding to attempt to produce characteristics he might consider desirable. But he obviously did not realise that this is not the same as the naturally occurring variation, nor can selective breeding ever provide a path to creating new species.

Breeders produce variations amongst animals. plants etc. for purposes absent in nature and often for the sheer delight in seeing how much variation can be achieved. When domesticated animals are returned to the wild, the most highly specialised breeds quickly perish and the survivors revert to the original wild type. A modern cow even cannot go a single day without being milked. What artificial selection shows is that there are definite limits to the amount of variation that even the most highly skilled breeders can achieve. But unsurprisingly (to us), breeding of domestic animals has produced no new species, pigeons still stay pigeons, dogs still dogs etc.[18]

We now know of course that all such variation is only subspecies variation caused by mating (gene shuffling), or epigenics (gene switching) - the ingenious mechanism that allows an organism to adapt to its environment, but within the limits of the information contained within its genome.

As stated by the late eminent French Professor of Zoology Pierre Grasse:

> (Artificial) selection gives tangible form to and gathers together all the varieties a genome is capable of producing, but this does not constitute an innovative evolutionary process.[19]

Before leaving natural selection, many examples are quoted by "Darwinians" as supposed evidence of 'evolution'. One of these (the one most often quoted), is the case first studied in 1896 in England by J W Tutt. This involved a peppered moth which had two varieties, a dark-coloured moth and a light-coloured moth. When trees became darkened due to industrial pollution, the lighter coloured ones stood out against the darkened trees and provided preferential lunch for birds as compared with their camouflaged companions. Soon no light-coloured moths remained. Evolutionists claimed this as evidence of natural selection causing permanent evolutionary change.

Obviously this certainly demonstrates natural selection, but not permanent evolutionary change. Most Darwinists today don't know or don't bother to mention the conclusion to the story. Later when the prevailing colour of the trees reverted to a mottled light colour with a reduction in industrial pollution; magically the light coloured moths were observed to re-appear, to join the many dark coloured ones. The status quo was maintained. In such a situation, clearly the genome of the moth contains both dark and light-coloured genes. Epigenics or (even gene shuffling caused by mating) would allow the expression of either gene appropriate to the environment. In other words this was a good example of subspecies variation to suit the environment, but nil evidence for the arrival of a **new** species caused by natural selection. Notably the moths still remained moths!

(Apparently there is now suggestion of fraud in the original reported data measuring of moth appearances on trees - as has been determined by further investigations. The moth in question apparently has a wider habitat than the trees mentioned in the story. Therefore any losses on dark trees would be of little consequence in effecting the survival of the white form, as white versions were freely available to return to the trees when the pollution effects disappeared.[20]

To sum up, despite the poor insignificant peppered moth becoming an unjustifiable celebrity and champion of Darwinists, it is just an unscientific distorted fantasy story still perpetuated by them in claiming it proves evolution. Sadly it still appears in modern school text books. "*Wikipedia*" though sensibly contradicts this by saying "Biologists agree that the peppered moth example shows natural selection causing evolution **within a species**, demonstrating rapid and obvious adaptiveness with such change, and accept that it is **not** proof of the theory of evolution as a whole".

Darwinists conveniently choose to ignore any difference between subspecies (or micro variation) whose cause is known, and macro variation (the arrival of new species), whose cause is unknown to all including all scientists.

I was horrified to see another similar case portrayed in a recent BBC Horizon documentary titled "Are We Still Evolving", when Dr Alice Roberts, Physical Anthropologist, and Professor Mark Hodson, of the University of Reading, both ecstatically highlighted what Roberts claimed was a modern case of "evolution in action". In digging in the soil adjacent to remains of a former copper mine in Cornwall, the Professor showed Dr Alice Roberts many worms who were quite happily living in arsenic contaminated soil, resulting from earlier mining. This, he claimed, was a wonderful example of evolution and he said that if a normal earthworm was placed in the soil it would surely soon die. He also stated that laboratory examination had indicated that there were some genetic changes. Dr Roberts then said that Mark "believed the worms to have evolved into a new species". What! A University Professor relying on supposition as evidence - without even bothering to easily test whether a normal earthworm could actually survive or not in the soil. Worse, claiming a new species, but not bothering to classically test the issue of whether it was a new species or not by simply and easily testing its ability to mate with a conventional earthworm. Rather than science, this is dogma! If it was a new species every paper on earth would be flush with the news, as science media atheists would at last to be able to claim some evidence for 'evolution' creating a new species. Obviously all that was observed was yet another example of normal subspecies variation as covered above in the peppered moth case. Since all still remained earthworms, it was completely unscientific to assert that some might be new species.

In the same television programme Dr Alice Roberts, the presenter, continued the television programme by saying that the differing skin colours of the human race (white, black, brown and yellow), was a "skin deep" example around us which provided evidence of modern evolution. She even drew Darwin's discredited *"Tree of Life"* sketch to depict her version of the 'evolution' of human species. She then said enthusiastically that she would show us an even better example of modern day evolution which went beyond being "skin deep", as it would show how evolution had changed those who lived in high altitudes such as "Sherpas" to function satisfactorily with the low oxygen levels encountered at high altitudes. Accompanied by another enthusiastic evolutionist - Professor Cynthia Beall of Western Reserve University, Cleveland, Roberts watched as the Professor took samples of blood from groups of Tibetans including Sherpas from a village close to Mt Everest. She wished to test her theory that the reason that they could breathe more easily at higher altitudes was because they had higher levels of hemoglobin blood levels than others. No appreciable differences were found, ruling out the hemoglobin theory. Beall then examined inner tissue above the lip of each member of the group, and found that the true reason for the better oxygen utilisation by the Tibetans, was a compensating denser network of capillaries throughout the body to cope with lower oxygen content in the lungs. This was then heralded ridiculously by the presenter as another brilliant example of modern day "evolution in action".

Unsurprisingly, as with all examples above, they are all well understood examples of subspecies variation, and certainly do not provide an affirmative case for the title of the programme "Are We Still Evolving". Significantly, slightly amusingly and inconsistently, no new Sherpas and other Tibetans living at high altitudes were claimed by Dr Roberts to have changed either partly or completely into another new species. Otherwise our credulity would have been stretched beyond belief, due to the absurdity of the having to explain why they were new species but obviously still able to mate with other humans. Amazingly Roberts, claims new species in the cases of earthworm environmental changes, but not for similar skin or capillary changes in humans.

It therefore appears that some scientists and evolutionists, are now suffering mental 'adaptions' themselves by no longer claiming that the mechanism for 'evolution' and creation of new species is due to mutations. Instead unscientifically, nowhere in the television programme was a mechanism offered to explain the cause of the variation observed. Instead the causes of all changes were explained as resulting from "natural selection". Towards the end of the Horizon documentary Dr Alice Roberts even claimed natural selection itself as evidence of evolution - ignoring the fact that natural selection simply cannot provide the new information content required to create new species. She also seems unaware of the fact that artificial selection, as **even** any breeder of animals knows, provides only variations limited to the species itself (i.e. within the species genome), and has never created a new species.

Clearly neo-Darwinists have long since given up trying to find facts to fit the theory, (as they are simply not there). Instead they are now unashameably trying to cherry pick or distort the facts to fit their theory.

Unbelievable as this is, Pierre Grasse was similarly unimpressed by neo-Darwinists as he pointed out:

The "evolution in action" of J. Huxley and other biologists is simply the observation of demographic facts, local fluctuations of genotypes, geographical distributions.

Often the species concerned have remained practically unchanged for hundreds of centuries! Fluctuations as a result of circumstances ...does not imply evolution, and we have tangible proof of this in many panchronic species (i.e. living fossils that remain unchanged for many years....[21]

We have many examples such as the Australian lungfish, the ginko tree etc.

Pierre Grasse's conclusion seems so obviously correct that it raises the issue of why do other 'experts' and supposedly intelligent people get it so wrong? Perhaps the main problem, particularly with scientists, is that their belief system is so wedded to materialism, that any suggestion of a hint of evidence in favour of a supernatural explanation is intolerable - particularly amongst atheists. There is also the point that a scientist's career is so demanding technically and science specialisation so great, that there is little time for them to give to other areas such as micro biology (This of course cannot excuse those whose career lies in biology).

My pet hate and reason why throughout this book I have written the word 'evolution' in inverted commas is that there are real problems with the word 'evolution'. Its use in biology appears to have been an invention by neo-Darwinists, as it was not used by Darwin in his book *On the Origin of Species* - where he only used the word "variation". The fact is that frustratingly, it is the only word in our lexicon that can conveniently be used as a single word to describe both micro (i.e. subspecies) variation and macro variation. In the Oxford Dictionary, it is defined for all applications as "development", and for biological purposes is given the specific dictionary biological definition of "origination of species **by development**". Therefore the frequent, widespread and popular use of the misnomer "evolution" inevitably suggests the Darwinian belief, i.e. species improvement to form new species.

Obviously this is scientifically incorrect, as observable reality demonstrated by the fossil record only shows increased fully formed species without any transitions. Instead just increased complexity and the arrival of fully formed species over time. Neither does the fossil record show any evidence at all of observable "development" - as favoured by the Oxford dictionary.

There is ample evidence to support one element of Darwin's theory - subspecies variation. This means examples of change within a species. But there is virtually no evidence for "macroevolution" - the claim that one species can transform into another.

Every time therefore we use the word 'evolution', we perpetuate the falsehood of Darwinism and reinforce the myth!

A1.2 **ATHEISM**

Professor Philip Johnson, a graduate of Harvard and the University of Chicago, has taught law for over 20 years at the University of California. He took up study of

Darwinism because he saw the books defending this theory were seen as dogmatic and unconvincing. As a specialist in logic analysis and false assumptions, he has brought a useful and somewhat independent contribution in commenting on Darwinism by publishing his own book entitled *Darwin on Trial*. His overall findings are that Darwinism is **as much a religion as Christianity** - which is somewhat mild compared with science's most respected philosopher Karl Popper's viewpoint, who simply labels it as "metaphysical".[22]

Johnson's argument that Darwinism is nothing but a religion, is highlighted by his view that:

> ..."Evolution" can mean anything from the uncontroversial statement that bacteria "evolve" resistance to antibiotics, to the grand metaphysical claim that the universe and mankind "evolved" entirely by purposeless, mechanical forces. A word that "elastic" that it is likely to mislead, by claiming we know as much about the grand claim as we do about the small one". [23]

All without reference to any experiments, facts, science, or fossil evidence to support the theory, amazingly, neo-Darwinists consider that evolution is so self-evident that it does not require proof. To rub salt into the wounds, Anthony Flew, one of the world's leading atheist philosophers and authors, famously argued that instead the burden of proof for design in the world fell on Christians to prove, not atheists to rebut.[24]

Hopefully my above arguments favoring "design" while not the proof demanded by Flew, would be sufficient even for a skeptical jury. But with regard to 'evolution', perhaps someone should tell Flew that by saying this, not only is he suggesting a possible lack of confidence by him in support for his atheist position, but he is making a fool of himself. This is because he and his atheist friends would find such a burden of proving evolution, if placed on themselves - impossible; as it is logically impossible to prove a falsehood.

However, Karl Popper's famous testability criteria for the validity of a theory by testing it against the data for falsification, has been well covered above, by highlighting the complete vacuum of evidential data available in the **fossil record** to support Darwinism. Further, on this issue of the fossil record, Johnson in his book recalls a remarkable lecture given by Colin Patterson at the American Museum of Natural History in 1981. Patterson was a senior paleontologist at the British History Museum. He asked his audience of **fossil record experts** a question which reflected his own doubts about much of what was thought to be secure knowledge about evolution:

"Can you tell me anything you know about evolution, any one thing that is true? I tried that question on the **geology staff** at the Field Museum of Natural

History and the only answer I got was silence. I tried it on the members of the Evolutionary Morphology seminar in the University of Chicago, a very prestigious body of evolutionists, and all I got was silence for a long time and eventually one person said "I do know one thing - it ought not to be taught in high school."

Johnson also states that:

"Another factor that makes evolutionary "science" seem a lot like religion is the evident zeal of Darwinists to evangelize the world by insisting that even non-scientists accept the truth of their theory as a matter of moral obligation." [25]

If indistinguishable from religion, and unsupported by evidence or facts, then Darwinism is merely dogma.

Johnson identifies Richard Dawkins, an Oxford Zoologist as one of the most influential figures in evolutionary 'science'. In Johnson's book he says that Dawkins

"...is unabashedly explicit about the religious side of Darwinism. His 1986 book *The Blind Watchmaker* is at one level about biology, but at a more fundamental level it is a sustained argument for atheism. According to Dawkins, "Darwin made it possible to be **an intellectually fulfilled atheist**" [26]

An "Amazon" reviewer of Spetner's book *By Chance* (referred to above), records Spetner's comments on Dawkins, as follows:

Spetner searched Richard Dawkins work for traces of solid science and found mainly false assumptions and technical inaccuracies instead. He notes that, "Like many passionate believers, Dawkins did not examine his evidence critically. Indeed, his vaunted cumulative selection thesis is riddled with unfounded assumptions. He built his case for it entirely on the power of the concept, with not one word of proof. His biomorph and lexical computer simulations are demonstrated not to represent natural selection as his uncritical disciples may believe, only artificial selection, as in pigeon breeding.

What if Darwin's quaint theory were advanced today for the first time? The proposal that a clumsy hypothetical mechanism modelled on eighteenth century economic theories and pigeon breeding practices could possibly account for the origins of every single element in the incredibly complex universe of microbiology unfolding before our eyes would be laughable. The hodgepodge theory of evolution has become a religious faith so deeply ingrained in its adherents they appear oblivious to its absurdities. This book (*By Chance*) relates how stunning advances in biotechnology in just the past two decades have dramatically widened the gulf separating the realities of empirical science from the myths of neo-Darwinism."

I have read many of Dawkins' books myself and find them deceptively written in a compelling and interesting way. For any reader, aware of his position as Professor of Zoology at Oxford University and his acceptance as a worldwide authority on 'evolution', there is a very real danger of being seduced by his authoritative and easy reading style of *Just So Stories*. It is only when one finds the logic in one or a number of his arguments lacking that doubt arises, and once realised, acceptance is replaced with concern. Although he seems very proud of his puerile and simplistic computer simulations, the flaws (as indicated above) are rather obvious.

It is sad to see pseudo-science disseminated so widely by atheistic neo-Darwinists such as Dawkins, to the point where the majority of people now falsely believe in the myth of Darwinism and 'evolution'. The fact is, that subspecies variation is real and provable, but the science behind the reason for the arrival of new species (macro variation), is currently unknown and **cannot be micro 'evolution'**.

I share zoologist David Suzuki's despair in thinking that the "Age of Reason" is over, as stated at on ABC Television in September, 2013 in Brisbane[27]. Just as he claims the views of climate deniers holds sway over substantive scientific evidence supporting man made global warming, we see science is similarly disregarded by many with objections against introducing fluoridation to improve dental decay, and inoculations to prevent disease in children, and similarly in the case where recycled water, despite being purified to a quality standard beyond that of rivers, lakes or dams; cannot be added to public water supplies in most countries.

The "Age of Reason" also certainly seems to be over as well, for the neo-Darwinian explanation for the 'science' behind the appearance of new species. Instead, the falsity and pseudo-science of their atheistic mechanism of chance, random small changes; is thrust upon us all due to their political atheistic agenda which includes the rebuttal of even replicated experimental science, such is their determination to disown any possibility of allowing a creator /God explanation.

David Suzuki considers that climate change deniers are "guilty of wilful blindness and intergenerational crime." I share his sentiment but also with regard to neo-Darwinism, as one can only wonder what a better world it would have been without this atheistic pseudo-science. Without the perpetuation of the blind alley of Darwinism we at least could have expected micro-biologists to have been stimulated to determine the real science behind macro-'evolution' by now, together with many other scientific discoveries perhaps in the areas of quantum physics and consciousness.

The viewpoint of Lynn Margulis, the world-renowned biologist on Darwinism (quoted above), included the following:

"History will ultimately judge Darwinists and neo-Darwinists as comprising a minor twentieth-century religious sect within the sprawling religious persuasion of Anglo-Saxon biology."

That said, for me this cannot come soon enough, together with the return of rationality, reason and true science - rather than speculative irrationality.

Appendix Two

A List of Some Constants Affecting Earth

(Ref: Astrophysicist George Greenstein's book *The Symbiotic Universe*)

1. If the centrifugal force of planetary movements did not precisely balance the gravitational forces, nothing could be held in orbit around the sun.

2. Any of the laws of physics can be described as a function of the velocity of light. Even a slight variation in the speed of light would alter the other constants and preclude the possibility of life on earth.

3. If water vapor levels in the atmosphere were greater than they are now, a runaway greenhouse effect would cause temperatures to rise too high for human life; if they were less, and insufficient greenhouse effect would make the earth too cold to support human life.

4. If Jupiter were not in its current orbit, the earth would be bombarded with space debris such as meteorites etc. Jupiter's gravitational field acts as a cosmic vacuum cleaner, attracting asteroids, comets and meteorites that otherwise might strike earth.

5. If the thickness of the earth's crust were greater, too much oxygen would be transferred to the core to support life. If it were thinner, volcanic and tectonic activity would make life impossible.

6. If the rotation of the earth took longer than 24 hours, temperature differences would be too great between night and day. If the rotation period were shorter, atmospheric wind velocities would be too great.

7. The 23-degree axis tilt of the earth is just right. If the tilt were altered slightly, surface temperatures on earth would be too great.

8. If the lightning discharge rate were greater, fire destruction would be intolerable; if it were less there would be too much nitrogen fixing in the soil.

9. If there was greater seismic activity, more life would be lost; if there were less, nutrients on the ocean floor and runoff would not be cycled back to the continents through tectonic uplift.

Appendix Three

The Double Slit Experiment

When one tries to determine the wave or particle (or other quantum) properties of electrons (or other subatomic particles) experimentally by beaming electrons (as in a TV set) through a barrier containing two double slits, it is found that they exhibit what is termed "complementary behavior" i.e. on a target screen/backing board they can either appear as a wave, or a particle, depending on the experimental arrangement.

With any one of the two slits closed, particle dots build up on the screen with predictably a greater density of dots appearing at the center compared with less dense fringes at the outside. With both slits open, wave like behavior results as an interference pattern forms on the screen similar to that which one observes when waves travel across a pond and encounter other waves.

If only a **single** electron is fired at the double slit, after sufficient have gone through the slits, incredibly an interference pattern still results. The only way in which it is thought that these individual electrons could form an interference pattern, is to accept the fact that each single electron is a virtual probability cloud like object which is interfering with itself while passing through both slits. Since it is known that all subatomic particles exhibit a cloud of random quantum fluctuations, this can at least explain the observed wave like behavior compared to the previous particle behavior, as the cloud must have been dragged across both slits. Once enough electrons have gone through, the interference pattern emerges as the waves interfere with each other and later impact on the screen one by one while being observed. It is considered that it is the act of conscious observation and participation by the experimenter which causes collapse of the Schrödinger probability wave form function in each case to create a particular probable outcome into an actual real entity as seen on the screen. Amazingly, each case above did not exist as a real entity until observed hitting the screen. i.e. consciousness creates reality.

If however, a measuring device is next placed just behind either of the two slits; instead of the interference pattern, the pattern on the screen reverts to that of the first experiment i.e. the particle nature of light appears with a greater density of dots in the centre and a decreasing number of dots surrounding it. In this case it is clear that conscious 'observation' caused by the experimenter using and observing the results of a measuring device placed behind the slits, forced immediate collapse of the probability wave to occur behind the slits rather than collapse occurring at the screen as in all the previous cases.

References

Chapter 1: The Case for a Creator or God

1. *The Mind of God: Science and the Search for Ultimate Meaning,* Paul Davies (Simon & Schuster Ltd, 1992), Page 223.
2. *The Fire in the Equations,* Kitty Fergusson, (Bantum Press,1994), Page 10
3. Ibid., page 26
4. *The Fire in the Equations,* Kitty Fergusson, (Bantum Press,1994), Page 62.
5. Ibid., Page 64)
6. *The New Story of Science,* Robert M. Augros & George N. Stanciu, Page 39, also "Confronting Sciences Logical Limits", John L. Casti, *Scientific American,* Oct.1966
7. Ref: http://science.discovery.com/famous-scientists-discoveries/10-eureka-moments.htm
8. Ibid.
9. Ref: http://profiles.nlm.nih.gov/ps/retrieve/Narrative/SC/p-nid/143)
10. *The Matter Myth,* Paul Davies & John Gribbin (Orion Productions 1992), Page 141
11. "Confronting Sciences Logical Limits", John L. Casti, *Scientific American,* Oct.1966
12. *Biocentrism,* Robert Lanza and Bob Berman, Page 6 (Benbulla books, 2009). See also *The Matter Myth,* Page 164, Paul Davies & John Gribbin (Orion Productions 1992)
13. *Natural Theology,* William Paley, 1828
14. *The Fire in the Equations,* Kitty Fergusson, (Bantum Press,1994), Page 163.
15. *Eves Bite,* Ian Wishart, Howling at the Moon Publishing Ltd, 2007, Page 58.
16. Ibid., Page 59.
17. *Horizon,* BBC Television Programme "Origins of Us" 2013.
18. *Eves Bite,* Ian Wishart, Howling at the Moon Publishing Ltd, 2007, Page 45.
19. *On the Origin of Species,* Charles Darwin, Penguin Classics, Edition 2009, Page175
20. *The Case For A Creator,* Lee Strobel, Zodervan 2004, Page 42
21. Ibid., Page 225
22. *Ancient Traces,* Michael Baigent (Viking, 1998), Page 36
23. *The Case For A Creator,* Lee Strobel, Zodervan 2004, Page 237
24. Ibid., Page 219
25. *The Crumbling Theory of Evolution,* by JWG Johnson, Page 93 Perpetual Eucharist Adoration Inc 1986, Australia.

26 *The Case For A Creator*, Lee Strobel, Zodervan 2004, Page 244
27 *The Crumbling Theory of Evolution*, by JWG Johnson, Page 90 Perpetual Eucharist Adoration Inc 1986, Australia.
28 *The Crumbling Theory of Evolution*, by JWG Johnson, Page 93 Perpetual Eucharist Adoration Inc 1986, Australia.
29 *Ancient Traces*, Michael Baigent (Viking, 1998), Page 36
30 *Evidence of Purpose*, John Marks Templeton Essays, Page 172 (How Blind the Watchmaker, David Wilcox)
31 *The Fire in the Equations*, Kitty Fergusson, (Bantum Press, 1994), Page 9
32 *Is There a God*, Richard Swinburne (Oxford University Press, 1996), Page 49
33 *The Mystery of Physical Life*, EL Grant Watson (Abelard Schuman, London, New York, 1964), Page 61
34 *God & the New Physics*, Paul Davies (Simon & Schuster Paperbacks 1983), Page 167
35 *The Whispering Pond*, Ervin Laszlo (Element Books Inc; 1996), Page 50
36 *The Big Questions*, Paul Davies (Penguin Books Australia Ltd, 1996), Page 132
37 *God's Secret Formula*, Peter Plichta, Page 206
38 *The Mind of God*, Penguin Books, 1992, Page 79-80
39 Ibid., 195
40 "Custom Universe", Compass ABC Television Programme, Australia, 2013
41 *God & the New Physics*, Paul Davies (Simon & Schuster Paperbacks 1983), Page 179
42 "Custom Universe", Compass ABC Television Programme, Australia, 2013
43 *Dreams of a Final Theory*, Steven Weinberg, Page 175
44 "Evidence of Purpose", John Marks Templeton, Essays. *Dare a Scientist believe in Design*, Owen Gingerich, Professor of Science, Harvard University Page 24
45 *Disturbing the Universe*, Freeman Dyson, (New York: Harper & Row), Page 250
46 *The Whispering Pond*, Ervin Laszlo (Element Books Inc; 1996), Page 50
47 *The Big Questions*, Paul Davies (Penguin Books Australia Ltd, 1996), Page 132
48 *I Don't Have Enough Faith to be an Atheist*", Norman L. Geisler & Frank Turek, Crossway, 2004, Page 98
49 *God's Secret Formula*, Peter Plichta, Page 206
50 *Dreams of a Final Theory*, Steven Weinberg, Page 193
51 *The Mind of God*, Professor Paul Davies, Page 43
52 Ibid., Page 44
53 *Between Inner Space and Outer Space*, John D. Barrow (Oxford University Press, 1999), page 46
54 *The Web of Life*, Fritjof Capra (Harper Collins, Hammersmith, London 1996), Page 326
55 *The Case for a Creator*, Zondevan, 2004, Le Strobel, Page 277
56 *The Fire in the Equations*, Kitty Ferguson, Bantum Press 1994, Page 274

Appendix 1, Chapter 1: Darwinism and Atheism

1 *The Bond*, Lynn McTaggart, Page 25

2   Ibid., Page 30
3   *The Bond*, Lynne McTaggart, Page 32
4   *On the Origin of Species*, Charles Darwin, Penguin Classics, Edition 2009, Page 20
5   *Courier-Mail* Newspaper, 7.9.2013 "Release from ARC Centre of Excellence for Coral Reef Studies".
6   *Eves Bite*, Ian Wishart, Page 40. Howling at the Moon Publishing 2007.
7   *The Crumbling Theory of Evolution*, by JWG Johnson, Page17 Perpetual Eucharist Adoration Inc 1986, Australia.
8   *Eves Bite*, Ian Wishart, Page 41. Howling at the Moon Publishing 2007.
9   Ibid., Page 53.
10 "*The Crumbling Theory of Evolution*, by JWG Johnson, Page 93 Perpetual Eucharist Adoration Inc 1986, Australia.
11 http://www.trueorigin.org/spetner2.asp
12 *Eves Bite*, Ian Wishart, Page 41. Howling at the Moon Publishing 2007.
13 *The Evolution of Life*, Stephen Jay Gould
14 Reference: R.D.K. Thomas, Rebecca M. Shearman, and Graham W. Stewart, "Evolutionary Exploitation of design options by the First Animals with Hard Skeletons," *Science* 288 (2000): 1239-42
15 *The Crumbling Theory of Evolution*, by JWG Johnson, Page 23 Perpetual Eucharist Adoration Inc 1986, Australia.
16 *Ref: On the Origin of Species,* Charles Darwin, Page 179
17 http://www.huffingtonpost.com/james-a-shapiro/cell-cognition_b_1354889.html
18 *The Facts of Life: Shattering the Myths of Darwinism*, by Richard Milton, Page 164 Fourth Estate 1992
19 *Darwin on Trial*, Philip E. Johnson, Page 18 Regnery Gateway 1991
20 http://en.wikipedia.org/wiki/Peppered_moth_evolution
21 *Darwin on Trial*, Philip E. Johnson, Page 27, Regnery Gateway 1991
22 *Unended Quest: an intellectual autobiography*, by Karl Popper, Fontana.1976, Page 171
23 *Darwin on Trial*, Philip E. Johnson, Page 9, Regnery Gateway 1991
24 Ref. *Eves Bite*, Ian Wishart, Page 65. Howling at the Moon Publishing 2007.
25 *Darwin on Trial*, Philip E. Johnson, Page 9, Regnery Gateway 1991
26 *Darwin on Trial*, Philip E. Johnson, Page 9, Regnery Gateway 1991
27 Australian "Q&A" ABC Television programme, Sept. 2013

Chapter 2: Non-Physical Reality etc.

Note: *e-Books quoted (i.e. Kindle Amazon books), unfortunately up until recently do not have page numbers. With recent technological developments only recent Kindle Amazon books released (2015), are provided with page numbers which can be used for references purposes.*

1   *Biocentrism*, Robert Lanza, BenBella Books. Inc. 2010, Page 1

2   *The God Theory*, Bernard Haisch, Page 38
3   *The Dancing Wu Li Masters*, Gary Zukav, William Morrow (1979), Page 219.
4   *The Facts of Life*, Richard Milton, Fourth Estate Ltd (1992), Page 255.
5   *The Holographic Universe*, Michael Talbot, Page 1
6   *The God Hypothesis*, Joe Lewels, Page 66
7   *The Holographic Universe*, Michael Talbot, Page 12
8   *Memory*, Elizabeth Loftus (Addison-Wesley publishing Coy.Inc.- 1980) Page 50
9   *The New Story of Science*, Robert M. Augros and George N Stanciu, Page 29, Regnery Gateway, Inc. (1984)
10 *The Holographic Universe*, Michael Talbot, Page 12
11 *Facing Reality*", John Eccles (Berlin: Springer-Verlag, 1970), Page 174
12 *The Holographic Universe*, Michael Talbot, Page 1
13 *On Mysteries of the Mind*, Edgar Cayce, Henry Reed (The Aquarian Press- 1990), Page 272
14 "Shufflebrain", Paul Pietsch, *Harpers* Magazine 244 (May 1972), Page 66
15 *The Holographic Universe*, Michael Talbot, Page 20
16 *The Conscious Universe*, The Scientific Proof of Psychic Phenomena, Dean Radin, PhD, Page 284
17 *The Cosmic Blueprint*, Paul Davies (William Heinesmann Ltd 1987), Page 189
18 Ibid., Page 189
19 *The Fifth Miracle*, Paul Davies (Allen Lane The Penguin Press, 1998), Page 209
20 *The Holographic Universe*, Michael Talbot, Page 37
21 *The Web of Life*, Fritjof Capra (HarperCollins Hammersmith London, 1996), Page 260
22 *The Secret Life of Plants*, Peter Tomkins and Christopher Bird (Allen Lane, 1974), Page 70
23 *The Rebirth of Nature*, Rupert Sheldrake (Park Street Press, 1991), Page 101
24 *Seven Experiments That Could Change the World*, Rupert Sheldrake Fourth Estate Ltd, 1994
25 *Consciousness and Human Identity*, John Cornwall (Oxford University Press, 1998)
26 "The Puzzle of Conscious Experience", Dr David J. Chalmers (Article, *Scientific American*, Dec.1995)
27 *Parallel Universes*, Fred Alan Woolf, Page 306
28 *The Conscious Universe: The Scientific Proof of Psychic Phenomena*, Dean Radin, Page 259
29 *Physics of the Soul*, Amit Goswami. Hampton Roads Publishing Company, Inc., Page13
30 *The Field*, Lynne McTaggart, HarperCollins, New York, 2008 Page 118
31 *The Conscious Universe*, Dean Radin, HarperCollins, 2009 Page 325
32 http://henry.pha.jhu.edu/haisch.html
33 *The Intention Experiment*, Sept 5, 2011 Lynne McTaggart, Page 35
34 *Biocentrism*, Robert Lanza, (Benbella Books, 2010), Chapter 3, Pages 19–23
35 *The Mind of God*, Paul Davies, Penguin Books 1992, Page 158

36 *The Matter Myth*, Paul Davies and John Gribbin, 1992, Page 207
37 *Science and the Near-Death Experience: How Consciousness Survives Death*, Chris Carter (Aug 23, 2010) Kindle Book
38 Ibid.
39 "Logic of Quantum Mechanics and Consciousness", 2013 by Michael B Mensky, Kindle Book: *Cosmology of Consciousness - Quantum Physics & Neuroscience of Mind*
40 *Quantum Physics, Near Death Experiences, Eternal Consciousness, Religion and Human Soul*, William Bray (Apr 28, 2010), Kindle Book

Chapter 3: The Quantum Communication System (PCAR) etc

1 *The Conscious Universe*, Dean Radin, HarperCollins 1997, page 321
2 Ibid., Page 172
3 http://www.quantumconsciousness.org/overview.html
4 *Physics of the Soul*, Amit Goswami. Hampton Roads Publishing Company, Inc., Page 37
5 *The Field* Lynn McTaggart, HarperCollins, 2008, Page 42.
6 Ibid., Page 47/49
7 Ibid., Page 26
8 Ibid., Page 89.
9 http://www.newdawnmagazine.com/articles/intuition-delusion-or-perception-toward-a-scientific-explanation-of-the-akashic-experience
10 *The Field*, Lynne McTaggart, HarperCollins, 2008, Page 95.
11 *The God Theory*, Bernard Haish, Page 54
12 *Jung on Synchronicity and the Paranormal*, C.C. Jung (Routledge, 1997), Page 14
13 *The Holotropic Mind*, Stanislav Grof (HarperCollins;1990), Page 168
14 *Phantoms in the Brain*, V.S. Ramachandran and Sandra Blakeslee)
15 *The Holographic Universe*, Michael Talbot, Page 198
16 Ibid., Page 198
17 *The Spiritual Universe*, Fred Alan Woolf (Simon & Schuster, New York, 1996), Page 266
18 *The Whispering Pond*, Ervin Laszlo (Element Books Inc;1996), Page 114
19 *The Field*, Lynne McTaggart, HarperCollins, 2008, Page 101.
20 *The Conscious Universe*, Dean Radin, HarperCollins, 2009, Page 143
21 http://www.princeton.edu/~pear/experiments.html
22 http://theintentionexperiment.com/
23 *The Conscious Universe*, Dean Radin, HarperCollins, 2009, Page 174
24 *The Holographic Universe*, Michael Talbot, Page 60
25 *The Rebirth of Nature*, Rupert Sheldrake (Park Street Press,1991), Page 144
26 Ibid., Page 101
27 http://journalofcosmology.com/Consciousness149.html

28. http://www.newdawnmagazine.com/articles/intuition-delusion-or-perception-toward-a-scientific-explanation-of-the-akashic-experience
29. *The Conscious Universe*, Dean Radin,1997 HarperCollins, New York Page 164
30. *The Secret Life of Plants*, Peter Tomkins, Christopher Bird, Harper & Row Inc, USA, Page 22
31. "The Neurophysiological of Remembering", Karl Pribam, *Scientific American*, 220 Jan 1969, Page 75
32. *Encounters with Qi,* David Eisenberg, with Thomas Lee Wright, (New York: Penguin, 1987), pp. 79-87.
33. *Strange People,* Frank Edwards, "People Who Saw without Eyes," (London: Pan Books, 1970).
34. "Soviet Experiments in Eyeless Vision", A. Ivanov, *International Journal of Parapsychology* 6 (1964); see also M. M. Bongard and M. S. Smirnov, *About the Dermal Vision'* of R. Kuleshova, *Biophysics 1* (1965).
35. *The Field*, Lynne McTaggart, HarperCollins, 2008, Page 87

Chapter 4: The Commonality of Science Amongst All Paranormal Phenomena etc

Note: *e-Books quoted (i.e. Kindle Amazon books), unfortunately up until recently do not have page numbers. With recent technological developments only recent Kindle Amazon books released (2015), are provided with page numbers which can be used for references purposes.*

1. http://www.uri-geller.com/books/geller-papers/g20.htm
2. http://www.mysteriouspeople.com/Nina_Kulagina.htm
3. *The Link: Extraordinary gifts of a Teenage Psychic*, Matthew Manning, Page 168, Corgi Books, 1975
4. http://www.mysteriouspeople.com/Nina_Kulagina.htm
5. *The Conscious Universe,* Dr Dean Radin,1997, HarperCollins, New York Page 174, and "Natures Mind: the Quantum Hologram" – a paper authored by Dr Edgar Mitchell. See: http://journalofcosmology.com/Consciousness149.html
6. *The Field*, by Lynne McTaggart, Page 127
7. http://www.arthurfindlaycollege.org/
8. "Natures Mind: the Quantum Hologram", Dr Edgar Mitchell,
    a. http://journalofcosmology.com/Consciousness149.html
9. "Natures Mind: the Quantum Hologram", Dr Edgar Mitchell,
    a. http://journalofcosmology.com/Consciousness149.html
10. https://www.google.co.nz/?gfe_rd=cr&ei=s2xMVIzlOMGN8QetnICgDg&gws_rd=ssl#q=the+monroe+institute
11. http://www.bcs.org/content/conwebdoc/16175 also
    a. "Natures Mind: the Quantum Hologram", Dr Edgar Mitchell,
    b. http://journalofcosmology.com/Consciousness149.html

12. "Natures Mind: the Quantum Hologram", Dr Edgar Mitchell,
    a. http://journalofcosmology.com/Consciousness149.html
13. *God & the New Physics*, Paul Davies, (Simon & Schuster, 1983), Page 124
14. *God and the New Physics*, Paul Davies (Simon & Schuster, 1983),
15. *The Tao of Physics*, Fritjof Capra, Fontana, 1976, Page 43,
16. *The Tao of Physics*, Frijof Capra (Fontana), 1976), Page 196
17. *Seth Speaks*, Jane Roberts,Page 48
18. *Seth Speaks*, Jane Roberts, Page 257
19. *Destiny of Sous*, Michael Newton, Kindle Book
20. "Subatomic Particles, Nuclear Structure and Chemistry", by Sandor Nagy, Institute of Chemistry, Eotvos Lorand University, Budapest, Hungry
    a. http://www.eolss.net/sample-chapters/c06/e6-104-15-00.pdf
21. *God and the New Physics*, Paul Davies (Simon & Schuster, 1983), Page 80
22. *Far Journeys*, Robert Monroe, Souvenir Press. 1985, Page 20
23. *Seth Speaks*, Jane Roberts, Page 257
24. *Destiny of Souls*, Michael Newton, Kindle Book
25. "Subatomic Particles, Nuclear Structure and Chemistry", by Sandor Nagy, Institute of Chemistry, Eotvos Lorand University, Budapest, Hungry
    a. http://www.eolss.net/sample-chapters/c06/e6-104-15-00.pdf
26. *God and the New Physics*, Paul Davies (Simon & Schuster, 1983), Page 80
27. *Far Journeys*, Robert Monroe, Souvenir Press. 1985, Page 20

Chapter 4, ANNEX: Further considerations of Time and Space

1. http://www.universetoday.com/111603/does-light-experience-time/ An article by Fraser Cain in discussion with Astrophysicist Dr Pamela Gay, May 7 2014.
2. *The Unknown Reality* Vol 1, by Jane Roberts, Page 59, Prentice-Hall, 1977
3. *The Unknown Reality* Vol 1, by Jane Roberts, Page 54, Prentice-Hall, 1977
4. "What is Time", article by Keith Mayes, http://www.thekeyboard.org.uk/What%20is%20Time.htm,
5. *Seth Speaks*, Jane Roberts, Page 267, Bantum Books/Prentice-Hall, 1974, also *The Unknown Reality*, Vol 1, by Jane Roberts, Page 55, Prentice-Hall, 1977
6. *The Unknown Reality*, Vol 1, by Jane Roberts, Page 62, Prentice-Hall, 1977
7. *God and the New Physics*, Paul Davies (Simon & Schuster,1983), Page 39
8. *The Unknown Reality*, Vol 1, by Jane Roberts, Page 62, Prentice-Hall, 1977
9. "Scientists suggest space-time has no time dimension", Apr 25, 2011 by Lisa Zyga http://phys.org/news/2011-04-scientists-spacetime-dimension.html
10. https://medium.com/the-physics-arxiv-blog/quantum-experiment-shows-how-time-emerges-from-entanglement-d5d3dc850933
11. *God and The New Physics*, Paul Davies. Page 48, Simon & Schuster Paperbacks, 1983

Chapter 5: Reasons for Reincarnation

Note: *e-Books quoted (i.e. Kindle Amazon books), unfortunately up until recently do not have page numbers. With recent technological developments only recent Kindle Amazon books released (2015), are provided with page numbers which can be used for references purposes.*

1. *Exploring Reincarnation*, Hans Ten Dam, Penguin Books, 1987. This copy, revised Ryder Books 2003, Page 361
2. *Between Inner Space and Outer Space*, John D Barrow (Oxford University Press, 1999), Page 46
3. *Masks of the Soul*, Benjamin Walker (Nene Litho, Earls Barton, 1981), Page 78
4. *Reincarnation* (Sylvia Cranston and Carey Williams (Julian Press, 1984), Page 7
5. *The Wheel of Life*, Elisabeth Kubler-Ross (Scribner: 1997), Page 281
6. *Dreams, Evolution. And Value Fulfilment* Vol. II, Jane Roberts (Prentice-Hall, 1986), Page 145
7. Ibid., Page 148
8. *Seth Speaks,* Jane Roberts (Prentice-Hall, June 1972), Page 472,
9. *Is There Life After Death*, Professor Robert Kastenbaum (1995 – Prion (Multimedia Books), Page 171
10. *The Edgar Cayce Reader*, Hugh Lynn Cayee, *Vol. II* (New York: Paperback Library, 1969), pp. 25-26
11. *Edgar Cayce: on Mysteries of the Mind*, Henry Reed (The Aquarian Press - 1990), Page 45
12. *Edgar Cayce: A Seer out of Season*, Harmon Hartzell Bro (New American Library, 1989) Page 195
13. *Seth Speaks* – Jane Roberts (Prentice-Hall, June 1972), Page 10, Also *Dreams, Evolution and Value Fulfilment*, Vol. 1, (Prentice-Hall, 1986), Page 144, Page 196
14. http://en.wikipedia.org/wiki/Jane_Roberts
15. *Seth Speaks,* Jane Roberts (Prentice-Hall, June 1972), Page 360
16. *Masks of the Soul*, Benjamin Walker (Nene Litho, Earls Barton, 1981), Page 27
17. *Life Between Life*, Joel L. Whitton MD, Joe Fisher (Grafton Books, 1987), Page 91
18. http://www.thenazareneway.com/reincarnation.htm
19. *Quantum Physics, Near Death Experiences, Eternal Consciousness, Religion, and the Human Soul* by William Bray (Dec 9, 2013) - Kindle eBook
20. http://en.wikipedia.org/wiki/Reincarnation
21. *The Purpose-Guided Universe: Believing In Einstein, Darwin, and God*, Bernard Haisch, Kindle Book, 2010
22. Ibid.
23. *The God Theory: Universes, Zero-Point Fields, and What's Behind It All*, Bernard Haisch, Pages xi, xii, 51,52.
24. Seth's concepts of God, http://www.spiritual-endeavors.org/seth/Andy4.htm

Chapter 6: ESP, Remote Viewing and Non-Ordinary States of Consciousness etc.

Note: *e-Books quoted (i.e. Kindle Amazon books), unfortunately up until recently do not have page numbers. With recent technological developments only recent Kindle Amazon books released (2015), are provided with page numbers which can be used for references purposes.*

1. *After life*, Colin Wilson (Harrup, London 1985), Page 143
2. *The Whispering Pond*, Ervin Laszio (Element Books, Inc. 1996), Page 96
3. Charles Tart, "Physiological Correlates of Psi Cognition", *International Journal of Neuropsychiatry* 5, No. 4 (1962).
4. E. Douglas Dean, "Plethysmograph Recordings of ESP Responses", *International Journal of Neuropsychiatry* 2 (September 1966).
5. *The ESP Papers*, Sheila Ostrander and Lynn Scroeder, (Bantum Books, May 1976) Page 108.
6. *Psychic Discoveries Behind the Iron Curtain*, Sheila Ostrander and Lynn Schroeder (Souvenir Press, 1997), Page 239
7. *The Conscious Universe: The Scientific Proof of Psychic Phenomena*, Dean Radin, PhD Page 88.
8. Ibid., Page 4.
9. *The Whispering Pond*, Ervin Laszio (Element Books, Inc. 1996), Page 114
10. *The Conscious Universe: The Scientific Proof of Psychic Phenomena*, Dean Radin, PhD, Page 107
11. *After life*, Colin Wilson (Harrup, London 1985), Page 143
12. *The Case Against Death*, Richard Lazarus, (Warner Books, 1993), Page 92
13. *The Conscious Universe: The Scientific Proof of Psychic Phenomena*, Dean Radin, PhD, Page 105.
14. *Mind Beyond The Body*, D. Scott Rogo (Penguin Books 1978), Page 85
15. *Margins of Reality*, Robert G. Jahn and Brenda J. Dunne, (New York: Harcourt Brace Jovanovich, 1987), Pages 160, 185.
16. *The ESP Papers*, Sheila Ostrander and Lynn Schroeder, (Bantam Books, May 1976), Page 121
17. *Psychic Discoveries Behind the Iron Curtain*, Sheila Ostrander and Lynn Schroeder (Souvenir Press, 1997), Page 347
18. *Psychic Warrior: Inside the CIA's Stargate Program*, David Moorhouse (St Martin Press, 1966, page 153.
19. *Cosmic Voyage*, Courtenay Brown (Hodder and Stoughton, 1997), Page 18
20. http://www.dailymail.co.uk/sciencetech/article-2643332/Beam-Scientists-sat-teleportation-possible-transfer-atoms.html
21. *Recollections of Death*, Michael B. Sabom, (New York: Harper & Row, 1982), p. 184.
22. *The Adventure of Self-Discovery*, Stanislov Grof (Albany, N.Y.:SUNY Press,1988), Pages 71-72.
23. *The Case Against Death*, Richard Lazarus (Warner Books, 1993), Page 218

24 *The Holographic Universe*, Michael Talbot, Page 230,
25 *New ASPR Research on Out-of-the-Body Experiences*, Karlis Osis, Newsletter of the American Society for Psychical Research 14 (1972).
26 *Mind Beyond the Body*, D. Scott Rogo (Penguin Books Ltd, 1978), Page 160
27 Ibid., Page 177
28 Ibid., Page 192
29 *Jung on Synchronicity and the Paranormal*, C.C. Jung , key readings - Roderick Main Routledge, 1997), Page 145
30 *Far Journeys*, Robert A Monroe, (Double Day and Coy, Inc, 1985), Page 63.
31 *Seth Speaks*, Jane Roberts, Bantam books, Prentice-Hall edition, 1972, Page152
32 *Mind Beyond the Body*, D. Scott Rogo (Penguin Books Ltd, 1978), Page 58.
33 *Far Journeys*, Robert A Monroe, (Double Day and Coy, Inc, 1985), Page 64.
34 *Cosmic Voyage*, Courtenay Brown (Hodder and Stoughton,1997), Page 43
35 *Journey's Out of the Body*, Robert A Monroe, Pages 101-115
36 *Cosmic Voyage*, Courtenay Brown (Hodder and Stoughton, 1997), Page 43
37 *Psychic Warrior*, David Moorhouse (St Martin's Press, 1966), Page 153
38 *Far Journeys*, Robert A Monroe, (Double Day and Coy, Inc, 1985), Page 77.
39 *Far Journeys*, Robert A Monroe, (Double Day and Coy, Inc, 1985), Page 73.
40 *The Holographic Universe*, Michael Talbot, Page 257
41 Ibid., Page 252
42 Ibid., Page 240
43 http://www.near-death.com/experiences/evidence01.html
44 *On Children and Death*, Elisabeth Kubler-Ross (New York: Maemillan, 1983), p. 208
45 *Life at Death*, Kenneth Ring (New York: Quill, 1980), pp. 238-39.)
46 *Best Evidence*, 2nd Edition, Michael Schmicker, Amazon Kindle Book,
46 Ibid.

Chapter 7: Past Life Recall - Spontaneous and via Hypnosis

1 http://www.dalailama.com/news/post/753-statement-of-his-holiness-the-fourteenth-dalai-lama-tenzin-gyatso-on-the-issue-of-his-reincarnation
2 *Children's Past Lives*, Carol Bowman, Element Books, UK, 1998, Page 119
3 *Life Before Life: Children's Memories of Previous Lives*, Jim B Tucker, St Martin's Press, New York, Page 30
4 *The Holographic Universe*, Michael Talbot, Harper-Collins, 1996, Page 217
5 http://www.near-death.com/experiences/reincarnation01.html
6 *Children's Past Lives*, Carol Bowman, Element Books, UK, 1998, Page 97
7 Ibid., Page 107
8 http://www.near-death.com/experiences/reincarnation01.html
9 *Life before Life, Children's Memories of Past Lives*, Jim B Tucker, St Martin's Giffin, New York, 2005, Page 8

10 http://www.near-death.com/experiences/reincarnation01.html
11 *Children's Past Lives*, Carol Bowman, Element Books, UK, 1998, Page 106-108
12 http://reluctant-messenger.com/reincarnation-proof.htm#swarnlata
13 *The Holographic Universe*, Michael Talbot, Harper-Collins, 1996, Page 219
14 This is an extract by an Amazon reviewer of Dr. Stevenson's Book, *Where Reincarnation and Biology Intersect*, May 21, 1997 See: http://www.amazon.com/exec/obidos/ASIN/0275951898/reluctantmess-20#customerReviews
15 *Children's Past Lives*, Carol Bowman, Element Books, UK, 1998, Page 103
16 http://reluctant-messenger.com/reincarnation-proof.htm#swarnlata
17 *Children's Past Lives*, Carol Bowman, Element Books, UK, 1998, Page 103
18 Ibid., Page 18
19 *The Whispering Pond*, Ervin Laszlo (Element Books Inc; 1996) Page 96.
20 *The Case for Reincarnation*, Joe Fisher (William Collins & Sons, May 1984, Page 49)
21 *Reliving Past Lives*, Helen Wambach (Hutchinson Publishing Group, Arrow edition 1978), Pages 16, 17, 37, 83
22 Ibid., Page 85
23 *Exploring Reincarnation*, Hans TenDam (Rider, 2003), Page 128
24 *The Case Against Death*, Richard Lazarus - (Warner Books, 1993) Page 273
25 *Exploring Reincarnation*, Hans Ten Dam (Rider, 2003), Page 128
26 *Reliving Past Lives*, Helen Wambach, Arrow Books Ltd, 1980, Page 12
27 Ibid., Page 94
28 Ref: http://www.viewzone.com/reincarnation.html
29 *Reliving Past Lives*, Helen Wambach, Arrow Books Ltd, 1980, Page 145.
30 *Americans Who Have Been Reincarnated*, H. N. Banerjee, (New York: Macmillan Publishing Company, 1980), Page 195.
31 *The Holographic Universe*, Michael Talbot, Page 213
32 *Reliving Past Lives*, Helen Wambach (Hutchinson Publishing Group, Arrow edition 1978), Pages 123
33 *Exploring Reincarnation*, Hans TenDam, Rider (2003), Pages (*Gender*) 49,55,76,80 etc.
34 *Reliving Past Lives*, Helen Wambach (Hutchinson Publishing Group, Arrow edition 1978), Pages 16, 17, 37, 83
35 *Exploring Reincarnation*, Hans TenDam, Rider (2003), Page 142
36 *Many Lives, Many Masters*, Brian Weiss (Simon & Schuster Inc, 1988) Page 38
37 *Trauma, Trance and Transformation*, M. Gerald Edelstein, (New York: Brunner/Mazel, 1981).
38 *Reliving Past Lives*, Helen Wambach (Hutchinson Publishing Group, Arrow edition 1978), Page 8
39 *Exploring Reincarnation*, Hans TenDam (Rider 2002), Page 137
40 *Children's Past Lives*, Carol Bowman, Element Books, UK, 1998, Page 178
41 *Memory*, Elizabeth Loftus (Addison-Wesley publishing Coy.Inc.- 1980), Page 6.
42 *Exploring Reincarnation*, Hans Tem Dam, (Rider, 2003), Page 128

43   *Memory*, Elizabeth Loftus (Addison-Wesley publishing Coy.Inc. 1980), Page 50.
44   *Exploring Reincarnation*, Hans TemDam, (Rider 2003), Page 128.
45   *The Case for Reincarnation*, Joe Fisher (William Collins & Sons, May 1984, Page 152)
46   *Exploring Reincarnation*, Hans Tem Dam, (Rider 2003), Page 200.
47   *Reliving Past Lives*, Helen Wambach, Arrow Books Ltd, 1980, Page 63.
48   *Children's Past Lives*, Carol Bowman, Element Books, UK, 1998, Page 58.
49   Ref: https://www.youtube.com/watch?v=HayY1yyXnn0
50   *Greatest Mysteries of the Modern World*, John Pinkney (The Five Mile Press Pty Ltd), 2004, Page 320-327
51   *Children's Past Lives*, Carol Bowman, Element Books, UK, 1998, Page 108

Chapter 8: Psychics and, Mediums

Note: *e-Books quoted (i.e. Kindle Amazon books), unfortunately up until recently do not have page numbers. With recent technological developments only recent Kindle Amazon books released (2015), are provided with page numbers which can be used for references purposes.*

1   http://www.coastal.edu/ashes2art/delphi2/misc-essays/oracle_of_delphi.html
2   http://en.wikipedia.org/wiki/Psychic_Kids, also http://www.tv.com/shows/psychic-kids/
3   *Breakthrough Scientific Evidence of Life After Death*, Gary E. Schwartz with William L. Simon, Atria Books, 2002
4   Wikipedia
5   *Breakthrough Scientific Evidence of Life After Death*, Gary E. Schwartz with William L. Simon, page 50, Atria Books, 2002
6   http://en.wikipedia.org/wiki/Cold_reading
7   *Breakthrough Scientific Evidence of Life After Death*, Gary E. Schwartz with William L. Simon, page 60, Atria Books, 2002 (Also see Appendices for all details on arrangements for various experiments and results which follow).
8   *Breakthrough Scientific Evidence of Life After Death*, Gary E. Schwartz with William L. Simon, page 222, Atria Books, 2002
9   Ibid., Page 216
10   Ibid., Page 350
11   Ibid., Page 256
12   http://www.badpsychics.com/2014/09/an-analysis-of-live-lisa-williams.html
13   *Breakthrough Scientific Evidence of Life After Death*, Gary E. Schwartz with William L. Simon, page 264 Atria Books, 2002
14   Ibid., Page 332
15   http://www.ascsi.org/feat/life_after/buried_crosses_mystery.htm
16   Wikipedia

17 *Is There Life After Death*, Professor Robert Kastenbaum, Page 150 (1995- Prion, Multimedia Books), also *The Survival Files*, Miles Edward Allen, A Kindle Book

Chapter 9: Life-between-Lives and Concluding Book Comments

1 *By Your Side* – Colin Fry, (Introduction, vii) Rider, 2010
2 http://newtoninstitute.org/become-an-lbl-therapist/tni-training/
3 *Journey of Souls: Case Studies of Life Between Lives (1994)*, Michael Newton - A Kindle (Amazon) book
4 *Adventures of the Soul: Journeys Through the Physical and Spiritual Dimensions*, James Van Praagh, A Kindle/Amazon iBook, Chapter 1
5 *The Seth Material*, Jane Roberts, Page 147, A Bantum Book, Prentice-Hill (1970)
6 http://www.the-gospel-truth.info/bible-teachings/the-true-identity-of-the-devil-satan/
7 *The Seth Material*, Jane Roberts, Page 145, , A Bantum Book, Prentice-Hill (1970)
8 http://www.carolmoore.net/articles/helenwambach.html
9 *Seth Speaks*, Jane Roberts, Page 351, Bantum Books, Prentice-Hall Inc. (June 1972)
10 *The Seth Material*, Jane Roberts, Page 272, A Bantum Book, Prentice-Hill (1970)
11 *Your Soul's Plan: Discovering the Real Meaning of the Life You Planned Before You Were Born*, by Robert Schwartz - a Kindle Amazon e-Book
12 *Messages from Michael*, by Chelsea Quinn Yarbro, Page 67 Berkely Books, PBJ Books Oct. 1980
13 Wikipedia
14 *The Immortal Mind: Science and the Continuity of Consciousness Beyond the Brain*, by Ervin Laszlo (2014?), A Kindle Book
15 http://www.dalailamaquotes.org/category/dalai-lama-quotes-on-kindness/
16 *Far Journeys*, Robert A. Monroe, Page 122, (Doubleday & Coy, New York, 1985)
17 *The Seth Material*, Jane Roberts, Page 3, A Bantum Book, Prentice-Hill (1970)

List of Books used by the author to check correlations for the life-between-life summary in the Chapter

Journey of Souls: Case Studies of Life Between Lives, Michael Newton
Destiny of Souls: New Case Studies of Life Between Lives, Michel Newton
Memories of the Afterlife, Michael Newton
The Seth Material, Jane Roberts
Seth Speaks, Jane Roberts
Far Journeys, Robert A. Monroe
Life After Death, Neville Randall
Messages from Michael, Chelsea Quinn Yarbo
Your Soul's Plan: Discovering the Real Meaning of the Life You Planned Before You Were Born, by Robert Schwartz

Chapter 9: ANNEX

1. *God and the New Physics*, Paul Davies, Page 98, Simon & Schuster, 1983
2. http://www.independent.co.uk/news/science/is-there-an-afterlife-the-science-of-biocentrism-can-prove-there-is-claims-professor-robert-lanza-8942558.html
3. http://www.naturalnews.com/028575_placebo_effect_medicine.html, also https://www.psychologytoday.com/blog/brain-sense/201201/the-placebo-effect-how-it-works
4. *The Nature of Personal Reality*, by Jane Roberts, Page 483. Prentice-Hall, 1974
5. Ibid., Page, 480.
6. Ref. Isaiah 13: 15-18, Deuteronomy20:10 -17 Koran: http://www.thereligionofpeace.com/quran/023-violence.htm) also, http://www.thereligionofpeace.com/Pages/Bible-Quran-Violence.htm
7. *The Nature of Personal Reality*, by Jane Roberts, Page 483. Prentice-Hall, 1974

Index

A
abortion 261
advanced entities 140, 257, 263
AfterlifeData 252
Afterlife Experiments, The, Dr Gary Schwartz 227
Akashic Field 239, 240, 288
Alpha, Beta and Theta states 176
Among Mediums: A Scientist's Quest for Answers, Dr Julie Beischel *See* Beischel, Julie
anathema 138, 139
Apocrypha 138, 139
Archimedes xxviii, 273
arrow of time 108
Asimov, Isaac 28
Aspect, Alan 37
A Theory in Crisis, Michael Denton 8
attention 36, 43, 45, 47, 51, 69–72, 83, 96, 99, 101–102, 113, 118, 168, 195, 200, 205, 241, 284–287, 299
attraction 14, 23, 140, 185, 280, 282, 289
automatic writing 225

B
bacteria 42, 66, 75, 80, 94, 108, 296, 298, 301, 304, 310
Barrow, John xxvi, 28, 128
'Beauty' in Physics viii, xxvii, 19, 20
Beischel, Julie 236, 237, 238, 239, 240, 241, 242, 248
belief systems xvii, 59, 103, 127, 138, 170, 189, 201, 224, 233, 266–268, 277–280, 282, 309
Best Evidence, Michel Schmicker 93
Bible, The 138, 139, 140, 146, 282
Big Bang, The xxvii, 5, 6, 7, 17, 18, 21, 22, 23, 25, 26, 33, 34, 49, 105, 107, 108, 120, 121, 144
biocentric viii, 30, 31

Biocentrism, Dr Robert Lanza 33, 49
Biological Big Bang 11
bio-photon emissions 59
birthmarks 191–194, 192, 193, 194, 195
Bohm, David 37, 41, 42, 65, 84, 135
Bohr, Niels xxviii, 66
Bootstrap Theory, The *See God and The New Physics*, Paul Davies
Borei, Emile 16, 22, 300 *See also* probability
Bowman, Carol 198, 200, 208, 216, 219, 223
Bray, William 47, 53, 93, 141, 178, 182
British Airship R101 245–246
Brown, Dr Courtenay 168, 178, 179
buckyballs 46
Buddhist belief 144, 260, 290

C
Cambrian
  era 10, 11, 302, 304
  Explosion 10, 11, 301, 302, 304
Capra, Frijof 109 *See also Tao of Physics*
Carter, Chris 50, 93, 168
Case for Reincarnation, The, Joe Fisher 218
Casti, John L. 4
Cathars 138, 139
causality 3, 6, 117, 120, 121
Cayce, Edgar 131, 132, 133, 134, 135, 136, 137, 146, 225, 242
cell speciation 59, 75
Chalmers, Dr James 44
children remembering past lives 192
Children's Past Lives, Carol Bowman 198, 219
CIA 161, 164, 165, 167, 168, 173, 179, 249
clairvoyance 7, 67–69, 76, 78, 81, 96, 98, 103, 155, 159, 163, 164, 166, 169, 173, 174, 175, 186, 187, 188, 225, 234, 242
clairvoyant 135, 136, 155, 166
cluster group 254, 259, 260

CMB (Cosmic Microwave Explorer) 21, 22
COBE (Cosmic Background Explorer) 21, 105, 108
cold reading 228, 229, 230, 231, 232, 237
collective mind 43, 133
Collective Subconscious 64
Collective Unconscious 68
communication system 38, 48, 55, 56, 59, 69, 76–78, 80, 81, 85, 93, 94, 96, 99, 100, 102, 113, 159, 163, 180, 187, 188, 206, 231–234, 236, 240
completeness of nature *See* Casti, John L.
consciousness (CU's) 136
Conscious Universe, The, Dean Radin 71, 161
Contingency Argument, The 6
contingent events 7, 104, 107, 111
correlation xxv, xxvi, 36, 41, 58, 69, 71, 77, 80, 89, 131, 135, 137, 141, 168, 180, 181, 188, 192, 195, 199, 203, 208, 212, 252, 255, 266
Council of Elders 259, 260, 261
Council of Trent 138
Crick, Francis xxviii, 13, 273, 298 *See also* DNA
Cruickshank, Kevin *See* Sensing Murder
curare 289
cytoskeletal microtubules 57

D

Danly, Laura 22
Darwin, Charles 8–12, 14, 100, 114, 143, 156, 162, 290, 295, 296, 297, 298, 299, 300, 301, 302, 304, 305, 307, 309, 310, 311
Darwinian xx, 8, 9, 10, 12, 13, 23, 34, 297, 302, 303, 305, 309, 312
revolution 8
Davies, Paul 3, 18, 20, 21, 22, 25, 27, 28, 29, 35, 49, 50, 96, 110, 117, 121, 122, 272, 274
Dawkins, Richard 21, 311, 312
deterministic 6, 41, 56, 145
Devil 138, 257, 259
Dirac 36
discarnates ix, 87, 92, 98, 102, 113, 114, 147, 170, 187, 225, 229, 230, 231, 235, 236–241, 251, 256, 266, 268, 285
Discontinuous motion 117
Divining 68
DNA xxvii, xxviii, 9, 10, 13–16, 59, 68, 100, 113, 127, 195, 262, 273, 296, 297, 298, 300, 303, 304, 305
Doors of Perception, The, Aldeous Huxley 63

Doppler, Christian 6
double-blind experiments 231
double - slit, the Double-slit experiment 45
Dowker, Dr Fay 6
dowsing 91, 160, 169, 286, 289
Dryden, John 129
Dyson, Freeman 24, 41

E

Eccles, Sir John 40
Edward, John 140, 226–230, 233, 267
EEG (electroencephalograph) 206
readings 59, 160
Einstein xxvii, 33, 36, 37, 49, 50, 104, 105, 106, 107, 119, 121, 143, 274
Einsteinian physics 104, 106, 108
electronic voice phenomena (EVP) 242
End of Materialism, The, Charles T Tart 93
entangled 36, 58, 68, 69
entanglement ix, 36, 38, 58, 61, 62, 71, 72, 77, 78, 111, 120
epigenics 9, 12, 100, 113, 240, 262, 296, 297, 298, 300, 301, 304, 306
event-line 103, 107, 111, 118
Eve's Bite, Ian Wishart 298
evolution xx, 7–13, 16, 23, 25, 29, 34, 119, 145, 156, 210, 251, 295, 298–312
Exploring Reincarnation, Hans TenDam 213, 214, 217

F

false beliefs 280
Faraday chambers 58
Faraday type caging 80
Far Journeys, *Journey Out of the Body*, and *Ultimate Journey*, Robert Monroe 176
Ferguson, Kitty xxiv, xxvi, 17, 30
Feynman, Richard P. 55
Fibonacci sequence 18
Field, The, Lynne McTaggart 60, 61, 62
filter, selective brain filter 63, 64, 69, 80, 85, 261, 263, 285, 287
Fire in the Equations, The, Kitty Ferguson xxiv, 17, 30
first cause ix, 3, 4, 21, 30, 31, 54, 87, 109, 114
Fisher, Joe 218, 300
fluoridation 281, 312
fossils 9–12, 22, 27, 300–305, 309, 310
free will 9, 41, 46, 56, 115, 145, 153, 253, 276

frequency
    matching 73, 135
    signature 72
fundamental constants 24, 26, 30, 33, 34

G

Gaia Hypothesis, Lovelock 28, 33, 136
Gandhi, Mahatma 130
Ganzfield Method 161, 162
Gao, Shan 116, 120
Garrett, Eileen 226, 245–248
Gates, Bill 14
gender 209, 228, 258
ghosts and poltergists 85, 87, 95, 96, 164, 227, 249, 256, 267
Giggle factor 168, 224
Gingerich, Owen 23 *See also* DNA
GM (Genetic Modification) experiments 297
God and The New Physics, Paul Davies 121, 274
God Does Play Dice with the Universe, Shan Gao 116
God Hypothesis, The, Joe Lewels 37
God Theory, The, Bernard Haisch 34, 143
Golden Mean, the 18
Goswami, Amit 45
Greenhouse Effect 29
Greenstein, George 26, 315
Group Consciousness 64, 66, 68, 69, 71
growth of crystals 75
guides 140, 249, 257, 258, 259, 261, 263, 268

H

Haisch, Bernard 34, 60, 61, 143, 144, 145
Hameroff, Stuart 57, 94
Hartzell, Bro Harmon 134
Heisenberg, Werner xxvii, xxviii, 4, 47, 66
Hell 259
Hemi - Sync process 175, 178
holographic ix, 35, 37–41, 52, 56, 60, 61, 63, 65, 73, 79, 80, 82, 83, 86, 91, 100, 101, 112, 121, 135, 137, 201, 216, 260, 267, 290
Holographic Universe, The, Michael Talbot 179, 181
Holographic Universe Theory 135
How Blind the Watchmaker, David Wilcox 17
Hoyle, Fred xxiii, 14, 16, 24, 28
Hubble, Edwin Russell 6
Huxley, Aldeous 63, 143, 145, 308
Hypnosis 103, 189, 200, 201, 202
hypnotherapists 90, 103, 146, 201–204, 206–208, 213–219, 222, 251–256, 268, 287
hypnotic regression xx, 103, 146, 170, 189, 200, 202, 204, 205, 207, 213, 216, 226, 251, 255, 264
hypnotism 113, 175, 200, 201, 204
hypnotist 103, 201, 202, 204–206, 216, 219, 220

I

immortality ix, 52, 54, 84, 85, 87, 108, 109, 110, 111, 114, 128, 142–144, 224, 259, 264, 268
independence of distance 36, 76, 83, 98
indeterminacy 4, 105
indigo children 98, 227, 266
information fields 43, 74, 79
information/knowledge xxix, 73, 133, 225, 251, 272, 280, 282–290
inspiration xxv, xxviii, 69, 72, 73, 146, 273, 283, 286
inspirational 51, 113, 142, 146, 273, 285
instinctive behaviour 42, 65, 66, 69, 78
intention viii, xxiii, 7, 12, 31, 50, 51, 54, 58, 60, 69–73, 77, 80, 83, 87, 96, 114, 207, 229, 242, 281
interconnectedness 52, 101, 135, 201, 260, 267, 269, 282
interconnectness 188
Intuition 76

J

Jahn, Robert 46, 51, 166
James, William xxvii, 28, 29, 33, 48, 50, 140, 144, 190, 213, 222, 226, 227–229, 232, 256, 280, 298, 304
Jeans, James 48, 144
Johnson, J.W.G. 14, 16, 289, 309, 310, 311
Journey of Souls, Dr Michael Newton 215, 253, 266
Jung, Carl 47, 64–66, 110, 133, 136, 173

K

Koran 138, 139, 146, 282
Kubler-Ross, Elisabeth 130, 184
Kulagina, Nina *See* telekinesis

L

Lanza, Dr Robert 33, 49, 84, 274, 275
Lashey, Karl 40, 82
Laszlo, Ervin 25, 62, 267

Law of Cause and Effect 17, 109
Laws of the Universe 20, 21
levitate 91, 92
Lewels, Joe 37
Life before Life, Children's Memories of Past Lives, Jim B. Tucker 193
Life Between Life, Professor Joel Whitton 214
life-between-lives 36, 90, 95, 109, 111, 249, 253–255, 261
Loewi, Otto xxviii
logical consistency xxvi, 17, 19, 127, 129, 142, 211, 215, 216, 273, 284
Logic of Quantum Mechanics and Consciousness, Mensky 51
Lovelock, James 29, 33, 136 *See also* Gaia Hypothesis, The

M

Magnetic Resonance Imaging (fMRI) 61, 74, 76
Many Lives, Many Masters, Dr Brian Weiss 215
Marcer, Peter 76, 100
Margenau, Henry 19
Matter Myth, The, Paul Davies 3
Mayes, Professor Keith 116
McTaggart, Lynne 60, 62, 71
mediums xx, xxviii, 87, 92, 102, 140, 141, 147, 225–242, 245, 251, 264–268, 272, 285–287
Mendeleev, Dimitri xxviii, 66, 273
Mensky, Michel B. 51, 64, 66, 101, 201, 241, 284, 285
mescaline 63 *See also* Aldeous Huxley
Meyer, Stephen C Meyer 14 *See also* DNA
microtubules 57, 78, 100
mind-matter influence 91
mind-mind 80, 242 *See also* mind-matter influence
Mitchell, Dr Edgar 76, 93
Moneagle, Joe 167, 179
Monroe, Robert 99, 100, 102, 170, 174–179, 182, 187, 201, 241, 251, 257, 259, 264, 269
Moorhouse, David 167, 168, 179
morphic fields and resonance 73, 74, 75, 76 *See also* Sheldrake, Rupert
mutations 8, 9, 34, 100, 114, 295, 296, 298, 299, 300, 301, 303, 305, 308
Mystery of the Buried Crosses, The, Hamlin Garland 244
mystics xxviii, 90, 113, 127, 131, 142, 143, 146

N

Near Death Experiences (NDE's) 7, 140, 141, 178, 180, 211, 256
new species 9–12, 16, 34, 74, 114, 262, 295, 297–299, 301–309, 312
Newton, Dr Michael 215, 253–256, 258, 260, 262, 266 *See also* Journey of Souls
Newtonian physics 3, 106
Newton Institute, The 253, 254
Newton, Isaac xxv, 20, 36, 50, 107, 115, 162, 180, 273
Nicholson, Sue 97 *See also* Sensing Murder
non-locality 37, 38, 40, 56, 59, 71, 76, 77, 78, 83, 86, 91, 101, 137, 188
non-physical reality 36, 43, 46, 56, 79, 86, 102, 103, 109, 110, 121, 130, 131, 133, 136, 173, 178, 201, 206, 208, 241, 257, 258, 261, 264, 268, 269, 276, 285, 288

O

Occam's razor xxviii, 33, 142, 235
On Children and Death, Dr Kubler-Ross 184
On the Origin of Species, Charles Darwin 11, 12, 296, 304, 309 *See also* Evolution
OOB (Out Of Body) 99
  phenomena 170, 171, 174, 175
  state 164, 169, 172, 173, 175, 176, 177, 185, 188
Oracle of Delphi 226
Origin of Life, The 13
Osis, Dr Karl 172, 182
Ouija board 135

P

Paleontologists 303
Paley, William 7, 8, 18
paramecium 57, 84, 94
paranormal vii, viii, ix, xvii, 7, 35, 36, 55, 76, 85–87, 89, 91–93, 96, 98, 99, 114, 159, 168, 169, 171, 187, 207, 223, 225, 232, 264, 265, 268, 276, 279, 282, 283, 286, 290
Parsimony xxvii
Past Life Regression 200, 202
PCAR (Phase conjugate adaptive resonance system) 55, 56, 69, 77, 78, 80–85, 90–103, 111, 112, 135, 159, 163, 170, 180, 181, 187, 188, 198, 206, 231, 232, 234, 236, 240, 241, 264
Pell, Cardinal 21
Penfield, Wilder 38, 39, 40, 62, 63, 135, 217
Penrose, Roger 25, 26, 41

Perennial Philosophy, The, Aldeous Huxley 143, 145
Perimeter Institute 5, 7
Periodic Table of Elements xxviii, 273
personal resonance 72, 73
phobias 192, 198, 199, 200, 202, 205, 207, 211, 215, 222
Physics of the Soul, Amit Goswami 45
Pietch, Paul 40
Pilbram, Dr 40, 135
Pippard, Sir Brian xxiv
placebo 58, 79, 279
plasma 36, 41, 42, 84, 94, 108
Pleistocene era 10, 12, 301
poltergeist 92
polygraph 42, 161
Popper, Karl 310
Popp, Fritz-Albert 59
positivity 277
Pribram 41, 65, 76, 82, 83
Price, Harry 229, 230, 245
probability xvii, xxiii, xxvii, 3, 9, 15, 16, 17, 18, 26, 27, 30, 34, 44–46, 51, 52, 55, 58, 91, 111, 116, 141, 161, 191, 194, 197, 227, 228, 230, 232, 235, 245, 273, 275, 276, 278, 284, 287, 300, 301, 305, 317, 318
Probability theory xxvii, 300
Provine, William 8 *See also* Evolution
"Psychic Detectives" 96
psychics xx, 67, 69, 80, 81, 87, 90–92, 96–99, 102, 103, 113, 118, 180, 225–227, 232–236, 240–242, 265–267, 272, 276, 285, 286
psychic training schools 98
psychometry 69, 78, 98, 103, 226, 234, 265
psychotherapists 205, 213 *See also* hypnotherapists
Puthoff, Harold 164, 166
Putoff, Hal 60, 160

Q

quantum fields 56, 59, 73, 76, 78, 91
quantum fluctuation 5, 108
Quantum Hologram (QH) 62, 77, 78
quantum holograph (QH) 71, 73, 76, 77, 81
quantum interference wave patterns 60
quantum tunneling 50
quantum zero point vacuum 5

R

Radin, Dean 70–72, 83, 93, 96, 161, 241

Radioactivity 4
Ramster, Peter 220, 221
random 3–5, 8, 9, 10, 12, 15, 17, 18, 22, 25, 41, 48, 69–71, 91, 100, 108, 109, 116, 160, 161, 166, 172, 201, 226, 235, 279, 295, 296, 300, 312, 317
randomness 4, 70, 116, 290
rater bias 237, 283
Rebirth of Nature, The, Rupert Sheldrake 74
recycled water 281, 312
REG experiments 70, 71, 282
regressions 104, 109, 202–204, 207–212, 215, 218, 219, 222, 249, 251, 254, 255, 257, 262, 266, 272, 287
regressive hypnosis 53, 146, 205
Reincarnation Experiments, The 219
Reliving Past Lives, Helen Wambach 206–208, 215, 218
remote viewing xx, 7, 78, 81, 98, 146, 161, 163–176, 178, 179, 201, 206, 224, 251, 264, 272
resonance 23, 55, 56, 73–81, 83, 94, 98, 102, 135, 136, 163, 231, 236, 258
revelationary xxviii, 142, 285, 286
Rhine, Professor J.B. 64, 69, 160, 173, 236
RNG 70, 91
Roberts, Dr Alice Roberts 10, 307, 308
Roberts, Jane xx, xxi, 109, 117, 130, 131, 135, 136, 137, 146, 149, 150, 154, 225, 266, 274, 287, 291 *See also* Seth
Rosicrucians 138, 139
Rote 179
rule of population biology 26
Russek procedure 231

S

Sabeti, Dr Pardis 10 *See also* Evolution
salamanders 40, 59
savant 63, 67, 69, 72–74, 103, 113, 272, 284, 289
Schempp, Walter 60–63, 74, 76, 77, 83, 99, 111, 135, 264, 265
Schmicker, Michael 93
Schmidt, Herman 51, 69–72, 91, 96
Schrödinger, Erwin xxvii, 44, 45, 50, 73, 116, 143, 277, 317
Schwartz, Dr Gary 227–234, 236, 241, 248, 266, 268, 283
Second law of Thermodynamics 5
self-organising systems 15

senses ix, 39, 40, 47–49, 61, 81, 83, 86, 87, 95, 113, 114, 136, 143, 162, 163, 180, 258
Sensing Murder 97, 180, 187
Seth xx, 85, 109, 116, 117, 130, 131, 134–138, 145, 146, 149, 150, 153–156, 175, 225, 251, 256, 258, 261–263, 266, 269, 273, 274, 282, 286–288, 291
Sheldrake, Rupert 56, 74–76, 83, 94, 135, 136
sin 138, 257, 269
Singh, Param 5
singularity 6, 122
skeptic 40, 95, 99, 189, 207, 228, 232–236, 253, 265, 283
soul vii, ix, xix, 44, 84, 85–87, 95, 108, 110, 114, 121, 127, 131, 134, 139, 140, 143, 253, 255–263, 266, 287, 291
spacelessly 65
Spontaneous Culture Links 68
SRI programme 165
Standard Model of Science, The xxiv, xxv, xxvi, 4, 5
Stevenson, Dr Ian 192–200, 221–223, 233
stigmata 195, 276
String theory xxvi
Subspecies variation 297
superposition 45, 51, 116
super-psi 239
super self 133, 136, 137
Suzuki, David 312
Swarnlata 195–198, 222
Swedenberg, Emmanual 164
Swedenborg 179, 180
Symbiotic Universe, The, Greenstein 26, 315
synchronicities 68

T

Talbot, Michael *See Holographic Universe, The*
Tao of Physics, Frijof Capra 109
Tart, Charles 79, 93, 172, 279
tautology 65, 115, 305
telekinesis 91
telepathy xx, xxvii, 7, 36, 38, 55, 56, 58, 61, 64, 69, 76, 83–85, 91, 94, 95, 96, 98, 146, 155, 159, 160, 162, 163, 166, 173, 176, 179, 180, 186–188, 192, 207, 225, 235, 236, 239, 242, 258, 265, 282
teleportation 170, 177, 181
TenDam, Hans 213, 214, 216, 217
termites 43, 69, 75, 83
Theory of Cause and Effect, The 3

Theory of Design 7, 8, 11, 13, 16, 18
Theory of Everything (TOE) 33, 121, 265
Tibetan monks 190, 276
time independence 91, 103, 232
timeless viii, ix, 7, 31, 51–54, 84–87, 90, 108–110, 114, 119, 120, 187, 208, 258, 259
timelessly 65
Tipler, Frank 28
Tlingits 193
transitional fossil 303
transitional species 10
traumas 202, 205, 215
Truth About Reincarnation, The, Peter Ramster 220
Tucker, Dr Jim B. 193, 194, 197, 200, 223
Turok, Neil 5
turtles xxv, 11, 224
Twenty Cases Suggestive of Reincarnation, Ian Stevenson 192
twins 68, 69, 72, 73, 160, 161

U

Uncertainty Principle 4, 47 *See also* Heisenberg, Werner
universe holograph and internet 65
Utts, Dr Jessica 161, 165, 176, 249

V

van Praagh, James 140
Vikings 278, 289
virtual 5, 60, 81, 275, 290, 317
Virtual reality games 274
Von Neumann, John 41, 47

W

Wambach, Dr Helen 203, 206–215, 218, 219, 221, 222, 251, 255
Watson, James xxvii, 298
wave function 4, 45, 47, 49, 50–52, 56, 143, 275, 276, 277
wave function collapse 51
Webber, Deb 97 *See also* Sensing Murder
Weber, Nancy 96, 226
Weinberg, Steven 44
Weiss, Dr Brian 215
What is Time?, Professor Keith Mayes 116
Whispering Pond, The, Laszlo 25
Whitton, Professor Joel 200, 214, 219
Wickramasinghe, Chandra 16
Wilcox, David 17
Williams, Lisa 53, 227, 235, 236

Windbridge 241
Windbridge Institute 236–238, 241, 242, 249, 268
Wishart, Ian *See Eve's Bite*
Woolf, Fred Alan 44
wormhole 141, 178, 256

X
xenoglossy 217, 218

Z
zener 282
Zeno's Paradox 47, 115, 116
Zero Point Field 60, 61, 62, 63, 65, 66, 68, 69, 72–75, 77–79, 81–86, 113, 135, 163, 198, 201, 208, 216, 239, 240, 241, 263, 265, 272, 288

www.ingramcontent.com/pod-product-compliance
Lightning Source LLC
Chambersburg PA
CBHW081148290426
44108CB00018B/2482